Oral Motor Assessment and Treatment

Ages and Stages

Diane Chapman Bahr
Loyola College in Maryland

With a chapter co-authored by

Argye Elizabeth Hillis
Johns Hopkins Hospital

Allyn and Bacon
Boston London Toronto Sydney Tokyo Singapore

Executive editor and publisher: Stephen D. Dragin
Series editorial assistant: Barbara Strickland
Marketing manager: Stephen Smith

Library of Congress Cataloging-in-Publication Data

Bahr, Diane Chapman.
Oral motor assessment and treatment : ages and stages / Diane Chapman Bahr ; with a chapter co-authored by Argye Elizabeth Hillis.
p. ; cm.
Includes bibliographical references and index.
ISBN 0-205-29786-2
1. Articulation disorders. I. Hillis, Argye Elizabeth. II. Title
[DNLM: 1. Dysarthria--diagnosis. 2. Dysarthria--therapy. 3. Feeding and Eating Disorders of Childhood--rehabilitation. 4. Psychomotor Disorders--rehabilitation. 5. Speech-Language Pathology--methods. WL 340.2 B151o 2001]
RC424.7 .B34 2001
616.85'5--dc21 00-044150

Printed in the United States of America

10 9 8 7 6 09 08 07 06

This book is dedicated to my loving
husband, Joe, who provided me with
continuous encouragement, assistance, and
support throughout the writing of this book.

Contents

Preface

In recent years, there has been a great surge of interest in the area of oral motor assessment and treatment. It almost seems as if an "oral motor explosion" has occurred, leaving the speech-language pathologist wondering:

- Where do I begin?
- Where can I find appropriate and adequate training in this area?
- What tools and materials should I buy?
- What techniques should I use?

These and many other questions regarding oral motor assessment and treatment are answered in this book.

Oral Motor Assessment and Treatment: Ages and Stages is meant to instruct clinicians who are beginning to use oral motor assessment and treatment in their practice (i.e., working clinicians and graduate student clinicians). The book will also help to "fill in the gaps" for clinicians who are using oral motor assessment and treatment in practice but do not fully understand why certain procedures, activities, or materials are used.

The field of oral motor assessment and treatment is a continuum that spans the age groups from birth to advanced age. This book discusses appropriate assessment and treatment techniques, materials, and tools for each age group and for the variety of populations within each age group.

Case examples and interactive case experiences are provided throughout the book. These assist the clinician in assimilating and integrating the information provided in each chapter. They also allow the clinician to apply the information immediately to sample clients. The interactive case experiences challenge the reader to think of the possibilities for each of the cases. Although I have provided case examples in the book as a guide for the reader, the answers to the questions posed in the interactive case experiences are for the reader to decide. This approach was chosen based on my experience in teaching professional seminars and graduate speech-language pathology classes.

This book also contains many tools that the clinician can use in oral motor assessment and treatment. Checklists, tables, and figures are provided to assist the clinician in accurately diagnosing muscle function and motor planning issues in a range of clients requiring oral motor assessment and treatment. Specific ideas for treatment are discussed relative to clients in specific age groups with a variety of disorders and severity levels. An overview of available assessment and treatment tools is provided to assist the clinician in choosing appropriate tools and materials.

The first chapter of this book was co-authored by Argye Elizabeth Hillis, MD, MA, Assistant Professor of Neurology at Johns Hopkins Hospital. The chapter presents neurology, anatomy, and physiology of the oral mechanism used in the processes of eating, drinking, and speech production. Neurological and anatomical development are discussed, as well as recent research regarding neural control for speech versus nonspeech tasks. Chapter 1 also reviews well-known information regarding the contribution of successive levels of the nervous system to oral motor function (e.g., upper motor neuron, lower motor, pyramidal system, extrapyramidal system, etc.). This body of information, in combination with specific information provided in the chapter about muscle and temporomandibular joint function, will assist the speech-language pathologist in understanding and making an appropriate assessment of the client's oral motor concerns. The tables in the chapter also describe the musculature involved in the different processes of eating and drinking, as well as specific sound production. Finally, the chapter focuses on syndromes that can affect an individual's oral motor function.

Chapter 2 presents physiologic considerations affecting oral motor assessment and treatment. The clinician will learn to understand the relationships between muscle tone, stability, mobility, planes of movement leading to rotation, and the different sensory systems. Each sensory system is described relative to oral motor function.

Discussed in Chapter 3 are the challenges and treatment considerations that affect individuals with oral motor concerns at a variety of ages and stages in life. The first half of the chapter addresses the challenges that have an impact on oral motor function. Treatment considerations are addressed in the second part of the chapter. These include critical learning periods; the impact of learning, fun, and rest during treatment; the connection between oral sensory input and attention; the use of music during treatment; movement and positioning ideas; the use of inhibition and facilitation techniques; the relationship between oral motor skill development and other treatment areas; the possible composition of the oral motor team; the use of universal precautions; and the parts of a typical oral motor treatment session.

Chapter 4 covers the assessment and treatment of oral motor concerns in individuals from birth to 2 years of age. A large amount of information is presented in this chapter, because this is considered a critical learning period for the development of oral motor skills in eating, drinking, and speech production. Some of the material in the chapter may also be applicable to individuals functioning in the birth to 2-year developmental range or to those individuals at any age who have severe to profound oral motor disorders. Highlights of this chapter include an oral motor case history form, a form for systematic evaluation of foods and liquids, an Oral Motor Assessment Checklist, and an oral massage sequence.

Chapter 5 covers the assessment and treatment of children in the 2- to 4-year age range. It contains a complete list of questions related to oral motor evaluation components for the clinician to use in developing an appropriate assessment tool. Specific assessment and treatment activities and materials are discussed in the chapter. The treatment section of the chapter also contains a gross motor and sensory activity checklist.

Chapters 6 and 7 discuss the assessment and treatment of children in the 4- to 6-year and 6- to 12-year ranges. Many assessment and treatment activities and materials have been developed for preschool-aged and school-aged children and are discussed in these chapters. Chapter 7 also addresses the application of oral motor assessment and treatment in the school setting, where the clinician is often working with groups of children and parents are not present for treatment.

Chapter 8 covers the assessment and treatment of adolescents and adults with oral motor concerns. This chapter completes the continuum of assessment and treatment that spans the age groups from birth to advanced age. Specific assessment and treatment tools, techniques, and materials are discussed. Highlighted in this chapter are the specific characteristics of dyspraxia and the different types of dysarthria. It also focuses on the treatment of adults dependent on others for care.

Report writing is discussed in Chapter 9. This final chapter includes common challenges encountered in report writing, a full diagnostic report format, as well as information on writing SOAP notes, treatment notes, and goals.

Appendix A contains an Assessment Tool Reference List that summarizes information presented on the assessment tools discussed throughout the book. Appendix B lists contraindications for massage. Information on moto-kinesthetic speech training is given in Appendix C, and Appendix D presents product sources, associations and organizations, continuing education, websites, and listservs. See www.oral-motor.com (Diane Chapman Bahr's website) for a direct link to many of the websites listed in this book.

Acknowledgments

Writing this book would not have been possible without the work completed by so many other individuals. I would like to acknowledge the contributions of those who have added to the base of knowledge in the area of oral motor disorders. Rona Alexander, Debra Beckman, Charlotte Boshart, James Bosma, Anthony Caruso, Michael Crary, Leslie Faye Davis, Joseph Duffy, Deborah Hayden, Judy Michels Jelm, Raymond Kent, Beth Langley, Leonard LaPointe, Linda Lombardino, Christopher Moore, Suzanne Evans Morris, Helen Mueller, Donald Robin, John Rosenbek, Sara Rosenfeld-Johnson, Maureen Stone, Edythe Strand, Robert Wertz, and many others have made significant contributions in this area. I wish to thank the book's editor and the following reviewers for a tremendous amount of assistance in refining the information presented in the book: Rona Alexander; Ronald Bloom, Hofstra University; Karen Walton Ebnit, Central Michigan University; Sara Rosenfeld-Johnson; David Sorenson, Idaho State University; and Travis T. Threats, Saint Louis University.

I also thank my colleagues and graduate students for their support during the book writing process and assistance in my learning process in the area of oral motor assessment and treatment. These include Jennifer Adams, John Barnes, Susan Barnett, Laura Baur, Cheryl Councill, Patsy Fann, Sally Gallena, Mina Goodman, Karen Keilholtz, Libby Kumin, Felicia Lightfoot, April Dawn Long, Susan Mazurek, Paula McGraw, Barbara Miller, Rebecca Miller, Suzanne Evans Morris, Margaret Outen, Lori Overland, Amy Pfleger, Sara Rosenfeld-Johnson, Lisa Schoenbrodt, Kathleen Siren, John Sloan, Carla Smith, Vickie Smith, Lori Sova, Lura Vogelman, Suzanne Wayson, Patricia Winders, and many others. I wish to express my heartfelt appreciation to my coauthor of Chapter 1, Argye Elizabeth Hillis, MD. In addition, I thank my many clients and students, who have allowed me to learn about the oral motor assessment and treatment process through my work with them. I am grateful to the clients pictured in the book (Michael, Carmen, Nicole, Daniel, Beth, and Charlie) and to their families for allowing me to use these photographs in the teaching process.

Finally, I wish to express my love and appreciation to my husband, Joe, who provided me with continuous support and inspiration throughout the writing process; my daughter, Kim, who assisted me when time was of the essence; and my other family members (Helen, Charlie, Al, and Bev), who have supported my growth throughout my lifetime. Thank you all for your assistance, support, and encouragement.

1

Neurological and Anatomical Bases

Argye Elizabeth Hillis, MD, MA
Diane Chapman Bahr, MS, CCC-SLP, CMT, CIMI

In recent years there has been a great surge of interest in the area of oral motor assessment and treatment. A large number of materials and tools have been developed to address this area. It almost seems as if an "oral motor explosion" has occurred, leaving the speech-language pathologist wondering:

- Where do I begin?
- Where can I find appropriate and adequate training in this area?
- What tools and materials should I buy?
- What techniques should I use?

These and many other questions regarding oral motor assessment and treatment are answered in this book.

The book is meant to instruct clinicians who are beginning to use oral motor assessment and treatment in their practice. It will also help to "fill in the gaps" for clinicians who are using oral motor assessment and treatment in practice, but do not fully understand why certain procedures, activities, or materials are used.

Oral motor assessment and treatment is a continuum that spans the age groups from birth to advanced age. These chapters discuss appropriate assessment and treatment techniques, materials, and tools for each age group and for the variety of populations within each age group. A developmental framework is used as a means of structuring the material presented in the book. Throughout the book, information is generally conveyed in a chapter where the reader can find the earliest developmental use of the material, but the material may apply to a variety of different age groups. For example, feeding, eating, and drinking are discussed in Chapters 4 and 5 with regard to infants and young children; however, many of the tools and techniques presented in these chapters can be used with older individuals who exhibit concerns in the area of feeding, eating, and drinking. Chapters 5 through 8 focus on oral motor activities and materials to improve speech production, because individuals typically use speech for communication purposes during this time period (i.e., age 2 through adulthood).

Case examples and interactive case experiences are provided throughout the book. These assist the clinician in assimilating and integrating the information provided in each chapter. They also allow the clinician to apply the information immediately to sample clients. The interactive case experiences challenge the reader to think of the possibilities for each of the cases. The authors have provided case examples in the book as a guide for the readers, but the answers to the questions posed in the interactive case experiences are for the readers to decide. This approach was chosen based on the main author's experience in teaching professionals and graduate speech-language pathology students.

The book also contains many tools that the clinician can use in oral motor assessment and treatment. Checklists, tables, and figures are provided to assist the clinician in accurately diagnosing muscle function and motor planning issues in the range of clients requiring oral motor assessment and treatment. Specific ideas for treatment are discussed relative to clients in specific age groups with a variety of disorders and severity levels. An overview of available assessment and treatment tools is provided to assist the clinician in choosing appropriate tools and materials.

THE IMPORTANCE OF UNDERSTANDING THE NEUROLOGICAL AND ANATOMICAL BASES OF MOTOR FUNCTION

An understanding of the neurological and anatomical bases of motor function is crucial to the assessment and treatment of oral motor disorders. This information assists the clinician in differential diagnosis based on clinical symptomatology. When assessing oral motor skills, it is important to examine characteristics of motor planning and execution through muscle function. These data are then utilized in a plan of treatment for remediation or facilitation. The skilled clinician can apply neurophysiological principles to the functional motor activities of feeding, eating, drinking, and speech production. Furthermore, the clinician can predict clinical performance when presented with definitive information regarding deviancy in anatomical or neurological substrates associated with motor performance.

This chapter will begin with a discussion of neural development of speech motor control and will include research regarding the neural control of the oral mechanism. A broad overview of neural control of oral movements, focusing on mechanisms underlying speech production, will be provided. The contribution of successive levels of the nervous system will be described from the cortex and corticobulbar tracts through subcortical structures, brain stem nuclei, lower motor neurons of each of the cranial nerves, neuromuscular junctions, and, finally, the muscles themselves. Common neurologic and neuromuscular diseases that generally affect function at each level (i.e., those that affect functioning of many nerves or many muscles involved in speech) will be noted. The chapter will address specific functions of individual cranial nerves and muscles as well as how each can be individually assessed. A discussion of anatomical development of the oral mechanism and the importance of tongue shape, vocal tract shape, and palatal contact for speech production is provided. Syndromes affecting the processes of eating, drinking, and speech production will also be addressed. Finally, the chapter will culminate with sample case studies and interactive case experiences. These illustrate how identification of impairment at a particular level of the nervous system or impairment to individual nerve or muscle can help to illuminate the diagnosis and focus treatment.

NEURAL DEVELOPMENT AND CONTROL

Neural Development of Speech Motor Control

"Neural development is far from well understood, and only fragmentary information is available on many of the structures and processes thought to be involved in speech production" (Kent, 1999, p. 46). Kent provides a thorough discussion of the current research in this area in the book *Clinical Management of Motor Speech Disorders in Children* (Caruso & Strand, 1999). Kent's (1999) information is summarized here.

According to Kent (1999, p. 46), the brain has a "full complement of neurons" by 5 months gestation, and by birth, "neuronal cell formation is complete." By 3 months of age, the amount of dendritic branching in the infant's brain is more advanced in the oral area of the cortical motor strip than in Broca's area and in the right hemisphere than in the left hemisphere of the brain. At approximately 6 months of age, a peak occurs in the development of the inner language areas of the cortex. "It is likely that the auditory-motor neural circuitry for vocalization is established largely during the second half of the first year of life" (Boysson-Bardies & Vihman, 1991; Kent, Netsell, Osberger, & Hustedde, 1987; Oller & Eilers, 1988; Rvachew, Slawinski, Williams, & Green, 1996, as cited by Kent, 1999, p. 47). "Adult-like metabolic activity is observed across [brain] regions" at approximately 8 to 9 months of age (Kent, 1999, p. 46). By 15 months of age, "a rapid acceleration in number of cortical synapses" occurs and the maturity of the hippocampus provides the child with the "neural system for memory" (Kent, 1999, p. 46). Dendritic branching matures in Broca's area and throughout the rest of the left hemisphere by the time the child is 2 years of age and plays a significant role in speech and language production. By 4 years of age, peaks are noted in overall brain metabolism and in the development of the outer language areas of the cortex. By age 6, the dendritic branching in Broca's area is more advanced than in the oral region of the motor cortex. At this age, the child can perform complex speech and oral motor tasks.

Neural Control for Speech versus Nonspeech Tasks

Moore and colleagues (Green, Moore, Ruark, Rodda, Morvee, & VanWitzenburg, 1997; Moore & Ruark, 1996; Moore, Smith, & Ringel, 1988; Ruark & Moore, 1997) have written extensively about the relationship or lack of relationship between the motor coordination required for speech and nonspeech tasks (e.g., sucking, chewing, and swallowing). The research completed by these individuals indicates that the motor coordination used for speech production appears to be controlled by different neural mechanisms than the motor coordination used for the nonspeech tasks involved in eating and drinking. The studies looked at lip and jaw muscle activity during speech and nonspeech tasks using electromyographic (EMG) recordings and generally found different types of muscle activity for speech versus nonspeech tasks. In adults, the mandibular muscle activity used in chewing predominantly required the reciprocal activation of antagonist muscles, whereas the mandibular muscle activity used in speech production required coactivation of antagonist muscles (Moore, Smith, & Ringel, 1988; Ruark & Moore, 1997). Muscle activity in young children generally resembled the muscle activity found in adults; however, the muscle activity of young children lacked refinement.

In 15-month-old children a similarity was found between the mandibular movements for reduplicative babbling and earlier developing nonspeech tasks such as chewing. This supports the possibility of shared neural control during early development. However, no similarity was found between the muscle activity required for nonspeech tasks and speech acts requiring increased sophistication such as variegated babbling (Moore & Ruark, 1996). Another study by Ruark and Moore (1997) on lip muscle activity in 2-year-old children generally supported the idea that speech and nonspeech behaviors are mediated by unique neural control mechanisms. However, some speech and nonspeech behaviors (e.g., chewing and bilabial speech tasks; lip-rounding and nonlabial speech tasks) yielded similar results in certain aspects of muscle activity. This may indicate that these processes share common neural control mechanisms.

The results of these studies seem to suggest that although common neural control may exist for speech and nonspeech tasks during early development, the control has generally been differentiated by the age of 2 years. This may support the idea that a critical learning period for oral motor development occurs during the birth to 2-year period. By this time, the structures and many of the pathways used for speech and nonspeech processes may be the same but the areas of neural control and the timing of muscle contraction appear to be different. The speech-language pathologist must consider this information when assessing and treating individuals with oral motor disorders. This is particularly important when facilitating speech production. Eating and drinking activities may be used to increase sensation, improve jaw stability and control, encourage tongue and jaw dissociation, and so on, but other activities will need to be incorporated in treatment to address the differences in muscle activity and neural control required for speech versus nonspeech tasks.

Infant Reflexes and Responses

Infant reflexes and responses "are useful as general indices of neural maturity and integrity" (Kent, 1999, p. 48). Either delayed appearance of reflexes or the presence of reflexes beyond the age when they typically disappear can signal neurological impairment. The reflexes and responses that may affect the development of oral control for eating and drinking are found in Table 1.1.

The reflexes listed in Table 1.1 are normal reactions exhibited by infants. Many of them appear to assist the infant in feeding. The reflexes and responses are an important aspect of infant movement until the infant's neurological system has matured enough to develop motor control. As the infant matures neurologically, the reflexes and responses become integrated by the motor system and many seem to disappear (DeMyer, 1994). However, some can reappear when a neurological insult or damage occurs (e.g., traumatic brain injury, degenerative neurological disease, etc.).

Reflexes help the infant to move prior to the maturation of the motor system, which occurs as the neurons become covered with myelin. Many of the reflexes assist the infant in survival. The rooting, suckling, swallowing, tongue, and grasp reflexes assist the infant in feeding. The infant uses the rooting reflex to locate the nipple. The suckling, swallowing, and tongue reflexes are used by the infant to obtain and manage the fluid expressed from the nipple. The grasp reflex is probably most important to infants living in societies where mothers spend significant time gathering food with the baby being carried at the front of the mother's body. It is believed that the grasp reflex assists the infant in holding on to the mother. The bite and transverse tongue reflexes appear to help the infant develop the initial movements required for the later developing processes of chewing and tongue lateralization. The palmomental and Babkin's reflexes appear to help establish the hand and mouth connection that becomes particu-

TABLE 1.1 Infant Reflexes Impacting Feeding Development

REFLEX	CRANIAL NERVES	ELICITED BY	MOVEMENT	POSSIBLE USE	CONTROL DEVELOPS	DISAPPEARS
Rooting	V, VII, XI, XII	Touch to cheek or lips	Head turn towards stimulus	Assists in nursing	1 month	3–6 months
Suckling	V, VII, IX, XII	Finger or nipple in mouth	Suckling	Assists in nursing	2–3 months	6–12 months (involuntary)
Swallowing	V, VII, IX, X, XII	Saliva or food in pharnyx	Swallow	Nutrition, etc.	18 months	Persists
Tongue	XII	Touch to lips and tongue	Protraction-retraction tongue movement	Assists in nursing		12–18 months
Bite	V	Moderate pressure on gums	Jaw closure and phasic bite response	Precursor to chewing		9–12 months
Gag	IX, X	Touch to posterior half of tongue or posterior wall of pharnyx	Mouth opening, head extension, depression of floor of mouth with elevation of larynx and diaphragm	Protective mechanism		Persists
Transverse Tongue	XII	Touch or taste to lateral border of tongue	Tongue moves toward stimulus	Precursor to tongue lateralization	6–8 months	
Palmomental		Touch to palm	Wrinkliing of mentalis	Hand-mouth connection		
Babkin's		Base of palm pressed	Mouth opens, eyes close, head moves forward	Hand-mouth connection for feeding		
Grasp		Finger placed in palm with slight traction	Hands grasp and holds tightly	To hold mother while feeding		6 months

Sources: R. J. Love and W. G. Webb, *Neurology for the Speech-Language Pathologist,* 3rd ed. (Boston: Butterworth-Heinemann, 1996), pp. 287–293; S. E. Morris and M. D. Klein, *Pre-Feeding Skills* (Tucson, AZ: Therapy Skill Builders, 1987), pp. 26–27; M. Samuels and N. Samuels, *The Well Baby Book: A Comprehensive Manual of Baby Care, from Conception to Age Four* (New York: Summit Books, 1991), p. 142.

larly important during self-feeding. The gag reflex protects the infant from swallowing items that are too large for the infant to swallow and prevents nasal regurgitation of liquids.

The role that primitive reflexes play in the development of normal voluntary movement is not clearly understood. Oral motor reflexes are likely to develop concurrently with complex, voluntary motor skills, as opposed to being the basis from which complex, voluntary motor skills develop, and this development probably extends into adulthood (Smith, Weber, Newton, & Denny, 1991). In fact, several authors have argued that primitive reflexes do not significantly contribute to early motor function in normally developing full-term infants, including the development of speech motor control (Bartlett, 1997; Moore & Ruark, 1996; Smith et al., 1991). Furthermore, Love, Hagerman, and Tiami (1980) found virtually no correlation between the number of abnormal oropharyngeal reflexes present and the severity of dysarthria (defined by a quantification of articulatory accuracy) in children with cerebral palsy. Therefore, it is only when immature oral and pharyngeal reflexes are part of the child's spontaneous feeding pattern that the reflexes have diagnostic and prognostic significance in neurological disease (Love & Webb, 1996). The speech-language pathologist should be careful not to generalize the impact that persistent or delayed infantile reflexes have on oral motor development beyond their potential impact on feeding. This is an area that requires further research.

Some reflexes persist throughout life, whereas others seem to disappear. The gag reflex and swallowing reflex are examples of those that persist and are protective. Other reflexes are apparent until as late as 18 months of age and then seem to disappear. The infant can demonstrate control over some of the reflexes prior to their apparent disappearance. This control is an indication of the ongoing process of neural maturation and integration. The infant will often begin to demonstrate control over the rooting reflex at 1 month of age. However, the rooting reflex does not generally disappear until 3 to 6 months of age. The infant may begin to demonstrate some control over the suckling reflex at 2 to 3 months of age. This response typically disappears as an involuntary response between 6 and 12 months of age. The transverse tongue response can begin to be controlled by the infant between 6 and 8 months of age. This response may be important for the initiation of tongue lateralization seen throughout life for the purpose of moving food to the molar surfaces for chewing as well as moving food from the molar surface and sulci back to the tongue for the creation of the bolus prior to swallowing.

At 18 months of age, the infant is believed to have volitional control of swallowing. However, the swallowing reflex fortunately persists throughout life. The tongue reflex generally disappears between 12 and 18 months of age. This is the reflex responsible for the suckle-swallow that the child uses during nursing to express milk from the nipple. Although the tongue and suckling reflexes typically disappear, many individuals continue to exhibit a tongue protraction-retraction pattern as part of their movement patterns well beyond the 12- to 18-month period. This pattern is often secondary to the limited development of more sophisticated oral motor patterns that usually replace the tongue protraction-retraction pattern. The bite reflex generally disappears at 9 to 12 months of age. This early response seems to be important for jaw closure and the phasic bite and release pattern that is seen in the development of chewing. The grasp reflex also normally disappears at about 6 months of age.

If an infant has some type of neurological disorder, either delayed or persistent reflex patterns are frequently observed. Children with cerebral palsy often exhibit the persistence of reflex patterns beyond an age when the patterns have generally disappeared in children without cerebral palsy. In these children, the rooting, suckling, tongue, bite, palmomental, Babkin's, and grasp reflexes may persist. These children often exhibit a poorly integrated or hyperactive gag response and a significant tongue protraction-retraction pattern. Children and adults who have a neurological disease or sustain some type of neurological damage (e.g., congenital disease such as Batten's disease, strokes due to sickle cell anemia, traumatic brain injury, degenerative disease such as amyotrophic lateral sclerosis) often reexhibit many of the reflex behaviors that were previously inhibited by the cortical motor system prior to the neurological damage.

As previously mentioned, most reflex behaviors tend to be integrated by the cortical motor system (i.e., the pyramidal system, described later in this chapter) over time as the infant develops rather than truly disappearing. The concept of integration versus true disappearance is an important one for the clinician to understand. Integration occurs as the neurological system matures and the individual gains more control over the motor system through experiences with the environment. If reflex patterns are not integrated for some reason, the patterns can remain.

The gag reflex (i.e., rapid elevation of the soft palate in response to stimulation of the tongue or pharynx) persists in the individual throughout life. This reflex is given specific attention in the assessment and treatment of both infants and adults. The gag protects the infant from swallowing items that may be unsafe for the infant (e.g., food that is too large, toy parts or pieces) and prevents nasal regurgitation of liquid. At birth, the gag response can be elicited by touching the posterior three-fourths of the infant's tongue (Morris & Klein, 1987). As the infant becomes more adept in the management of food, the gag is not as easily elicited. The gag response is then elicited further back on the child's tongue and in the pharynx. This response is inhibited over time via the oral experiences of the infant. However, it remains a protective mechanism for the child and the adult. Individuals with neurological damage tend to exhibit hyperactive gag responses or diminished gag responses, depending on the location of the damage to the system. Individuals with upper motor neuron damage tend to exhibit hyperactive gag responses (secondary to loss of inhibition from the cortex), whereas individuals with lower motor neuron damage tend to exhibit hyporesponsive gag responses. Upper motor neurons and lower motor neurons are discussed in another portion of this chapter.

Some practitioners working with clients on swallowing activities may think that individuals without an apparent gag reflex may be unsafe with swallowing activities. Although the gag response tends to protect the airway from items too large to be effectively managed and swallowed, the pharyngeal phase of the swallow needs to be evaluated separately from the gag response. It is the pharyngeal phase of the swallow that usually determines the safety of swallowing activities. The pharyngeal phase of the swallow can be assessed in a cursory manner during feeding, but this phase is best evaluated via a modified barium swallow procedure in an individual at risk for aspiration. Some of the clinical signs indicating that an individual may be at risk for aspiration include a history of upper respiratory illness, particularly pneumonia, a wet-sounding vocal quality, a weak-sounding cough, or excessive coughing during or after meals.

As previously discussed, primitive reflexes may persist or be delayed in infants and children exhibiting neurological impairments. The Infant Reflex Checklist (Table 1.2) may be used to evaluate the presence, absence, or quality of reflex patterns in infants.

SPEECH MOTOR PLANNING: THE CORTEX OF THE BRAIN

Speech production begins in the cortex, with the decision to speak and the formulation of the content of speech. Formulating a verbal message probably recruits a vast cortical area, including left frontal and parietal areas. Then, selection of specific spoken word forms is believed to take place in or around Wernicke's area, in the left posterior superior temporal gyrus. Putting the words together into grammatical sentences is likely to occur in or around Broca's area, in the left inferior frontal gyrus. Planning the movements to articulate words and sentences is thought to occur in Broca's area and the underlying operculum and insular cortex. These neuroanatomical correlates of oral motor functions for speech production have been identified by functional imaging studies that show which areas of the brain are activated during specific language tasks, such as positron emission tomography (PET) studies (described by Chertkow & Bub, 1994; Howard, Patterson, Wise, Brown, Friston, Weiller, & Frackowiak, 1992; Peterson, Fox, Posner, Mintun & Raichle, 1988) or functional magnetic resonance imaging (fMRI) studies (described by Binder & Rao,

TABLE 1.2 Infant Reflex Checklist

REFLEX	CRANIAL NERVES	ELICITED BY	MOVEMENT	PRESENT (+) ABSENT (–) DELAYED (D) PERSISTENT (P)	MOVEMENT OBSERVED/ COMMENTS
Rooting	V, VII, XI, XII	Touch to cheek or lips	Head turn toward stimulus		
Suckling	V, VII, IX, XII	Finger or nipple in mouth	Suckling		
Swallowing	V, VII, IX, X, XII	Saliva or food in pharynx	Swallow		
Tongue	XII	Touch to lips and tongue	Protraction-retraction tongue movement		
Bite	V	Moderate pressure on gums	Jaw closure and phasic bite response		
Gag	IX, X	Touch to posterior half of tongue or posterior wall of pharnyx	Mouth opening, head extension, depression of floor of mouth with elevation of larynx and diaphragm		
Transverse Tongue	XII	Touch or taste to lateral border of tongue	Tongue moves toward stimulus		
Palmomental		Touch to palm	Wrinkling of mentalis		
Babkin's		Base of palm pressed	Mouth opens, eyes close, head moves forward		
Grasp		Finger placed in palm with slight traction	Hand grasps and holds tightly		

Sources: R. J. Love and W. G. Webb, *Neurology for the Speech-Language Pathologist,* 3rd ed. (Boston: Butterworth-Heinemann, 1996), pp. 287–293; S. E. Morris and M. D. Klein, *Pre-Feeding Skills* (Tuscon, AZ: Therapy Skill Builders, 1987), pp. 26–27.

1994). These correlates have also been identified by associations between particular lesion sites and specific types of problems in speech production (Geschwind, 1965; Alexander, 1997). Strokes or tumors in Broca's area, for example, typically result in substantial problems in motor planning of oral movements with resultant nonfluent, poorly articulated speech (although swallowing is usually normal). Neurological findings are inconclusive regarding the area of the brain that impacts the motor planning deficit seen in children, called *developmental apraxia of speech* (Crary, 1993). Some researchers have argued that developmental apraxia of speech is a linguistic deficit. More recently, others have considered it a motor deficit (Caruso & Strand, 1999). Developmental apraxia of speech will be discussed as a motor impairment in this book.

MOTOR SPEECH EXECUTION: THE PYRAMIDAL SYSTEM

Information from Broca's area and other cortical regions involved in language and motor planning is sent (via connecting neurons) to the motor strip, a region of cortex that lies just in front of the central sulcus. This area of the brain cortex contains the cell bodies of the *upper motor neurons*—the nerve cells that control all volitional movements involving striate muscles. All oral motor function is ultimately produced by muscles of the mouth, face, pharynx, and larynx that are controlled by *cranial nerves.* Each cranial nerve has a set of upper motor neurons, or nerve cells, which connect with a set of lower motor neurons that share a specific motor function. The system comprised of upper and lower motor neurons and their connections is called the *pyramidal system.*

Important parts of the neuron are (1) dendrites that receive impulses from other neurons, (2) a cell body that contains the important machinery for keeping the cell alive, (3) an axon that transmits impulses to nerve terminals, and (4) nerve terminals that transmit impulses to other neurons and to muscles. Each upper motor neuron passes its message along its lengthy axon, which runs through the *internal capsule* (a tract of axons sandwiched between the basal ganglia). Each axon of an upper motor neuron devoted to speech production runs through the internal capsule at its genu, or bend, before entering the brain stem, where it crosses to the other side. Finally, the upper motor neuron synapses (i.e., communicates with other neurons) at its cranial nerve nucleus in the brain stem. Each upper motor neuron synapses with a *lower motor neuron* that, in turn, passes the message originating in the cortex to the muscle, via the *neuromuscular junction.*

The neuromuscular junction consists of the nerve terminals of the lower motor neuron, the *synaptic space,* and the *motor end plate*. The nerve terminals release packets of the neurotransmitter, *acetylcholine,* which diffuse across the synaptic space to the acetylcholine receptor in the muscle. When an adequate number of acetylcholine receptors are activated by acetylcholine, the muscle contracts and produces a movement. These crucial components of the pyramidal system are illustrated in Figure 1.1.

Damage to the Upper Motor Neurons

When there is an acute injury to the upper motor neurons, the immediate effect is loss of function of both the upper and lower motor neuron, resulting in decreased tone (flaccidity), weakness, and loss of even reflexive movements of the muscle innervated by that nerve. However, over the days to weeks after the acute injury, the function of the uninjured lower motor neuron returns and is not inhibited by the upper motor neuron from the cortex. This loss of inhibition with *chronic upper motor neuron injuries* results in increased tone (spasticity), reduced range of movement, and exaggerated reflexes (hyperreflexia) in the muscles innervated by that nerve. Often, the muscle remains strong, but is not under volitional control, because it is "disconnected" from the command center in the cortex. In contrast, both acute and chronic injury to lower motor neurons cuts off all input to the muscle, resulting in flaccid paralysis with weakness and loss of reflexive movements in the corresponding muscles. Atrophy and muscle twitches, called *fasciculations,* rapidly develop after lower motor neuron lesions. These basic characteristics of lesions at different levels of the nervous system are listed in Table 1.3.

All muscles controlled by the cranial nerves—except the sternocleidomastoid, trapezius, and those of the lower half of the face and tongue—receive input from both sides of the cortex. Unilateral strokes or other unilateral lesions cause only noticeable dysfunction of the lower face (facial droop) and imprecise lingual articulation due to this bilateral innervation. A low-pitched or harsh phonation may also be heard. In contrast, bilateral cortical lesions (e.g., due to multiple strokes, head injury, metastatic cancer, cerebral palsy, or infections such as toxoplasmosis) or lesions in the brain stem above the nuclei of cranial nerves VII, IX, X, and XII cause bilateral upper motor neuron (spastic) dysar-

FIGURE 1.1 A Motor Neuron, Showing the Cell Body, Axon, and Myoneural (Muscle-Nerve) Junction (a motor-end plate [the junction between a neuron and a muscle fiber] is shown on the lower right)

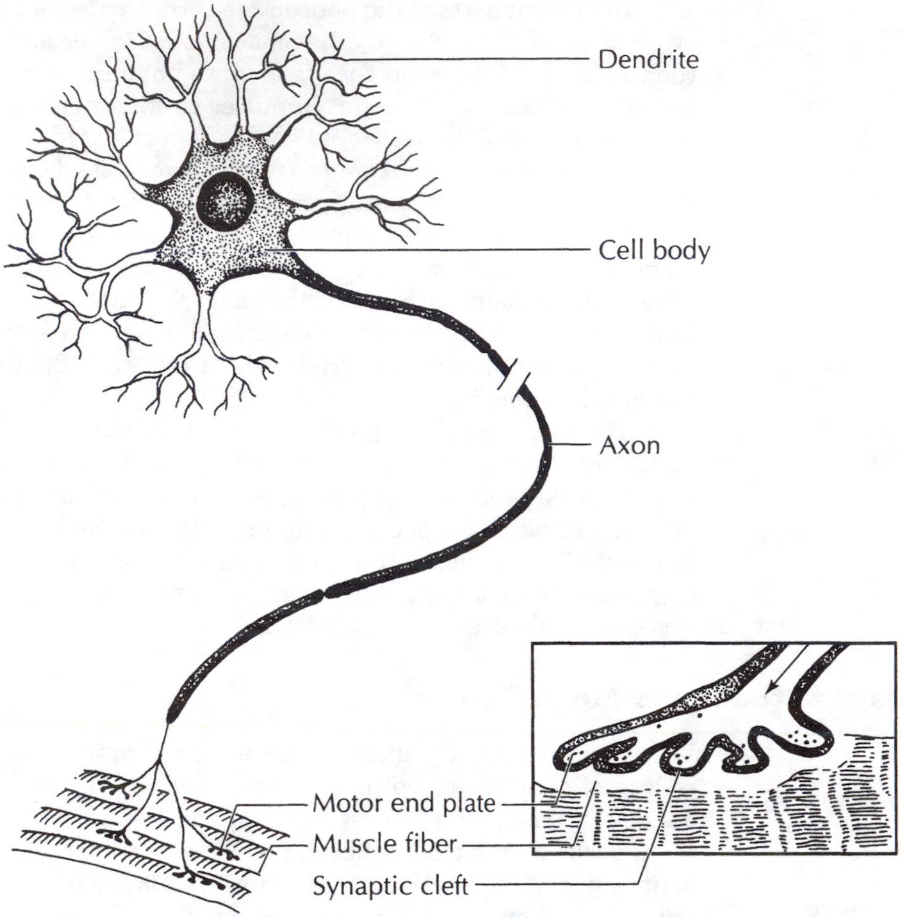

Source: R. H. Brookshire, *An Introduction to Neurogenic Communication Disorders,* 5th ed. (Saint Louis, MO: Mosby Year Book, Inc., 1997), p. 15. Reprinted by permission.

thria, also known as *pseudobulbar palsy*. Spastic dysarthria is characterized by (1) slow, imprecise articulation with prolongation and distortion of phonemes and words; (2) harsh, monotone phonation with reduced variation of stress and loudness; and (3) hypernasality (Darley, Aronson, & Brown, 1975). Because of the loss of inhibition from the cortex, pseudobulbar dysarthria is often accompanied by reflexive laughing and crying, basically indistinguishable from emotional lability except that it may not have any emotional trigger.

A number of degenerative diseases of the nervous system that affect the higher levels of the pyramidal system, such as olivopontocerebellar atrophy and progressive supranuclear palsy, can also result in pseudobulbar dysarthria. More prevalent disease states that generally affect the upper motor neurons are focal lesions that compress or interrupt blood flow to the upper motor neuron somewhere along its path. Common lesions of this type include tumor, stroke, abscess, and focal trauma. Multiple sclerosis affects the rate at which the mes-

TABLE 1.3 Characteristics of Damage at Different Levels of the Nervous System

LEVEL OF DAMAGE	STRENGTH	TONE	RANGE OF MOTION	RATE OF MOTION	PHONATION	ARTICULATION	RESONANCE
UMN: acute	Low	Low	Normal or low	Normal or slow	Breathy, harsh	Imprecise	Hypernasal
UMN: chronic	Low or normal	High	Low	Slow	Harsh, strained, low pitch	Imprecise	Hypernasal
LMN	Low	Low	Normal or high	Normal	Breathy, soft	Imprecise	Normal or hypernasal
Cerebellar	Normal	Low or normal	Normal	Slow	Inappropriate pitch & volume changes	Imprecise; distorted vowels	Variable hypernasal/ hyponasal
Hyperkinetic	Normal or low	High or low	High	Slow	Inappropriate pitch & volume changes	Imprecise; distorted vowels	Variable hypernasal/ hyponasal
Hypokinetic	Normal or low	High	Low	Brief, rapid bursts	Harsh, low volume	Imprecise; consonant repetitions	Normal

UMN= upper motor neuron; LMN = lower motor neuron

sage is communicated down the axon, by disrupting the *myelin sheath* that speeds transmission in the upper motor neurons.

Damage to the Lower Motor Neurons

Lower motor neuron dysfunction results in predominant weakness and reduced muscle tone, with relatively preserved rate and range of movement. Muscle atrophy often occurs late in the course. Lower motor neuron diseases affecting cranial nerves V, VII, IX, X, and XII result in flaccid dysarthria, characterized by hypernasality, imprecise consonants, breathiness, monopitch, reduced loudness, and short phrases (Darley et al., 1975). Common diseases that affect lower motor neurons are brain stem strokes, Guillain Barre syndrome (which primarily disrupts the myelination of the lower motor neurons), Lyme disease, sarcoidosis, and carcinomatous meningitis. A relatively common type of brain stem stroke that markedly disrupts oral motor function is Wallenburg's syndrome, due to an infarct in the lateral medulla. The nucleus ambiguous, which is crucial for speech and swallowing control, and the lower motor neurons of cranial nerves VII, IX, and X are affected by lesions in the lateral medulla. Moebius syndrome is a "congenital facial diplegia" involving cranial nerves VI and VII bilaterally (Love & Webb, 1996, p. 171), which can affect the child's development of facial expression, eating and drinking skills, and speech. Werdnig-Hoffman disease is an infantile form of spinal muscle atrophy, which is a progressive degeneration of lower motor neurons, especially of the cranial nerves.

Damage to Both the Upper and the Lower Motor Neurons

Amyotrophic lateral sclerosis (ALS; also known as Lou Gehrig's disease) affects both upper and lower motor neurons. One form of the disease, bulbar ALS, begins in the brain stem, causing prominent mixed spastic and flaccid dysarthria. The speech is most often characterized by imprecise consonants and distorted vowels; hypernasality; harsh, monotone phonation; slow rate; and short phrases. Unlike flaccid or spastic dysarthria, however, there are also inappropriate silences and prolonged consonants (Darley et al., 1975). Polio used to be another common cause of upper and lower motor neuron disease, often involving cranial nerve function.

Disease of the Neuromuscular Junction

By far the most prevalent disease that affects the neuromuscular junction is myasthenia gravis. This disease, seen mostly in young women or in older adults (although there is a childhood form of the disease), results from autoimmunity against one's own acetylcholine receptors in the motor end plate. The muscle cannot continue to contract, resulting in rapid muscle fatigue due to the reduced number of receptors. It is this rapid fatigability that distinguishes the dysarthria related to pathology in the neuromuscular junction from the dysarthria related to pathology in the lower motor neurons themselves. When the acetylcholine released by the lower motor neuron no longer activates a receptor in the muscle, the outcome is the same as when the lower motor neuron failed to release the acetylcholine. For example, when a person with myasthenia gravis attempts to sustain counting, the individual may begin with normal speech but rapidly deteriorate into flaccid dysarthria. Speech and other movements become progressively weak as activity is prolonged. Thus, in the course of speaking, the person develops worsening hypernasality, breathiness, and slurred consonant articulation.

Often the dysarthria can be quickly reversed by intravenous administration of the medication, edrophonium chloride (Tensilon), which prolongs the effectiveness of acetylcholine by preventing it from being broken down in the synaptic space. Reversal of deficits with administration of edrophonium during a sustained activity such as speech is often used in making the diagnosis of myasthenia gravis. Use of a similar, but long-acting medication, pyridostigmine (Mestinon), is used to treat the symptoms of myasthenia gravis.

Botulism, due to ingestion of botulinum toxin, can also cause profound oral motor dysfunction, due to blocking of the presynaptic release of acetylcholine. The other major disease of the neuromuscular junction, Lambert-Eaton syndrome, also results in reduced release of acetylcholine from the lower motor neuron, but does not typically affect oral motor function.

Disease of Muscles (Myopathy)

Diseases of the muscles themselves can also cause dysarthria and dysphagia. Polymyositis and dermatomyositis are inflammatory diseases of muscle that can affect bulbar (speech and swallowing) musculature. They result in diffuse weakness, typically greater in proximal than distal muscles. Similarly, myotonic (muscular) dystrophy is another relatively common myopathy that occasionally affects speech musculature (Brookshire, 1997). The salient speech characteristics of these disorders are similar to flaccid dysarthria: breathy, monotone voice with reduced loudness, imprecise consonants, and hypernasality. Severe polymyositis or dermatomyositis often require tracheostomy due to reduced respiratory function and/or inability to protect the airway due to laryngeal dysfunction. Treatment that suppresses the immune system often results in at least temporary improvement of oral motor function in myositis but not in inherited myopathies like myotonic dystrophy.

MOTOR SPEECH COORDINATION: THE CEREBELLUM

The cerebellum does not initiate movements, but coordinates motor speech by regulating the timing, force, rate, and direction of motion, predominantly through inhibiting excess activity. It receives input and modulates output from the cortex and subcortical structures. The midportion of the cerebellum, between the anterior and posterior vermis, is believed to be crucial for speech and oral motor control (Brown, Darley, & Aronson, 1970). Lesions to this region, diffuse degeneration of the cerebellum, or bilateral cerebellar strokes result in ataxic dysarthria, also called *scanning speech.* This type of dysarthria is characterized by slow rate with equal and excess stress on each word, intermittent articulatory breakdown with imprecise consonants and distorted vowels, as well as harsh voice quality. There is often variable hyper- and hyponasality due to impaired ability to coordinate soft palate movement with movements of the lips and tongue. Diseases that often affect the midportion of the cerebellum include multiple sclerosis, alcohol and medication toxicity, as well as tumors. Strokes that damage only one side of the cerebellum may acutely cause ataxic dysarthria, but rapid recovery is typical. Diffuse cerebellar degeneration can be caused by cancer (paraneoplastic cerebellar degeneration), by inherited progressive neurologic disease (e.g., olivopontocerebellar atrophy), or by toxins (e.g., alcohol). Cerebellar involvement is also frequently seen in individuals with cerebral palsy.

MOTOR SPEECH MODULATION: THE EXTRAPYRAMIDAL SYSTEM

The extrapyramidal system is a finely tuned network of inhibitory and excitatory mechanisms that regulate tone, posture, and complex movements. It includes the basal ganglia (caudate nucleus, putamen, and globus pallidus), subthalamic nucleus, red nucleus, and substantia nigra. The motor nuclei of the thalamus also contribute to this system and its communication with the cerebellum. The normal function of this system includes inhibition of extraneous or unintentional movements of the lips, tongue, and jaw that can disrupt speech, in addition to facilitation of intentional movements. Depending on which components of the system are impaired, lesions can result in two major types of movement disorders that are reflected in speech production: hyperkinetic dysarthria and hypokinetic dysarthria.

Hyperkinetic Dysarthrias

Hyperkinetic dysarthrias can be loosely subdivided into slow and quick forms, but there is a great deal of overlap. Quick hyperkinesias include myoclonic jerks, tics, chorea, and hemiballistic movements. Slow hyperkinesias include athetosis, dystonia, and some other focal dyskinesias (Darley et al., 1975).

Quick hyperkinesias interfere with speech production by causing unwanted jerks of the jaw, lips, or tongue or by causing unintentional tongue protrusion that interrupts normal speech articulation and causes distortions of vowels and phonation. Wide variations are noted in speaking rate and muscle tone. The variability in movements causing distortions of phonemes, excess loudness, and pitch variation often impede speech intelligibility and prosody. Slow hyperkinesias result in similar unintentional movements of the articulators, but the movements build slowly to a peak and are sustained for several seconds to minutes. The smooth, repetitive writhing and twisting motions of athetosis and the gradual, prolonged muscle contractions in dystonia prevent execution of desired speech movements and cause extraneous movements that disrupt ongoing speech. Prominent characteristics of slow hyperkinetic dysarthria are imprecise consonants, distorted vowels, harsh or strained-strangled phonation, intermittent articulatory breakdowns, and inappropriate silences.

The most frequent cause of hyperkinetic dysarthria is cerebral palsy, which has many etiologies, including congenital infections, prenatal or perinatal anoxia, and exposure to toxins. Hyperbilirubinemia (neonatal jaundice) used to be a common cause of kernicterus or deposition of bilirubin in the basal ganglia and brain stem nuclei, but this condition is now usually prevented by early recognition and treatment of jaundice.

Hypokinetic Dysarthrias

The hallmark of hypokinetic dysarthria is reduced range of movement in all the articulators. It is virtually always caused by Parkinson's disease, in which there is a loss of dopamine neurons in the substantia nigra bilaterally. Occasionally, this type of dysarthria is observed in patients with parkinsonism (some symptoms of Parkinson's disease caused by multiple strokes, toxins, encephalitis, or other neurodegenerative diseases that result in dysfunction or less specific loss of the dopamine-producing neurons). The salient features of hypokinetic dysarthria are restricted movements with minimal energy, frequent hesitations, false starts, and repetitions of phonemes, all subsequent to the rigidity of the muscles in Parkinson's disease or parkinsonism. The rate of speech is variable; there can be bradykinesia (slowness of movements) or short bursts of rapid speech with minimal range of motion of the articulators. Speech production, like other movements, often improves with administration of medications that bolster or replace dopamine, such as levodopa (e.g., Sinemet).

Now that the general function of each component of neural control of oral motor function (focusing on speech production) has been reviewed, the specific functions of each cranial nerve and muscle involved in oral motor function will be discussed. The child's anatomical development of the oral system as well as the structure and function of the temporomandibular joint will also be addressed. The information will be related to the processes of eating and drinking as well as speech production.

CRANIAL NERVES

The functions of each of the 12 cranial nerves should be familiar to the clinician who will assess and treat individuals with oral motor dysfunction. The sensory function of the olfactory nerve (I) allows the individual to smell food and other aromas. The person's interest in food may change significantly if he or she is hyperresponsive or unresponsive to smell. The optic nerve (II) carries visual information from the retina to the visual pathway that reaches the occipital lobe; damage results in loss of visual acuity or constriction of the visual fields in the affected eye(s). The oculomotor (III), trochlear (IV), and abducens (VI) nerves control eye movements, permitting search of the visual field. Difficulties with visual function can affect the individual's interest in food, the ability to self-feed, as well as visual scanning and tracking skills used in any number of activities of daily living. The acoustic nerve, now called the vestibulo-cochlear nerve (VIII), is responsible for vestibular function as well as hearing. Auditory function can have an impact on the individual's ability to attend, focus, and concentrate, as needed for eating, drinking, swallowing, speaking, and learning language. Difficulties with vestibular function may affect an individual's ability to maintain the head in alignment during eating, drinking, and speech production. Dizziness or nausea related to vestibular dysfunction may have an impact on his or her appetite or ability to participate in many activities of daily living. The spinal accessory nerve (XI) is responsible for turning the head and shrugging the shoulders, important for positioning the head in space and shoulder stability needed for jaw stability and graded jaw movement.

The cranial nerves that supply the oral musculature are particularly important to consider when working with individuals with oral motor disorders. The trigeminal nerve (V) is responsible for chewing (i.e., jaw closing and lateral jaw movement) as well as sensation to the face and mouth. It innervates the temporalis, the masseter, the medial pterygoid, the lateral pterygoid, as well as some other muscles. Damage to the lower motor neuron can result in unilateral muscle weakness, muscle atrophy, and jaw deviation to the side of the lesion. The person will often support the jaw with a hand while speaking or chewing for long periods. Damage to the upper motor neuron on one side rarely affects chewing or speaking, because the muscles of mastication receive bilateral upper motor neuron innervation (i.e., connection from the cortex of both hemispheres). Damage to bilateral upper motor neuron V results in spasticity, increased muscle stretch reflex (the jaw jerk), slowness, and reduced range of jaw opening. The function of the trigemial nerve (V) can be evaluated by palpation, observation, movement of the jaw against resistance, and testing sensation of the face.

The upper and lower motor neurons of the facial nerve (VII) synapse at the motor nucleus in the pons. This nucleus is responsible for wrinkling the forehead, closing the eyes, closing the mouth, smiling, tensing the cheeks, pulling down the corners of the mouth as in a frown, tensing the anterior neck muscles, and causing contraction of the stapedius muscle to protect the inner ear from trauma in response to loud noise. The muscles of the upper face (e.g., the frontalis muscle) receive innervation from bilateral facial nerve nuclei, whereas muscles of the lower face (e.g., the orbicularis oris and the buccinator) are innervated only by the facial motor nucleus on the contralateral side. Therefore, unilateral upper motor neuron damage results in weakness (facial droop), limited range of motion, and slowness of labial movements on the opposite side, but little or no involvement of the muscles of the forehead (since the frontalis receives input from the intact ipsilateral motor nucleus). The range and speed of movement of the lips is much greater in reflexive movements, such as laughing or crying, than in volitional movements such as speech, since reflexive movements do not involve the damaged upper motor neuron.

Lower motor neuron damage to the facial nerve results in flaccid weakness of both the upper and lower face on the side of the lesion, with no preservation of reflexive movements. Isolated paralysis of the facial nerve of unknown cause is known as *Bell's Palsy.* Persons with Bell's Palsy have (usually self-limited) weakness of the forehead, eye, and lip musculature on one side and may complain of sensitivity to loud noises. The eyes often will not close completely even during sleep. The function of the facial nerve (VII) can be evaluated by observation and asking the client to wrinkle the forehead, close the eyes tightly, smile, pucker, puff out the cheeks, and pull down the corners of the lips. The solitary nucleus of the facial nerve is responsible for taste on the anterior two-thirds of the tongue and a small portion of the nasopharynx as well as for the function of the salivary glands. Its function can be evaluated by placing sugar with a cotton-tipped applicator on the front of the tongue, and querying the person about the taste.

The glossopharyngeal nerve (IX) is responsible for sensation to the outer ear and taste on the posterior one-third of the tongue. It also contributes to pharyngeal constriction through innervation of the stylopharyngeus muscle and to sensation in the nasopharynx, oropharynx, and carotid sinus via the solitary nucleus and spinal trigeminal nucleus. Isolated dysfunction of either upper or lower motor neurons of nerve IX are not clinically apparent. Evaluation of the glossopharyngeal nerve requires assessment of pharyngeal sensation, typically by testing the gag reflex. To illustrate, suppose the person feels the stimulation of the posterior pharyngeal wall and is disturbed by it, but shows no palatal elevation. In this case, it can be concluded that the glossopharyngeal sensory function is intact, but the lower motor neuron component of the vagus nerve is impaired. Lack of sensation in the pharynx, on the other hand, implies damage to the glossopharyngeal sensory component. The motor function of nerve IX cannot be tested in isolation from the motor function of the vagus nerve (X).

The vagus nerve (X) is responsible for palatal elevation and depression, vocal fold opening and tensing, laryngeal excursion, pharyngeal constriction, and movement of the cricoid cartilage to change pitch. The vagus innervates all muscles of the velum, larynx, and pharynx except the stylopharyngeus. These muscles all have bilateral input from the cortex, so that unilateral upper motor neuron vagus damage is barely detectable, except perhaps as transient harsh phonation. Bilateral upper motor neuron damage results in hypernasality due to limited range and slowness of palatal movement, low-pitched and harsh or strained-strangled voice quality with little pitch variation, and hyperactive gag reflex. Lower motor neuron damage may result in absence of the gag reflex, reduced movement of the soft palate, absent or delayed swallow reflex, and breathy voice quality. Failure to elevate the larynx, close the vocal cords, and move the epiglottis to protect the larynx often results in aspiration of liquids (and less often, solids). Failure to elevate the palate often results in nasal regurgitation of liquids. The function of the vagus nerve (X) can be evaluated through observation of palatal movement with phonation, testing of the gag reflex, evaluation of voice quality, and assessment of swallowing.

The hypoglossal nerve (XII) is responsible for all tongue movements. It innervates the vertical, transverse, inferior longitudinal, superior longitudinal, styloglossus, genioglossus, and hyoglossus muscles. Upper motor neuron damage results in transient muscle weakness, delayed but prolonged increased muscle tone, reduced range of motion, as well as slowness and imprecision of lingual articulation. Lower motor neuron damage may result in muscle atrophy, decreased muscle tone, and muscle weakness on the side(s) of the lesion. There may also be deviation of the tongue to the side of the lesion, fasciculations, and imprecise articulation of lingual sounds. The function of the hypoglossal nerve (XII) lower motor neurons can be evaluated through observation for muscle atrophy, fasciculations, and tongue asymmetry. Strength can be assessed via tongue lateralization, protrusion, elevation, and retraction against resistance. Rapid sequential speech movements, as in the repeated production of / təkə /, can be used to evaluate rate and precision of lingual articulation. Sustained phonation helps to assess vocal fold function. Upper motor neuron function can be tested in the same ways, focusing on the rate and range of motion of the tongue movements.

Cranial nerve function can be assessed via the typical oral peripheral exam. However, many of the protocols do not specifically address all of the issues just discussed. Current assessments of oral motor function are relatively thorough in the evaluation of eating, drinking, and speaking, but do not adequately address localization of function delineated in Table 1.4.

TABLE 1.4 The Cranial Nerves

NUMBER	NAME	SUMMARY OF FUNCTION
I	Olfactory	Smell
II	Optic	Vision
III	Oculomotor	Innervation of muscles to move eyeball, pupil, and upper lid
IV	Trochlear	Innervation of superior oblique muscle of eye
V	Trigeminal	Chewing and sensation to face
VI	Abducens	Abduction of eye
VII	Facial	Movement of facial muscles, taste, salivary glands
VIII	Acoustic (Vestibular)	Equilibrium and hearing
IX	Glossopharyngeal	Taste, swallowing, elevation of the pharynx and larynx, parotid salivary gland, sensation to upper pharynx
X	Vagus	Taste, swallowing, elevation of palate, phonation, parasympathetic outflow to visceral organs
XI	Accessory	Turning of head and shrugging of shoulders
XII	Hypoglossal	Movement of tongue

Source: R. J. Love and W. G. Webb, *Neurology for the Speech-Language Pathologist,* 3rd ed. (Boston: Butterworth-Heinemann, 1996), p. 140. Reprinted by permission.

ANATOMICAL DEVELOPMENT OF THE OROPHARYNGEAL-LARYNGEAL MECHANISMS

This portion of the chapter will briefly cover some of the essential milestones of the oral, pharyngeal, and laryngeal developmental process. Particular attention will be given to the difference between the newborn and the adult oral, pharyngeal, and laryngeal mechanisms as well as the changes in development that occur in the first three years of life. The child's vocal tract approaches an adult-like configuration during the first three years of life (Kent, 1999, p. 45). This is a period of incredible growth and change in the child's vocal tract, allowing the child to develop increasingly sophisticated oral movements seen in the processes of eating, drinking, and speaking.

Figure 1.2 as well as the following list show the anatomical differences between the newborn and the adult mouth and pharynx:*

1. The oral space of the newborn is small.
2. The lower jaw of the newborn is small and somewhat retracted.
3. Sucking pads are present in infants but not in adults.
4. The tongue takes more relative space in the newborn due to the diminished size of the lower jaw and the presence of sucking pads in the cheeks.

*From Suzanne Evans Morris and Marsha Dunn Klein, *Pre-Feeding Skills,* p. 10, Copyright © 1987 by Therapy Skill Builders, a division of The Psychological Corporation. Reproduced by permission.

FIGURE 1.2 Anatomical Differences between the Newborn and the Adult Mouth and Pharynx

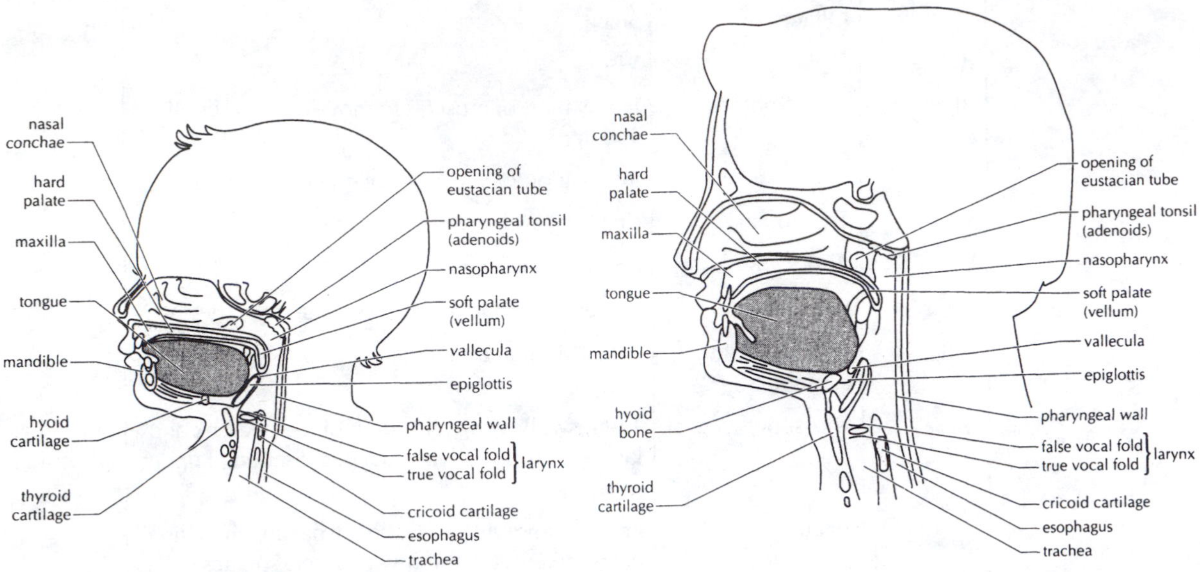

Mouth and pharynx of the newborn **Mouth and pharynx of the adult**

Source: Suzanne Evans Morris and Marsha Dunn Klein, *Pre-Feeding Skills,* p. 8, Copyright © 1987 by Therapy Skill Builders, a division of The Psychological Corporation. Reproduced by permission.

5. The tongue shows restrictions in movement partially because of the restricted intraoral cavity in which it resides.
6. Newborns are obligate nose breathers. They do not breathe through their mouths.
7. The epiglottis and soft palate are in approximation in the newborn as a protective mechanism.
8. Newborns often can breathe and swallow at the same time.
9. The larynx is higher in the neck of the newborn than in the older infant or adult. This eliminates the need for sophisticated laryngeal closure to protect the airway during swallowing.
10. The eustachian tube in the infant lies in a horizontal position. It assumes a more vertical angle in the adult.

(Note: Researchers today are not as certain that newborns can, in fact, breathe and swallow at the same time [item 8 above].)

The oral space (i.e., area that can be filled with air or fluid) inside the newborn's mouth is extremely small. The child's tongue and sucking pads fill the mouth. This helps create a safe oral stage for the infant. The newborn's tongue moves in a primitive protraction-retraction (i.e., front/back) pattern to extract mother's milk from the breast or formula from a bottle. The small bony oral structure and the relatively large tongue and cheek pads assist the newborn in the creation of adequate intraoral pressure needed to take the fluid from the breast or bottle into the mouth.

The next part of the system consists of several pharyngeal mechanisms that help keep the newborn safe from aspiration during the pharyngeal stage of the swallow. In the pharynx the newborn's epiglottis and soft palate approximate. This allows the newborn to breathe through the nose without risk of aspiration of fluid from the mouth. When a swallow occurs, the epiglottis easily covers the infant's trachea. The larynx is in a relatively high position in the newborn's neck. The newborn's larynx does not need to rise in the same manner as seen in the older infant or adult during a swallow secondary to the location of the larynx. The positioning of the epiglottis and larynx provide natural protection of the airway for the newborn during swallowing.

The infant's eustachian tube is positioned more horizontally than the adult's eustachian tube. This is an important consideration, as fluids can enter the infant's eustachian tube from the pharynx and move into the middle ear space. This could cause otitis media (i.e., middle ear infections) and is a reason for feeding an infant in a more upright position as opposed to total recline (i.e., keeping the infant's ear above the infant's mouth; Rosenfeld-Johnson, 1999a). Very young infants can be fed at a 45-degree angle, and older infants can be fed at angles between 45 and 90 degrees.

Infants who are born prematurely often have difficulties with feeding based on anatomical as well as physiological differences. Many of these infants have underdeveloped sucking pads, limited tongue movements, poor lip seal, difficulties organizing the suck-swallow-breathe sequence as well as difficulties with muscle tone and proximal stability (Morris & Klein, 1987). This creates a problem in the oral phase of the feeding process. Infants who are premature often have difficulty attaining adequate intraoral pressure, since the oral structures are not as well developed as those of full-term infants. Without adequate intraoral pressure, the infant will often have difficulty establishing a nutritive suck. Although the infant born prematurely may have a suckle-swallow response, the suckle may not be strong enough to extract the liquid from the breast or bottle.

During the first three years of life, infants born full term become more adult-like as their oral structures develop (Kent, 1999). Some of the structural changes seen in the child during this time include:

1. Enlargement of the oral space
2. Growth of the lower jaw and other bony structures of the face
3. Disappearance of the sucking pads
4. Increased muscle tone and more skilled movement in the tongue
5. Lowering of the larynx
6. Separation of the epiglottis and soft palate
7. Development of more sophisticated movement (i.e., elevation) of the larynx during swallowing

The child's oral space becomes larger during the first three years of life, secondary to growth of the bony structures and the general maturation of the oral mechanism. The sucking pads disappear as the child develops more sophisticated oral control. The primary dentition begins to emerge around 6 months of age, with the first primary molars achieving "occlusal contact at about 16 months" of age, marking "the appearance of a stable jaw closing pattern" (Kent, 1999, p. 38). The development of jaw stability is crucial for the processes of eating, drinking, and speech production. The dentition provides important contact points for lingual articulation used in sound production (Boshart, 1999; Kent, 1999, Rosenfeld-Johnson, 1999a). For example, the child stabilizes the tongue in the back molar region for rapid coarticulated speech. The child's increasing ability to actively maintain lip closure and the approximation of the cheeks near the teeth assist the child in attaining the intraoral pressure needed for a mature swallowing pattern and precise speech production. A rapid growth of the child's lips occurs between the first and second years of life (Kent, 1999). The child's tongue movements become increasingly dissociated from jaw movements during the first three years of life, allowing him or her to use the tongue to retrieve food from the sulci and molar areas as well as produce a variety of speech sounds.

As the child develops, the larynx is lower in the neck and the epiglottis and soft palate no longer approximate. By age 3, the child generally has a swallow that resembles the sophisticated swallow of the adult, as the larynx and pharynx are well developed (Kent, 1999). The larynx now rises in the neck to protect the airway during the swallow. The soft palate rises to prevent nasal reflux, and the epiglottis provides a limited amount of protection of the airway.

Kent (1999) describes the development of the oral mechanism between 3 years of age and adulthood. During the period of development from ages 3 to 7, the overall oral system continues its gradual growth. By 4 years of age, the child's vocal tract has nearly achieved its adult-like form, and by 5 years of age, the child's vocal tract is essentially the same shape as that of the adult. The child's skull almost reaches adult size around age 6, and the child's permanent teeth begin to emerge at this time. From ages 7 to 10, the lower face goes through a noticeable growth spurt. By age 8, the child's jaw moves with adult-like precision, and by age 9, the child's velopharyngeal closure pattern may change secondary to nasopharyngeal tonsil atrophy. Rapid growth is seen in the individual's tongue and lips between the ages of 9 and 13. The permanent teeth continue to erupt until 14 years of age, with the exception of the wisdom teeth. Growth of the mandible, tongue, and lips continues until 18 years of age or later in males and approximately 16 years of age in females.

STRUCTURES INVOLVED IN EATING, DRINKING, AND SPEECH PRODUCTION

Muscle and temporomandibular joint function are important to the processes of eating, drinking, and speaking. The muscles work in a coordinated fashion so that graded lip, jaw, and tongue movements as well as jaw and tongue stability and graded jaw movement can be attained. The temporomandibular joint is also responsible for jaw movement. Jaw instability and difficulties with graded jaw movement are frequently noted in individuals with oral motor concerns. The mandible moves and the maxilla remains stationary during eating, drinking, and speaking. An individual must learn to actively stabilize the mandible in a variety of positions so that the tongue can move separately from the jaw during these processes. The person with jaw instability frequently has difficulty with tongue and jaw dissociation and tongue stability. It is important for the clinician to understand the functions of the muscles involved in the processes of eating, drinking, and speech production in order to provide effective oral motor assessment and treatment. The oral musculature has a significant impact on the development and positioning of the bony oral structures. The function of the temporomandibular joint is also important to understand. The activity of this joint and the musculature of the oral mechanism significantly affect all oral motor function. By assessing muscle function and the mobility of the temporomandibular joint, the clinician can better address discrete oral motor concerns during treatment.

Jaw and Facial Muscles

The digastric, mylohyoid, geniohyoid, and lateral pterygoid muscles lower and protrude the jaw. The digastric and geniohyoid muscles depress the jaw. They can be palpated by placing the fingertips on the tissue under the jaw and opening the jaw. The mylohyoid muscles also depress the mandible and cannot be palpated. The lateral pterygoid muscles depress the mandible as well as draw the mandible forward and sideways. These can be palpated by placing a gloved finger inside the individual's cheek area and asking him or her to lower, protrude, and lateralize the jaw (see Figure 1.3).

The appendix called "Physiologic Phonetics" in *Anatomy for Speech and Hearing* (4th ed.) by John M. Palmer (1993) provides an excellent summary of the muscles and muscle functions required to produce specific speech sounds. The movements of the digastric (anterior belly), mylohyoid, geniohyoid, and lat-

FIGURE 1.3 Mandibular Depressors

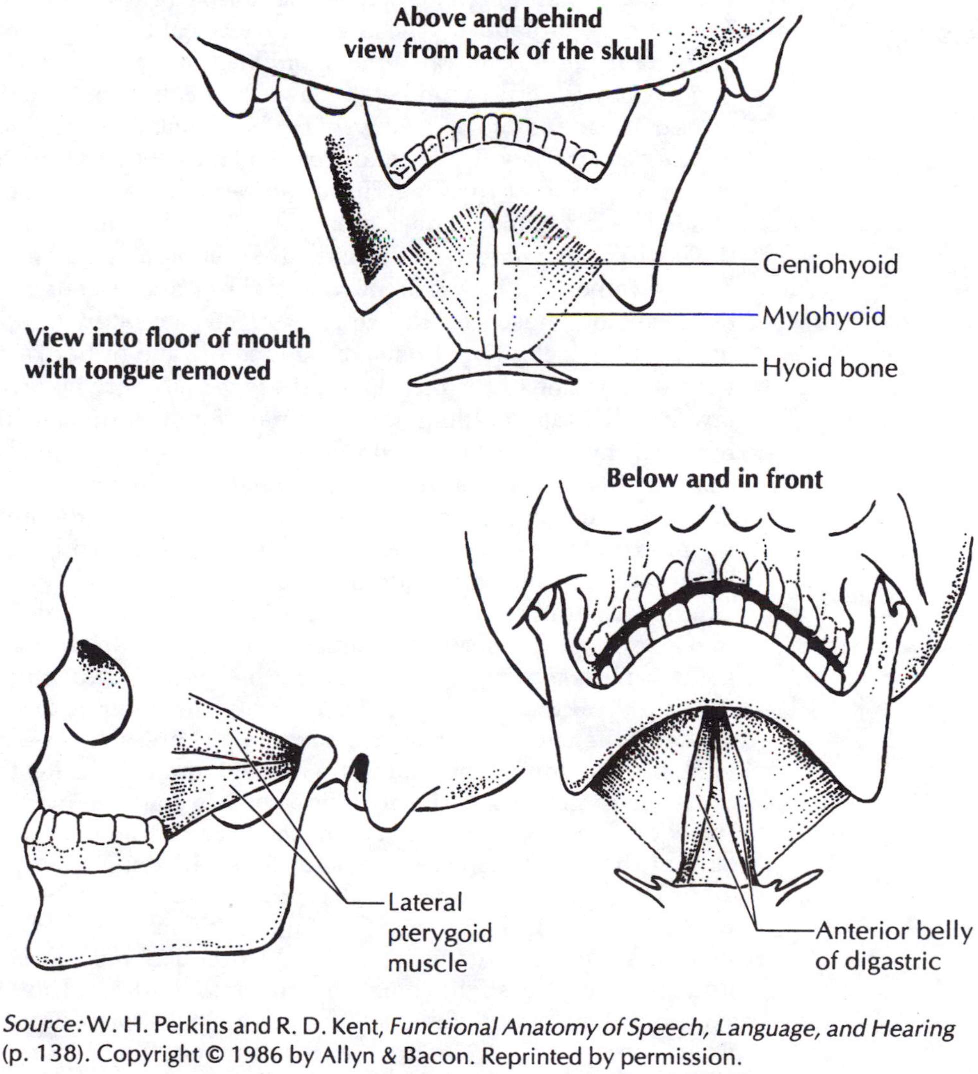

Source: W. H. Perkins and R. D. Kent, *Functional Anatomy of Speech, Language, and Hearing* (p. 138). Copyright © 1986 by Allyn & Bacon. Reprinted by permission.

eral pterygoid muscles are important for the production of the speech sounds /i/, /ɪ/, /ɔ/, /o/, /ʊ/, /u/, /ʌ/, /ɝ/, /b/, /p/, /f/, /v/, /n/, /ŋ/, /θ/, /ð/, /ʃ/, /ʒ/, /l/, /r/, /j/, /hw/, /w/, and /h / requiring slight depression of the mandible. The movements of these muscles also assist in the production of the /e/, /ɛ/, and /a/ sounds requiring moderate depression of the mandible as well as the /æ/ sound requiring considerable depression of the mandible (see Table 1.5 on pages 24–26).

Although the areas of neural control may be different for the processes of eating and drinking versus the process of speech production, common musculature is used. Based on the actions of the digastric (anterior belly), the mylohyoid, and the geniohyoid (i.e., mandibular depression or assistance with mandibular depression), these muscles are believed to assist with jaw stabilization; mouth opening to accept the bottle, cup, spoon, and so on; as well as graded jaw movements used for the processes of sucking, munching, and chewing. The lateral pterygoid muscles assist with these processes as well as the processes of suckling and diagonal-rotary chewing. The lateral pterygoid muscles draw the mandible forward and sideways in addition to depressing it. Suckling involves the front and back movement of the jaw, and diagonal-rotary chewing involves side-to-side movement of the jaw.

The temporalis, masseter, and medial pterygoid muscles close the jaw by raising the mandible. The temporalis muscles raise and retract the mandible. They can be palpated on the lateral surfaces of the skull above each ear as the individual closes or retracts the mandible. The masseter muscles close the jaw and assist with protraction of the jaw. They can be palpated on the lateral surfaces of the mandible in the area of the back molars as the individual closes and/or protracts the jaw. The medial pterygoid muscles raise the mandible and assist with protrusion of the jaw. These can be palpated by placing a gloved finger inside the individual's cheek area and asking him or her to close and protrude the jaw. The movements of the masseter, temporalis, and medial pterygoid muscles are important for the production of the /s/ and /z/ sounds, which require dental occlusion. Based on the actions of the masseter, temporalis, and medial pterygoid muscles (i.e., raising the mandible and either retracting or assisting with protraction of the mandible), these muscles are believed to be involved in jaw stabilization; grading jaw movement for suckling, sucking, biting, munching, and chewing; as well as lip closure (i.e., they bring the lips into approximation) during the processes of eating and drinking (see Figure 1.4).

The buccinator, orbicularis oris, and the mentalis muscles contribute to facial expression as well as the processes of eating, drinking, and speaking. The buccinator muscles maintain the positioning of the cheeks near the teeth and can be palpated by touching the cheeks as the individual moves the lips. The movements of the buccinator muscles are important for the production of the sounds /f/ and /v/ requiring tension in the lower lip. During the processes of eating and drinking, the buccinator muscles are believed to assist with the tightening of the cheeks to provide the intraoral pressure needed for suckling and sucking, the adjustment of the lip corners and cheeks for the retention of food and fluid in the mouth, the prevention of food spillage into the buccal cavity during chewing, and the movement of food from the side to the center of the tongue so that the tongue can create a bolus for swallowing.

The orbicularis oris muscles provide lip closure and can be palpated by touching the lips as the individual moves them. The movements of the orbicularis oris muscles are important for the production of the sounds /ɝ/, /ʃ/, /ʒ/, /r/, and /j/ requiring slight labial protrusion; /ɔ/, /o/, and /ʊ/ requiring moderate labial protrusion; /u/, /hw/, and /w/ requiring strong labial protrusion; /p/, /b/, and /m/ requiring strong lip compression; and /f/ and /v/ requiring slight elevation and tension in the lower lip. The orbicularis oris muscles have a significant

FIGURE 1.4 Mandibular Elevators

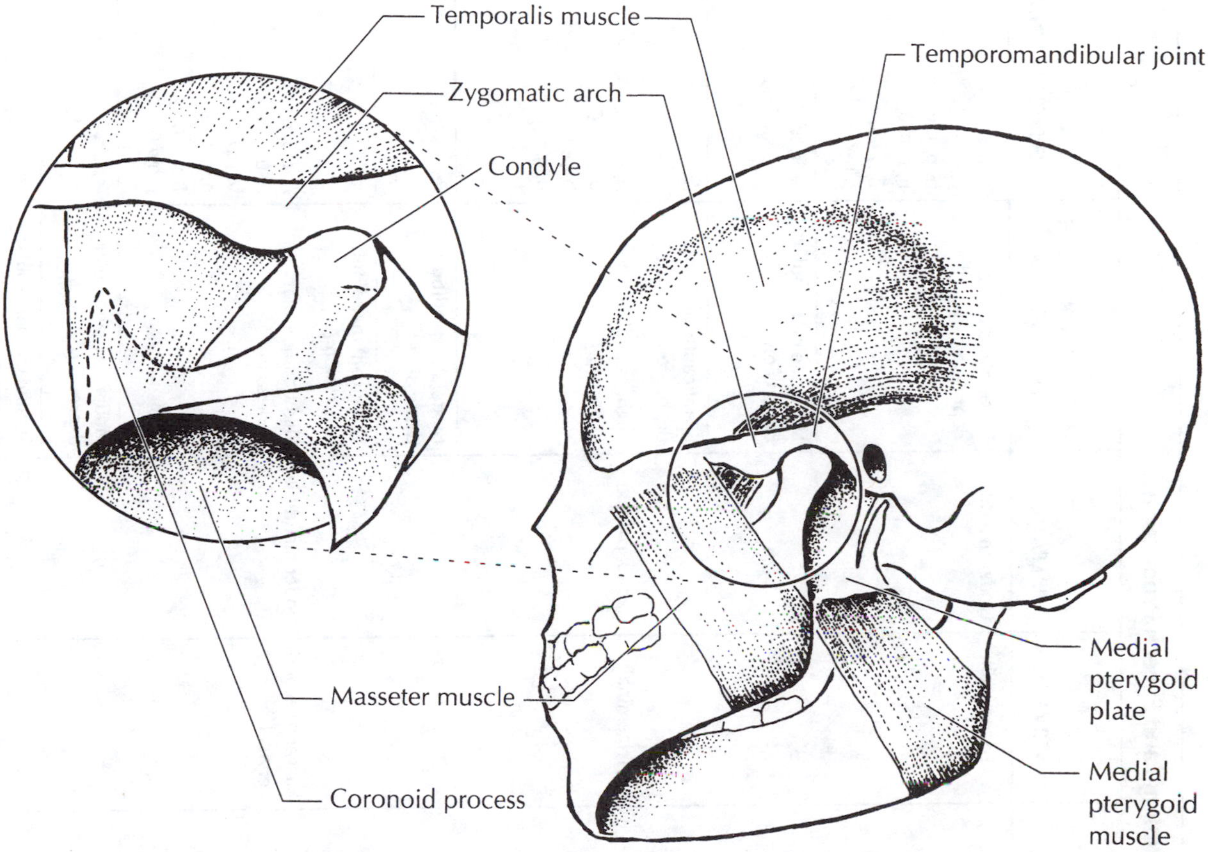

Source: W. H. Perkins and R. D. Kent, *Functional Anatomy of Speech, Language, and Hearing* (p. 137). Copyright © 1986 by Allyn & Bacon. Reprinted by permission.

role during the processes of eating and drinking. They help sustain lip closure on the nipple and lip contact on the cup. They grade lip rounding and tension during drinking as well as upper lip movement used in clearing food from a spoon. The orbicularis oris muscles also provide sustained lip closure during the processes of chewing and swallowing as well as graded lip closure during the oral management of foods. Gradations of lip closure necessarily occur secondary to the presentation of different food textures, the changing placement of food within the mouth, and an individual's skill in tongue movement to position food in the mouth.

The mentalis muscles wrinkle the chin and evert the lower lip. These can be palpated by touching the chin as the individual tenses the lips or pushes out the lower lip. The movements of the mentalis muscles are important for the production of the /ɛ/ sound requiring moderate lip parting; the /ɝ/, /ʃ/, /ʒ/, /r/, and /j/ sounds requiring slight labial protrusion; the /ɔ/ and /o/ sounds requiring moderate labial protrusion; the /u/, /hw/, and /w/ sounds requiring strong labial protrusion; and the /f/ and /v/ sounds requiring slight elevation of the lower lip. The mentalis muscles evert the lower lip during breast, bottle, and cup drinking (see Table 1.5).

TABLE 1.5 Jaw and Facial Muscles Involved in Eating, Drinking, and Speech Production

MUSCLE	ORIGIN	INSERTION	GENERAL ACTION	INNERVATION	PALPATION	ACTION FOR SPEECH PRODUCTION	SPEECH SOUNDS	FUNCTIONS IN EATING AND DRINKING
Digastric (anterior belly)	Mandible (inner surface near symphysis)	Intermediate tendon (at hyoid bone)	Depresses mandible	V (Trigeminal)	Under mandible	Slight mandibular depression	/i, ɪ, ɔ, o, ʊ, u, ʌ, ɝ, b, p, f, v, n, ŋ, θ, ð, ʃ, ʒ, l, r, j, hw, w, h/	Jaw stabilization; opening mouth for spoon, cup, bottle, etc.; graded jaw movements during sucking, munching, and chewing
						Moderate mandibular depression	/e, ɛ, a/	
						Significant mandibular depression	/æ/	
Mylohyoid	Mandible (mylohyoid line)	Hyoid bone (median raphe and body)	Assists in depressing mandible	V (Trigeminal)	Cannot palpate	Slight mandibular depression	/i, ɪ, ɔ, o, ʊ, u, ʌ, ɝ, b, p, f, v, n, ŋ, θ, ð, ʃ, ʒ, l, r, j, hw, w, h/	Jaw stabilization; opening mouth for spoon, cup, bottle, etc.; graded jaw movements during sucking, munching, and chewing
						Moderate mandibular depression	/e, ɛ, a/	
						Significant mandibular depression	/æ/	
Geniohyoid	Mandible (mental spine)	Hyoid bone (body)	Depresses mandible	First and second cervical	Under mandible	Slight mandibular depression	/i, ɪ, ɔ, o, ʊ, u, ʌ, ɝ, b, p, f, v, n, ŋ, θ, ð, ʃ, ʒ, l, r, j, hw, w, h/	Jaw stabilization; opening mouth for spoon, cup, bottle, etc.; graded jaw movements during sucking, munching, and chewing
						Moderate mandibular depression	/e, ɛ, a/	
						Significant mandibular depression	/æ/	

Lateral Pterygoid	Pterygoid plate (lateral surface)	Mandible (TMJ capsule)	Depresses mandible, draws mandible forward and sideways	V (Trigeminal)	Interior cheek area	Slight mandibular depression	/i, ɪ, ɔ, o, ʊ, u, ʌ, ɝ, b, p, f, v, n, ŋ, θ, ð, ʃ, ʒ, l, r, j, hw, w, h/	Jaw stabilization; opening mouth for spoon, cup, bottle, etc.; graded jaw movements during suckling, sucking, munching, and diagonal-rotary chewing
						Moderate mandibular depression	/e, ɛ, a/	
						Significant mandibular depression	/æ/	
Temporalis	Lateral surface of temporal bone	Mandible (coronoid process and ramus)	Raises and retracts mandible	V (Trigeminal)	Lateral surface at temple	Jaw closure for dental occlusion	/s, z/	Jaw stabilization; graded jaw movements during suckling, sucking, biting, munching, and chewing; lip closure
Masseter	Zygomatic arch	Mandible (lateral surface of ramus)	Raises mandible, assists protraction	V (Trigeminal)	Lateral mandible in area of back molars	Jaw closure for dental occlusion	/s, z/	Jaw stabilization; graded jaw movements during suckling, sucking, biting, munching, and chewing; lip closure
Medial Pterygoid	Pterygoid plate (medial surface)	Mandible (medial surface of ramus)	Raises mandible, assists protraction	V (Trigeminal)	Interior cheek area	Jaw closure for dental occlusion	/s, z/	Jaw stabilization; graded jaw movements during suckling, sucking, biting, munching, and chewing; lip closure
Buccinator	Maxilla, mandible	Lips	Maintains cheeks near teeth	VII (Facial)	Cheeks	Lower lip tension	/f, v/	Tightening of cheeks with inward compression during suckling and sucking, adjustment of lip corners and cheeks to retain food and fluid in mouth, use of cheeks during chewing to prevent food spillage into buccal cavity, assistance in moving food from side to center of tongue to create bolus for swallowing

TABLE 1.5 Continued

Orbicularis Oris	Maxilla, mandible, lips, buccinator	Mucous membranes, muscles inserting into lip	Closes lips	VII (Facial)	Around lips	Slight labial protrusion	/ɝ, ʃ, ʒ, r, j/	Sustained lip closure on nipple; sustained lip contact on cup; gradations in lip rounding and tension while drinking from breast, bottle, or cup; graded upper lip movement in clearing food from spoon; sustained lip closure during chewing and swallowing; gradations in lip closure during chewing secondary to food texture or placement and tongue skill
						Moderate labial protrusion	/ɔ, o, ʊ/	
						Strong labial protrusion	/u, hw, w/	
						Strong lip compression	/b, p, m/	
						Slight elevation and tension in lower lip	/f, v/	
Mentalis	Mandible (mental tuberosity)	Integument of chin and orbicularis oris	Wrinkles chin, everts lower lip	VII (Facial)	Chin	Moderate labial parting	/ɛ/	Lip eversion in breast, bottle, and cup drinking
						Slight labial protrusion	/ɝ, ʃ, ʒ, r, j/	
						Moderate labial protrusion	/ɔ, o,/	
						Strong labial protrusion	/u, hw, w/	
						Slight lower lip elevation	/f, v/	

Sources: S. E. Morris, "Developmental Implications for the Management of Feeding Problems in Neurologically Impaired Infants," *Seminars in Speech and Language, 6* (1985): pp. 293–315; J. M. Palmer, *Anatomy for Speech and Hearing,* 4th ed. (Baltimore: Williams & Wilkins, 1992), pp. 62, 261–270; K. W. Sieg and S. P. Adams, *Illustrated Essentials of Musculoskeletal Anatomy* (Gainesville, FL: Megabooks, Inc., 1985), pp. 134–135; W. R. Zemlin, *Speech and Hearing Science: Anatomy and Physiology* (Englewood Cliffs, NJ: Prentice-Hall, Inc., 1968), pp. 558–566.

The clinician will often note muscle dysfunction in individuals with oral motor difficulties. Muscles may be low in tone or high in tone. Muscle weakness and limited range of motion is frequently observed in individuals with oral motor deficits. Hypermobility in the temporomandibular joints may exist as the result of lax ligaments. Immobility may also be seen in the temporomandibular joints. By understanding the function of the temporomandibular joints and the functions of the muscles involved in jaw stability and mobility, the clinician can better determine the appropriateness of specific assessment and treatment approaches discussed in future chapters. The temporomandibular joints will be discussed in the next section.

Temporomandibular Joints (TMJ)

The temporomandibular joints are synovial joints. Synovial joints allow relatively free movement between the bones that comprise the joint. In order to have normal jaw function, there needs to be (1) structural freedom provided by the synovium and (2) normal seating of the mandibular head and mandibular fossae (Nelson, Meek, & Moore, 1994). A smooth, articular cartilage covers the temporomandibular joint surfaces on each side. A capsule within each joint, the synovium, is lined by a membrane that secretes lubricating fluid. Temporomandibular joints also have kinesthetic sensation so that the individual is continuously aware of each joint's position (Palmer, 1993). The complex temporomandibular joint with its intricate geometric arrangement of muscles allows the mandible to depress, elevate, protrude, retract, lateralize, and rotate. The movements of the mandible can influence lip posture, tongue position, the configuration of the oropharynx, and possibly laryngeal height (Zemlin, 1998).

Temporomandibular joints contain three ligaments that protect the joints from separation and provide some elasticity to the joints. The temporomandibular ligament is the primary ligament that limits movement of the joint (Zemlin, 1998). The sphenomandibular ligament and the stylomandibular ligament are accessory ligaments to the temporomandibular ligament. Sensory nerve endings in the ligaments indicate when pain is present in each joint. Lax ligaments in the temporomandibular joints may fail to maintain each joint's approximation and alignment and can significantly affect oral motor function. This may be found in individuals with Down syndrome. Unilateral temporomandibular joint immobility is fairly common in individuals with cerebral palsy and traumatic brain injury (Nelson et al., 1994). This results in asymmetry during oral motor function for these individuals. Some clinical indicators of immobility in at least one of the temporomandibular joints include opening and closing the mouth using a hinge-like movement, loosing saliva from the mouth, and difficulty chewing or placing food onto the molars for chewing (Nelson et al., 1994).

Intrinsic Tongue Muscles

The intrinsic tongue muscles are completely contained within the tongue and are responsible for the refined movements of widening, flattening, elongating, shortening, narrowing, thickening, and lateralizing the tongue (see Figure 1.5). These muscles lift the sides, raise and depress the tip, as well as form a convex and concave dorsum in the tongue changing the shape and contour of the tongue.

The vertical muscles widen and flatten the tongue. These movements are important for the production of the sounds /θ/, /ð/, /ʃ/, and /ʒ/. These sounds

FIGURE 1.5 Intrinsic Tongue Muscles

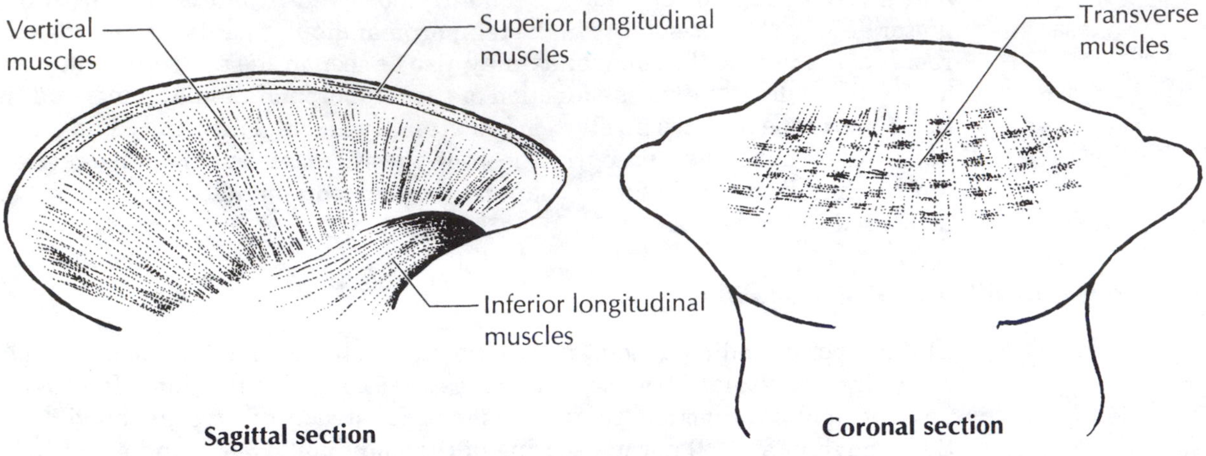

Source: W. H. Perkins and R. D. Kent, *Functional Anatomy of Speech, Language, and Hearing* (p. 134). Copyright © 1986 by Allyn & Bacon. Reprinted by permission.

require flattening of the tongue dorsum. During the processes of eating and drinking, the vertical muscles are believed to be responsible for tongue flattening observed during suckling and sucking of liquids and semisolid foods. The tongue also spreads to accept the spoon into the mouth and as part of the swallowing process (see Table 1.6).

The transverse muscles elongate, narrow, and thicken the tongue as well as lift the sides of the tongue. These movements are important for the production of the sounds /ɝ/, /l/, and /r/, which require elevation of the sides of the tongue. They are also important for the production of the sounds /s/, /z/, and /j/, which require grooving of the tongue. The transverse muscles play a role in the processes of eating and drinking. Tongue grooving is noted during the suckling and sucking of liquids and semisolid foods. Shallow tongue cupping is observed during the acceptance of the spoon into the mouth. Tongue cupping is also an important aspect in bolus formation (i.e., when the food or fluid is collected by the tongue) prior to swallowing.

The inferior longitudinal muscles create a convex dorsum, depress the tongue tip, and shorten the tongue. These movements are important for the production of the sounds /i/, /ɪ/, /e/, /ɔ/, /ʃ/, /ʒ/, and /r/, which require depression of the tongue apex. They are also important for the production of the sounds /ʊ/, /u/, and /ʌ/, which require depression of the anterior tongue dorsum. The inferior longitudinal muscles are believed to participate in the gradation of tongue humping during chewing and bolus management. This is particularly important when collecting the bolus in the mouth prior to the swallow. The tongue elevates posteriorly so that the bolus can be formed in the mouth. Once the bolus is collected, the tongue releases the bolus into the pharynx. The inferior longitudinal muscles may also assist the tongue in clearing food from the lower lip and lower sulcus.

The superior longitudinal muscles shorten the tongue, raise the tongue tip and edges, and form a concave dorsum. These movements are important for the production of the sounds /t/ and /d/, which require the elevation of the tip and

TABLE 1.6 Intrinsic Tongue Muscles

MUSCLE	ORIGIN	INSERTION	GENERAL ACTION	INNERVATION	ACTION FOR SPEECH PRODUCTION	SPEECH SOUNDS	FUNCTIONS IN EATING AND DRINKING
Vertical	Mucous membrane of tongue dorsum	Tongue sides and inferior surface	Widens and flattens tongue	XII (Hypoglossal)	Tongue dorsum flattening	/ θ, ð, ʃ, ʒ, /	Tongue flattening during suckling and sucking; tongue spreading to accept spoon and to swallow
Transverse	Lingual septum	Mucosa of tongue dorsum and lateral margins	Elongates and narrows tongue; elevates sides	XII (Hypoglossal)	Side of tongue elevation	/ʒ̃, l, r/	Tongue grooving during suckling and sucking; shallow tongue cupping to accept spoon; tongue cupping for bolus formation
					Tongue grooving	/s, z, j/	
Inferior Longitudinal	Hyoid bone; tongue root	Tongue apex	Creates convex dorsum, depresses tip, shortens tongue	XII (Hypoglossal)	Tongue apex depression	/i, ɪ, e, ɔ, ʃ, ʒ, r/	Gradations in tongue humping during chewing and bolus management; clearing food from lower lip and lower sulcus
					Anterior tongue dorsum depression	/ʊ, u, ʌ/	
Superior Longitudinal	Near epiglottis	Tongue sides and apex	Shortens tongue, raises tongue tip and edges, forms concave dorsum	XII (Hypoglossal)	Tongue tip and lateral margin elevation	/t, d/	Tongue front to palate contact and release in true suck; elevated tongue tip position at rest and during swallowing; tongue grooving during suckling and sucking; shallow tongue cupping to accept spoon; tongue cupping for bolus formation; tongue tip elevation during food lateralization and in clearing food from upper lip or upper sulcus
					Tongue tip, lateral margin, and central apical elevation	/ʧ, ʤ/	
					Tongue apex elevation	/l/	

Sources: S. E. Morris, "Developmental Implications for the Management of Feeding in Neurologically Impaired Infants," *Seminars in Speech and Language, 6* (1985): pp. 293–315; J. M. Palmer, *Anatomy for Speech and Hearing,* 4th ed. (Baltimore: Williams & Wilkins, 1993), pp. 69, 79, 80, 83, 261–270; W. R. Zemlin, *Speech and Hearing Science: Anatomy and Physiology,* 4th ed. (Boston: Allyn & Bacon, 1998), pp. 253–254.

lateral margins of the tongue; the sounds /ʧ/ and /ʤ/, which require the elevation of the tip, lateral margins, and central apical portion of the tongue; and the /l/ sound, which requires the elevation of the tongue tip. The superior longitudinal muscles seem to have a significant role in the processes of eating and drinking. They are believed to assist the processes requiring tongue tip elevation and tongue cupping or grooving. The front of the tongue makes contact with the palate during true sucking. The tongue tip elevates to the alveolar ridge for a normal, mature tongue resting position as well as mature swallowing. Tongue tip elevation also occurs during tongue lateralization and when clearing food from the upper lip or upper sulcus. Tongue grooving occurs during the suckling and sucking of liquids and semisolids. Shallow tongue cupping occurs when the individual accepts the spoon into the mouth. Tongue cupping is also important for the adequate formation of the bolus prior to swallowing (see Table 1.6).

Extrinsic Tongue Muscles

The extrinsic tongue muscles are responsible for changes in tongue position in the mouth (see Figure 1.6). These muscles elevate, depress, protrude, and retract the tongue and are important in the processes of eating, drinking, and speech production.

The styloglossus muscles move the tongue upward and backward. They may also assist the tongue in forming a concave dorsum. These movements are important for the production of the sounds /i/, /ɪ/, /e/, and /ɛ/ requiring elevation of the posterior dorsum of the tongue; /ɝ/ requiring tongue border elevation; /t/ and /d/ requiring elevation of the tongue tip and borders; /k/, /g/, and /ŋ/ requir-

FIGURE 1.6 Extrinsic Tongue Muscles

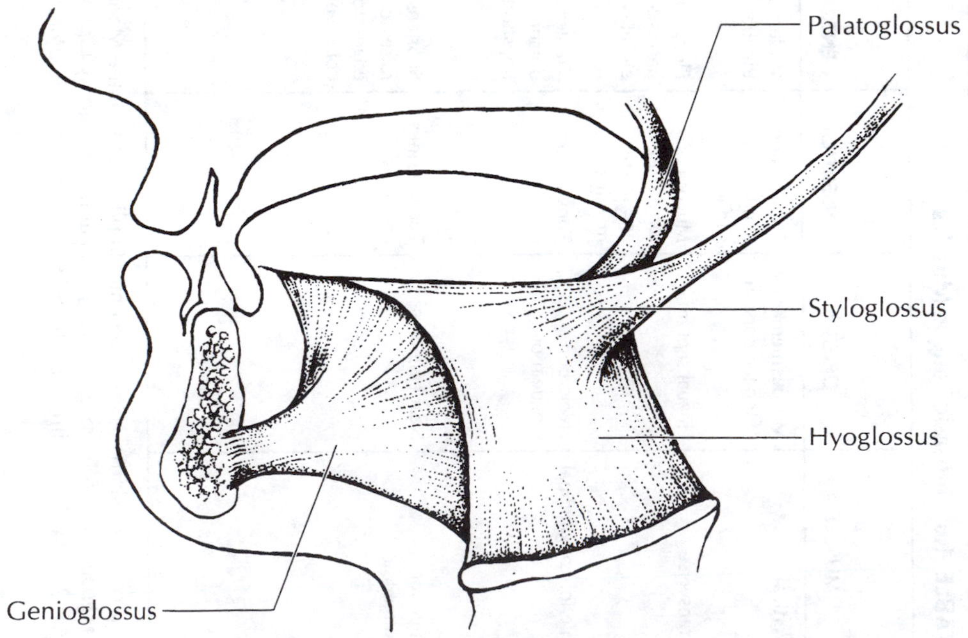

Source: W. H. Perkins and R. D. Kent, *Functional Anatomy of Speech, Language, and Hearing* (p. 135). Copyright © 1986 by Allyn & Bacon. Reprinted by permission.

ing elevation of the middle of the tongue; /n/ and /l/ requiring elevation of the apex of the tongue; and /ʧ/ and /ʤ/ requiring elevation of the tip, lateral margins, and central apical portion of the tongue. During the processes of eating and drinking, the styloglossus muscles are believed to assist with the graded tongue movement needed during chewing and bolus management. This is particularly important when collecting the bolus in the mouth prior to the swallow. The tongue elevates posteriorly so that the bolus can be formed in the mouth. Once the bolus is collected, the tongue releases the bolus into the pharynx. The styloglossus muscles may also assist with tongue front to palate contact and release during the true suck; elevated tongue tip to alveolar ridge position used in a mature tongue resting position and a mature swallowing pattern; as well as tongue blade, front, and tip elevation used during the lateralization of food in the mouth. If the styloglossus muscles assist in forming a concave tongue dorsum, they may also assist in tongue grooving noted during suckling and sucking of liquids and semisolid foods, shallow tongue cupping to accept the spoon into the mouth, as well as tongue cupping during bolus formation (see Table 1.7).

The genioglossus muscles depress, retract, and protrude the tongue. These movements are important for the production of the sounds /i/, /ɪ/, /e/, /ɔ/, /ʃ/, /ʒ/, and /r/ requiring depression of the apex of the tongue; /æ/, /a/, /ɔ/, /ʊ/, /u/, and /ʌ/ requiring depression of the anterior tongue dorsum; /o/ requiring depression of the tongue dorsum; /s/ and /z/ requiring extension of the apex of the tongue; and /θ/ and /ð/ requiring protrusion of the tongue tip. During the processes of eating and drinking, the genioglossus muscles may assist with the tongue protraction-retraction pattern used in the early suckle-swallow response and movement of food toward the pharynx for swallowing. When the genioglossus muscles depress the tongue into a bowl shape, they are believed to assist with tongue grooving and cupping for the suckling and sucking of liquids and semisolid foods, the acceptance of the spoon into the mouth, and bolus formation.

The hyoglossus muscles also depress and retract the tongue. These muscles perform functions similar to those of the genioglossus muscles. The movements of the hyoglossus muscles assist in the production of the /i/, /ɪ/, /e/, /ɔ/, /ʃ/, /ʒ/, and /r/ sounds requiring the depression of the tongue apex; /æ/, /a/, /ɔ/, /ʊ/, /u/, and /ʌ/ requiring depression of the anterior tongue dorsum; and /o/ requiring tongue dorsum depression. The hyoglossus muscles are also believed to play a significant role in the processes of eating and drinking. They are thought to assist tongue depression for the acceptance of the nipple or spoon. Tongue depression also occurs during activities involving the cupping or grooving of the tongue (e.g., suckling, sucking, bolus formation, etc.). The hyoglossus muscles may assist in the protraction-retraction pattern used during the suckle-swallow as well as in the movement of food back toward the pharynx for swallowing.

The glossopalatine muscles raise the posterior portions of the tongue and lower the soft palate. These movements are important to the production of the /i/, /ɪ/, /e/, and /ɛ/ sounds requiring elevation of the tongue dorsum; the /ɝ/, /l/, and /r/ sounds requiring tongue border elevation; the /k/, /g/, and /ŋ/ sounds requiring elevation of the tongue middle; and the /j/ sound requiring a grooved tongue. During the processes of eating and drinking, the glossopalatine muscles may assist with graded tongue movements used in chewing and bolus management (i.e., elevation of the posterior tongue while food is formed into a bolus prior to the swallow). These muscles may participate in tongue grooving and cupping important for the suckling and sucking of liquids and semisolid foods, the acceptance of the spoon into the mouth, and bolus formation. Tongue blade elevation is used during the lateralization of food in the mouth (see Table 1.7).

TABLE 1.7 Extrinsic Tongue Muscles

MUSCLE	ORIGIN	INSERTION	GENERAL ACTION	INNERVATION	ACTION FOR SPEECH PRODUCTION	SPEECH SOUNDS	FUNCTIONS IN EATING AND DRINKING
Styloglossus	Styloid process of temporal bone	Lateral border of tongue	Draws tongue upward and backward, may assist in forming concave dorsum	XII (Hypoglossal)	Posterior tongue dorsum elevation	/i, ɪ, e, ɛ/	Gradations in tongue humping during chewing and bolus management; tongue front-to-palate contact and release in true suck; elevated tongue tip position at rest and during swallowing; tongue blade, front, and tip elevation during food lateralization; tongue grooving during suckling and sucking; shallow tongue cupping to accept spoon; tongue cupping for bolus formation
					Tongue border elevation	/ɝ/	
					Tongue tip and border elevation	/t, d/	
					Midtongue elevation	/k, g, ŋ/	
					Tongue apex elevation	/n, l/	
					Tongue tip, lateral margin, and central apical elevation	/ʧ, ʤ/	
Genioglossus	Superior mental spine on posterior surface of mandibular symphysis	Lingual fascia, tongue dorsum, body of hyoid bone	Posterior fibers protrude tongue tip, anterior fibers retract tongue, entire muscle contraction depresses tongue into bowl shape	XII (Hypoglossal)	Tongue apex depression	/i, ɪ, e, ɔ/ ʃ, ʒ, r/	Tongue protraction-retraction pattern used in suckle-swallow, movement of food back toward pharynx for swallow, tongue grooving during suckling and sucking; shallow tongue cupping to accept spoon; tongue cupping for bolus formation
					Anterior tongue dorsum depression	/æ, a, ɔ, ʊ, u, ʌ/	
					Tongue dorsum depression	/ o/	
					Tongue apex extension	/s, z/	
					Tongue tip protrusion	/θ, ð /	

Hyoglossus	Greater cornu and corpus of hyoid bone	Lateral submucous tissue of posterior half of tongue	Depresses and retracts tongue, may elevate hyoid bone	XII (Hypoglossal)	Tongue apex depression	/i, ɪ, e, ɔ, ʃ, ʒ, r/	Tongue depression to accept nipple and spoon, tongue protraction-retraction pattern used in suckle-swallow, movement of food back toward pharynx for swallow, tongue depression for activities involving tongue cupping and grooving
					Anterior tongue dorsum depression	/æ, a, ɔ, ʊ, u, ʌ/	
					Tongue dorsum depression	/o/	
Glossopalatine	Sides of tongue (blend with transverse, styloglossus, and hyoglossus)	Anterior surface of soft palate	Raises posterior tongue to groove dorsum, lowers soft palate	X (Vagus)	Posterior tongue dorsum elevation	/i, ɪ, e, ɛ/	Gradations in tongue humping during chewing and bolus management, tongue grooving during suckling and sucking; shallow tongue cupping to accept spoon; tongue cupping for bolus formation, tongue blade elevation during food lateralization, soft palate movements during eating and drinking
					Tongue border elevation	/ɜ̃, l, r/	
					Midtongue elevation	/k, g, ŋ/	
					Tongue grooving	/j /	

Sources: S. E. Morris, "Developmental Implications for the Management of Feeding in Neurologically Impaired Infants," *Seminars in Speech and Language, 6* (1985): 293–315; J. M. Palmer, *Anatomy for Speech and Hearing,* 4th ed. (Baltimore: Williams & Wilkins, 1993), pp. 69, 80, 83, 261–270; W. R. Zemlin, *Speech and Hearing Science: Anatomy and Physiology,* 4th ed. (Boston: Allyn & Bacon, 1998), pp. 254–256.

TONGUE SHAPE, VOCAL TRACT SHAPE, AND PALATAL CONTACT FOR SPEECH PRODUCTION

Speech scientists Maureen Stone and Andrew Lundberg (1998) used ultrasound imaging and electropalatography (EPG) data to study tongue shapes and palatal contact used in the production of consonant and vowel sounds. Three-dimensional tongue shapes were reconstructed from the ultrasound images and compared to palatal contact made during the production of 18 English speech sounds. This is important information for the assessment and treatment of oral motor difficulties affecting speech production. The clinician can use this information to determine adequate tongue position when assessing and teaching sound production.

Stone and Lundberg (1998) point out that the tongue is composed entirely of muscle and is moved and shaped by both the extrinsic and intrinsic tongue muscles. "Tongue shape is systematically related to tongue position because tongue volume can be redistributed but not increased or decreased" (p. 4). The importance of jaw and subsequent tongue position are discussed in a variety of chapters throughout the book. It should be noted that the results of the Stone and Lundberg study were based on data gathered from a single subject (i.e., a normal adult female, age 26, from Maryland with a slight regional accent).

Stone and Lundberg found four categories of three-dimensional tongue surface shapes (see Table 1.8). The speech sounds /i/, /ɪ/, /e/, /ɝ̃/, /u/, /ʃ/, and /n/ were produced with a front-rising tongue shape. Complete grooving was noted

TABLE 1.8 Tongue Shape during Speech Production

TONGUE SHAPE	DESCRIPTION	PALATAL CONTACT	SPEECH SOUNDS
Front-rising	Anterior and midtongue elevation, level or arched coronal shape, posterior tongue and tongue root grooved	Bilateral contact in alveolar or palatal vault	/i, ɪ, e, ɝ̃, u, ʃ, n/
Complete grooving	Continuous tongue grooving		/ɛ, æ, u, θ, s/
Back-rising	Dorsal tongue displaced upward, tongue grooved at midline		/ʊ, o, a, ʌ, ɔ, k/
Two-point displacement	Elevated anterior and posterior tongue, short groove in midtongue		/l/

Source: Table created from information presented in M. Stone and A. Lundberg, "Three-Dimensional Tongue Surface Shapes of English Consonants and Vowels," in M. P. Cannito, K. M. Yorkston, and D. R. Beukelman (Eds.), *Neuromotor Speech Disorders: Nature, Assessment, and Management* (Baltimore: Paul H. Brookes Publishing Company, 1998), pp. 3–25.

during the production of the /ɛ/, /æ/, /u/, /θ/, and /s/ sounds. The speech sounds /ʊ/, /o/, /a/, /ʌ/, /ɔ/, and /k/ were produced with a back-rising tongue shape, and the /l/ sound was produced with a two-point displacement tongue shape.

The data from electropalatography revealed that the American English vowels studied by Stone and Lundberg (i.e., /i, ɪ, e, ɛ, u, ɝ/) were produced via bilateral tongue contact. Three tongue-to-palate contact patterns were found during the production of consonant sounds. The /s/, /ʃ/, /r/, /j/, /w/, and /θ/ sounds were produced with bilateral tongue to palate contact; the /l/ sound was produced with crosswise palatal contact; and the /n/ and /ŋ/ sounds were produced using a combination of bilateral and crosswise palatal contact.

Studies conducted by speech scientists have provided pieces of information needed to fully understand the processes involved in speech production. Ong and Stone (1998) comment that the information on vocal tract dimensions and shapes is important in "understanding the speech production mechanism" and "improving the speech of patients with dysarthria" (p. 2).

Ong and Stone reconstructed three-dimensional airway volumes from magnetic resonance (MRI) and computed tomography (CT) images for the speech sounds /r/ and /l/ using a single subject design. They discussed the relationship of these shapes to acoustic, ultrasound, and electropalatographic information. Speech-language pathologists frequently work with children and some adults who demonstrate difficulties producing the /r/ and /l/ sounds. Individuals who continue to have difficulty producing these sounds beyond the normal developmental period frequently exhibit an oral motor basis for the concern. The details from studies such as the one by Ong and Stone provide the clinician with information needed to treat individuals who present with these difficulties.

Ong and Stone (1998, p. 2) describe the /r/ sound as a voiced linguapalatal glide characterized by a change in resonance as the tongue glides past the palate and briefly makes lateral contact. The retroflex /r/ is described as the "curling back" of the anterior tongue segment with palatal contact posterior to that of the "bunched /r/." The "bunched /r/" is produced by arching the tongue toward the palatal vault.

The /l/ sound is described by Ong and Stone as a voiced lingua-alveolar lateral or glide. This sound is produced with a compressed region of the tongue posterior to the tongue tip that contacts the alveolar ridge. The posterior tongue is convex in shape during the production of the /l/ sound.

Although the speech sounds /r/ and /l/ are different in tongue shape and palatal contact, they are reported to be similar acoustically. This is believed to be related to similarities in the shape of the vocal tract according to Ong and Stone. The knowledge of these characteristics of the /r/ and /l/ sounds can change the clinician's approach to treatment. The clinician can use this information to better describe tongue shape and tongue positioning to the client.

SYNDROMES THAT CAN AFFECT ORAL MOTOR FUNCTION

Oral motor impairments are seen in individuals with certain syndromes. It is important for the speech-language pathologist working in the area of oral motor assessment and treatment to be knowledgeable about the characteristics of these syndromes. The syndromes may be "viral, bacterial, genetic, chromosomal, teratogenic (a foreign agent causing embryonic or fetal structural abnormalities), or traumatic" (Shipley & McAfee, 1992, p. 51) in nature. Table 1.9 summarizes the characteristics of some syndromes that may result in oral

TABLE 1.9 Syndromes and Characteristics That May Result in Oral Motor Concerns

SYNDROME	CHARACTERISTICS THAT MAY RESULT IN ORAL MOTOR CONCERNS
Apert Syndrome	Premature fusion of cranial sutures, underdevelopment of midface, cleft palate, hyponasality, mouth breathing, forward tongue positioning, articulation concerns
Cornelia de Lange Syndrome	Small, dysmorphic nose; thin, downturned upper lip; cleft palate; underdeveloped mandible; severe speech concerns
Cri du Chat Syndrome	Narrow oral cavity
Down Syndrome	General hypotonia, flat facial profile, small oral cavity, hard palate abnormalities, malocclusion, tooth grinding, lax ligaments in temporomandibular joint, open-mouth posture, mouth breathing, tongue protrusion, abnormalities of the neuromuscular junctions of the tongue, poor control of oral movements, delayed speech development, dysarthria, motor planning concerns
Ectrodactyly-Ectodermal Dysplasia-Clefting Syndrome	Cleft lip and palate, velopharyngeal incompetence, dental abnormalities, underdeveloped maxilla
Fetal Alcohol Syndrome	Short, upturned nose; underdeveloped maxilla and/or mandible; hypotonia; poor motor coordination; articulation concerns; high incidence of cleft palate
Floating-Harbor Syndrome	Triangular face, prominent nose, expressive language delay
Fragile X Syndrome	Prominent forehead; long, narrow chin; delayed speech and motor development
Goldenhar Syndrome	Underdeveloped face and/or head, facial asymmetry, underdeveloped mandible, facial palsy, cleft palate, velar asymmetry and/or paresis, articulation and resonance concerns
Moebius Syndrome	Bilateral facial paralysis (involvement of the facial and hypoglossal nerves); tongue lateralization, elevation, depression and protrusion problematic; eating, drinking, and articulatory concerns; high incidence of cleft palate and underdeveloped mandible
Noonan Syndrome	Increased distance between eyes; lingual and oral malformations; small, upturned nose; wide mouth; "cupid's bow" lips; micrognathia; narrow upper and lower jaw; high arched hard palate; malocclusion and other dental concerns; articulation concerns
Oro-Facial-Digital Syndromes	Clefting of lip or lip and palate, short labial frenulum, absent central incisors, underdeveloped mandible, micrognathia, tongue malformations, speech impairments
Oto-Palatal-Digital Syndrome	Micrognathia; upper airway obstruction; cleft palate; missing teeth; eating, drinking, and articulation concerns
Pierre-Robin Sequence	Underdeveloped mandible, downward placement of tongue, cleft palate, bifid uvula, speech delays, resonance concerns

Prader-Willi Syndrome	Hypotonia, speech delays, dysarthria and/or motor planning concerns
Refsum Syndrome	Ataxic dysarthria; articulation, voice, rate, and prosody issues
Rett Syndrome	Motor planning concerns
Stickler Syndrome	Underdeveloped midface; micrognathia; submucosal or overt cleft palate; eating, drinking, articulation, and resonance concerns
Treacher Collins Syndrome	Underdeveloped mandible and/or maxilla; submucosal or overt cleft palate; short or immobile uvula; malocclusion; underdeveloped teeth; open bite; beak-shaped nose; eating, drinking, and articulation concerns
Turner Syndrome	Narrow maxilla and palate, micrognathia
Van der Woude Syndrome	Pits or mounds on lower lip; cleft lip or palate; upper lip shaped like "cupid's bow"; velopharyngeal incompetence; eating, drinking, articulation, and resonance concerns
Velocardiofacial Syndrome	Hypotonia; long face; prominent nasal bridge; long, tubular nose; narrow palpebral fissures; small mouth; downturned upper lip; cleft lip and/or palate; bifid uvula; eating, drinking, articulation, and resonance concerns; dysarthria; motor planning concerns
Waardenburg Syndrome	Cleft lip or palate, prognathic mandible
Williams Syndrome	Short palpebral fissures; depressed nasal bridge; small, upturned nose; long philtrum; prominent lips; open-mouth posture; small, missing, or poorly aligned teeth; eating, drinking, and articulation concerns

Sources: S. O. Carneol, S. M. Marks, and L. Weik, "The Speech-Language Pathologist: Key Role in the Diagnosis of Velocardiofacial Syndrome," *American Journal of Speech-Language Pathology, 8* (1999): 23–32; L. Kumin and D. C. Bahr, "Patterns of Feeding, Eating, and Drinking in Young Children with Down Syndrome with Oral Motor Concerns," *Down Syndrome Quarterly, 4* (2) (1999): 1–8; J. F. Miller and M. Leddy, "Down Syndrome, the Impact of Speech Production on Language," in R. Paul (Ed.), *Exploring the Speech-Language Connection* (Baltimore: Paul H. Brooks, 1998), pp. 163–167; N. Y. Muir, G. B. Allard, and C. Greenburg, "Oral Language Development in a Child with Floating-Harbor Syndrome," *Language, Speech, and Hearing Services in Schools, 30* (1999): 207–211; K. G. Shipley and J. G. McAfee, *Assessment in Speech-Language Pathology: A Resource Manual* (San Diego, CA: Singular Publishing, Inc., 1992), pp. 52–61; R. Yarrom, U. Sagher, Y. Havivi, I. J. Peled, and M. R. Wexler, "Myofibers in Tongues of Down Syndrome," *Journal of Neurological Science, 73* (1986): 279–287.

motor concerns affecting the processes of eating, drinking, and speaking. It is important to note that the syndromes listed in Table 1.9 also have characteristics other than the ones noted. A full discussion of each syndrome is beyond the scope of this book. However, the characteristics that may result in oral motor concerns will be discussed.

Individuals exhibiting structural abnormalities involving the development of the maxilla and/or mandible frequently exhibit oral motor concerns. Structural abnormalities affect the shape of the oral cavity. The importance or the shape of the vocal tract was discussed in the previous section of this chapter. Difficulties such as cleft palate or hard palate abnormalities (e.g., a v-shaped hard palate) can significantly affect the individual's eating, drinking, and speaking skills. The hard palate forms the roof of the intraoral space and is an important target for the tongue during rest, swallowing, and speech production. The dentition of the maxillary arch also typically provides important points of contact for the tongue during rest and speech production. Irregularities in dentition can affect the individual's biting and chewing abilities as well as the individual's speech production. Difficulties with velopharyngeal closure and hyponasality often significantly affect the individual's resonation and speech intelligibility. Lip abnormalities or difficulties with lip function can impact on the individual's lip closure during swallowing and speech production. Open-mouth posture resulting from low muscle tone, paralysis, paresis, lax ligaments, or mouth breathing will often affect graded jaw movement and tongue position. When the tongue is out of position, swallowing and speech production are usually unrefined. The individual's tongue may not move independently from his or her jaw when this occurs. Independent tongue movement is extremely important for all oral motor processes. Tongue malformations as well as muscle tone and tongue mobility issues can impact tongue shape for speech production and tongue movement during eating (e.g., tongue lateralization) and drinking (e.g., effective swallowing). Motor planning difficulties can also significantly affect speech production. These and many other oral motor issues will be covered in this book.

CASE EXAMPLES

The following two cases reveal the importance for understanding the anatomical and neurological bases of oral motor function. The speech-language clinician who understands this information will be better prepared to interpret assessment data and plan treatment strategies.

Carolyn

Carolyn was a 22-month-old child with Moebius syndrome. She exhibited normal hearing and no history of middle ear infections. Her receptive language skills appeared to be age appropriate. Carolyn had bilateral sixth (abducens) and seventh (facial) nerve palsies as well as questionable involvement of cranial nerve XII (hypoglossal). Secondary to these cranial nerve palsies, Carolyn did not use facial expression when interacting with others. Her parents, therefore, did not benefit from the nonverbal communication provided by a child's facial expression. Carolyn's oral movements were also limited, which made eating, drinking, and speaking a challenge.

Carolyn exhibited an open mouth posture, drooling, and low muscle tone in her cheeks secondary to the damage of cranial nerve VII (facial). She also pocketed food in her cheeks and bit on the spoon and cup to attain jaw stability. Carolyn did not use her upper lip to clear food from the spoon. She lost some liquid from her mouth when drinking from the cup. These difficulties indicate involvement of Carolyn's orbicularis oris and her buccinator muscles.

Carolyn's tongue was thick and bunched. She did not elevate her tongue tip nor did she lateralize food to the molar surfaces with her tongue. This seemed to support the questionable involvement of cranial nerve XII (hypoglossal). Carolyn demonstrated more significant involvement of the intrinsic muscles of the tongue than the extrinsic muscles. She retracted her tongue to swallow food and could produce the /æ/, /a/, /k/, and /g/ sounds. These are characteristics of the extrinsic tongue muscles. She had difficulty producing the variety of speech sounds and tongue movements for eating indicative of functional use of the intrinsics.

Carolyn's cranial nerve V (trigeminal) seemed to be intact. This nerve is responsible for innervation of the temporalis, masseter, medial pterygoid, lateral pterygoid, and glossopalatine muscles. Sensory input via cranial nerve V (trigeminal) relays the position of the food bolus in the mouth, while the motor branch of cranial nerve V (trigeminal) controls chewing movements (Love & Webb, 1996). Carolyn used an "up-down" munching pattern to manage her foods and retracted her tongue to swallow the bolus.

Based on the difficulties exhibited by Carolyn, a variety of treatment strategies were implemented. Appropriate gross motor activities were incorporated into Carolyn's treatment and daily activities to improve postural tone needed for stability in the body and oral musculature. (These were recommended by her physical therapist.) The increased stability in her body and oral structures allowed for improved lip and tongue mobility needed for improved eating, drinking, and speech production. She began to produce the bilabial sounds /m/ and /b/. She elevated her tongue blade to her alveolar ridge to produce an immature approximation of the /t/ and /d/ sounds.

Oral massage was provided three times each day prior to an activity where she was required to use her oral mechanism (e.g., eating, drinking, sound play, etc.). The oral massage seemed to improve sensation in Carolyn's oral structure as she began to move her oral structures with greater sophistication than previously noted. She also participated in a variety of oral motor activities involving the use of food to encourage jaw stabilization, tongue elevation and lateralization, as well as lip closure.

Carolyn's eating, drinking, and sound production skills improved significantly. She began lateralizing her tongue to move food within her mouth. Her drooling decreased. A decrease was noted in her pocketing of food in her cheeks, her biting on the cup for stability, and her loss of liquid from the cup. She produced a greater variety of speech sounds and produced them more frequently. The prognosis for Carolyn's development of adequate oral motor skills for eating, drinking, and speech production is good based on her initial response to oral motor treatment.

Eddie

Eddie was a 59-year-old man who had bilateral subcortical strokes, including the internal capsule on each side, one month prior to being evaluated by a speech-language pathologist. He exhibited normal hearing and auditory comprehension skills. He had profound pseudobulbar palsy (bilateral upper motor neuron dysarthria) as well as spastic quadriplegia. There was greatly increased tone in all of his facial and oral muscles. Eddie could barely open his mouth volitionally. He could open it very slowly to a maximum range of about a centimeter, due to upper motor neuron (UMN) involvement of bilateral trigeminal nerves. He could not smile or retract his lips on command, due to UMN involvement of bilateral facial nerves. His palate did not elevate at all when he spoke because of bilateral UMN damage to the glossopharyngeal (IX) and the vagus (X) nerves. His phonation was harsh, low pitched, low volume, and monotone as a result of bilateral UMN impairment of the vagus nerve (X). Further, Eddie could protrude his tongue only half a centimeter with slow rate, attributable to UMN lesions of bilateral hypoglossal nerves (XII).

In contrast to the profoundly reduced rate and range of volitional movements of his jaw, lips, velum, and tongue, Eddie's reflexive movements showed normal or increased range and rate, indicating sparing of the lower motor neurons and reflex arcs in each of the cranial nerves. His jaw opened fully during a reflexive yawn, and he had a broad smile or frown during reflexive laughing and crying. His laughter and tears were frequent. This is consistent with emotional lability or "pseudobulbar laughing and crying" associated with bilateral UMN lesions. Furthermore, he had a hyperactive gag reflex consistent with UMN damage.

Eddie could not talk or eat because of his severe difficulty with volitional oral motor function. He communicated using a printed word board or notebook. He was fed by a gastrostomy tube. However, he had intact reflexive gag, swallow, laryngeal elevation with swallowing, and epiglottic tilt. Therefore, he could swallow without any aspiration (as demonstrated by videofluoroscopy) when food was placed on the back of his tongue. In order to place food on the back of his tongue, the speech-language pathologist had to make him laugh, so that his mouth would open widely enough to position the food.

To reduce tone and increase range of movement of the lips and other facial muscles, biofeedback was used. Electrodes were placed on the obicularis oris muscles and translated activity of the muscles (at rest) into sound. Louder, more frequent pulses of sound were associated with increased resting activity, or higher muscle tone. Eddie learned to reduce the tone of his muscles at rest. This allowed him to open his mouth to accept food and to regain functional speech. He continued to speak slowly, with imprecise articulation and reduced range of movement of the articulators. He also continued to have persistent, severe hypernasality and nasal escape of air that limited intraoral pressure for the production of stop consonants due to limited range of velar movement. These problems were partially relieved by a palatal lift prosthesis, a bulb attached to the back teeth that elevated the velum mechanically. The palatal lift prosthesis improved not only Eddie's speech intelligibility and resonance but also his loudness and swallowing ability due to the presence of improved intraoral pressure. It also eliminated nasal regurgitation of liquid.

Eddie continued to work with the speech-language pathologist on improving function of labial and lingual muscles to improve articulation over the next year. He eventually achieved nearly 100% intelligibility and could manage both foods and liquids fully by mouth. The gastrostomy tube was removed.

INTERACTIVE CASE EXPERIENCES

Interactive case experiences are provided throughout the book to allow the reader to practice using the information from the chapter. These experiences challenge the reader to think of the possibilities for each of the cases. The authors have provided case examples in the book as a guide for the reader, but the answers to the questions in the interactive case experiences are for the reader to decide.

Given the information about the following cases, discuss the possible damage to nerves and muscles that may be responsible for the concerns noted.

Drew

Drew is a 30-year-old male who presents with moderate to severe cognitive communication deficits secondary to traumatic brain injury after a motor vehicle accident in which one year ago he was thrown from a car. His hearing is normal; however, his auditory comprehension and processing are impaired. Drew's brain injury consisted of a right frontal/temporal contusion as well as midbrain and brain stem contusions.

Drew has a left visual field deficit, left hemiparesis, a tracheostomy tube, and a PEG (percutaneous endoscopic gastrostomy) feeding tube. He has a history of pneumonia. He is currently unable to speak secondary to tracheostomy placement. He attempts to mouth words in structured situations. When mouthing words, Drew opens his mouth in wide excursions and would probably sound quite dysarthric if his speech could be heard. He responds accurately to yes/no questions and can point to appropriate words and pictures with facilitation. Drew can also gesture recognizable functions for objects. He seems to understand most of what is said to him.

Drew presents with moderate oral phase and mild pharyngeal phase neurogenic dysphagia. He appears to have decreased motor control and sensation in the oral and pharyngeal areas. He manages a mechanical soft diet with liquids thickened to a nectar consistency. He does not have the oral or pharyngeal control to manage regular thin liquids. When drinking, Drew bites on the cup or the straw to gain jaw stability. He exhibits occasional coughing and choking.

At rest, Drew exhibits generally low muscle tone throughout his facial musculature with the exception of an upper lip retraction. He finger-feeds appropriate foods and spoon-feeds himself with assistance. He opens his mouth in wide excursions to accept food. While eating, he has difficulty controlling his drool. Drew has limited lip mobility and strength. He can clear food from a spoon with his upper lip if the person assisting with his feeding touches the spoon on the body of his tongue and allows time for his upper lip to move down to clear the spoon.

When eating foods of increased texture, such as crackers, Drew lateralizes the foods to both molar surfaces with his tongue. When eating foods of decreased texture, such as eggs, he primarily uses a front-to-back tongue-pumping pattern. His tongue moves better to the right than to the left when lateralizing food. Drew's tongue appears thick and bunched rather than thin and grooved. He exhibits mixed muscle tone in his tongue. After a meal, Drew is unaware that food remains in his mouth. Food often remains in the sulci and his high narrow palate.

Amber

Amber is a 12-month-old child who was born following a full-term pregnancy. Her general health at birth was described as excellent. She has normal hearing and no history of middle ear infections. Amber exhibits a developmental delay of unknown origin that is affecting her development of receptive and expressive language skills. She currently produces spontaneous vocalizations consisting primarily of back vowel sounds.

Amber exhibits postural instability secondary to low muscle tone in the trunk of her body. When seated in a chair, she presents with a "slouched" posture. Her mouth remains in a closed position at rest, and she does not drool. Amber exhibits low muscle tone in her lips and cheeks. She has poor lip mobility; however, her lips are symmetrical.

During feeding, Amber opens her mouth in a wide excursion to accept the spoon. She moves her jaw in an up and down munching pattern to manage food. Her lips close on the spoon, but her upper lip is not active in clearing the food from the spoon. Amber appears to be unaware of food that remains on her face, as she does not attempt to remove it with her lips, tongue, or hand. While she appears to have decreased oral sensation, she does not like her face or mouth to be touched by others.

Amber's tongue appears low in muscle tone. When she swallows food, her tongue protrudes slightly before retracting the bolus. Amber can transfer food with her tongue from midline to each side of her mouth. Her lips remain open during chewing, which results in loss of food.

Amber prefers to eat soft and smooth foods with sweet or salty tastes. She occasionally chokes or gags on foods of increased texture. She drinks thickened liquids from a bottle and cutout cup, as she has difficulty managing regular thin liquids.

2

Physiologic Considerations

In the assessment and treatment of oral motor function, it is important for the clinician to consider the physiological functions of the entire body. The body contains many complex, interrelated systems. One system significantly affects another system, and this has an impact on the individual's learning process.

In this chapter, the relationship between stability and mobility in the body as well as the effects of muscle tone on these processes will be addressed. The importance of straight planes of movement leading to rotational movements in the body and in the mouth will also be discussed. The various sensory processes (i.e., vestibular, tactile, proprioceptive, olfactory, gustatory, auditory, and visual) will be defined and described relative to oral motor assessment and treatment.

The chapter provides background information from individuals who completed much of the original work in the areas of neuro-developmental treatment and sensory integration. The work of Karel Bobath, Berta Bobath, A. Jean Ayres, and others is cited and discussed. Although much of this work was completed a number of years ago, it continues to provide the bases for current techniques used in oral motor assessment and treatment.

Neuro-developmental treatment was "developed by Berta and Karel Bobath . . . as a means of treating underlying neuro-motor deficits related to tone, movement, and posture of both a neurological and a developmental nature" (Scherzer & Tscharnuter, 1982, as cited in Langley & Thomas, 1991, p. 1). Clinicians using this form of treatment analyze the components of movement that are essential in performing an activity. They then work toward facilitating changes in muscle tone, inhibiting atypical movement patterns, and facilitating more typical and functional movement patterns in the individual being treated (Langley & Thomas, 1991).

"A. Jean Ayres developed sensory integration theory to better explain the relationship between behavior and neural functioning, especially sensory processing or integration" (Fisher & Murray, 1991, p. 1). The theory is used to explain the brain-behavior relationship between deficits in sensory processing (i.e., the individual's ability to interpret sensory information received from the body and/or the environment) and learning (Fisher & Murray, 1991). Further information on neuro-developmental treatment and sensory integration theory will be presented in Chapter 3.

THE RELATIONSHIP BETWEEN STABILITY AND MOBILITY

The concepts of *stability* and *mobility* are important for the speech-language pathologist to understand when working with individuals who have oral motor concerns. Stability must occur in the proximal areas of the body (e.g., trunk, shoulder girdle, etc.) so that mobility can occur in the distal areas of the body (e.g., mouth, hands, etc.). These concepts are well known in the fields of occupational therapy and physical therapy. The central nervous system controls the mechanisms from which stability and subsequent mobility arise in the body. Stability in the body is related to muscle tone as well as the coordinated contraction of the musculature. Mobility could be described as the execution of motor acts. According to Karel Bobath (1971), virtually every motor act is automatic and outside of the individual's consciousness, because the central nervous system activates the musculature immediately after a motor act is initiated. Motor acts can be efficiently executed or inefficiently executed. If an individual does not have stability in the body, motor acts are likely to be inefficient and/or imprecise.

The righting and equilibrium reactions are two types of automatic reactions that assist the individual in the establishment of normal postural tone, postural control, and adequate reciprocal muscle innervation important for normal movement. Although these reactions develop throughout childhood, the majority of the development occurs in the first 12 months of a child's life (Boehme, 1990b). Righting reactions assist an individual in maintaining a normal head position in space; normal head, neck, and trunk alignment; and normal trunk and limb alignment. These provide the individual with head control and the ability to rotate the body around a central axis, an important skill discussed separately in this chapter. Righting reactions also enable the individual "to assume or regain a body position" (Koomar & Bundy, 1991, p. 292). The more complex and highly integrated equilibrium reactions "produce compensatory shifts of tone to maintain or restore balance" (K. Bobath, 1971, p. 517). Equilibrium reactions enable the individual "to maintain a body position when it has been threatened by perturbations to the body or the support surface" (Bly, 1983; Weisz, 1938, as discussed in Koomar & Bundy, 1991, p. 292). If the righting or equilibrium reactions are not occurring normally, the individual will have difficulty with maintaining stability and attaining mobility in the body.

"Normal movement is achieved through a delicate balance between stability and mobility" (Morris, 1987b, p. 79). Postural stability and control are required for fluid and efficient voluntary movement. Voluntary movement is achieved via graded adjustment of agonist and antagonist muscle contraction in the body (i.e., coactivation, cocontraction, or reciprocal innervation of the musculature). Weight is shifted or transferred in the body during movement, and there must be a balance between stability and mobility for efficient weight shifting to occur (Boehme, 1990b). Some muscles stabilize, whereas others move the bones of the skeleton. Postural control "relies on the proper mechanical alignment of the skeleton, with the pelvis acting as the cornerstone" (Boehme, 1990b, p. 209).

Reciprocal innervation or cooperative action of the musculature is necessary for "postural fixation of proximal parts of the body and the regulation of the smooth interaction of the muscles of the moving distal parts" (K. Bobath, 1971, p. 516). The trunk is proximal to the head-neck area and the extremities. The head-neck area is proximal to the jaw, tongue, lips, and cheeks. The individual must attain dynamic stability (i.e., where one part of the body remains stable but active while allowing other parts of the body to move) in the proximal areas of the body to achieve efficient movement in the distal areas of the body. Many examples of this principle are seen in the movement of different areas of the body. The trunk of the body needs to be stable but active for efficient movement to occur in the head-neck area and the extremities. The head-neck area needs to be stable but active for efficient movement to occur in the jaw, tongue, lips, and cheeks. The jaw needs to be stable but active for efficient movement to occur in the tongue, lips, and cheeks for eating, drinking, and speech production. The hyoid bone needs to be stable but active so that the tongue can move appropriately for swallowing (Mohr, 1990).

The stability and mobility of the trunk are particularly important to consider when working with individuals with oral motor concerns. Functional activities—such as eating, drinking, and speaking—depend on trunk control as the basis for movement. Difficulties with trunk control can affect the individual's ability to maintain head control and effectively use the oral mechanism. Upper trunk movements are normally dissociated from lower trunk movements. Therefore, the upper trunk can rotate while the lower trunk and pelvis can remain stable. Thoracic vertebrae 7 and 8 (T7 and T8) are the point of dynamic stability for the dissociation of the trunk (Mohr, 1990). Many individuals with oral motor concerns exhibit difficulty with dynamic stability in this area of the trunk. The speech-language pathologist can work closely with the physical therapist and/or occupational therapist to learn techniques to address the individual's difficulties with postural control.

Several individuals have specifically discussed the development of oral stability (Morris, 1985; Nelson, Meek, & Moore, 1994). Oral stability develops secondary to the development of stability and control in the neck and shoulder girdle. The neck and shoulder girdle also provide stability for the larynx and muscles of respiration. "Stability as a basis for oral mobility and precision centers around the development of jaw control" (Morris, 1985, p. 296). A stable jaw allows the individual to perform the skilled lip and tongue movements used for eating, drinking, and speech production. Jaw stability is generally established by 24 months of age (Morris, 1985). Individuals with oral motor concerns frequently exhibit jaw instability and resulting limitations in tongue and lip mobility.

There is developmental process involved in the attainment of stability and mobility in the body. "Positional or external stability emerges first" in children (Morris, 1985, p. 295). One body part is supported by another or by an external source (e.g., a surface such as a floor or mat, a person holding or supporting the individual, etc.). With the maturation of the child's brain and muscle function, "postural or internal stability develops" (Morris, 1985, p. 295). If an individual has neurological concerns resulting in difficulties with muscle tone and/or function, the individual may not have the postural or internal stability needed for mobility and may rely on positional or external support. This is seen in adult as well as pediatric clients.

The development of active antigravity muscle control allows the development of stability and subsequent mobility to occur. Alexander (1987), Oetter, Richter, and Frick (1995), and Redstone (1991) have described this development. Active, antigravity muscle control develops cephalo-caudally in the body during the first 8 to12 months of life. "Antigravity extension has developed at the head, neck, and thoracic spine" (Alexander, 1987, p. 90), and flexion has developed in the front of the upper trunk by the time an infant is 3 months of age (Redstone, 1991). At this point, the infant demonstrates decreased shoulder elevation and depressed scapulae, providing the upper trunk with increased stability. The infant's head, neck, and spine demonstrate improved alignment, and the infant's ability to lift the head has improved. The balance of capital flexion (flexing the neck and head) and cervical elongation (extending the neck and head) assists the infant in attaining stability in the laryngeal area needed for adequate respiration and phonation. The alignment of the head and neck region also impact on the position and movement of the tongue.

The infant's head, neck, shoulder girdle, trunk, and pelvic control improve from ages 3 to 5 months. During this stage, the infant is developing "bilateral antigravity head and neck flexion, antigravity thoracic and lumbar extension, scapular stability, humeral adduction with flexion, hip flexion with external rotation and abduction-adduction, and abdominal musculature activity" (Alexander, 1987, p. 90). Dissociated movements between the head and shoulder girdle develop, and an increase in head control is seen. Between the ages of 4 and 6 months, the infant begins to develop extensor control in the hip area. Improved abdominal control, rotation in the trunk, scapular stability, and respiratory control result in an increase in vocal sound production by the infant.

From ages 6 to 12 months, the infant develops "the controlled use of both flexion and extension" (Redstone, 1991, p. 37). Trunk control is seen in most infants by 8 months of age and is based on the adequate development of shoulder and pelvic stability as well as trunk rotation. Pelvic stability and abdominal control appear to develop at the same time as control of the abdominal musculature stabilizes the pelvic area. The infant uses controlled abdominal and thoracic movements for graded expiration of air for sound production resulting in vocal play. "By 7 to 8 months of age, the infant has developed active head, neck, shoulder girdle, rib cage, trunk, and hip musculature activity that provides the foundation for better coordination of respiration with oral functioning for sound production" (Alexander, 1987, p. 91). By 12 months of age, the child exhibits adult-like breathing patterns and first words emerge. The use of speech "leads to finer grading of expansion by chest wall musculature and ligaments of the larynx" (Oetter et al., 1995, p. 27).

As previously stated, the development of stability begins proximally and moves distally in the body. The individual must begin with a stable trunk and balanced muscle function on both sides of the body. When an individual exhibits oral motor concerns resulting in eating, drinking, and speaking difficulties, the clinician can look at the physical functioning of the person's entire body for clues regarding the underlying causes of the dysfunction. "What you want at the lips, you mediate at the hips." This saying was coined by an instructor of neurodevelopmental treatment (NDT) named Leslie Faye Davis.

MUSCLE TONE

Boehme (1990b, p. 210) describes muscle tone as "the degree of stiffness" in the musculature "to stabilize or move the skeleton" in the presence of gravity. Muscle tone needs to be "high enough to resist gravity" while "the ability to move in a carefully controlled and skilled manner" is maintained (K. Bobath, 1971, p. 516). The central nervous system constantly adjusts muscle tone throughout the body. This allows the individual to attain postural control against the force of gravity through reciprocal innervation, cocontraction, or coactivation of the agonist and antagonist musculature. Individuals attain postural stability in the presence of gravity through "balanced extensor and flexor muscle tone in the trunk" (Bly, 1983, as cited in Redstone, 1991, p. 36) of the body. Individuals with oral motor concerns frequently exhibit hypotonicity (low muscle tone), hypertonicity (high muscle tone), or some combination of these in the body.

Individuals with hypotonia demonstrate postural instability resulting in insufficient head, neck, and trunk control to "support functional movement" (Boehme, 1990a, p. 3). Postural instability can limit the individual's movement in all planes (i.e., straight planes, lateral planes, and rotational planes). The individual with hypotonicity demonstrates a poor balance between the activity of the flexor and extensor muscles in the body and "lacks ligament, muscle, and tissue resistance" as well as graded control in "initiating, sustaining, and terminating functional movement" (Boehme, 1990a, p. 3). Decreased muscle tone "reduces the stability around the joints that is necessary for skilled movement" (Morris, 1987b, p. 79). Individuals with low muscle tone frequently attempt to compensate for reduced stability around the joints through hyperextension or fixing. For example, the individual may hyperextend the head to compensate for postural instability, and this may result in hyperextension of the jaw and forward tongue movement (Redstone, 1991). Many individuals with oral motor concerns exhibit low muscle tone proximally (e.g., in the trunk of the body) and hyperextension or fixing patterns in the more distal areas of the body (e.g., in the jaw, upper extremities, and lower extremities).

With regard to whole-body movement, "muscle tone is by far the most important factor affecting the age at which [gross motor] skills are achieved. The lower a child's tone, the longer acquisition will be delayed" (Winders, 1997, p. 226). Individuals with low muscle tone demonstrate specific concerns with trunk and shoulder stability. They have "little scapular stability on the rib cage" (Boehme, 1990a, p. 3). Scapular stability is needed for the efficient distal function of the head-neck area and extremities. According to Boehme (1990a), inactive abdominal oblique musculature can fail to elongate the intercostal muscles, and the rectus abdominis musculature may be used by the individual with hypotonia in an attempt to stabilize the trunk. This can lead to inefficient respiration and whole-body movement. Therefore, respiration may not be sufficient to sustain vocalization and breathing may be shallow and/or noisy.

Children with hypotonicity in the trunk of the body often exhibit sternal depression during inspiration and flared ribs (Redstone, 1991). These tonal concerns in the trunk of the body can significantly affect the individual's ability to develop appropriate respiratory support for speech production. Children with hypotonicity frequently have limited oral play experiences resulting in sensory discrimination concerns and oral hyporesponsivity. On the other hand, oral hyperresponsivity may result from "the use of head and neck hyperextension with tongue retraction" (Boehme, 1990a, p. 4). Children and adults with hypotonia often demonstrate oral motor difficulties in eating, drinking, speaking, and the use of facial expression.

Elevated muscle tone (hypertonicity) requires the individual to "move against tension and resistance" (Morris, 1987b, p. 79). Brain damage (e.g., upper motor neuron damage) can cause increased muscle tone, atypical cocontraction of the musculature, and "abnormal patterns of muscular coordination" (K. Bobath, 1971, p. 520). According to Boehme (1990b), individuals with high muscle tone tighten the musculature and limit movement to small ranges of weight shifting, while demonstrating significant fixing in the spine. These individuals also demonstrate restricted movement around joints, and their movements generally lack fluidity. Individuals with hypertonicity in the trunk of body often demonstrate "shallow and rapid breathing" along with a barrel-shaped chest from many muscles contracting simultaneously (Redstone, 1991, p. 39). Hypertonicity in the individual's oral area restricts the movements of the jaw, lips, and tongue needed for eating, drinking, and speech production.

The tonic reflexes generally present themselves in an atypical manner when hypertonicity is present in the individual (K. Bobath, 1971; Love & Webb, 1996; Morris, 1987b). This is often seen in individuals with cerebral palsy and traumatic brain injury. The tonic labyrinthine reflex is activated by neck flexion and can result in shoulder retraction, neck and trunk extension, and tongue thrust. The asymmetric tonic neck reflex is activated by a stretch in the neck musculature during a head turn. The individual's extremities extend on the side of the body the individual is facing and flex on the other side of the body. The symmetric tonic neck reflex is activated when the head and neck are extended. The individual's arms move into extension and the legs move into flexion as a result of head-neck extension. Individuals exhibiting these reflexes have difficulty positioning the body effectively to act on the environment. The presence of these reflexes can significantly affect the individual's oral motor function.

"Associated reactions are released abnormal postural reflexes" (K. Bobath, 1971, p. 523) frequently resulting from undue effort, fear, or gravitational insecurity. These are "largely responsible for the permanent increase of spasticity in children and adults" (p. 524). Associated reactions are a major contributor to the development of contractures and deformities. According to Bobath, it is important to diminish undue effort, fear, and gravitational insecurity during treatment. When postural tone is improved "through the inhibition of the abnormal postural reflexes," the individual's "options for normal movement" significantly improve (Morris, 1987b, p. 79).

Some individuals exhibit fluctuating muscle tone. According to Boehme (1990b), these individuals have difficulty maintaining adequate tension in the musculature during functional movement. Fluctuating muscle tone can, therefore, result in postural instability, deficits in midrange control, and disorganized body movement.

Appropriate therapeutic handling can facilitate more typical muscle tone and movement patterns. Berta Bobath (1971) and Suzanne Evans Morris (1987b) discuss the treatment of muscle tone and subsequent movement issues. According to Berta Bobath (1971, p. 528), "Postural tone and motor patterns can be changed." The central nervous system can be influenced by therapeutically handling the individual from the periphery. However, treatment techniques should be continued only if improvement in muscle tone and active movement occur in a single treatment session. If this does not occur, then different treatment techniques should be implemented. According to Morris (1987b, p. 79), "Treatment includes the simultaneous stimulation and facilitation of normal postural reactions and of other automatic responses that provide the major contribution to the sensory model of normal movement patterns." Feedback is provided to the individual regarding muscle tone and movement for the purpose of improving body image and postural control. Atypical muscle tone and movement patterns need to be addressed in the body prior to addressing these in the mouth.

Percussion, bouncing, tapping, resistance, icing, and brisk movement activities are some ways to facilitate or increase tone in the individual's body. These must be carefully done when individuals exhibit hypertonicity in any area of the body. "Stimulation must be graded carefully, using it only when postural tone is too low and immediately stopping when it becomes abnormally high" (B. Bobath, 1971, p. 529). When an individual exhibits increased or high muscle tone, techniques such as slow rocking, massage, and warming can be used to inhibit or decrease muscle tone.

Gross motor activities may increase muscle tone in the body and fine motor activities may decrease muscle tone in the body of the individual with hypotonia or the individual with "normal" muscle tone. Vigorous whole-body activities can increase trunk tone. Activities that involve the use of the mouth or hands may decrease the muscle tone in the body. These are important concepts to consider during oral motor assessment and treatment of individuals with hypotonia or "normal" muscle tone. For example, when an individual is seated in a chair, completing fine motor tasks (e.g., reading, writing, speaking, eating, or drinking), the person's general muscle tone may decrease. If this occurs, the individual may not have or maintain the stability in the body to efficiently complete the task. The incorporation of a gross motor task at this point may assist the individual in gaining or regaining the stability needed to complete the task with increased efficiency.

INTERACTIVE EXPERIENCE

1. Imagine yourself seated in a comfortable chair at the end of a busy day. You are feeling tired and you notice that you are "slouching" in the chair. You could decide to take a nap, but you decide that you want to feel revitalized. Are you going to take a brisk walk, or are you going to read a book? Why?
2. Imagine that you are feeling very anxious and are having a difficult time going to sleep. Will you get up and do some vigorous exercise, or will you read a book? Why?

Discussion

With regard to question number 1, you may decide to take a brisk walk, because the gross motor activity has the potential of raising the muscle tone in the body. This would be alerting to the system. Reading a book is a fine motor activity, may further decrease the tone in the body, and may actually make you feel sleepy.

Regarding question number 2, you may decide to read a book to relax if you are having difficulty sleeping. This fine motor activity has the potential of decreasing the muscle tone in the body. However, you would want to be careful of the content of the book selected. If the book contains material that is very interesting or alerting to you (e.g., a mystery story), you may have more difficulty sleeping. Many individuals engage in fine motor tasks for relaxation (e.g., needlework, writing, carving, etc.).

MOVEMENT

Movement occurs with weight shift in the individual's body. According to Morris and Klein, "Infants tend to develop in straight planes of movement first, before they develop lateral or diagonal and rotary skills" (2000, p. 63). "Weight shift in straight planes through anterior-posterior movement precedes lateral and diagonal shifts to allow children to move in all planes" (Langley & Thomas, 1991, p. 15). These planes of movement are related to the individual's development of midline control. Infants shift weight through a small range and then through larger and larger ranges around the midline as they develop controlled movement (Langley & Thomas, 1991).

The infant's early movement patterns consist of "a combination of alternate pulls from the extensor or flexor muscle systems" (Morris & Klein, 2000, p.

63). As the infant gains stability by leaning against a support (e.g., a surface or another body part), graded control of straight plane, anterior-posterior movement develops. The infant develops controlled lateral movements by 5 to 6 months of age in prone (Alexander, 1990). Rotation begins to appear in the body around 6 or 7 months of age and is usually established by 8 months of age (B. Bobath, 1971; K. Bobath, 1971). Between 6 and 8 months of age, the young child's "ability to weight shift in all planes of movement increases," and "the foundation of muscular activity" for later developing movement activities (e.g., standing, walking, running, etc.) is apparent "at approximately 8 months of age" (Alexander, 1987, p. 90).

"Rotation within the body axis" is "basic to every human activity" (K. Bobath, 1971, p. 518). It is an important component of most sophisticated body movement. "Midline control is not complete without some ability to rotate," and "dissociation does not begin until there is control of rotation around the body axis" (Mohr, 1990, p. 2). Both midline control and dissociated movement are important aspects of eating, drinking, and speech production.

In young children, rotation can be seen as the child crosses midline to reach for objects while in prone, supine, and sitting positions. Crawling and walking also involve rotational movements. If a child does not develop rotation proximally in the larger muscles of the body, it is unlikely that rotation will occur in the finer muscle groups, such as those required for eating. Adults with oral motor concerns often have previously established lateral and rotational movements upon which the clinician can frequently reestablish skills.

Oral movements "develop from straight planes toward lateral and rotary movements" (Morris & Klein, 2000, p. 64). The suckle-swallow pattern seen in the infant involves a straight plane, protraction-retraction of the tongue. Early chewing movements, often referred to as a "munching" pattern, involve straight plane, opening and closing of the jaw. Tongue lateralization is an example of dissociated lateral movement seen in the fine motor system of the mouth during eating. The ability to lateralize the tongue without lateral jaw movement indicates that an individual can move the tongue separately from the jaw. Dissociated tongue movement is required for eating and speech production.

Rotary chewing is the most sophisticated level of chewing and begins as a combination of lateral and diagonal movements. Lateral tongue and rotary jaw movements usually occur in concert with one another. Rona Alexander (1990) describes the development of the chewing process. According to Alexander, unsophisticated lateral tongue movements and lateral-diagonal jaw movements are seen in the 7-month-old child. The 10-month-old child can transfer food with the tongue from the side of the mouth to the center and from the center of the mouth to the side. At age 10 months, the child can also move the jaw in a variety of directions (i.e., up and down, forward and backward, as well as laterally, diagonally, and circularly). Side-to-side tongue lateralization and increased circular-diagonal jaw movements are noted at ages 12 to 15 months. "Well integrated rotary jaw movement with controlled grinding and shearing activity" continues to develop during the first three years of the child's life (Alexander, 1990, p. 67).

The separation of jaw and tongue movement is very important for speech production. However, the tongue movements for speech production are different from those for eating and drinking. Speech is the most refined fine motor act accomplished by the body and requires a rapid succession of dissociated lip, tongue, and jaw movements. If the jaw is unstable, the lips and tongue often do not move separately from the jaw; and if jaw, lip, and tongue movements lack grading, speech difficulties frequently occur.

Assessment of oral motor function frequently involves assessment of eating, drinking, and speaking. Although the oral movements for eating and drinking are not identical to the movements required for speech production and seem to have different areas of neural control and different timing of muscle contraction, observation of the individual's oral movements during a meal can give the clinician clues regarding the function of the oral musculature.

SENSORY SYSTEMS

The adaptation of existing movement patterns to new activities depends on sensory input (B. Bobath, 1971). "Man in toto stands in an environment which constantly stimulates him and demands a response" (K. Bobath, 1971, p. 516). The importance of sensory input is often not fully understood by speech-language pathologists providing oral motor assessment and treatment. The focus of oral motor assessment and treatment is often on movement or motor output rather than the sensory input needed for accurate motor output. Josephine Moore (as cited by Burpee, 1999) describes the tremendous importance of sensory input relative to motor output. According to Moore (as cited by Burpee, 1999):

- "The central nervous system has five to ten times as many sensory fibers as motor fibers."
- The sensory fibers do the learning. "Sensory systems are estimated to learn 100 times faster than motor fibers."
- "The central nervous system listens to multisensory input, while unisensory input is apt to be ignored."
- "The central nervous system listens to new information or a change in information and 'turns off' to sameness."

These ideas need to be considered when assessing and treating individuals with oral motor concerns. The sensory systems must be appropriately addressed in the assessment and treatment process so that effective motor learning can occur. The importance of each sensory system, the relationship among the systems, and the manner in which sensation is believed to be processed in the brain and body are discussed in this portion of the chapter.

Sherrington (1913) stated that the central nervous system is an "organ of integration" as it integrates sensory stimulation and coordinates motor responses (as cited in K. Bobath, 1971, p. 516). Burpee (1999, p. 8) defines *sensory integration* as "a neurological process involving the analysis, synthesis, and organization of sensory stimulative input." Trott, Laurel, and Windeck (1993) also discuss the process of sensory integration as follows: The individual's brain and body must integrate information received via all of the senses as well as from movement and gravity. Motor activities are often performed automatically without conscious effort as a result of the integration of information from the sensory systems. Through this integration, the individual knows the location of the body relative to the environment and how the body can act on the environment by attending to relevant stimuli and disregarding stimuli that is considered irrelevant.

Burpee (1999) describes a three-step, hierarchical, overlapping process that fosters sensory integration and allows the individual to interact appropriately and effectively with the environment. "Sensory registration, sensory integration, and self-regulation with sensory affective attunement" (Burpee, 1999, p. 8) comprise step 1. Sensory registration incorporates the processes of arousal, orientation to sensory stimuli while evaluating the stimuli for its significance, and preparing the body for action if the stimuli is considered relevant (Koomar & Bundy, 1991). As previously noted, "Sensory integration is a neurological process involving the analysis, synthesis, and organization of sensory stimulative input" (Burpee, 1999, p. 8). "Self-regulation is the ability to achieve, monitor, and change state to match the demands of the environment/situation" (Oetter et al., 1995, p. 31). The individual attains self-regulation while being attuned to emotions that affect this process. Step 2 is comprised of "body and self-awareness with modulation of muscle tone and the development of basic postural control/stability/mobility" (Burpee, 1999, p. 8). Step 3 is comprised of "environmental awareness with praxis (highly dependent on body awareness, developing tone, and postural control followed by the development of motor planning through ideation, sequencing, planning, and execution)" (Burpee, 1999, p. 8). This complex, overlapping, three-step process expresses the importance of sensation and sensory processing in the individual's attainment of effective movement and interactions with the environment.

In a book entitled *Adult Hemiplegia: Evaluation and Treatment* (1970) Berta Bobath describes the relationship between sensation and movement:

> Movements are in response to sensory stimuli which act upon the central nervous system from the outside world through the exteroceptors, vision, touch, and hearing. These sensory messages are integrated at the cortical level and produce a coordinated motor response in keeping with the demands of the environment. Movements are guided throughout their course by vision and by sensory cues from the proprioceptors of muscles, tendons, and joints. (p. 2)

Bobath (1970) also points out that "the influence of sensory disturbances on the ability to initiate and perform normal movements is profound" (p. 2). Individuals with sensory integration concerns "have difficulty organizing information and performing the many complex tasks necessary for learning and functioning in the world" (Trott et al., 1993, p. 1).

The integration of the sensory systems can be attained through movement. Neural mechanisms are "incomplete unless the motor component is executed satisfactorily" (Ayres, 1972b, p. 68). Therefore, movement disorders—such as those related to tonal issues in the body (e.g., hypotonia, spasticity, etc.)—lead to disorders in sensory integration. This supports the ideas expressed by the Bobaths discussed earlier in this chapter. Figure 2.1 is a "model of motor control and the circular process of sensory integration" (Fisher, 1991, p. 86). This represents a combination of theories about the mechanisms involved in an individual's attainment of active movement throughout the body, including the movements of the oral mechanism.

Motor commands are generated in the brain from an "intention to act" (p. 86). In active movement, the motor command is sent to the muscles as well as to the sensory centers of the brain where a "reference of correctness" (Matthews, 1988, as cited in Fisher, 1991, p. 85) is provided. The reference of correctness is believed to be a neural memory of "how it feels" to move in a particular manner as well as "what is achieved" when movement occurs in that manner (Brooks, 1986, as discussed in Fisher, 1991, p. 85). This memory provides information to the motor planning area (i.e., premotor cortex) of the brain. Information is sent to the motor cortex from the premotor cortex. The motor command is generated and the efference copy, a feedforward mechanism, is established. The efference copy is thought to be "a special type of internal feedback (feedforward) which, when compared to the reference of correctness, can be used to correct errors that

FIGURE 2.1 Schematic Model of Motor Control and the Circular Process of Sensory Integration

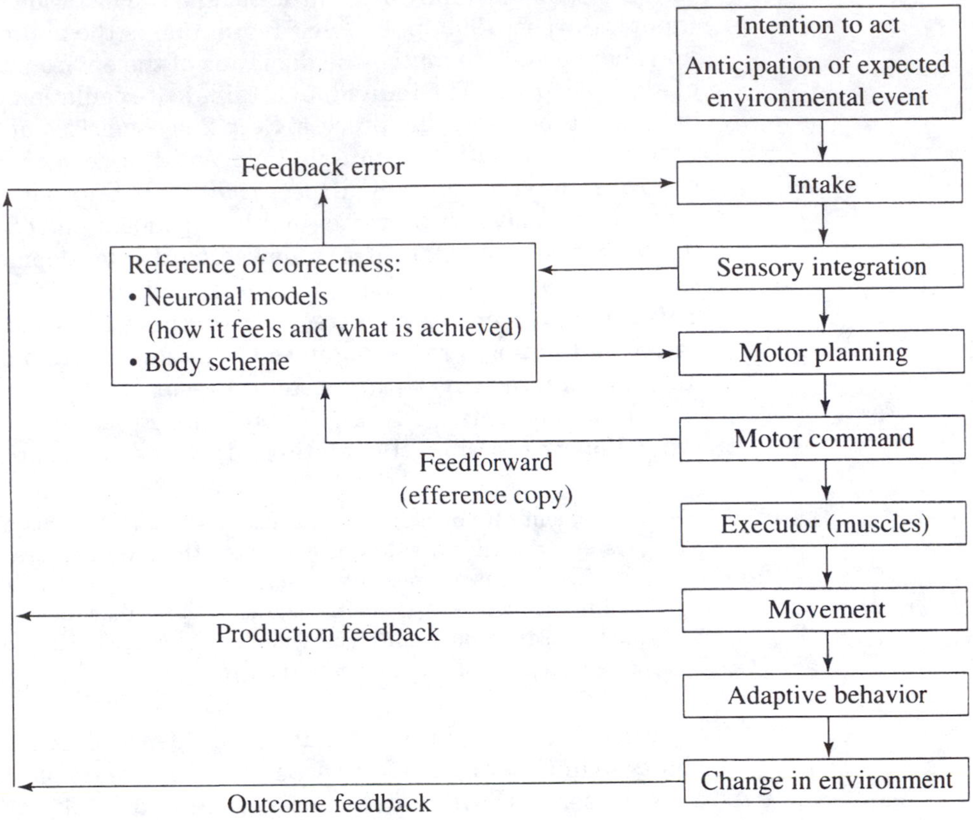

Source: Reprinted, with permission, from A. G. Fisher "Vestibular-Proprioceptive Processing and Bilateral Integration and Sequencing Deficits" in A. G. Fisher, E. A. Murray, and A. C. Bundy (Eds.), *Sensory Integration: Theory and Practice* (Philadelphia: F. A. Davis Company, 1991), p. 86.

are detected prior to the actual production of the action" (Fisher, 1991, p. 88). When the individual performs active movement, several feedback mechanisms are in place. Production feedback is thought to be generated by "the muscles as they contract" and by the "movement of the body or body parts in space" (Schmidt, 1988, as discussed by Fisher, 1991, p. 87). Outcome feedback is believed to be generated by changes in the environment resulting from the movement. Both production feedback and outcome feedback are evaluated by the body and brain. Detection of feedback errors signal the system to make corrections. The functioning of these feedback mechanisms is particularly important when an individual is learning new motor skills (Fisher, 1991).

Many individuals with oral motor issues exhibit difficulties with the integration of sensory input. This may result in hyperresponsivity, hyporesponsivity, or some combination of these, depending on the type of sensory stimulation challenging an individual's sensory systems at a particular time. Hyperresponsivity occurs when sensory input is allowed to "flood" the central nervous system and results in a "disorganized response to sensory input" (Royeen & Lane, 1991, p. 120). Individuals experiencing this may appear "overly active, hyperverbal, distractible, and disorganized" (Royeen & Lane, 1991, p. 120). Hyperresponsivity to sensory input often results in sensory defensiveness. *Sensory defensiveness* can be defined as "a tendency to react negatively or with alarm to sensory input that is generally considered harmless or non-irritating" (Wilbarger & Wilbarger, 1991, p. 3). According to Wilbarger and Wilbarger (1991), there are several forms of sensory defensiveness. These include "tactile defensiveness, oral defensiveness, gravitational insecurity, postural insecurity, visual defensiveness, auditory defensiveness," as well as "unusual sensitivities to taste and/or smell" (p. 4). Sensory defensiveness may be the result of hyperresponsivity. It may also be a learned behavior that began with hyperresponsivity or possibly an experience that was perceived as negative by the individual. For example, an individual may not accept certain food textures because he or she was given these prior to having the oral skills to manage the food. Sensory defensiveness is considered a sensory modulation disorder.

In addition to sensory defensiveness, individuals with oral motor concerns also can experience sensory overload. The concept of thresholds, or "levels of arousal," can assist the clinician in understanding the idea of sensory overload (Wilbarger & Wilbarger, 1991, p. 5). The typical individual exhibits a particular threshold in each sensory system where that system becomes alerted, or "turned on." Each system may also have a threshold where the system becomes overloaded, or "turned off." In the typical individual, the band of acceptance for sensory input may be rather broad. In the individual with sensory integration concerns, this band may be narrow. Therefore, the individual may appear hyperresponsive to a particular type of sensory input at one point in time and unresponsive to input provided to the same sensory system at another point in time. A particular sensory system can, therefore, "turn on" with very little stimulation and also "turn off" as stimulation increases.

Another type of sensory modulation disorder results from hyporesponsivity to sensory stimuli, which frequently presents as "sensory dormancy" (Royeen & Lane, 1991, p. 120). According to Royeen and Lane (1991, p. 120) sensory dormancy is the result of "excessive inhibition of incoming sensory input and a lack of sensory arousal." Individuals exhibiting sensory dormancy may appear to be quiet individuals who generally comply with the demands placed on them; however, their behavior is often disorganized and immature in nature (Royeen & Lane, 1991). These individuals may appear to lack initiative and may have difficulty socializing with peers. Individuals who demonstrate hyporesponsivity frequently demonstrate disorganized and unrefined eating, drinking, and speaking skills. They tend to place large amounts of food in the mouth and make imprecise articulatory contacts.

Sensory dormancy resulting from hyporesponsivity and sensory defensiveness resulting from hyperresponsivity represent two ends of the sensory modulation continuum with "normal" responsiveness occurring between these two ends of the continuum. The limbic system in the brain is believed to play an important part in sensory modulation. This would explain the emotional and social issues that often accompany sensory defensiveness, the presence of sensory defensiveness or dormancy across sensory systems, and the extreme shifts from defensiveness to dormancy that can occur within an individual (Royeen & Lane, 1991).

There are seven sensory systems that require consideration during the assessment and treatment of oral motor concerns. A definition, description, and discussion of these systems relative to oral motor assessment and treatment is provided in the next part of this chapter. Figure 2.2 demonstrates the interrelated nature of five of the seven sensory systems discussed in this chapter.

The Vestibular System

The vestibular system is activated by body movements through space and resulting changes in head position to automatically coordinate the movement of the eyes, head, and body (Sensory Integration International, 1991). It was one of the earliest sensory systems to develop phylogenetically in the human being and is well developed by 20 weeks gestation in the human fetus (Ayres, 1972b). Ayres (1972b) stated:

> The vestibular system enables the organism to detect motion, especially acceleration and deceleration and the earth's gravitational pull. The system helps the organism know whether any given sensory input—visual, tactile, or proprioceptive—is associated with movement of the body or is a function of the external environment. (p. 56)

The vestibular system assists the body in "maintaining muscle tone, coordinating the two sides of the body, and holding the head upright against gravity" (Sensory Integration International, 1991). It also reportedly stimulates the

FIGURE 2.2 The Senses, Integration of Their Inputs, and Their End Products

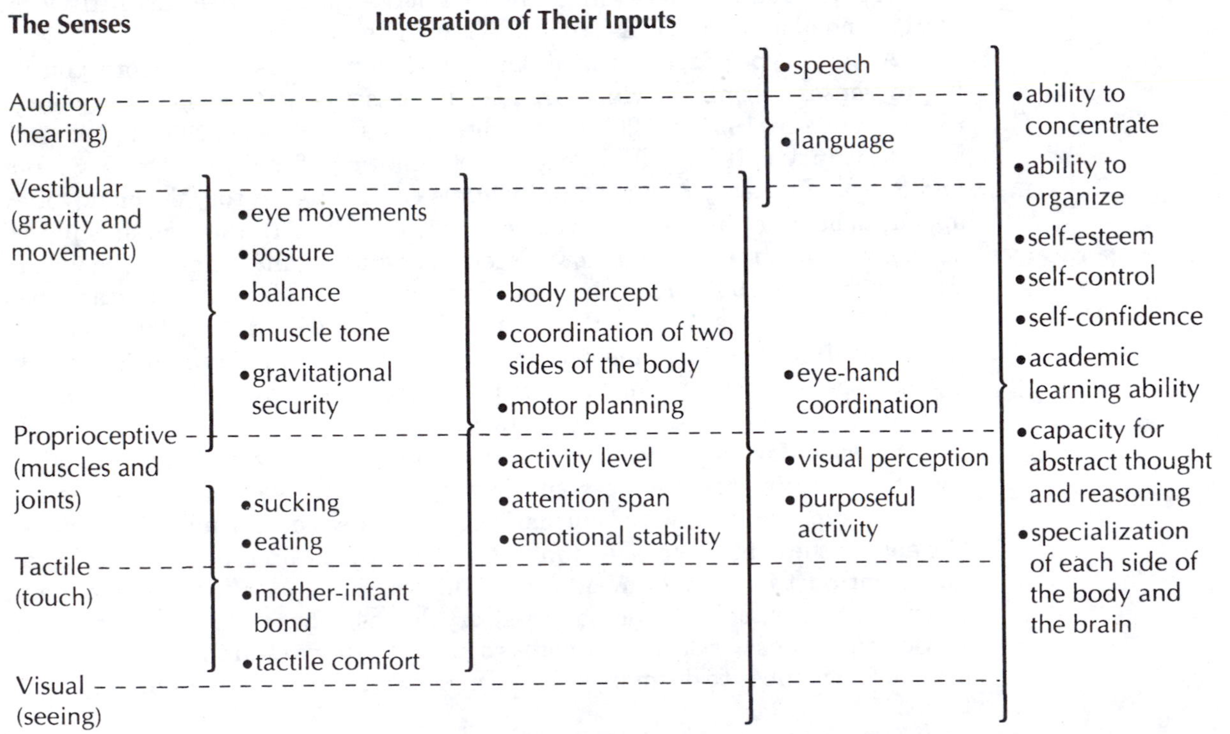

Source: A. Jean Ayres, *Sensory Integration and the Child* (Los Angeles: Western Psychological Services, 1979), p. 60. Material from *Sensory Integration and the Child* copyright © 1979 by Western Psychological Services. Reprinted by permission of the publisher, Western Psychological Services, 12031 Wilshire Boulevard, Los Angeles, California, 90025, U.S.A. Not to be reprinted in whole or in part for any additional purpose without the expressed, written permission of the publisher. All rights reserved.

reticular activating system, which is responsible for the individual's level of alertness or arousal.

The interrelated nature of the different sensory systems is expressed in Ayres's definition in the previous paragraph. Information from the vestibular system is integrated with information from other sensory systems at the level of the brain stem and cortex. According to Ayres (1979, p. 37), the vestibular system is "the unifying system" that prepares "the entire nervous system to function effectively," because "all other types of sensation are processed in reference to this basic vestibular stimulation." Trott and colleagues (1993, p. 6) state that "input from the vestibular system paces the functioning of the entire central nervous system and prepares it for other sensory input."

The vestibular system has a strong influence on maintaining muscle tone in the body (Ayres, 1972b; Sensory Integration International, 1991). This occurs specifically through the neuromuscular reflexes previously discussed in this chapter. Vestibular input provides the physical reference that assists the individual in making sense of visual information (Trott et al., 1993). Research by Aarons and Goldenberg (1964) suggested a connection between muscle tone and visual perception, and Ayres (1972b) hypothesized that disordered muscle tone may interfere with an individual's visual perceptual abilities.

Based on research by Stilwell, Crowe, and McCallum (1978), Trott and colleagues (1993, p. 7) state that "vestibular processes in the lower (subcortical) levels of the brain support processes that occur in higher (cortical) levels of the brain, including speech and language." They further hypothesize that "negative experiences with movement caused by a vestibular system dysfunction may, therefore, cause children to have trouble with speech and language" (p. 7). Language may not develop at the expected rate or follow the expected pattern of development in children with vestibular disorders (Trott et al., 1993). The vestibular system also affects an individual's ability to use gesture and body language, since these require adequate muscle tone and coordinated use of both sides of the body (i.e., bilateral integration).

"The vestibular system is a source of specialized proprioceptive inputs" (Fisher, 1991, p. 71). As originally defined by Sherrington in 1906, the term *proprioception* refers to the "perception of sensations that originate in receptors that are simulated by an organism's own movement" (Fisher, 1991, p. 71). Clinically, it is difficult to differentiate between the contributions from the vestibular and the proprioceptive systems to "postural control and motor performance" (Fisher, 1991, p. 71). A thorough description of the vestibular system and its relationship to the visual and proprioceptive systems can be found in the text *Sensory Integration: Theory and Practice* (1991) edited by Anne G. Fisher, Elizabeth A. Murray, and Anita C. Bundy. These systems are said to work together to provide three major functions: "subjective awareness of body position and movement in space; postural tone and equilibrium; and stabilization of the eyes in space during head movements" (p. 77). In order for an individual to have adequate oral motor control, these functions need to be in place. (See previous discussions in this chapter on muscle tone, stability, mobility, and movement. The proprioceptive system will be discussed in greater detail later in this chapter.)

A person may exhibit sensory modulation concerns in the vestibular system. The individual with a hyperreactive vestibular system may be very sensitive to and cautious about movement through space. The individual with a hyporeactive vestibular system may "crave" intense or constant movement experiences. The speech-language pathologist can work with an occupational therapist trained in sensory integration techniques to assess the client's responses to activities involving vestibular input. Based on this assessment, appropriate movement activities can be used in treatment to improve postural tone and stability needed for improved oral motor function.

Gross motor and other movement activities done at the beginning of treatment sessions and/or interspersed during treatment sessions can provide vestibular stimulation. To stimulate the individual with a hyporeactive vestibular system, the clinician can provide the client with rigorous, controlled movement activities, such as jumping, swinging, spinning, and so on. The type of movement must be carefully selected so that the individual does not become overstimulated by activities that may be too rigorous. Clients may also have previous medical conditions (e.g., atlanto-axial instability often seen in individuals with Down syndrome) that preclude the use of certain rigorous movement activities. Consult with the individual's physical therapist or physician prior to initiating vigorous activities with these individuals. Slower movement activities, such as rocking and swaying, can be calming to someone who is hyperreactive to vestibular stimulation. As previously discussed, the organization of the vestibular system can bring about positive results clinically in the speech and language system, the visual system, as well as the proprioceptive and tactile systems. After treatment of the vestibular system, clients have been observed to communicate more readily and use their visual skills more accurately.

Many individuals requiring oral motor treatment require treatment of the vestibular system secondary to the unifying nature of the vestibular system with regard to the other sensory systems. The potential effects of vestibular dysfunction on muscle tone and postural control may significantly affect the individual's ability to produce adequate oral movements used in eating, drinking, and speech production. As previously mentioned, occupational therapists trained in sensory integration therapy assess and treat disorders of the vestibular system. It is important for the speech-language pathologist to seek input from the occupational therapist regarding the types of vestibular activities needed by an individual during treatment. The speech-language pathologist may also wish to become trained in the use of sensory integration techniques.

The Tactile System

The tactile system provides input to the individual about cutaneous sensations on the surfaces of the body, including "touch, pressure, texture, heat, cold, pain, and movement of the hairs on the skin" (Ayres, 1979, p. 34). This is the earliest developing sensory system phylogenetically in the human being (Ayres, 1979; Fisher, Murray, & Bundy, 1991; Montagu, 1986). The skin is the oldest, largest, and most sensitive sensory organ of the body (Montagu, 1986). Skin covers the entire body, including the inside of the mouth and nostrils. Ayres (1979, p. 35) states that touch is "important for overall neural organization." Montagu (1986, p. 3) says that touch is the "mother of the senses."

According to Ayres (1972b), the tactile system also significantly contributes to the "perception of other types of sensation" (p. 61). A study by Melzack, Konrad, and Dubrovsky (1969) demonstrated that the tactile system influences the functioning of both the visual and auditory systems (Ayres, 1972b). Tactile system maturation is said to be related to overall neural development and resulting human behavior. The function of the tactile system reportedly indicates "the degree of central nervous system integration" (Ayres, 1972b, p. 62). Changes in tactile perception can indicate general results from brain injury (Wheeler, Burke, & Rietan, 1963). The neurologist performs testing procedures, such as double simultaneous stimulation (i.e., "two symmetrical points on the body" touched simultaneously), to assess these changes as indicators of neurologic damage (Brookshire, 1997, p. 58).

Charlotte Boshart (1999, p. 69) states that "tactile sensation is the foundation of movement" and that "repetitive oral touch stimulates and perpetuates repetitive movement." Repetitive movement is important in the processes of eating, drinking, and speaking.

The extremely acute tactile sensitivity of the tongue requires special consideration by the speech-language pathologist. Boshart (1999) states that the tongue tip and the back of the tongue have the greatest amount of tactile acuity compared to the rest of the tongue. The heightened sensation is believed to be partially related to "the type and/or number of sensory nerve endings" in these areas (p. 70). The tongue tip plays an important role in speech production, eating, and drinking. The protective gag response generally occurs with stimulation to the back of the tongue. The back of the tongue is also the area of tongue stabilization during speech production. During rapid coarticulated speech production, the tongue is spread in the back of the mouth and stabilizes in the area of the back molars. Graded movement of the posterior tongue is also an important component in the production of many speech sounds. "Of all sensations, the tactile sensation is the most vital in speech [production]. Speech is a 'touching' activity!" (Boshart, 1999, p. 68).

Much of the information from the tactile system is mediated in the brain stem to assist the individual in the establishment of efficient movement patterns and in the adjustment of the reticular activating system. Emotions are influenced by the tactile system (Ayres, 1979), and there are close connections between the tactile and limbic systems (Ayres, 1972b). Touch can be comforting or disturbing to an individual. This is dependent on the type of touch provided and the individual's perception of the tactile stimulation provided. The tactile system is comprised of the discriminative system and the protective system (Trott et al., 1993). The discriminative system determines the location and the source of the tactile input. The protective system engages the fight or flight response if the source of the tactile input threatens or is perceived to threaten the individual. "In order for the tactile system to function efficiently, the discriminative and protective systems must perceive information correctly and work in balance" (Trott et al., 1993, p. 3).

It is important to consider the discriminative and protective systems during the assessment and treatment of individuals with oral motor issues. Tactile discrimination typically varies within the mouth. In "an intra-oral two-point discrimination analysis on various locations in the mouth," Ringel and Ewanowski (1965, as cited in Boshart, 1999, p. 71) found that the front of the mouth was more sensitive than the back of the mouth. Ringel and Fletcher (1967, as cited in Boshart, 1999, p. 71) found that the tongue was more accurate in texture judgment than the lips. When tactile discrimination is a concern, the individual may have difficulty with the fine motor function of articulation. The articulation of speech sounds requires precise tactile discrimination. Individuals exhibiting tactile discrimination concerns may also stuff their mouths with food or be unaware of drool or food on their faces. These individuals appear to have decreased sensory awareness or hyporesponsivity. When an individual has difficulty with the protective system, tactile input that is typically nonthreatening may be perceived as threatening. Individuals who demonstrate these concerns may not want to eat foods of certain textures, as these may be perceived as threatening. These individuals are often described as "picky" eaters. Individuals exhibiting concerns with the protective system generally do not like touch in and around the facial area and are often described as exhibiting hyperresponsivity and/or tactile defensiveness.

Many individuals with oral motor concerns have difficulties with tactile thresholds that may affect eating, drinking, and speaking. Touch/pressure stimulation (e.g., massage) can be used to decrease hyperresponsivity and tactile defensiveness or increase sensory discrimination in the client with a hyporesponsive system. Firm touch tends to be calming. Light touch tends to be alerting. For individuals who tend to be hyperresponsive to touch, phasic (i.e., on/off) touch seems to be more readily accepted than sustained touch. This type of touch can be applied in a series of firm on/off presses or firm presses with a rotary component. After the individual adjusts to the application of phasic touch, firm sustained touch can then be applied. For individuals who are not easily alerted, light touch may be used. As with all sensory techniques, the application of touch must be carefully applied to move the individual toward a calm alert state (i.e., homeostasis).

Temperature is perceived through the tactile and proprioceptive systems. Warm temperatures tend to be calming, whereas cold temperatures tend to be alerting. Muscles tend to relax when warmth is applied and tend to contract when cold is applied. "Temperature preferences are related to . . . tactile preferences. Having extreme preferences about temperature or difficulties with temperature regulation may be indicative of [sensory] processing problems" (Trott et al., 1993). Food temperatures are important to consider when working with individuals with oral motor concerns. Cold foods can be alerting, whereas warm foods can be calming to an individual. Individuals with oral motor concerns can exhibit sensory modulation difficulties relative to food temperatures. Some individuals with oral motor concerns have difficulty tolerating temperature differences in foods. These individuals may more readily accept foods at "neutral room temperature" (Boshart, 1999, p. 82). Other individuals with oral motor concerns may require intense temperature changes in foods to demonstrate awareness of or interest in the food. They may respond best to cold or frozen foods and may risk burning the mouth on foods that are very hot.

Texture is perceived through the tactile and proprioceptive systems. Sensation from these systems assists an individual in responding motorically to different food textures. Chewy food textures (e.g., dried fruit, bagels, and meat) require more sophisticated oral motor patterns than soft food textures (e.g., pudding and applesauce). For individuals who reject certain food textures, foods can be systematically modified, moving from foods accepted by the individual toward foods that are not. These concepts will be more fully discussed in Chapters 4 and 5.

The Proprioceptive System

The proprioceptive system provides the individual with inner awareness in the muscles, tendons, ligaments, and joints. Sensation from these areas is generally processed at an unconscious level. The proprioceptive system is myelinated by 20 to 28 weeks of gestation, and the fetus demonstrates reflexive responses to proprioceptive input by 16 weeks gestation (Burpee, 1999). "The word proprioception refers to the sensory information caused by contraction and stretching of muscles and by bending, straightening, pulling, and compression of the joints between bones" (Ayres, 1979, p. 35). Proprioception allows the human being to monitor body and body part spatial orientation, the rate and timing of movements, the force exerted by the muscles, as well as the rate and extent of muscle stretch (Fisher, 1991; Sensory Integration International, 1991). It "is heightened during muscle contraction," but also provides feedback to the brain and body about muscle tone when the body is at rest (Boshart, 1999, p. 73). According to Ayres (1979), "the proprioceptive system is almost as large as the tactile system" (p. 35) and is critical to the integration of sensory input in the body. Proprioceptive information is processed simultaneously with tactile information.

The majority of proprioceptive information provided to the body is generated by the "muscle spindles, mechanoreceptors of the skin, and centrally generated motor commands" (Fisher, 1991, p. 85). Mechanoreceptors are those "which respond to mechanical pressure or deformation of the receptor and adjacent tissues" (Zemlin, 1998, p. 394). Centrally (i.e., brain) generated motor commands result in volitional or purposeful movements made by the individual. The joint receptors are no longer considered the main source of proprioceptive information in the body. Therefore, Fisher (1991) suggests that active muscle contraction against resistance may be a better treatment technique than joint compression and traction (i.e., manual techniques usually applied by physical and occupational therapists that compress or expand a joint) to elicit proprioceptive feedback in many individuals. However, this information must be carefully applied to individuals with significant neuromotor impairments (e.g., individuals with cerebral palsy, traumatic brain injury, progressive neurological disease, etc.), as some of these individuals may not respond positively to activities involving active movement against resistance.

Eating, drinking, and speaking are "spatial activities" (Boshart, 1999, p. 73). Difficulties with oral proprioception results in poor oral control in space. This will affect the movements of the jaw, lips, and tongue and can significantly affect the oral motor processes of eating, drinking, and speaking. Henke (1967, as cited in Boshart, 1999, p. 73) suggested that proprioceptive feedback is important in the timing and rate of speech production. Individuals with oral motor concerns often exhibit concerns regarding the integration of proprioceptive input. Difficulties with the inner awareness in the muscles, tendons, ligaments, and joints can affect the individual's ability to attain stability and mobility throughout the body and oral mechanism.

It is interesting to note that proprioceptive feedback to the brain is believed to assist with visual perception (Ayres, 1972b). According to Hebb (1949), the proprioceptive information from the eye muscles to the brain is believed to assist with visual form and space perception. Individuals who exhibit difficulties receiving appropriate proprioceptive feedback from their bodies tend to use the visual system to compensate by looking at what the body is doing (Ayres, 1979).

Fisher (1991) briefly discusses the term *kinesthesia,* which was once defined as "conscious joint proprioception" as opposed to "unconscious proprioception" in the muscle spindles and tendons (Ayres, 1972b; Burpee, 1999; Fisher, 1991, p. 84). More recently, the terms *proprioception* and *kinesthesia* have been used synonymously.

The proprioceptive system can be stimulated through movement, massage, and joint compression or traction. Many individuals with oral motor concerns require deep proprioceptive input. This input brings awareness and helps the individual become more sensorially organized. The speech-language pathologist can receive training in techniques to elicit increased proprioception.

Clients attain proprioceptive input during movement activities. Rigorous controlled movements, such as those found in jumping, bouncing, and running, generally provide deep awareness in the muscles and the joints. These movements can facilitate improved muscle tone in individuals with hypotonia. (See the discussion in the previous sections on muscle tone and the vestibular system.) Gentle movement, such as rocking, can decrease muscle tone in individuals demonstrating hypertonicity. It can also provide important information about the ease of a particular movement for individuals with all types of muscle tone. For example, Feldenkrais's "Awareness through Movement" activities provide the client with information regarding the ease and efficiency of movement. These activities were developed by Moshe Feldenkrais, who originated the functional integration system to improve the "functions of the human motor system" (Kimmey, 1985, cover). Movement done with ease and efficiency requires less effort on the behalf of the client. This can lead to greater willingness to continue the particular movement. The Bobaths, who developed neurodevelopmental treatment (NDT), also stressed the concept of establishing ease and efficiency of movement. It must again be stressed that the speech-language pathologist should consult with the individual's occupational therapist and/or physical therapist when choosing appropriate movement activities for the client.

Oral movement activities can provide increased proprioception in the mouth. Heavy chewing activities can provide deep input into the jaw musculature and temporomandibular joint. Blowing and sucking activities as well as a variety of other oral exercises can also naturally increase proprioception in the muscles, ligaments, tendons, and joints of the oral mechanism. Specific oral motor activities are chosen according to the client's muscle tone and movement patterns.

In addition to active movement, touch/pressure can be used to facilitate proprioception in the oral area. Prior to activities requiring the use of the mouth, touch/pressure can be used to inhibit the hyperresponsive sensory system or to facilitate the hyporesponsive sensory system. Touch/pressure to the face, lips, cheeks, tongue, and hard palate can be done with the fingertips and/or an oral massage brush, depending on the area receiving input and the client being served. The use of touch/pressure does not always necessitate the direct placement of the clinician's hands on the individual but can be facilitated during a variety of activities using a variety of pieces of equipment (e.g., therapy balls, therapy brushes, etc.). These techniques will be more specifically discussed in the chapters on treatment.

The Olfactory System

The olfactory system is responsible for the integration of information received through the sensation of smell. According to Ayres (1979), the sense of smell seems to be well organized in the human being at birth and to "play an important role during the first month of life" (p. 17). Infants appear to identify their mothers using the sense of smell. However, the olfactory sense does not appear to change significantly over the course of early development (Ayres, 1979).

The olfactory system developed early in human evolution, and the cortex of the brain "evolved as an extension of the first cranial (olfactory) nerve" (Ayres, 1972b, p. 73). This system has not significantly changed in size throughout the evolution of humans. The olfactory lobes are located in the rhinencephalon in the brain, which is "phylogenetically quite primitive" (Zemlin, 1998, p. 544). The olfactory receptors are hair cell chemoreceptors located in the "mucosa at the roof of the nasal cavity" (Kapit & Elson, 1993, p. 160). The olfactory tract terminates "in the interior frontal lobe and medial temporal lobe," which is thought to account for "olfactory relationships with memory, eating, survival, sex, and other emotional behavior" (Kapit & Elson, 1993, p. 160).

The olfactory system is believed to affect the performance of the limbic and the reticular activating systems. The olfactory bulbs located on the medial surface of the frontal lobe of the brain are considered to be part of the limbic system. "The limbic system receives sensory information from, and returns its output to, the reticular formation in the brain stem, and it connects to the frontal lobes and hypothalamus" (Zemlin, 1998, p. 334). The system is said to mediate the sense of smell. The importance of the olfactory system is just beginning to be understood with the use and study of treatments such as aromatherapy.

The senses of smell and taste are interrelated. Adults report that food tastes decrease when they cannot smell the food. This would occur because the tongue can detect the tastes of sweet, sour, salty, and bitter, but the sense of smell provides further information about the food. As previously mentioned, babies use smell to identify their mothers. Smell is one of the earliest senses used to experience the environment. Certain smells can be very alerting, whereas others can be soothing or calming. "Strong" odors (e.g., ammonia) are usually alerting; subtle scents (e.g., vanilla) can be calming. However, the response to smell is quite individual. Some individuals are alerted by a familiar odor, such as the smell of baking bread, while others may feel calmed by this. For smell, as well as the other senses discussed in this chapter, association and learned responses seem to play an important roll in an individual's response to particular stimuli. Therefore, what may be alerting to one individual may be calming to another and vice versa.

Some individuals may be sensitive to certain scents or airborne substances. Certain scents from perfumes, cleaning solutions, and so on may cause sneezing or other reactions in some individuals. Pollen, mold, and dust mites are well known irritants for many individuals. These are important environmental considerations for learning. It is difficult to learn in environments where individuals are demonstrating environmental sensitivities or allergies. Many individuals with oral motor concerns have histories of asthma and/or allergies. Treatment in an area such as a basement, where many of these environmental concerns exist, may affect the attention, focus, and concentration of individuals with these sensitivities.

Individuals exhibiting oral motor disorders frequently exhibit difficulties in the integration of information from the olfactory system. Hyperresponsivity to smell can result in the rejection of food or interpersonal interaction based on the individual's selectivity. An individual may reject foods and fluids that do not have an acceptable aroma. Interactions with people may be rejected based on a sensitivity to the aromas of cologne, soap, and so forth. The person with a hyporesponsive olfactory system may be disinterested in food because the aroma of the food is not perceived. These individuals may respond best to intense aromas. The sense of smell is therefore important to consider in the assessment and treatment of individuals exhibiting oral motor issues.

The Gustatory System

The gustatory system is responsible for the integration of information received through the sensation of taste. Taste receptors are located in various areas of the tongue "and to a lesser extent, on the soft palate and lingual side of the epiglottis" (Kapit & Elson, 1993, p. 160). Taste buds are chemoreceptors and are stimulated by molecules in dissolved material from food and liquid that enter through pores in the structures (i.e., tongue, soft palate, and epiglottis) (Kapit & Elson, 1993; Zemlin, 1998). These pores, called *papillae,* contain the taste buds (Boshart, 1999). "Each papillae contains several taste buds, and each taste bud consists of several receptor cells (about 30) arranged like closed petals of a flower" (Boshart, 1999, p. 85). Receptor cells live approximately 7 to 10 days.

New receptor cells replace the dying receptor cells. Each taste bud contains immature receptor cells around the outside, mature receptor cells near the inside, and some dying cells (Beidler & Smallman, 1965, as cited in Boshart, 1999, p. 85). "There are [approximately] 10,000 taste buds in the mouth" (Boshart, 1999, p. 85). Taste bud development continues after birth. Infants may "respond differentially to bitter, sweet, and sour stimuli," but they reportedly "are indifferent to salty taste" (Boshart, 1999, p. 88). As an individual ages, the number of taste buds decrease (Coren, 1979, as cited in Boshart, 1999, p. 85). Many older adult clients complain about food lacking taste, and this may be related to a decrease in the number of taste buds. Taste sensation is sent to the brain stem from the mouth via cranial nerves VII, IX, and X (i.e., facial, glossopharyngeal, and vagus). The interpretation of taste occurs in the postcentral gyrus (i.e., sensory cortex).

Tastes are discriminated in different locations on the tongue (see Figure 2.3). Sweet tastes are detected near the tongue tip, salty tastes are detected near the front and sides of the tongue, sour tastes are detected on the sides of the tongue, and bitter tastes are detected on the back of the tongue and soft palate (Boshart, 1999; Kapit & Elson, 1993). The brain detects the bitter sensation prior to detecting other taste sensations as a protective mechanism. "Many poisons and toxic substances are bitter" (Boshart, 1999, p. 86).

A variety of other factors can affect an individual's ability to taste foods and liquids. Taste is affected by temperature. Room-temperature foods and liquids reportedly have more flavor than cold or hot foods and liquids (Boshart, 1999). Saliva also plays an important role in the taste process, as "it transports

FIGURE 2.3 Taste Sensation on the Tongue

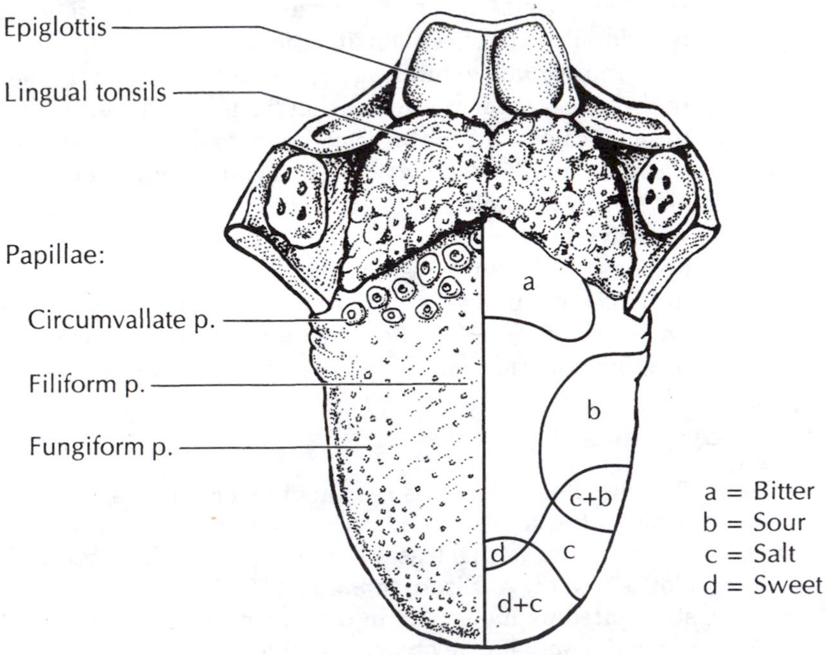

Source: From *The Anatomy Coloring Book* by Wynn Kapit and Lawrence M. Elson; Copyright © 1977, by Harper & Row Publishers. Reprinted by permission of Addison-Wesley Educational Publishers.

the food and liquid to the taste receptors" (Boshart, 1999, p. 89). In order to taste food or liquid accurately the taste buds must be stimulated by having the taste stimuli carried to them via saliva, muscle action, and intra-oral suctioning (Boshart, 1999). Food or liquid must remain in the mouth for a period of time so that this process can occur. The taste of food or liquid is also said to be enhanced by tongue movement against the hard palate and alveolar ridge as well as the presence of air in the oral cavity (Boshart, 1999).

For many people, strong tastes are alerting and mild tastes are calming. Individuals with oral motor difficulties often exhibit concerns with the integration of information from the gustatory system. Those who are hyperresponsive to taste may accept foods only within a narrow taste range and are often easily overloaded with a change in taste. Tastes outside of this range, such as the taste of the same food item made by another company, may be unacceptable. Some individuals have low taste thresholds and respond well to foods of a neutral quality with flavors of a low intensity. Individuals with low taste thresholds who are truly overwhelmed by small changes in taste require a task-analyzed, systematic program of taste modification to address their needs. (See information presented in Chapter 4 on this topic.) However, individuals who seem hyporesponsive to taste may require foods that have an intense quality (e.g., spicy foods). This may be secondary to a decrease in taste sensation or an increase in taste threshold. Some individuals will reject food or liquid with a mild taste, because they require high taste sensation for the gustatory system to respond. They may adapt quickly to tastes and may need more time between bites to reset the system so that they do not crave more intense taste with each bite (Boshart, 1999). Other individuals may have a decrease in the sense of taste secondary to vitamin A depletion or reduced saliva production (Boshart, 1999). The loss of taste, called *ageusia,* can have many ramifications for individuals with oral motor concerns. These issues will be further discussed in the Chapters 4 and 5. Charlotte Boshart has written about the topic of taste in her book *Treatise on the Tongue: Analysis and Treatment of Tongue Abnormalities* (1999).

The Auditory System

The auditory system is responsible for the integration of auditory information received by the sense of hearing. After mechanical transmission through the middle ear, sound is received by receptors in the inner ear. Sound is vibratory in nature and is perceived through both the auditory and tactile systems (Trott et al., 1993). Auditory information is transmitted to the brain stem from the inner ear, where information from the vestibular, proprioceptive, tactile, and visual systems are also processed (Ayres, 1979). The center for processing visual information in the brain stem is in close proximity to the area where auditory information is processed. Information is exchanged between the auditory and visual processing areas in the brain stem. "Some of the auditory impulses [also] travel to other parts of the brain stem and cerebellum for integration with other sensations and motor messages" (Ayres, 1979, p. 34). Once this integration occurs, the auditory information is sent to several areas of the cerebral cortex. The central auditory nervous system "includes nuclei and pathways in the brain stem, subcortex, primary and association areas of the cortex, and corpus collosum" (American Speech-Language-Hearing Association, 1996, p. 43). It is "a complex system with multiple components and levels of parallel and sequential but interactive organization" (American Speech-Language-Hearing Association, 1996, p. 43).

The auditory system is comprised of mechanisms and processes called *central auditory processes.* These include auditory localization, discrimination, and pattern recognition; the time aspects of audition (e.g., auditory sequencing); and listening performance when competing or degraded auditory stimuli are present (American Speech-Language-Hearing Association, 1996). The process of auditory integration permits meaning to be attached to words. In conjunction with the sensory information received from the other sensory systems, auditory input also impacts on the individual's level of alertness (Trott et al., 1993). According to Ayres (1972b), the processing of sound in the brain is a primal survival mechanism in the human being. This would be particularly important to an individual living in a primitive environment where sounds may reflect the presence of some type of danger or possible food source. However, the processing and production of speech and language involve extremely complex operations in the brain that seem to go beyond this primal survival mechanism.

"Auditory information can be the most difficult [information] for the brain to organize, integrate, understand, and use" (Trott et al., 1993, p. 28) secondary to the complexity of the auditory system and its complex relationship with the various other sensory systems. The ways in which an individual uses auditory information reflect the brain's integration of information from the other sensory systems (Trott et al., 1993).

A strong relationship is thought to exist between the vestibular and auditory systems. The auditory system evolved from a "system closely related to the current vestibular system" (Ayres, 1972b, p. 72). It is likely that the integration of auditory and vestibular information occurs at the brain stem level. "Sensory integration therapists stimulate the vestibular system with movement and vibration to improve auditory and language processes" (Ayres, 1979, p. 41). Ayres (1972a) conducted a study to assess "the effects of sensory integration treatment programs on children with sensory integrative disorders and on children with auditory-language problems" (as cited in Fisher & Murray, 1991, p. 7). The children receiving sensory integration therapy demonstrated significant gains in sight-reading and auditory-language skills compared to matched control subjects (Fisher & Murray, 1991). The gains were believed to be related to increases in auditory perceptual and sequential memory skills. In another study, Ayres (1976, 1978, as cited in Fisher & Murray, 1991) concluded:

> Central vestibular processing disorders were a common basis of learning problems, and . . . children with central vestibular processing disorders (including depressed durations of postrotary nystagmus) may respond more readily to programs that include the use of sensory integration treatment techniques than will children with prolonged durations of postrotary nystagmus. (p. 8)

Postrotary nystagmus occurs after vestibular stimulation involving rotation. Occupational therapists use the duration and the timing of nystagmus (i.e., rhythmic horizontal eye movements) to determine adequate or inadequate function of the vestibular system. Densem, Nuthall, Bushnell, and Horn (1989, as cited in Fisher & Murray, 1991) suggested that further research needs to be completed in this area, focusing on outcome measures, how the intervention works, and for whom it works.

Many individuals with speech and language difficulties exhibit auditory processing concerns. The intensity and quality of sound can affect the individual's auditory processing. Some people do not tolerate loud sounds (e.g., some individuals with autism or traumatic brain injury), some people may be alerted by sounds that are often filtered out by others (e.g., individuals with attention deficit disorder), and some people require intense or increased auditory input (e.g., individuals who prefer loud music or who play music or the television when studying or going to sleep) (Trott et al., 1993). Sound has many parameters that can be adjusted to suit an individual's auditory preferences so that auditory processing can effectively occur.

"Central auditory processing disorder (CAPD) is a modality specific perceptual dysfunction that is not due to peripheral hearing impairment" (Cacace & McFarland, 1998, p. 355). This disorder is often treated by speech-language pathologists and audiologists. "Modality specific perceptual dysfunction" means that individuals with CAPD exhibit specific deficits in the processing of acoustic information but *do not* exhibit similar deficits in the processing of similar sensory information in other sensory modalities. Cacace and McFarland (1998) question the diagnosis of many children who have been identified as having CAPD:

> Children with diverse learning problems, including difficulties in learning to read, in acquiring spoken language, and in attention, can show abnormal performance on commercially available tests of central-auditory processing. When this occurs, it is worth questioning whether such children are appropriately classified as having CAPD in view of the evidence that they may also have information-processing deficits when assessments are performed in other sensory modalities. (p. 366)

Therefore, children with learning difficulties often have sensory integration concerns beyond those found in the auditory system. This information reflects the interconnected nature of the various sensory modalities discussed in this chapter and the need to assess the other sensory systems in addition to the auditory system in individuals demonstrating speech and language deficits. Individuals demonstrating oral motor concerns often exhibit concomitant difficulties with auditory integration as well as the integration of the other sensory processes. Some clinicians also question whether an individual's difficulties with speech output are related to motor or auditory processing concerns. Both areas play an important role in speech production and must be accurately assessed and treated by the speech-language pathologist.

Individuals with auditory integration and processing concerns have been successfully treated via sensory integration therapy as well as specific treatments designed to address CAPD. Some specific methods of auditory integration training have also been developed. These methods include the Berard method, the Tomatis method, and the Samonas method. It is currently beyond the scope of this book to discuss these methods. However, music can be used to modify the auditory environment for some individuals with sensory concerns. This topic will be discussed in detail in Chapter 3.

The Visual System

The visual system is responsible for the integration of visual input received by the eyes. According to Ayres (1972b), "The human being is not only a highly visual animal, he is conscious of being visual" (p. 73). Visual information is received by the retina and sent via neural pathways to the "visual processing centers in the brain stem" (Ayres, 1979, p. 33). The information is integrated with information from the other sensory systems (e.g., tactile, proprioceptive, and vestibular systems) in the brain stem. Visual information is further integrated in the cerebellum to allow movement in the eyes and neck for visual tracking. The information is also processed and integrated with other sensory systems within a variety of structures in the cerebrum, including the reticular formation, the thalamus, and the visual cortex (Ayres, 1972b, 1979).

The left half of each visual field for each eye sends impulses to the right cerebral hemisphere, and the right half of each visual field for each eye sends impulses to the left cerebral hemisphere. Integration of the two halves of the visual field seems to require communication between the two cerebral hemispheres (Ayres, 1972b). Some visual perceptual and reading disorders are believed to be related to a disruption in this interhemispheric communication.

In the book *SenseAbilities: Understanding Sensory Integration,* Maryann Colby Trott, Marci K. Laurel, and Susan L. Windeck (1993) discuss the importance of visual integration and the connection between the visual system and the other sensory systems. According to Trott and colleagues (1993), the ways in which the individual uses visual information reflect the brain's integration of information from the other sensory systems. Visual information is used to assist the individual in establishing personal space or boundaries, body position in space, and movement through space. The integration of information from the visual, tactile, and vestibular systems assists the individual in the establishment of personal space or boundaries. "Efficient processing of vestibular information is strongly related to the [individual's] ability to use visual information. It is the efficient integration of vestibular information that contributes to the understanding of spatial relationships" (Trott et al., 1993, p. 27). This assists the individual in using left to right and top to bottom progression in the complex tasks involved in reading and writing.

Individuals demonstrating oral motor concerns may also exhibit difficulties with visual integration and perception. Many of these individuals require environmental, lighting, or material changes to suit their visual preferences. Some may require intense visual stimulation, whereas others may require a neutral visual environment to attend, focus, and concentrate. Light assists the individual in initiating and maintaining alertness, and color assists the individual in orienting, attending, and learning (Trott et al., 1993). The visual environment can alert or calm the person and must be considered during assessment and treatment. A change in visual stimulation or the visual environment may allow the individual to more readily participate in these processes.

The visual environment can be easily modified. Lighting can be changed to accommodate an individual's preferences and enhance the learning environment. Some people prefer a brightly lit environment; others prefer soft lighting. Bright light is often associated with warm temperature (Trott et al., 1993). Some individuals demonstrate improved attention, focus, and concentration in an environment with natural lighting, full spectrum lighting, or incandescent lighting. Currently, research is being conducted on the use of full spectrum lighting versus florescent lighting in learning environments, home environments, and the workplace. Full spectrum lighting is believed to increase attention and achievement as well as reduce fatigue, depression, and chronic infections. Florescent lighting may be overstimulating and distracting for some people. This type of lighting may send out a sound that is heard by individuals with sensitive hearing, and the flicker of the lighting may affect visual processing for some people.

The amount of visual stimulation within an environment can affect an individual's learning process. Environments with a large amount of visual stimulation may be overstimulating for some individuals. These may be environments with many pictures on the walls or many items in the room. Individuals with attention concerns, such as those with autistic spectrum disorders or those with traumatic brain injury, often have difficulty maintaining attention in a "cluttered" environment.

Color can also affect the individual's response to the environment. Soothing, neutral colors tend to calming. Bold, intense colors seem to be alerting. The affect of color on attention, focus, and concentration may be related to the individual's level of development as well as personal preference. "Children tend to prefer intense primary colors" (Trott et al., 1993, p. 25). Adults seem to prefer to work in environments painted in pastel colors. Colors may also affect the individual's mood and emotional responses. Much research has been conducted on this topic but is beyond the scope of this book.

In addition to the effects of the visual environment on an individual, many people with postural stability and subsequent oral motor concerns also exhibit visual motor issues. It is important to recall that changes in body position and posture can significantly affect visual processes, such as visual scanning and tracking. When the individual's head and neck are not actively stable secondary to postural instability, he or she may have difficulty with these visual processes. Visual movements are distal fine motor movements and generally require the individual to attain postural stability for this distal control. The individual uses the processes of visual tracking and scanning when eating and drinking as well as during many other activities of daily living.

The speech-language pathologist may wish to consider the affects of lighting, color, and amount of visual stimulation when selecting an environment in which to work and when preparing materials to be used with the client. The relationship between the functional use of the visual system (i.e., visual scanning and tracking) and postural stability is another important consideration during assessment and treatment.

THE RELEVANCE OF SENSORY INTEGRATION TO ORAL MOTOR ASSESSMENT AND TREATMENT

As previously mentioned, individuals with oral motor concerns frequently demonstrate difficulties with sensory integration. They often exhibit uneven sensory responses and poor adaptive responses. The speech-language pathologist can assess the individual's ability to organize and integrate information from the different sensory systems. As a result of this assessment, the speech-language pathologist can then facilitate the organization and integration of sensory information so that the individual can produce appropriate adaptive responses in the areas of eating, drinking, and speaking. If the speech-language pathologist is not trained in sensory integrative assessment and treatment, an occupational therapist or another clinician trained in this area can assist the speech-language pathologist.

Using the "Environmental Sensory Variable Analysis" Morris and Klein (2000, p. 287) analyze individuals' sensory environments. They look at the calming and alerting effects of environmental factors on each of the sensory systems. In addition to the analysis of the client's sensory environment, it is important to observe how environmental factors affect the clinician (i.e., the assessment and treatment dyad). Assessment and treatment are a "dance" between these individuals. The concept of a "dance" is used here because dancing involves coordination between partners. If one partner is out of synchrony with the other, the "dance" is not well executed. Coordination of the sensory environment can allow both partners to work well together and to establish synchronicity.

When modifying the sensory environment for clients during oral motor assessment or treatment, one environmental change can be made at a time. This allows the clinician to determine the appropriate combination of alerting and calming factors for the individual as well as the assessment and treatment dyad. If several individuals are being treated in the environment, these factors must be considered for each individual. The variables affecting the sensory environment must also be considered for all members of the treatment team. A great deal of effective co-treatment occurs in current therapeutic environments, and it is important for the environment to be conducive to improved attention, focus, concentration, and learning for all persons involved in the process.

Difficulties in the organization and integration of sensory responses can affect both muscle function and motor planning in the oral mechanism. This is generally the result of specific damage to and/or poor connections in the central nervous system. Individuals with muscle function concerns exhibit difficulties with oral stability, strength, and grading of movement. Individuals with motor planning concerns demonstrate difficulties with the sequencing of oral movements. Adequate sensory perception and integration is needed for adequate oral muscle function and motor planning.

CASE EXAMPLES

The clients (Carolyn and Eddie) discussed in Chapter 1 exhibited a variety of concerns in the areas presented in this chapter. These contributed to their difficulties with oral motor function. The following case examples will look at the stability, mobility, muscle tone, movement, and sensory issues presented by Carolyn and Eddie. It should be noted that positioning and oral motor techniques described in this section relate specifically to the needs presented by Carolyn and Eddie. These techniques may or may not be appropriate for other clients. Refer to Chapters 4 through 8 for further information on specific oral motor treatment techniques.

Carolyn (22-Month-Old Child with Moebius Syndrome)

Stability and Mobility Carolyn had mild low muscle tone in the trunk of her body; therefore, she had difficulty attaining the stable postural base of support needed for more refined oral movements. When sitting in an appropriately sized chair with her hips, knees, and ankles at 90 degrees, she could use her mouth with increased efficiency for eating, drinking, and sound production. The positioning allowed for improved respiration and phonation in addition to improved oral motor function. Carolyn also attained a stable body position for improved oral motor function when sitting on the floor in side sitting with one hand and arm supporting her body. This position helped stabilize her hips and shoulder girdle.

Muscle Tone Carolyn's muscle tone in her body improved with gross motor activities. Her muscle tone was markedly improved after she jumped on a mini-trampoline, climbed over and through pieces of equipment in an obstacle course, and bounced on a "bouncing" horse. She also allowed manual tapping and manual vibratory stimulation to be applied to the areas of her masseter, buccinator, and orbicularis oris musculature. This seemed to improve the muscle tone in her cheeks and lips.

Movement Carolyn demonstrated generally adequate straight planes of movement and lateral movement in the trunk of her body. However, she exhibited mild difficulties with diagonal movement and rotation. She inconsistently crossed midline to retrieve objects. She usually reached with her right hand to retrieve objects on her right and reached with her left hand to retrieve objects on her left. Orally, she demonstrated difficulties with lateral, diagonal, and rotary movement. Carolyn did not lateralize food with her tongue, and she used an "up and down" munching pattern when she ate.

Sensory Responsiveness, Organization, and Integration Carolyn had mild difficulties with the integration of vestibular input. She required careful monitoring when playing on gross motor equipment, as she seemed to crave intense vestibular and proprioceptive input. On pieces of equipment, such as the mini-trampoline and the "bouncing" horse, she jumped or bounced "wildly" if not carefully monitored. Regarding the tactile system, Carolyn seemed hyperresponsive to tactile input, as she did not readily tolerate superficial touch to her arms, shoulders, face, or mouth. However, she seemed to desire deep proprioceptive input. She allowed gentle but firm presses to be applied to her arms and hands, and her mother reported that Carolyn loved to receive "bear hugs."

Carolyn did not seem particularly responsive to different smells. She preferred sweet foods and often rejected foods of other tastes. Regarding her auditory system, extraneous noise or sounds in the environment easily distracted Carolyn. However, she responded well to music played during treatment. Her attention, focus, and concentration noticeably improved when classical baroque music was played in the background. Carolyn appeared to be a visual learner. She responded well to the use of visual cueing strategies to assist in her production of speech sounds. Overall, Carolyn exhibited some disorganization in her processing of sensory information and required specific treatment strategies to facilitate the integration of these systems.

Eddie (59-Year-Old Man with Bilateral Subcortical Strokes)

Stability and Mobility Eddie had mild low muscle tone in the trunk of his body (premorbid status) and moderate spasticity in all four of his extremities (postmorbid status). Therefore, he had difficulty attaining the stable postural base of support needed for refined oral movements. His stability improved when he attended physical therapy or occupational therapy prior to speech therapy or a meal. Appropriate gross motor activities and upper body exercises seemed to improve his overall postural tone as well as his shoulder stability needed for improved oral motor function. Eddie's oral motor function also improved when he was positioned in a chair with a solid seat and solid back with his hips, knees, and ankles at 90 degrees of flexion.

Muscle Tone The high muscle tone in his oral structures accounted for Eddie's difficulties with eating, drinking, and speaking. His oral muscle tone improved through the use of oral massage and biofeedback. When Eddie exhibited difficulty maintaining adequate postural tone, a movement program suggested by his physical therapist was implemented. This involved movements of his trunk that increased his trunk tone while not increasing the muscle tone in his mouth.

Movement Eddie demonstrated generally adequate movement of his body in straight planes. However, he exhibited reduced rotation in his body and minimal arm swing and trunk rotation as he became ambulatory. He participated in activities suggested by his physical therapist to improve trunk rotation (e.g., reaching across midline to obtain desired objects). Orally, he exhibited limited tongue lateralization and primarily used a tongue protraction-retraction pattern (a straight plane movement) to manage food when he began eating again. His jaw moved rigidly in an up and down pattern (a straight plane movement) as he managed the food prior to swallowing. As he developed improved oral strength, stability, and control, his rotary chewing pattern and tongue lateralization returned.

Sensory Responsiveness, Organization, and Integration Eddie moved slowly and deliberately when he began walking again, possibly indicating some vestibular concerns. He exhibited decreased tactile and proprioceptive sensory awareness, as he required deep touch/pressure to the oral musculature before a response occurred (e.g., increased awareness, decreased muscle tone, improved oral movement). His liquids were initially thickened to provide greater tactile input. Eddie reported that food no longer tasted or smelled the same to him as before his strokes. His visual and auditory systems seemed to be intact. Eddie generally exhibited concerns with sensory responsiveness that affected his ability to organize and integrate the information from the various sensory systems. Specific treatment strategies were implemented to assist Eddie in this process.

INTERACTIVE CASE EXPERIENCES

Interactive case experiences are provided throughout the book to allow the reader to practice using the information from the chapter. These experiences challenge the reader to think of the possibilities for each of the cases. The author has provided case examples in the book as a guide for the reader, but the answers to the questions in the interactive case experiences are for the reader to decide.

1. Review the information presented in the interactive case experiences from Chapter 1 on Drew and Amber. From the information presented, what do you know about the areas of stability/mobility, muscle tone, movement, as well as sensory responsiveness, organization, and integration? What additional information would you like to know?
2. Given the information about the following cases, discuss the changes seen in the clients as a result of changes to the sensory environment.

Jerry

Jerry is a 32-year-old patient with a traumatic brain injury. He has normal hearing and moderate cognitive-communicative deficits. He is confused and agitated (i.e., Rancho Level IV). Jerry has difficulty remaining on task in treatment. He is easily distracted by sounds in the environment and becomes angry when tasks become difficult for him. Jerry also becomes agitated when the environment is visually cluttered. Bright lights seem to bother him. When agitated, he bangs his fists on the table and yells at the clinician.

Jerry was treated in a room with incandescent and natural lighting. He was presented with one material at a time, and the therapy room was uncluttered. Hemi-Sync Music (discussed in Chapter 3) was played as a background during treatment. Jerry began attending to tasks for up to 10 minutes. He did not exhibit any behavioral outbursts while the music was playing. However, when the music turned off, Jerry became agitated within several minutes. The music was also played while Jerry ate his meals. He ate his meals in a visually simple environment with two other patients; however, fluorescent lighting was present in the dining area. Jerry was generally calm during the meal and approached the meal in an organized manner. He had significantly fewer outbursts than previously noted with the environmental changes described above.

The nursing staff asked to have the music played on the unit throughout the day, as the music was calming to the staff as well as the patients. The use of music was helpful in establishing a calm environment for Jerry, the other patients, and the staff. Fortunately, in this case, all individuals in the environment benefited from the use of the Hemi-Sync Music. However, different music may be more appropriate for other groups of patients and staff, depending on their responses to the music. Also, the music was played in the environment to establish desired attending and interactive behaviors with Jerry. However, these behaviors will need to be generalized to the typical environment (without music) once they are well established.

Sara

Sara is a 3-year-old client with pervasive developmental disorder. She has a history of middle ear infections and a resulting fluctuating hearing loss, and she is delayed in speech and language development. Sara exhibits extreme cognitive disorganization and her sensory systems seem poorly integrated. Initially, Sara was treated in a classroom environment with fluorescent lights and many windows. Without environmental modifications, Sara ran around the room and had difficulty attending to structured tasks and play activities.

Sara's treatment was moved to a small treatment room without windows. The environment was visually simple. No pictures were on the walls and the carpet was a single, neutral color. Overhead incandescent lighting was used and could be adjusted for brightness. Sara responded best in moderate lighting. Treatment for Sara began with a movement activity, which provided her with intense vestibular and proprioceptive stimulation (e.g., jumping on a mini-trampoline with hands held, having her body gently but firmly rolled into a mat with her head and face free). Super-Learning Music (discussed in Chapter 3) was played as a background during treatment. With these environmental modifications and treatment strategies in place, Sara would sit in a chair or on a mat for up to 5 minutes while interacting with toys and activities. Sara also began interacting more appropriately with the clinician. She made fleeting eye contact with the clinician where she previously made no eye contact. Sara completed structured tasks with demonstration and began playing more appropriately with activities such as Play Doh, toy people, and farm animals.

3

Challenges and Treatment Considerations

There are a variety of challenges and treatment considerations that affect individuals with oral motor concerns at different ages and stages in life. In the first half of this chapter, challenges impacting on oral motor function that affect individuals of all ages exhibiting oral motor concerns will be discussed. Treatment considerations are addressed in the second part of the chapter. These include:

- Critical learning periods
- The impact of learning, fun, and rest during treatment
- The connection between oral sensory input and attention
- The use of music during treatment
- Movement and positioning ideas
- The use of inhibition and facilitation techniques
- The relationship between oral motor skill development and other treatment areas
- The possible composition of the oral motor team
- The use of universal precautions
- The parts of a typical oral motor treatment session

CHALLENGES IMPACTING ORAL MOTOR FUNCTION

A number of challenges can affect an individual's oral motor function. Sensory issues and postural concerns were discussed in Chapter 2. In this section of Chapter 3, oral structural concerns (i.e., cleft lip and/or palate) as well as difficulties with graded jaw movement, oral movement for eating and drinking, imitative oral movement, and oral movement for speech production will be addressed. Patterns that limit oral motor function will also be discussed. Interactive experiences are provided to assist the reader in synthesizing the information presented.

Oral Structural Concerns

A number of oral structural concerns have been discussed throughout the book. These primarily relate to jaw position/alignment and occlusion. However, the area of cleft lip and/or palate will be briefly discussed here, as many books have been written on this topic. Individuals with cleft lip and/or palate can benefit from appropriate oral motor assessment and treatment. When working with these individuals, the clinician should consult with the oral-facial team with the permission of the individual and/or family. The clinician would want to discuss the nature of the repair(s) and potential oral motor treatment ideas with the team, the client (if appropriate), and the client's family. With regard to treatment, *carefully applied* oral motor work may actually decrease the amount of scar tissue that forms after surgery. These techniques can be learned in workshops on myofascial release (see a description in Chapter 4) and massage. Oral massage may also increase the individual's oral awareness. However, oral massage and myofascial release techniques should be discussed with the team *prior to their implementation.* The individual's surgeon can tell the clinician when these techniques can be safely applied relative to the person's healing process. Other oral motor activities, such as those involving blowing and sucking, should also be discussed prior to implementation.

Difficulties with Graded Jaw Movement

The jaw needs to be stable but active for efficient movement to occur in the tongue, lips, and cheeks. Therefore, the jaw is the stable base from which the tongue, lips, and cheeks move. Many individuals with oral motor concerns exhibit difficulties with graded jaw movement. This is often related to the postural alignment, stability, and control issues discussed in Chapter 2. The jaw is a critical and often ignored structure in the functions of eating, drinking, and speaking. This is the reason that graded jaw movement is being discussed in a section of its own in this chapter.

Low muscle tone in the oral musculature and loose ligaments in the temporomandibular joint (TMJ) can significantly contribute to difficulties with jaw stability and graded jaw movement. Low muscle tone in the cheeks can be seen in individuals who lack muscle definition in the cheeks, giving the cheeks a "chubby" or "floppy" appearance. Loose ligaments in the TMJ are often indicated by large, unrefined excursions of the jaw in any plane (e.g., laterally, vertically, etc.). However, it should be noted that large excursions of the jaw could also result from difficulties with muscle function. Individuals with low oral muscle tone and/or loose ligaments in the TMJ may also tense and hold the jaw in a particular position while completing an oral motor activity (e.g., biting on a cup or straw for stability while drinking, holding the jaw in a high position while speaking). Hypertonicity and fluctuating muscle tone can also significantly affect jaw stability and graded jaw movement. These can inhibit the individual's jaw from moving in a smooth, graded manner. The jaw may become fixed in certain positions (i.e., opened, closed, high, medium, low). Increased tension is noted in the individual's musculature when hypertonicity is present. This tension will vary in individuals with fluctuating muscle tone.

Issues with jaw stability may result in difficulty moving the lips, cheeks, and tongue separately from the jaw. Mobility of the cheeks, lips, and tongue is a distal motor function based on dynamic stability provided by the jaw. When the jaw is not actively stable, the cheeks, lips, and tongue often cannot move independently. Dissociated cheek, lip, and tongue movement is important for the development and use of sophisticated eating, drinking, and speaking skills. Individuals with jaw stability and control difficulties often move the jaw, lips, cheeks, and tongue as a unit. This can be seen in eating when individuals use a munching pattern (i.e., up and down jaw movement) with little tongue lateralization or active lip movement as opposed to a rotary chewing pattern with adequate tongue lateralization and active lip movement. It should be noted that munching is seen in typically developing infants at approximately 6 to 7 months of age while the infant is developing jaw stability and control. Rotary jaw movements are seen in the typical 9-month-old child and are well established by 3 years of age.

The tongue and jaw may also move as a unit during swallowing. This occurs when an atypical protraction-retraction pattern, commonly called a *tongue thrust* or *tongue-pumping pattern,* is used by the individual to move food back to the pharynx. The lips and cheeks are not usually active during this process. Although the movement involved in tongue thrusting or tongue pumping may seem similar to the movement used by the infant during suckling, it is qualitatively quite different. Young infants use a suckling pattern to pump fluid into the mouth from the bottle or breast. The suckling pattern involves 50 percent retraction and 50 percent protrusion of the tongue (Rosenfeld-Johnson, 1999a). The tongue and jaw move basically as a unit. By approximately 6 months of age, infants use 75 percent retraction and 25 percent protraction during suckling (Rosenfeld-Johnson, 1999a). The tongue and jaw begin to dissociate. By 12 months of age, the sucking pattern has typically replaced suckling (Morris & Klein, 1987). Sucking involves up and down tongue movement and active use of the lips. Suckling is a developmental process and should be differentiated from atypical tongue thrust or tongue pumping seen in individuals with oral motor concerns.

The speech of individuals with jaw stability and control issues usually sounds very immature and/or unrefined. Again, the jaw, cheeks, lips, and tongue often move as a unit. The jaw carries the tongue to the locations of articulatory contact, as opposed to the tongue moving independently to make these contacts. The tongue may be stabilized in an inappropriate location or remain in the bottom of the mouth during speech production. The individual with these concerns often exhibits limited cheek and lip movement during speech production. Although the cheeks are not often considered articulators, the cheek musculature assists in the activation of the lips.

When attempting to move the tongue and the lips separately from the jaw, individuals with oral motor difficulties often position the jaw in a fixed manner or find some form of external stability. For example, a person may fix the jaw in a fully open position before attempting independent tongue movements (e.g., lateralization, elevation, depression, etc.) or may clench his or her teeth together to gain stability when attempting independent lip movements. The individual may lean on his or her hand to gain stability while performing speech movements. A stable but active jaw is particularly important for accurate speech sound production and the coarticulation necessary for connected speech production.

Speech requires the most refined fine motor control in the body. Efficient and effective speech is produced with very small movements in the mouth. In addition to graded jaw movement, appropriate tongue positioning is needed for adequate swallowing and speech production. In the infant, "the tongue practically fills the entire oral space" and may touch the cheeks in some children for stabilization (Boshart, 1999, p. 115). The tongue helps maintain the shape of the hard palate by resting against it (Rosenfeld-Johnson, 1999a). A significant amount of development occurs in the tongue and jaw musculature between birth and 5 years of age. At approximately 5 years of age, "the tongue assumes and acclimates to a lingua-palatal position" (Boshart, 1999, p. 115) at rest. In this position, the tip and apex of the tongue are in contact with the alveolar ridge and hard palate. The lateral margins of the tongue are also stabilized on the lingual sides of the back molars (Boshart, 1998, 1999). The molars should be 1 to 3 millimeters apart when the mouth is at rest (Boshart, 1998, 1999). When the tongue rests in this position, it can easily move to the precise locations needed for speech production. This tongue-resting position is also important for swallowing.

Tongue movements for articulation require little strength but tremendous precision. From an appropriate resting position, the tongue can move independently from the jaw to stabilize against the back maxillary teeth (i.e., molars) when producing specific speech sounds and coarticulatory movements. Individuals with jaw stability and control issues often do not attain an appropriate tongue-resting posture or tongue position for speech production and, therefore, have difficulty achieving the refined movements needed for effective speech production.

In addition to jaw stability and control issues, an open mouth posture resulting from chronic upper respiratory concerns can move the jaw and tongue out of alignment for effective speech production as well as efficient use of oral motor patterns during eating and drinking. Difficulties with occlusion may result from jaw stability and control issues. Congenital conditions (e.g., cleft palate) can also impact on jaw and tongue position.

Difficulties with Oral Movements during Eating and Drinking

Individuals with oral motor concerns frequently exhibit difficulties with oral movements during eating and drinking. These individuals often use unsophisticated and unrefined oral motor patterns that may actually be functional for the management of food and liquid. Although the neural control and the timing of muscle contraction for the processes of eating and drinking versus speech production may be different, observation of eating and drinking patterns assist the clinician in assessing the movements of the oral mechanism that may inhibit speech production. Speech appears to be an overlaid function on the mechanism originally used for eating and drinking. Concerns with muscle tone in the oral structures, jaw stability and control, cheek and lip mobility, tongue and jaw dissociation, as well as tongue stability and control are frequently seen in individuals with oral motor concerns. These difficulties often affect the processes of eating, drinking, and speech production.

A number of oral motor concerns are frequently noted when food is eaten by *spoon*. The individual's jaw may open in wide excursions. His or her jaw may not open and close symmetrically or in a smooth, graded manner secondary to jaw instability, muscle function concerns, and so on. The individual's lips may be inactive or may not completely clear the spoon. His or her lips may not remain closed, and spillage from the mouth may occur while eating foods from a spoon. These concerns are frequently due to limited lip strength and mobility. The protraction-retraction pattern, frequently called a *tongue thrust,* is often observed in individuals with oral motor concerns while eating spoon foods. The individual's tongue does not adequately form the bolus, and the tongue generally moves as a unit with the jaw when this pattern is present. It should be noted that the tongue thrust pattern can emerge from an initial pattern of tongue retraction. It is often seen in children who attempt to use suckling movements of the tongue without adequate development of the tongue musculature.

When taking *bites* of food, individuals with oral motor concerns frequently bite into the food and then proceed to pull the food away from the mouth with their hands. The individual may not open and close the jaw symmetrically or in a graded manner. These concerns are frequently related to jaw stability, jaw movement, and occlusion issues. Young children usually begin taking bites of food with the front teeth, as these are the first to erupt. However, many individuals take bites using the side teeth as opposed to the front teeth. This is often seen in people with oral motor concerns, as these individuals tend to have less jaw strength and graded motor control than the typical population. A person with oral motor concerns may also tend to take bites on the side, because his or her tongue tip does not lateralize food for chewing (Rosenfeld-Johnson, 1999a). Malocclusion can preclude the use of the front teeth when taking bites of food.

Individuals with oral motor difficulties frequently do not develop adequate rotary *chewing*. This may be related to the lack of well-developed rotational patterns in the body. An up and down munching pattern is often observed in these individuals beyond the age when munching is typically seen. Some lateral tongue movement may be observed. However, the lateral tongue movements are usually noted to a preferred side, with little transfer of food across midline to the other side of the mouth for thorough chewing. The tongue also tends to move in a center-to-side pattern as opposed to a tongue tip-to-side pattern in individuals with muscle weakness (Rosenfeld-Johnson, 1999a). The individual's lips may be apart when chewing foods, and some food loss may occur.

Bolus formation is often problematic for individuals with oral motor concerns. A bolus is formed when food is collected by the tongue in an organized manner from various locations within the mouth prior to swallowing. When an individual exhibits oral motor concerns, food often remains on the tongue or may be pocketed in the cheeks or sulci instead of being swallowed. This is frequently the result of poor oral sensory awareness and imprecise oral movement. Food remaining on the tongue can be secondary to the presence of the tongue thrust pattern. Food remaining in the cheeks can be related to poor tongue lateralization, low muscle tone in the cheek musculature, and lack of oral awareness. The individual may also be unaware of food remaining on the lips and make no attempt to clear this with the tongue or teeth.

While *drinking,* a person with oral motor concerns may bite on the cup or straw as an attempt to stabilize the jaw. If a tongue thrust pattern is present, the individual's tongue may be under the cup rim or the straw. If the individual's lips are weak, he or she may lose liquid from the mouth while drinking. Swallowing incoordination is frequently present in individuals with oral motor concerns, and their swallowing can be effortful and dysrhythmic. This may be apparent if "gulping" or "choking" occurs. Swallowing difficulties are frequently related to poor coordination of respiratory, oral, and pharyngeal function. The individual may use a single-sip-swallow pattern rather than coordinated consecutive swallows when drinking from a cup. Many people, however, can drink with consecutive swallows from a straw when they cannot drink with consecutive swallows from a cup. They often place the straw onto the tongue and use the protraction-retraction pattern of the tongue thrust to accomplish the consecutive swallows.

Difficulties with Imitative Oral Movements

Individuals with oral motor concerns frequently exhibit difficulties with imitative oral movements (e.g., lip rounding and spreading; tongue extension, retraction, elevation, and depression; etc.). Many of the oral motor issues seen during eating and drinking activities are primarily related to muscle function concerns. However, the difficulties seen during imitative oral movements or imitative speech movements may be the result of muscle function concerns and/or motor planning issues. Issues with tone, strength, and dissociated movement are some of the muscle function concerns seen in individuals with oral motor disorders. The attempted imitation of nonspeech oral movements by the person with oral motor concerns can provide important information for the clinician regarding the type of concern exhibited by the individual.

During the *jaw movement* of opening and closing the mouth, the individual with oral motor concerns may open and close the mouth in wide excursions, indicating jaw instability, difficulty with graded jaw movement, low oral muscle tone, and/or lax ligaments in the temporomandibular joints. The person may also move the head along with the movements of the jaw, indicating that jaw movements are not dissociated from head movements. He or she may have difficulty holding the mouth open at midrange or opening and closing the mouth in a smooth, graded manner. The difficulty in opening the jaw in midrange may be related to concerns with jaw stability and/or control, whereas difficulty with opening and closing the jaw in a smooth, graded manner may be either a muscle function or motor planning concern.

The difference between a motor planning and muscle function issue can frequently be determined when the individual's jaw is stabilized in some manner. If the activity is completed in a smooth, graded manner while the jaw is stabilized, then the individual is probably exhibiting a jaw stability concern. If the individual continues to demonstrate ungraded, groping movements of the oral structure while the jaw is stabilized, then a motor planning concern may be present (Jelm, 1995b).

Another way to tell the difference between a muscle function and motor planning concern is to evaulate the differences in the quality of movement seen during imitative oral motor tasks and automatic oral motor tasks, such as eating and drinking. Individuals with motor planning concerns often have great difficulty moving the jaw imitatively but can move the jaw effectively while eating and drinking. It is important to note that difficulties with imitative jaw movement may be related to a combination of muscle function and motor planning concerns. These and other issues will be discussed in detail in Chapters 4 through 8.

Imitative *lip movements* may also be difficult for individuals with oral motor concerns. These individuals may exhibit difficulties with pressing and holding the lips together, which may indicate a concern with lip strength or jaw position. Difficulty with touching the top teeth to the lower lip, touching the bottom teeth to the top lip, or moving the lips separately from the jaw may indicate concerns with dissociation. Difficulty with rounding the lips, smiling or spreading the lips, or maintaining or alternating these postures may indicate concerns with muscle tone, strength, coordination, or motor planning. If the individual produces these movements in a weak manner, then muscle function is probably the concern. If groping or struggle behaviors are noted, then motor planning may be the issue. If the person can adequately perform the lip movements when jaw stability is provided, then the difficulty with the movement is probably a muscle function concern as opposed to a motor planning concern. However, if the groping and struggle persists when jaw stability is provided, then the individual probably has a motor planning difficulty (Jelm, 1995b). Again, it is important to note that difficulties with imitative lip movement may be related to a combination of muscle function and motor planning concerns.

Many of the lip movements described here are used in the processes of eating, drinking, and speaking. Lip rounding and spreading are used in speech production. The individual must have the ability to maintain and rapidly alternate lip postures while speaking. Lip rounding is also used during straw drinking, whereas lip spreading is used during cup drinking. The individual's top teeth contact the lower lip in the production of the sounds /f/ and /v/ as well as when clearing food from the lower lip while eating.

A person may exhibit a variety of difficulties with *tongue movement* during imitative oral motor tasks. Limitations may be observed in the individual's ability to protrude, retract, elevate, depress, and lateralize the tongue independently from the jaw or in a precise manner. He or she may not be able to move the tongue to specific locations inside or outside of the mouth without touching the lips or without moving the jaw in the same direction of movement. This may again be related to difficulties with muscle tone, muscle strength, the grading and coordination of movement, and/or motor planning. If the individual's tongue can move separately from the jaw once jaw stability is provided, then jaw stability is often a concern. If the individual continues to exhibit groping and struggle behaviors during tongue movement when jaw stability is provided, then motor planning must be considered as a possible cause (Jelm, 1995b). Many of the tongue movements described here are used in the processes of eating, drinking, and speaking. For example, tongue protraction is used for the production of the "th" sound and for clearing food from the lips, tongue retraction is used during the swallowing process, tongue elevation and depression is critical in the production of the majority of speech sounds, and tongue lateralization is used during chewing and bolus formation.

Difficulties with Oral Movements during Speech Production

Individuals with oral motor concerns frequently exhibit difficulties with oral movements during speech production. They may move the jaw in wide excursions rather than in a smooth, graded manner where the jaw is in various midrange locations during speech production. An individual's lips may close in a weak manner, resulting in weak lip sounds. An upper lip retraction will affect the person's production of bilabial sounds, and a labio-dental placement for these sounds may then be used by the individual. If the articulators make weak oral approximations, then the individual may not have enough intraoral pressure to adequately produce coarticulated speech. In the case of weakness or paralysis, the person's lips and tongue may move asymmetrically.

Difficulties with dissociation of the oral structures can significantly affect speech production. The individual's lips and tongue may not move separately from the jaw. When the tongue and jaw move together, the person's speech has a primitive or immature quality. This often means that the jaw and tongue are not in appropriate positions for speech production. If the jaw and tongue are not actively stable, then it is difficult for the person to produce precise speech.

Individuals with oral motor concerns frequently have difficulty producing the sounds of speech in words, phrases, and sentences. At the word level, they may have difficulty putting the sounds together in single syllable words and may produce only word approximations. They may have difficulty producing sequences of syllables in multisyllabic words or diadochokinetic activities (i.e., /pʌpʌpʌ/, /tʌtʌtʌ/, /kʌkʌkʌ/, /pʌtʌkʌ/). This may be related to a muscle function concern and/or a motor planning concern. The quality of the utterance will assist the speech-language pathologist in determining the type of problem. If the speech sounds immature, slurred, and/or dysarthric in nature, then the speech difficulty is most likely a muscle function issue. If the speech consists of inconsistent articulatory errors, transpositions of sounds in words, and silent posturing or groping behaviors, then a motor planning issue may be present. Other characteristics of a motor planning concern include difficulties with the prosodic features of speech such as rate, rhythm, and stress as well as a decrease in intelligibility as the length of the utterance increases. Motor planning will be more thoroughly discussed in Chapters 4 through 8.

Limiting Oral Motor Patterns

According to Suzanne Evans Morris and Marsha Dunn Klein in *Pre-Feeding Skills,* the following oral motor patterns may limit the development of adequate oral motor skills:*

- Exaggerated jaw movement
- Jaw thrust
- Jaw clenching
- Jaw retraction
- Tonic bite reflex
- Tongue retraction
- Exaggerated tongue protrusion
- Tongue thrust
- Thick, bunched, low-tone tongue
- Lip or cheek hypotonicity
- Lip retraction
- Lip pursing
- Hypersensitivity
- Hyposensitivity
- Sensory defensiveness
- Sensory overload

Exaggerated jaw movement, jaw thrust, jaw clenching, and jaw retraction are patterns related to difficulties with jaw stability and control. *Exaggerated jaw movement* is ungraded jaw movement where the jaw moves in wide excursions. It is frequently seen in individuals with low oral muscle tone, loose ligaments in the temporomandibular joints, and movement incoordination. It can also be seen in individuals exhibiting extensor patterns in the jaw. Individuals with cerebral palsy, traumatic brain injury, stroke, other neurological disorders, and Down syndrome may exhibit exaggerated jaw movements. *Jaw thrust* is defined as "a strong downward extension of the lower jaw" (Morris, 1982, p. 142). It is often seen in individuals with significant neurological concerns. Individuals may exhibit jaw thrust when opening the mouth in anticipation of food or when opening the jaw to speak. "The jaw may appear to be stuck in the open position" and the individual may have difficulty closing the mouth to speak or take in food (Morris, 1982, p. 142). *Jaw clenching* is "the tight involuntary closure of the jaw which makes the opening of the mouth difficult" (Morris, 1982, p. 143). It is frequently observed in individuals with "strong flexor patterns" or a tonic bite reflex (Morris, 1982, p. 143). *Jaw retraction* is "the pulling back of the lower jaw so that the molars do not make proper contact" during eating, drinking, or speech production (Morris, 1982, p. 143). It may reflect an individual's attempt to stabilize the jaw; however, it moves the jaw out of alignment.

The *tonic bite reflex* is always an atypical pattern. It is "a strong closure of the jaw when the teeth or gums are stimulated" (Morris, 1982, p. 142). The individual with a tonic bite is often unable to release the bite. This is usually seen

*From Suzanne Evans Morris and Marsha Dunn Klein, *Pre-Feeding Skills,* p. 97, Copyright © 1987 by Therapy Skill Builders, a division of The Psychological Corporation. Reproduced by permission.

in individuals with severe neurological damage (e.g., cerebral palsy, traumatic brain injury, etc.). The tonic bite can greatly impinge on the individual's ability to manage food and liquid.

Tongue retraction is "the strong pulling back of the tongue into the pharyngeal space" (Morris, 1982, p. 143). This pattern may be related to "shoulder retraction" and "neck extension" (Morris, 1982, p. 143). It may also be the result of an individual's attempt to stabilize the tongue and/or protect the airway. The individual may retract the tongue in an attempt to control the amount of food or liquid reaching the pharynx and ultimately the airway. Tongue retraction can be seen in individuals who do not have adequate tongue control for the method of feeding (e.g., children who are bottle fed using nipples that allow a relatively fast liquid flow, adults who are "bird fed" with their necks hyperextended).

Exaggerated tongue protrusion and *tongue thrust* occur in individuals who use the protraction-retraction pattern of the tongue to manage food, liquid, and their own saliva. The individual's tongue moves primarily in a repetitive front-back pumping pattern as opposed to the more controlled pattern of bolus formation, where the tongue is cupped, collects the food into an organized bolus, and then moves the food back to the pharynx. *Tongue thrust* is defined by Morris and Klein (1987, p. 88) as "a very forceful protrusion of the tongue from the mouth." This is often observed in individuals with severe neurological concerns (e.g., individuals with traumatic brain injury or cerebral palsy). "Exaggerated tongue protrusion maintains the easy flow of movement seen in the normal suckle pattern; however, the protrusive movement is exaggerated" (Morris & Klein, 1987, p. 87). This pattern is often observed in individuals exhibiting mild to moderate low muscle tone in the oral structures, which includes a certain percentage of the typical population. It is also common in certain populations (e.g., individuals with Down syndrome). Please note that Morris and Klein (1987) differentiate the terms *exaggerated tongue protrusion* from *tongue thrust,* whereas myofunctional therapists tend to refer to exaggerated tongue protrusion as tongue thrust.

A *thick, bunched, low-tone tongue* "lacks the normal thin, cupped, or grooved configuration that assists efficient sucking" and bolus formation (Morris & Klein, 1987, p. 211). The tongue may appear thick and bunched as the result of intrinsic tongue muscle dysfunction. These muscles are responsible for the flattening and thinning of the tongue to create the "cupped or bowl-shaped configuration" as a "passageway for efficient movement of the liquid or food to the back of the mouth for swallowing" (Morris, 1982, p. 144). This is often seen in individuals with neurological concerns (e.g., individuals with cerebral palsy, stroke, and traumatic brain injury). Individuals with Down syndrome often exhibit low muscle tone in the tongue that is mistaken as a "large" tongue. The person's tongue is often a normal size but the low muscle tone and small jaw give the tongue the appearance of being large. Mild low muscle tone may also be seen in the tongues of some children with articulatory concerns and no other apparent difficulties. Individuals with low muscle tone in the tongue generally exhibit imprecise articulation of speech sounds secondary to concerns with intrinsic tongue muscle function. The extrinsic tongue musculature is unable to stabilize the tongue without the support of the intrinsic tongue musculature. This is often related to inadequate stability in the upper trunk, shoulder girdle, and head-neck area.

Lip or cheek hypotonicity is common in many individuals with oral motor concerns. "Hypotonia in the cheeks reduces the strength and skill with which the lips can move during" eating, drinking, and speech production (Morris & Klein, 1987, p. 218). Low muscle tone in the buccinator muscles may cause the individual to pocket food in the cheek areas. Low muscle tone in the masseter, medial pterygoid, and/or lateral pterygoid muscles may significantly affect jaw stability and controlled jaw movement. Low muscle tone in the musculature controlling the lips may affect the individual's ability to effectively swallow secondary to decreased intraoral pressure. Saliva or drool may fall from the person's mouth. The production of bilabial sounds are often weak and imprecise in individuals with low muscle tone in the cheek and lip musculature. These difficulties can be seen in a wide range of people, from children with articulation difficulties to adults with neurogenic disorders. The children with articulation difficulties who exhibit low muscle tone in the cheek area are often seen as having cute, chubby cheeks or "baby fat." Adults with low muscle tone in the cheek area often present with "floppy" or "droopy" cheeks.

Lip retraction can result from hypertonicity in the lips and cheeks, where the lips and cheeks tend "to be pulled into a tight, retracted position" and the lips "form a tight horizontal line over the mouth" (Morris & Klein, 1987, p. 216). It is seen in a variety of different populations (e.g., children with cerebral palsy, children and adults with traumatic brain injury and other neurological deficits, etc.). Some individuals exhibit an upper lip retraction where the upper lip is pulled upward and the individual appears to be smiling. This often results from tension in the facial musculature that meets the top lip. The tensing of the upper lip and facial musculature may be part of a fixing pattern that was developed by the individual as an attempt to stabilize the jaw. According to Rosenfeld-Johnson (1999a), when the jaw is held in a fixed position, lip mobility is affected. Some people develop a high, fixed jaw posture as a compensatory strategy for poorly graded jaw movement. This may be related to the fact that the majority of speech sounds are produced in a high jaw position.

Upper lip retraction can be seen in individuals with otherwise low oral muscle tone. It can also be seen in people with a tongue thrust pattern, as these individuals frequently have an overbite and high, narrow hard palate. Individuals exhibiting an overbite may have difficulty closing the upper lip over the teeth, and this may reinforce the lip retraction. Individuals with an upper lip retraction frequently demonstrate difficulty with the production of bilabial sounds and with the use of the upper lip to actively clear food from a spoon. These individuals frequently compensate for the difficulty in bringing the lips together for bilabial sounds by attempting to produce these sounds by making articulatory contact with the upper teeth and lower lip. It is interesting to note that the speech sounds produced by many people in this manner frequently sound acoustically adequate. When eating from a spoon, these individuals frequently clear the spoon with the upper teeth as opposed to the upper lip. The person may have difficulty attaining the intraoral pressure required for swallowing, since upper lip retraction may prevent him or her from closing the lips. The individual may swallow less frequently and drool.

Lip pursing results from the individual attempting to "counteract the effects of lip retraction" (Morris & Klein, 1987, p. 216). The person's lips pucker as though they were pulled together by a drawstring (Morris & Klein, 1987). Lip pursing is most commonly seen in individuals who have neurological deficits. "The use of effort to speak or eat in spite of the lip retraction can result in lip pursing" (Morris & Klein, 1987, p. 216). Lip pursing can affect the individual's ability to control the lips during eating, drinking, and speech production.

Hypersensitivity, hyposensitivity, sensory defensiveness, and sensory overload have been discussed relative to each of the sensory systems in Chapter 2. The individual who is *hypersensitive* or *hyperresponsive* to stimulation often responds dramatically to a low level or small amount of that stimulation. Those who are *hyposensitive* or *hyporesponsive* to stimulation frequently require a great deal of a particular type of sensory stimulation in order to respond. Some individuals may not actually be hypersensitive to a particular stimulus but may exhibit sensory defensiveness to that stimulus. In this situation, the individual will demonstrate a response to the stimuli that is stronger than would be expected and may exhibit a fight or flight response (Morris & Klein, 1987). *Sensory defensiveness* may be the result of previous hypersensitivity to the stimulus and/or a previous experience with the stimulus that may have been perceived as negative. *Sensory overload* may be a "more severe form of sensory defensiveness" (Morris & Klein, 1987, p. 233). Individuals demonstrating sensory overload may tolerate the stimulus under certain circumstances but become overwhelmed by the stimulus when too much is provided. They have difficulty functioning "in a multi-sensory environment" as they have problems "in filtering out unnecessary sensory input" and determining foreground from background information (Morris & Klein, 1987, p. 233).

Individuals with oral motor concerns frequently exhibit a variety of these sensory issues relative to the variety of sensory systems. It is believed that these sensory concerns occur as the result of difficulties with sensory awareness, regulation, and integration. Refer to Chapter 2 for a thorough discussion of this information.

INTERACTIVE EXPERIENCE: LIMITING PATTERNS

The following activity will assist the reader in identifying the musculature, cranial nerves, speech sounds, and eating/drinking processes involved in and affected by the limiting oral motor patterns discussed in this chapter. Professionals can better understand the limiting pattern and determine an appropriate treatment if the physiology and neurology related to the concern is identified.

List the muscles, cranial nerves, sounds in speech, and eating/drinking processes involved when the limiting oral motor patterns in the following activity are present in an individual exhibiting oral motor concerns. Use the tables in Chapter 1 to assist in completing this task. A sample for completing this exercise is provided.

Sample

LIMITING PATTERN	MUSCLES INVOLVED	CRANIAL NERVES INVOLVED	SPEECH SOUNDS INVOLVED	EATING/ DRINKING PROCESSES INVOLVED
Jaw Thrust	Digastric	V (Trigeminal)	All	All
	Mylohyoid	V (Trigeminal)		
	Geniohyoid	First and second cervical		
	Lateral pterygoid	V (Trigeminal)		

Discussion of Sample

Jaw thrust is the sudden forceful opening of the jaw (Morris & Klein, 1987). This involves all of the jaw musculature but particularly the muscles that depress the jaw. The majority of these muscles are innervated by cranial nerve V (trigeminal). When treating an individual with a jaw thrust, the digastric, mylohyoid, geniohyoid, and lateral pterygoid muscles can be specifically addressed through massage, myofascial release, proprioceptive neuromuscular facilitation, and other treatment techniques discussed in Chapters 4 through 8. It is important to think about the specific muscles and nerves involved in a limiting oral motor pattern so that effective treatment can take place. All speech sounds and all eating/drinking processes would be affected by jaw thrust. This pattern takes the jaw out of an appropriate position for these to occur.

Activity

LIMITING PATTERN	MUSCLES INVOLVED	CRANIAL NERVES INVOLVED	SPEECH SOUNDS INVOLVED	EATING/ DRINKING PROCESSES INVOLVED
Jaw thrust				
Jaw clenching				
Jaw retraction				
Tonic bite				
Tongue retraction				
Exaggerated tongue protrusion				
Tongue thrust				
Lip retraction				
Lip pursing				

INTERACTIVE EXPERIENCE: POSTURE, TEXTURE, PATTERNS, AND FEEDING

The following activities will assist the reader in becoming aware of the reader's own oral motor patterns while managing food and liquid. In addition, the reader can experiment with the challenges and patterns that affect oral motor function. Suzanne Evans Morris and Marsha Dunn Klein (1987) have similar activities in the first edition of *Pre-Feeding Skills*. They have also written a new book entitled *Mealtime Participation Guide* (Klein & Morris, 1999), which contains participation experiences along with discussion questions and interpretations of the material to guide a group experience.

Posture Assume the following postures/positions and take a bite of food or a drink of liquid. How effective is your ability to orally manage and swallow the food or fluid in each position? Are some positions more comfortable than other positions and why? Are some positions more effective than other positions and why? This activity requires you to assume slightly exaggerated postural differences, as the individual with a typical system tends to compensate well for subtle changes in posture. However, the individual with oral motor dysfunction often has difficulty compensating for postural issues and may actually overcompensate.

(Note: Use caution while eating and drinking and assuming the different postures. Extension of the neck generally opens the airway and can create an unsafe position for swallowing. This is the one reason that it is important to encourage appropriate positioning for individuals with oral motor disorders while they are eating and drinking.)

- Customary/"normal" sitting position
- 90/90/90 degrees of flexion at hips, knees, and ankles
- Slightly exaggerated flexion in the neck and trunk
- Slightly exaggerated extension in the neck and trunk *(Optional: Complete this activity at your own risk. Do not complete this activity if you have any difficulty with swallowing.)*

Texture Take a bite of each type of food listed here or a drink of some liquid. Describe what you do with each orally. Which foods do you chew? Do you chew on one side/molar surface or both? Do you have a preferred side or molar surface for chewing? Do you chew some textures only on one side or molar surface? What do you do with your lips when you remove soft foods from a spoon? When you take bites of crunchy or chewy foods, do you use your central incisors or do you take the bites using your side teeth? If it is difficult to bite through the food, do you bite down on the food with your teeth to stabilize the food and then pull the food away from the teeth with your hand? How do you manage soft foods differently from foods of increased texture? Do you chew soft foods or not? Where is your tongue and what does it do when you swallow food or liquid? Is there food left on your tongue after the swallow? Do you drink liquid from a cup with consecutive swallows, or do you tend to take a single sip and swallow one sip at a time?

- Soft foods (e.g., pudding, yogurt, etc.)
- Crunchy foods (e.g., crackers, pretzels, etc.)
- Chewy foods (e.g., bagels, dried fruit, etc.)
- Liquids (e.g., juice, water, etc.)

Limiting Patterns Create the limiting oral motor patterns listed here. Assume physiologic flexion (i.e., flex your trunk and neck), allowing your oral structure to become as relaxed and "limp" as possible. This position will hopefully help you simulate low oral muscle tone. Take several bites of the different food textures listed in the previous exercise and drink some liquid. Are some textures more difficult to manage than other textures when you use this pattern? Is fluid more difficult to manage when you use this pattern compared to your typical pattern of drinking? Next, keep your tongue in the bottom of your mouth and thrust your tongue when you swallow each bite of food or as you swallow liquid. How does this pattern feel to you? If you have exaggerated tongue protrusion (commonly called a *tongue thrust pattern* by myofunctional therapists), it may feel quite natural. If you do not have exaggerated tongue protrusion, it may feel quite awkward. As you eat different textures of food and drink liquid, move your lips and jaw together as a unit. Do not allow them to move separately. What does this do to your ability to adequately manage the food and liquid? Next, move your tongue and jaw together while you eat a variety of food textures and drink some liquid. Do not allow these structures to move separately. Are some textures easier to manage? Are some more difficult? How does it feel to drink liquid this way?

- Low oral muscle tone
- Exaggerated tongue protrusion/tongue thrust
- Undifferentiated lips and jaw
- Undifferentiated tongue and jaw

Feeding Feed another person while experimenting with the preceding postures, textures, and patterns. What is it like to feed another person? What is it like to be fed by another person? Which positions are most conducive to feeding another person and why? Which positions are least conducive to feeding another person and why? Which textures are easiest to feed to another person and why? Which textures are most difficult to feed to another person and why? How do the different oral motor patterns affect the feeding of the individual?

INTERACTIVE CASE EXPERIENCES

Identify the challenges that impact oral motor function (e.g., postural concerns, difficulties with graded jaw movement, etc.) and the limiting oral motor patterns (e.g., jaw thrust, jaw clenching, etc.) in the following clients. What changes in the individual's environment might circumvent these challenges and limiting patterns? This experience is meant to challenge the reader to think of the possibilities for each case and to provide some practice with the information presented in this and previous chapters.

Ben

Ben is a 4-year-old child with Down syndrome. He has fluctuating hearing loss secondary to eustachian tube malfunction and fluid retention in his middle ear spaces. His receptive language skills are delayed by approximately one year.

Ben sits with a rounded back when seated in a chair with a "scooped" seat. He rests his head in his shoulders and his neck is hyperextended. When Ben takes a bite of food, he opens his jaw wide. When eating food from a spoon, his lips close but do not actively clear the spoon. His tongue lateralizes food to the left side of his mouth but not his right. His tongue moves center-to-side and his tongue tip does not appear to be actively positioning the food on the molars during tongue lateralization. During chewing, he primarily uses an up and down munching pattern and chews food with his side teeth rather than his back molars. He uses exaggerated tongue protrusion when swallowing food. Frequently, he grinds his teeth and can move his jaw easily from side to side. While drinking from a straw, Ben's tongue is usually under the straw and moves in a protraction-retraction pattern. When drinking from a cup, he takes one sip at a time and he bites down on the cup.

Ben is beginning to talk. He says a variety of word approximations consisting primarily of consonant-vowel or vowel-consonant combinations. However, when he speaks, his tongue frequently remains in the bottom of his mouth. His entire jaw moves when he produces speech sounds. The sounds in his word approximations are immature sounding. When asked to imitate oral movements, Ben makes an attempt to move his lips and tongue to imitate the clinician. He exhibits a significant amount of groping and struggle when doing this. However, when his jaw is stabilized by the clinician, the quality of his movements improves significantly.

Ben really enjoys having his teeth brushed. He readily accepts deep touch pressure to his face and mouth. When the clinician withdraws the stimulation, Ben pulls the clinician's hands back to his face. He particularly appears to enjoy the feel of the Nuk oral massage brush in his mouth. Ben appears to have difficulty attending to tasks when florescent lighting is present in a room. He does not appear to like loud sounds or loud music.

Mary

Mary is a 65-year-old woman with progressive supranuclear palsy. She has essentially normal hearing and adequate auditory comprehension skills. Mary sits with an upright posture; however, she exhibits a large amount of rigidity in her body. The muscles in her shoulder girdle are particularly tense. This makes it difficult for her to feed herself. Her oral musculature is generally rigid and weak. This limits her ability to adequately manage food/liquid and to speak.

Mary eats ground and pureed foods and drinks liquids thickened to a nectar consistency. She has difficulty managing regular food and liquid textures. When eating and drinking, Mary uses a protraction-retraction, "tongue pumping" pattern. Mary's jaw movements are limited while eating, drinking, and speaking. She reportedly has decreased oral sensation. Foods are said to taste bland to her, even though spices are added to her food. She reports that she really enjoys the oral brushing program, particularly when the clinician applies firm pressure.

Mary also has difficulty using her vision. She has difficulty seeing items in her lower field of vision. She attempts to imitate some oral movements such as moving her tongue from side to side inside her mouth and pursing her lips. However, her oral movements are very slow and imprecise. The precision of her movements does improve when Mary has the visual feedback provided by looking in a mirror.

Mary's speech is very dysarthric in nature. She speaks in short phrases and sentences. Her speech is intelligible 75 percent of the time when the context is known. When Mary speaks, her tongue moves very slowly to make the appropriate articulatory contacts. Her entire jaw tends to move along with her tongue when she talks.

TREATMENT CONSIDERATIONS

A variety of topics related to treatment are presented in this portion of the chapter. The speech-language pathologist may want to consider these ideas when planning treatment. Critical learning periods are important to consider when treating infants and toddlers. An understanding of how learning, fun, and rest affect treatment can assist the clinician in effectively planning treatment sessions. Information on the connection between oral sensory input and attention is interesting to consider when planning treatment. Music can also be used during treatment to facilitate attention, focus, and concentration. Movement and positioning ideas can assist the clinician in working with the client's posture, stability, and mobility issues. The concepts of inhibition and facilitation are key concepts in treatment. They help the clinician focus on what responses and patterns to increase and what responses and patterns to decrease. Some other treatment areas that can be incorporated into oral motor treatment are also presented. These include the areas of neuro-developmental treatment, sensory integration therapy, articulation therapy, the remediation of intelligibility issues, and augmentation communication. As with any type of treatment, the oral motor team is important to consider. The potential members of the team are presented here. This section concludes with a discussion of a typical oral motor treatment session.

Critical Learning Periods

Children are believed to have critical or sensitive learning periods for the development of certain skills (Walter, 1994). This means that the human being is believed to develop these skills most easily during this period. The critical learning period for language development is believed to occur between the ages of birth and 5 years. The critical learning period for oral motor development would appear to occur between birth and age 2 or 3. It is during this time that children develop the majority of the skills required for eating, drinking, and speech production. This is why most children begin putting words together around the age of 2 years. Their eating, drinking, and speaking skills are fairly more refined by age 3.

The concept of critical learning periods is important when planning treatment for children with oral motor difficulties. Early intervention is critical from birth to age 3, for this is the time when the human being seems to be "programmed" for the development of eating, drinking, and speech production skills. Thus, it is easier for the child to develop more appropriate oral motor skills during this critical learning period than it would be to develop the same skills at a later time.

In his book entitled *The First Three Years of Life,* Burton White (1985) states:

> After seventeen years of research on how humans acquire their abilities, I have become convinced that it is to the first three years of life that we should now turn most of our attention. My own studies, as well as the work of many others, have clearly indicated that the experiences of those first three years are far more important than we had previously thought. In their simple everyday activities, infants and toddlers form the foundations of *all* later development. . . . To begin to look at a child's educational development when he or she is two years of age is already too *late*. (p. 5)

Stanley Greenspan has written a variety of books focusing on the importance of the period from birth to age 3. Five of his six core stages of development fall within this period. Jeannetta D. Burpee (1999), occupational therapist, summarized Greenspan's stages as follows. The first stage, "self-regulation and interest in the world," is generally accomplished by 3 months of age. The second stage, "intimacy, attachment, and falling in love," is typically accomplished by 5 months of age. The third stage, "intentional two-way communication," is typically accomplished by 9 months of age. The fourth stage, "complex communication and behavioral organization," is usually accomplished by 13 to 18 months of age. The fifth stage, "emotional ideas and representational capacity," is typically accomplished by 24 to 30 months of age. The sixth stage, "emotional thinking," is generally accomplished by 36 to 48 months of age. However, Greenspan and Wieder (1998) point out:

> Children achieve these milestones at different ages—there is wide variation even among children without challenges. What is important is not so much the age at which a child masters each skill, but that each one is mastered, for each skill forms a foundation for the next. (p. 89)

Developmental critical learning periods do not apply to adults. However, knowledge of the progression of an individual's disorder could lead to the use of critical treatment periods. For example, the person with a traumatic brain injury will usually recover in a step-wise fashion with periods of dramatic improvement and periods where a plateau has been reached. Oral motor treatment may be most effective during the time when the patient is progressing more rapidly. The treatment may be less intense during the period of a plateau, allowing the patient to "rest" the system and integrate the information.

Learning, Fun, and Rest

Learning takes place most easily when an individual is enjoying the activity. It is easier for him or her to remember information acquired in a "fun" atmosphere than in a stressful one. Adults and children tend to remember something that is humorous or enjoyable. Oral motor treatment sessions can be "fun." There are many enjoyable oral motor activities for children using food, mouth toys, and so on. Adults often enjoy oral massage and other oral facilitation techniques.

Rest is important for the assimilation of information. When people are bombarded with information, they tend to become overloaded. However, if sufficient breaks are provided during therapy sessions, clients have the time to integrate the material presented. Rest can be incorporated into therapy sessions by changing activities. Rest does not necessarily mean ceasing all activity. It may mean giving certain sensory systems used for particular therapy tasks "a break" while engaging other sensory systems. For example, therapy may begin with a gross motor activity involving primarily the proprioceptive and vestibular systems. The next treatment activity may be oral massage, which involves the tactile and oral proprioceptive systems. Once the system is "warmed up" with the massage, specific oral movement activities can be introduced. The typical oral motor treatment session discussed later in this chapter utilizes the idea of rest.

The Connection between Oral Sensory Input and Attention

The connection between oral sensory input and attention is discussed by Trott and colleagues (1993) and Oetter and colleagues (1995). "Oral input provides a subtle way to help [individuals] maintain focused attention" (Trott et al., 1993, p. 17). Gustatory, tactile, and proprioceptive input from certain foods, liquids, or other items placed in the mouth can bring about improved attention, focus, and concentration for the individual. When involved in cognitive tasks, it is not unusual for an individual to seek out oral stimulation. Some individuals will bite on a pen, chew gum, eat hard candy, and so on. This connection between oral input and increased attention, focus, and concentration is used in some educational settings where children are allowed to chew gum or eat crunchy foods while working on cognitive tasks. In the therapy setting, the clinician may want to have a client participate in chewing activities while completing certain cognitive tasks. Using this strategy, the clinician can address an oral motor goal and a cognitive goal at the same time. For a thorough discussion of each sensory system, refer to the information in Chapter 2.

The Use of Music during Treatment

Music is extremely useful in the treatment of individuals with oral motor concerns. It can be used in the background or foreground during treatment, to set the pace for massage and movement activities and to create a learning environment to facilitate an individual's ability to attend, focus, and concentrate. Morris thoroughly discusses this topic in a chapter entitled "Facilitation of Learning" in the book *Neurodevelopmental Strategies for Managing Communication Disorders in Children with Severe Motor Dysfunction* (1991).

Baroque classical music and folk music often have a rhythm of 50 to 70 beats per minute. These two types of music can approximate the natural body rhythms of heart rate, walking rate, and a baby's sucking rate when the body is functioning "normally" and is not under stress. The Lind Institute studied the use of baroque music in establishing an environment conducive to learning. This group developed a series of musical tapes and CDs called *Super-Learning Music*. Gary Lamb also created some audio CDs and tapes with a 60-beat-per-minute tempo to be used in learning environments. Music that approximates the natural rhythms of the body is believed to bring the body into balance so that improved attention, focus, and concentration can be achieved.

Robert A. Monroe developed "a patented auditory guidance system" called Hemi-Sync® to elicit increased attention, focus, concentration, and openness for learning (Morris, 2000). Morris (2000) discusses research and other clinical findings regarding the use of Metamusic (i.e., music containing Hemi-Sync®) during treatment in an article on her website <www.new-vis.com> entitled "Opening the Door with Metamusic."

Music for relaxation is another type of music available on audiocassette tape and CD, which can be useful in establishing a therapeutic learning environment. This type of music does not necessarily have a particular rhythm. Although some of the music consists of familiar songs or tunes, the tempo of some of the songs has been slowed significantly. Music for relaxation can often be purchased in the "New Age" section of the music store.

During oral motor assessment and treatment, the use of certain types of music may facilitate a change in the client's muscle tone. Decreased muscle tone is often the result of relaxation. Clients exhibiting spasticity or rigidity may benefit from the use of music that promotes relaxation. Metamusic, Super-Learning Music, and other music used for calming and relaxation can be played quietly in the background during treatment and at times during assessment. Using music during treatment also tends to level the auditory environment. While the music is playing, sounds that may otherwise distract the client are often not heard or attended to. This includes sounds from outside the treatment room and ambient noise inside the treatment room (e.g., the sound from the overhead lights or the heating system).

In addition to using music in the background, music can be used as a foreground in therapy. For example, folk music can be used to set the rhythm for gross motor/movement activities or oral massage. This strategy works particularly well with children. However, adults also seem to enjoy activities set to music and are accustomed to participating in exercise programs set to music.

Other types of music, such as rock and roll and "techno" music, may be used to alert an individual and encourage movement. However, some types of rock music (e.g., heavy metal) may go against the natural body rhythms and may not encourage the skill that the clinician desires in the client. It is most important that the clinician observe the client to determine which types of music seem organizing for the individual. Musical preferences are very personal for each individual, and the clinician must choose music that increases attention, focus, and organization for the client as well as the clinician. These individuals create the treatment dyad and the environment should be conducive to learning for both individuals. (See the appendix for product sources.)

INTERACTIVE EXPERIENCE: RESPONSE TO MUSIC TYPES

Listen to the following music types and record your responses to the music. Is the music calming, focusing, and organizing for you? Does the music relax you too much? Does the music cause you to feel disorganized or "out of sync" in some way? What do you feel in the muscles of your body?

- Quiet, centering (e.g., "New Age")
- Super Learning (e.g., music from the Lind Institute and Gary Lamb)
- Metamusic (e.g., music from the Monroe Institute)
- Folk
- Rock
- Other

Movement and Positioning

Postural concerns are quite common in individuals of all ages with oral motor issues. Muscle tone and stability issues can significantly affect postural control. (See detailed information presented in Chapter 2.) Movement activities and positioning are important to consider when working with these individuals. The types of movement activities chosen can affect the individual's muscle tone and stability. If the individual is properly positioned, improved stability and mobility can be facilitated.

For individuals with generalized low muscle tone throughout the body, appropriate vigorous gross motor activities can improve postural tone. However, fine motor activities can reduce muscle tone in individuals with generalized low muscle tone. People experience this in their daily lives. For example, a brisk walk would be the activity of choice for someone who is feeling tired, experiencing reduced postural tone, and wanting to increase alertness. Fine motor activities—such as reading, writing, and speaking—are often activities of choice when individuals feel tense and experience increased tension in the body. This is an important idea to remember in treatment, since speech is the most refined fine motor function in the body. If the clinician is asking the client to complete one oral or speech motor task after another, a reduction in overall muscle tone in the body may be noted in individuals with generalized low muscle tone. In addition to overtaxing an already compromised system, postural control may decrease based on this treatment regime. When working with individuals demonstrating hypertonicity or fluctuating muscle tone in the body (e.g., individuals with cerebral palsy, traumatic brain injury, etc.), this concept must be carefully applied, as many movement activities may increase muscle tone in these individuals. Slow, easy movement activities tend to decrease muscle tone. Specific treatment ideas will be discussed in Chapters 4 through 8 to address this area.

Appropriate positioning is also important for an individual to attain postural control. If the individual is having difficulty maintaining an upright position against gravity, then an antigravity position—such as side lying, supine, or prone—may be the position of choice for initial treatment. Gravity places force on the body that may lead to increased postural difficulties for the individual. If the individual is seated in a chair during treatment, the type of chair is often important. A chair with a solid, level seat; solid back; appropriate seat depth; and appropriate height can provide the individual with a stable base of support. This can allow the individual to be positioned with 90 degrees of flexion at the hips, knees, and ankles, allowing the greatest opportunity for postural control in many individuals.

A solid, level seat is particularly important to provide when positioning individuals exhibiting postural concerns. This allows the individual to receive information through the "sits" bones (i.e., ischial tuberosities) in the pelvis that communicate with the other important bones in the postural chain (e.g., the other bones of the pelvis, the bones of the spinal column, the bones of the shoulder girdle, etc.). Many chairs do not have solid, flat seats, appropriate seat depths, or appropriate heights. Numerous chairs in pediatric facilities actually tilt the child's pelvis and encourage flexion in the body, which impacts on postural control. The angle of the chair back is another important consideration. Some adapted chairs and wheelchairs allow the individual to be positioned in a slightly reclined position while maintaining 90-degree hip, knee, and ankle flexion. This position decreases the impact that gravity has on the individual, and improved oral motor function may be attained.

The table height during treatment or meals can also be an important positioning consideration. A table surface positioned at the level of the individual's elbows may be ideal in many situations. At times, however, a table surface closer to chest level may be used to facilitate postural control. By resting the arms on the raised table surface, the individual can obtain increased proprioceptive input through the shoulder girdle. The weight bearing involved in this activity can facilitate postural alignment.

Another technique to encourage upright trunk positioning and postural alignment involves the placement of visual materials. If visual materials are placed on an upright, slanted reading stand or another upright (i.e., vertical) surface, the individual will often hold the head and neck in an upright position that can facilitate postural alignment. Computer screens have the advantage of presenting material vertically. The vertical orientation of visual material allows individuals to use their vision in a more efficient manner. When the head is upright and aligned properly with the rest of the body, the individual can use visual fine motor skills more effectively than when the head is out of alignment. For example, it is easier to visually track the written line and to move the eyes from line to line without skipping lines. Again, distal fine motor function is improved with increased postural control.

INTERACTIVE EXPERIENCE: USE OF VISUAL SKILLS

Read several pages in a book while your body is placed in a flexed position (i.e., head down, back rounded). Read several more pages while your body and head are upright and properly aligned. Place your reading material on a stable, vertical surface, and read several more pages. Notice the effort it takes to read in each position. Which position required the greatest effort? Which position afforded you relative ease? In which position were you most likely to loose your place?

Inhibition and Facilitation

Therapeutic inhibition and facilitation techniques are well known to individuals who practice neuro-developmental treatment. To inhibit a response means to decrease the strength of the response or to stop the response from occurring.

To facilitate a response means to strengthen or encourage a desired response. During oral motor assessment and treatment it is important to observe the variety of responses that the individual is exhibiting and decide which responses are important to inhibit and which responses are important to facilitate.

The type of stimulation will often determine whether a technique is inhibitory or facilitative. Slow, deep massage can facilitate circulation and awareness in the skin and musculature. It can also inhibit muscle contraction and hypersensitivity to touch. Massage consisting of quick stretches can facilitate awareness in the skin and musculature as well as facilitate muscle contraction. Appropriate rigorous gross motor activities can facilitate overall muscle tone in individuals exhibiting generalized hypotonia. Fine motor activities can facilitate relaxation in the body of the individual with typical muscle tone. Slow, systematic changes in stimuli such as food tastes or textures can facilitate acceptance of those tastes or textures. Larger changes in these types of stimuli may actually inhibit acceptance.

Certain reflexive behaviors (e.g., a hyperresponsive gag response) can be inhibited by massaging the individual's tongue stopping just short of the gag response each time and working further back on the tongue during each successive approach or session. Atypical movement patterns (e.g., an asymmetric tonic neck reflex or a tonic bite reaction) can be inhibited by facilitating more appropriate and effective responses and movement patterns. The tonic bite reaction can also be inhibited via systematically applied oral massage.

The following form can be used to plan treatment. In column 1, list the individual's behaviors or responses that require some type of modification for more efficient function. If the response needs to be inhibited, ideas for this can be listed in column two. If a response needs to be facilitated, ideas for this can be listed in column three.

BEHAVIORS AND RESPONSES OBSERVED	TECHNIQUES TO INHIBIT THE RESPONSE	TECHNIQUES TO FACILITATE THE RESPONSE

INTERACTIVE EXPERIENCE: INHIBITION AND FACILITATION

To complete this experience, refer to previously presented information in Chapters 2 and 3. This experience will assist you in assimilating the information presented in these two chapters. You may wish to add ideas to this list as you read Chapters 4 through 8 on treatment.

List ways to inhibit the following:

- A tonic bite reaction
- A hyperresponsive gag response
- An upper lip retraction
- High tone in muscles of the face

List ways to facilitate the following:

- Increased postural stability and control
- Increased oral tactile awareness
- Increased oral proprioceptive awareness
- Increased muscle tone in the muscles of the face
- Jaw stability and control
- Tongue and jaw dissociation

Use of Information from Other Treatment Areas in Oral Motor Treatment

Neuro-Developmental Treatment

Neuro-developmental treatment (NDT) was developed by Karel and Berta Bobath. It is a "means of treating underlying neuromotor deficits related to tone, movement, and posture of both a neurological and a developmental nature" (Scherzer & Tscharnuter, 1982, as cited in Langley & Thomas, 1991, p. 1). "The technique seeks to alter tone qualities, inhibit abnormal movement patterns, and facilitate more normal, functional movement patterns through analysis of the movement components critical to the performance of a particular task" (Langley & Thomas, 1991, p. 1). The Bobaths' work was influenced by "Kabat and Knott's (1948) concepts of Proprioceptive Neuromuscular Facilitation (PNF); Rood's (1954) emphasis on tactile stimulation; and Peto's stress on symmetry, the use of hands and shoulder girdle, and trunk stability, as well as preparation for functional skill" (Hari & Akos, 1988, as cited in Langley & Thomas, 1991, p. 3). The Bobaths originally used this process with individuals exhibiting severe movement concerns. However, the process can be used with individuals demonstrating even mild movement issues and has great application to the area of oral motor assessment and treatment.

The concepts of "mobility based on stability" as well as "inhibition and facilitation" are essential ideas used in neuro-developmental treatment. These ideas have been discussed previously in this book. Morris (1991) provides an eloquent description of the NDT process when she states:

> Neuro-developmental treatment (NDT) is built on the concept that the templates for normal patterns of movement are inherent in the human nervous system. The child or adult who has experienced damage to a portion of the brain still theoretically retains the underlying patterns that lie predominantly within the postural reflex mechanism. These normal templates for movement become hidden or buried by the release of abnormal patterns of tone and movement that are no longer inhibited by action of the higher centers of the brain. The NDT approach seeks a balance that will enable the normal patterns to emerge. This is achieved by inhibiting or reducing the effect of these interfering patterns of tone and movement while simultaneously facilitating the more mature responses of the righting and equilibrium reactions. Through this process of facilitation of movement, the therapist creates the possibility for the child [or adult] to learn how to move more easily. (p. 270)

Sensory Integration Therapy

Sensory integration (SI) therapy is another important approach used with individuals exhibiting oral motor issues. Ayres originally developed this process for use with individuals with learning disabilities. However, the process has been used with individuals demonstrating a wide range of disabilities. Ayres (1972b) states:

> The central principle in sensory integrative therapy is providing planned and controlled sensory input with usually—but not invariably—the eliciting of a related adaptive response in order to enhance the organization of brain mechanisms. The plan includes the utilization of neurophysiological mechanisms in a manner that reflects some aspect of the developmental sequence. (p. 114)

In the treatment of children, the developmental sequence is extremely important. However, this is probably not an important factor in the treatment of adults.

As noted previously, it is important to observe the individual's responses to sensory stimuli. These systems include the vestibular, proprioceptive, tactile, gustatory, olfactory, visual, and auditory systems. The speech-language pathologist has usually been trained to work with the auditory and visual systems. However, individuals with oral motor concerns frequently exhibit poor integration of information received by the vestibular, proprioceptive, tactile, gustatory, and/or olfactory systems in addition to the visual and auditory systems. Therefore, the use of sensory integration therapy is very important in the treatment of many individuals with oral motor disorders. Refer to Chapter 2 for further information regarding the impact of the sensory systems on oral motor function.

Sensory integration therapy uses a systematic approach to organize function in each of the sensory systems. The individual's responses to stimuli presented to each sensory system are evaluated. Therapeutic activities and environmental changes provide the type of stimulation needed by the individual to make an adaptive response to the environment. Many of these activities enhance the individual's attention, concentration, and overall cognitive organization. For example, appropriately applied vestibular stimulation has been observed to increase visual function and expressive language output in some children. *(Note: It is important that the clinician work with a therapist trained in sensory integrative techniques when applying vestibular stimulation.)* Massage to the arms, hands, and face has been observed to increase alertness in some clients with low-level brain injury. The use of Metamusic played in the background during treatment has been observed to increase attention, focus, and concentration and decrease agitation in certain clients (e.g., some individuals with traumatic brain injury at Rancho Level IV and right hemisphere syndrome).

Articulation Therapy

Oral motor assessment and treatment can be an extremely important component of articulation therapy. Many individuals with articulation concerns exhibit poor oral sensory awareness, mild muscle function concerns, and motor planning difficulties. Observing these individuals during the tasks of eating, drinking, imitative oral movements, and speech production often reveals a variety of problematic oral motor patterns. While eating and drinking, these individuals often use the protraction-retraction pattern for swallowing food and liquid. They often maintain the tongue in the bottom of the mouth at rest and move the tongue and jaw together during eating, drinking, imitative oral movements, and speech acts. Mild postural stability and jaw stability concerns as well as mild low oral muscle tone are frequently noted in these individuals.

Accurate oral motor assessment can provide the clinician with important information that will enhance the progress of the individual in articulation treatment. For example, individuals exhibiting /r/ distortions frequently do not fully dissociate the movements of the tongue and jaw. Some of these individuals also seem to have difficulty with the control and range of movement in the posterior part of the tongue. Oral motor treatment specifically focusing on issues such as these will often improve the speed of therapeutic progress and the likelihood of remediation. A variety of materials and programs for the remediation of articulation concerns have been based on oral motor techniques and will be discussed in Chapters 4 through 8 in this book.

Remediation of Intelligibility Issues

Remediation of intelligibility concerns in children and adults can frequently be greatly enhanced by oral motor assessment and treatment. An individual's speech intelligibility is often affected by imprecise articulatory production and rate of speech. Careful assessment of the individual's eating and drinking skills, imitation of oral movements, and speech production can often provide information regarding the basis of the intelligibility issue. Many people with intelligibility concerns exhibit muscle function and/or motor planning concerns.

Individuals with muscle function concerns frequently exhibit many of the characteristics discussed previously in this chapter and in Chapter 2 (e.g., postural concerns, difficulties with graded jaw movement, oral muscle tone issues, poor oral awareness, difficulties with tongue and jaw dissociation, etc.). Tonal concerns in the oral musculature can affect the position of the jaw as well as the movement of the articulators. If the jaw and tongue are not in an appropriate resting position, it is difficult for the individual to move the articulators to appropriate points of contact. If the person's tongue remains in the bottom of the mouth and the entire jaw moves along with the tongue, speech intelligibility will be affected. Limitations in lip movement can significantly affect speech intelligibility. These and other issues prohibit individuals with muscle function concerns from making precise articulatory contacts during speech production and significantly affect speech intelligibility.

Individuals with motor planning concerns often exhibit inconsistent misarticulations; transpositions of sounds in words; occasional clear words heard once and not again; sound additions, repetitions, and prolongations; sound errors in the initial position of words (particularly in consonant clusters); difficulties with appropriate voicing of sounds; as well as several other characteristics (Brookshire, 1997). They seem to require speech to become routinized or automatic in order for them to obtain accurate speech production.

Oral motor treatment can help individuals with muscle function concerns to strengthen weak musculature, increase oral awareness, and develop more precise oral movements for eating, drinking, and speaking. It may help individuals with motor planning concerns to develop needed speech routines/motor plans for more intelligible speech production. Therefore, oral motor treatment is often an appropriate treatment approach for the remediation of intelligibility concerns. Specifics regarding the assessment and treatment of intelligibility issues are provided in Chapters 4 through 8.

Augmentative Communication

The use of sign language and other forms of augmentative communication can be important for individuals with oral motor issues. Augmentative communication strategies can assist these individuals in effectively communicating wants, needs, desires, thoughts, and ideas. The occupational therapist and physical therapist can work with the speech-language pathologist in the development and implementation of a functional communication system, as many individuals requiring the use of augmentative communication also demonstrate motor concerns throughout the body.

For children with oral motor issues, sign language and picture communication can provide the child with a way to communicate while articulatory and intelligibility concerns are being resolved. These strategies take the pressure off using a system of communication (i.e., speech) that does not work well. In most cases, the augmentative communication system will actually facilitate speech production. This is particularly true when the child has a motor planning difficulty. Sign language and picture communication can serve as cues to facilitate speech production. These and other cueing strategies are discussed in Chapters 4 through 8. Without augmentative forms of communication, children with oral motor concerns have very limited means for demonstrating receptive knowledge and getting feedback on their understanding of the world. This limits the child's ability to develop language.

Adults with intelligibility concerns have used signal language such as Amer-Ind (Skelly, 1979) to help work through speech motor planning difficulties. Amer-Ind is also useful for individuals with limited hand use, as the signals are generally simpler to produce than signs found in different forms of sign language. Sign language as well as letter, word, and picture communication boards can also help the individual to communicate more precisely and completely when speech is unintelligible to the listener. While individuals are receiving oral motor treatment to improve intelligibility, augmentative forms of communication can help them to communicate more effectively. The use of augmentative communication can also take the pressure off communication, allowing for greater ease during work with intelligibility. Augmentative communication is again particularly useful with individuals exhibiting motor planning concerns, as it can facilitate improved intelligibility of speech. Motor planning issues in adults will be discussed in Chapter 8. It is important to note that some adults may not be comfortable with the use of certain forms of augmentative communication. This area must be carefully explored with each individual client.

Many resources are available in the area of augmentative communication. A few suggested resources are listed here:

- *Augmentative and Alternative Communication: Management of Severe Communication Disorders in Children and Adults* by David Beukelman and Pat Mirenda (1992)
- *Total Augmentative Communication in the Early Childhood Classroom* by Linda Burkhart (1993)
- *Handbook of Augmentative and Alternative Communication* by Sharon Glennen and Denise DeCoste (1997)
- *Augmenting Basic Communication in Natural Contexts* by Jeanne Johnson, Diane Baumgart, Edwin Helmstetter, and Chris Curry (1996)
- *Assistive Technology: Essential Human Factors* by Thomas King (1999)
- *Augmentative and Alternative Communication: A Handbook of Principles and Practices* by Lyle Lloyd, Donald Fuller, and Helen Arvidson (1997)

The Oral Motor Team

The oral motor team should consist of the client and all individuals involved in the oral motor assessment and treatment of the client. The team will change, depending on the setting. Note that all team members may not be available in each setting. A team for an adult in an acute care hospital setting may include the patient, family members, physicians, nurses, other care providers, a speech-language pathologist, an occupational therapist, a physical therapist, and others as appropriate (e.g., audiologist, ophthalmologist). The team for an adult in a rehabilitation setting may include many of those just listed and a physiatrist (i.e., doctor of physical and rehabilitative medicine). The oral motor team for a child in a school setting may include the child, the parent(s), caregiver(s), special education teacher, regular education teacher, speech-language pathologist, occupational therapist, physical therapist, augmentative communication specialist, and others as appropriate.

An oral motor specialist may also be part of a treatment team. This individual is usually a speech-language pathologist or occupational therapist who has specific training in oral motor assessment and treatment and has a number of years of experience in this area. The oral motor specialist is usually trained in a variety of treatment modalities, such as neuro-developmental treatment, sensory integration therapy, myofascial release, proprioceptive neuromuscular facilitation, myofunctional therapy, and others. This individual can help guide the team toward the use of the most efficient and effective treatment techniques for the individual with an oral motor concern.

Oral motor treatment is most effective when a team approach is used. Oral motor programs usually need to be a part of an individual's daily routine. By using the team approach, it is more likely that the treatment program will be carried out in a consistent manner with the appropriate intensity. This type of program can be compared to a fitness routine. An athlete cannot expect to keep the body "in shape" or develop the body if the fitness routine is not completed on a regular basis (i.e., usually daily but at least three to five times per week). Changes in oral motor function cannot be expected to occur if the individual is not completing the prescribed oral motor activities regularly.

Universal Precautions

When working in and around an individual's mouth, it is important to use universal precautions. A list of these can be obtained from any health care facility or school. Appropriate hand-washing techniques must be used by anyone completing oral motor assessment and treatment procedures. When performing massage or other oral motor techniques in the area of the individual's lips or inside the individual's mouth, gloves must be worn. It is also important to wear gloves when working around the outside of the individual's mouth if the individual drools or has any open sores or lesions. For example, men who shave their faces may have small cuts on the face that may not be seen by the clinician.

Some individuals respond in a negative manner to gloves being worn by the clinician or others. These are often children who have been hospitalized and may associate the wearing of gloves with medical procedures. These individuals will need to learn that gloves are not threatening and are part of the oral motor assessment and treatment process. This can be done through play activities and by consistent use of gloves by all individuals completing oral massage or other oral motor activities requiring touch to the oral area. Some individuals are also sensitive to latex products. Gloves are available in vinyl as well as different colors, scents, and flavors. A variety of glove types can be purchased through a local medical supplier and companies such as Innovative Therapists International, Speech Dynamics, Inc., and others. (See product sources in Appendix D.)

Typical Oral Motor Treatment Session

The typical oral motor treatment session for individuals with oral motor issues may consist of four segments. The timing and the sequence of these segments are flexible and should be modified according to the client's needs. However, the timing and sequence have been provided for the speech-language pathologist who is beginning to use this approach to oral motor treatment. As the speech-language pathologist develops skill and his or her own style in this area of treatment, the timing and sequence may change. Similar approaches to treatment have been noted in the work of Czesak-Duffy (1993), Strode and Chamberlain (1997), Rosenfeld-Johnson (1999a), and others.

Typical Oral Motor Treatment Session

- Gross motor activity
- Oral massage
- Specific oral motor activities/exercises
- Specific speech and language activities

The first segment of the session may consist of approximately five minutes of appropriate *gross motor activity.* These activities are targeted to improve postural tone and stability necessary for improved eating, drinking, and speaking. The physical therapist, occupational therapist, or other motor specialist on the team can recommend specific gross motor activities to address the individual's specific postural concerns.

Specific exercises or activities may improve strength in the individual's back, abdominal, and chest muscles needed for postural control. Upper-body exercises or activities may be recommended for the development of the shoulder girdle. This is often an area of weakness in individuals with oral motor disorders. A light-weight or theraband program prescribed by a motor specialist can involve both isometric (i.e., resistance) and isotonic (i.e., active movement) activities to strengthen the muscles of the trunk and shoulder girdle. Controlled and appropriate rigorous movement activities—such as calisthenics, aerobics, vigorous dancing, and the like—can increase muscle tone in the body of the individual with hypotonia and thereby improve postural function. As previously noted, clients may have previous medical conditions (e.g., alanto-axial instability often seen in individuals with Down syndrome) that preclude the use of certain rigorous movement activities. Consult with the individual's physical therapist or physician prior to initiating vigorous activities with these individuals. For the individual with hypertonicity or fluctuating muscle tone, movement activities must be chosen to facilitate ease and efficiency of movement while inhibiting atypical muscle tone.

The gross motor segment of the treatment session can be omitted if the client has just completed a period of gross motor work. It is often ideal to schedule an oral motor treatment session just after the individual has completed gross motor activity in physical therapy, occupational therapy, recreational therapy, physical education, and so on.

The second segment of a typical oral motor treatment program would involve the use of *oral massage.* The oral massage can be completed in three to five minutes. This is an important step in the oral motor treatment process because the oral massage brings blood supply into muscle and connective tissue. When the muscles are not working well, the blood supply to them may be compromised. When blood does not pump "regularly" through the tissue, nutrients cannot be brought to the tissues, and waste products such as lactic acid (i.e., a by-product of muscular activity) cannot be carried away from the tissue. Lymphatic supply may also be compromised in these individuals.

The increase in blood supply to the musculature and connective tissue is generally accompanied by an increase in sensation to the area. This increase in sensation appears to continue for about 30 minutes, but improved response to sensation in the oral area may actually last longer. Wilbarger and Wilbarger (1991) state that the effects of appropriately applied brushing on the body may "last for about two hours" (p. 16). They prescribe the brushing for the treatment of sensory defensiveness. Increased as well as improved response to sensation is extremely important for oral motor activities and exercises that follow this portion of treatment.

Oral massage is varied to address the specific needs of the client. For example, oral massage can facilitate an improved response to tactile sensation. If a client is hyperresponsive to touch in the oral area, carefully applied oral massage can help the individual become more accepting of touch. In this situation, the type of touch accepted by the individual is explored. Many individuals who are sensitive to touch accept firm, phasic (i.e., "on and off") touch as opposed to touch that involves consistent or ongoing contact (e.g., long, effleurage massage strokes). The massage generally begins in an area on the individual's body where touch is readily accepted (e.g., the arms or back). The massage then progresses toward the area of hypersensitivity (e.g., the face or the mouth).

The general oral massage can be varied to address issues such as low or high muscle tone. Tapping (i.e., tapotement), vibration or friction, and icing can be used as part of the general oral massage to facilitate oral muscle tone, whereas the application of warmth and long, slow massage strokes can be used to inhibit high muscle tone. (The specifics of general oral massage will be discussed in Chapter 4.)

General oral massage can improve the individual's response to sensation, improve muscle tone, and/or improve awareness in the face and mouth for the purpose of improving the individual's acceptance of food textures, tastes, and temperatures. This may also improve the individual's ability to perform more precise oral movements needed to improve eating and drinking skills as well as speech production.

Once the individual accepts the general oral massage, more specific techniques can be used to release fascial restrictions and stimulate muscle function. Myofascial release, proprioceptive neuromuscular facilitation, and Beckman facilitation techniques can be used for this purpose. These treatment approaches will be discussed as they apply to different populations in Chapters 4 through 8. Note that there are circumstances under which massage work should not be used with a client. See Appendix B for a listing of cautions, contraindications, and comments regarding this issue.

Specific oral motor activities and exercises make up the next segment of the treatment regime. These consist of activities devised for each particular client, depending on his or her oral motor needs. Exercises or activities to improve respiratory support for speech production, jaw stability and/or graded jaw movement, tongue and jaw dissociation, the precision of tongue and lip movement, intraoral pressure, and so on can be introduced into this segment. These exercises are generally completed within a 5- to 10-minute period so that the remainder of the session can be spent on specific speech and language activities. Exercises and activities for improved oral motor function will be discussed according to the individual's age and level of function in Chapters 4 through 8. These activities are prescribed as part of the treatment session to improve oral strength, mobility, and coordination for the ultimate purpose of improving the individual's ability to eat, drink, or produce speech. Activities are chosen based on each individual's specific oral motor strengths and needs.

Specific speech and language activities follow the segment of the session containing the oral motor activities and exercises specified for the client. In a 45-minute session the gross motor and oral motor activities may take 15 to 20 minutes, leaving 20 to 25 minutes for more traditional speech and language treatment. A 45-minute treatment session is recommended for oral motor treatment. This amount of time works well for very young children as well as adults. If a session is limited to 30 minutes, then 15 minutes may be used for gross motor and oral motor activities and 15 minutes would remain for specific speech and language work. It should be noted that speech and language can be facilitated as appropriate throughout the treatment session. Although many specific speech activities will be covered in this book, the full range of speech and language activities that may follow oral motor activities cannot possibly be covered. These activities will be determined by the clinician based on individual client needs.

INTERACTIVE CASE EXPERIENCES

Identify other treatment areas that may benefit the following clients (e.g., neuro-developmental treatment, sensory integration therapy, articulation therapy, remediation of intelligibility concerns, sign language, augmentative communication, etc.). What team members could be part of an oral motor team for each individual? What segments of the typical oral motor treatment session would benefit each client? What oral motor skills or behaviors would need to be inhibited in each client? What oral motor skills or behaviors would need to be facilitated for each client? This experience is meant to challenge the reader to think of the possibilities for each case and to provide some practice with the information presented in this chapter.

George

George is a 60-year-old client with Parkinson's disease. He has a mild sensory neural hearing loss and normal auditory comprehension. His speech frequently unintelligible secondary to the presence of hypokinetic dysarthria. He presents with reduced range of·motion in his artiuclators, imprecise consonant production, repetitions of phonemes, frequent hesitations and false starts in his speech, monopitch, reduced loudness, and vocal tremor. The rate of his speech is variable, and he produces short bursts of rapid speech. His speech improves somewhat with the administration of medication (i.e., Sinemet).

Jenny

Jenny is a 5-year-old child who has been diagnosed with sensory integrative disorder, oral dyspraxia (i.e., she demonstrates groping and struggle behaviors when imitating oral movements), and developmental dyspraxia of speech. She has normal hearing but a history of middle ear infections. Jenny has above-average receptive language skills.

Jenny sits in a "w" sit pattern when sitting on the floor. When seated in a chair, she moves constantly, as if she is trying to increase the muscle tone in the trunk of her body. When asked to imitate oral movements, such as placing her tongue on her alveolar ridge, she has great difficulty imitating the precise movement. She is easily overwhelmed when oral motor tasks and activities are required of her. Jenny's oral movements while eating and drinking are within normal limits. She exhibits inconsistent multiple misarticulations. Her intelligibility decreases as her length of utterance increases.

Jenny generally accomplishes routine tasks with ease. She has difficulties with transitions and frequently refuses to try new activities or tasks. When Jenny can be encouraged to try new activities, she generally enjoys the activities once she is involved in them. She has a low frustration tolerance level and becomes easily frustrated when she cannot accomplish tasks with ease. When she becomes overwhelmed by tasks, she will sit under the table or will pull her shirt over her arms and legs so that she is swaddled by the shirt. Jenny participates readily in gross motor and language activities. She is a very imaginative child and suggests many creative ideas and solutions.

4

Birth to Age 2

A Critical Learning Period for Oral Motor Development

This chapter will cover the assessment and treatment of oral motor disorders in individuals from birth to 2 years of age. A large amount of information is presented in this chapter, because the birth to 2-year level is considered a critical learning period for the development of oral motor skills for eating, drinking, and speech production. Some of the material in this chapter may also be applicable to individuals functioning in the birth to 2-year developmental range or those individuals at any age who have severe to profound oral motor disorders.

Rhonda S. Walter, MD, discusses the concept of critical or sensitive learning periods in her chapter entitled "Issues Surrounding the Development of Feeding and Swallowing" (1994). She summarizes the work of Illingworth and Lister (1964) who based their work on animal studies. Critical learning periods are described as "fairly well delineated times when a specific stimulus must be applied to produce a particular action" (Walter, 1994, p. 27). This implies that it is more difficult for an individual to learn a particular behavior pattern after a critical or sensitive period has passed. Walter states that "although these concepts are unproven from a 'hard science' standpoint, they offer an interesting explanation for feeding delays and deviant feeding behavior in children" (Walter, 1994, p. 28). As discussed in Chapter 1, oral motor development appears to continue until the individual is at least 16 to18 years of age. Birth to 2 or 3 years of age seems to be a critical learning period for oral motor development. However, many refinements and changes occur in this system throughout childhood and adolescence. All of these stages will be discussed in Chapters 4 through 8.

A developmental framework was used as a means of structuring the material presented in this book. Information will be conveyed in the chapter where the reader can find the earliest developmental use of the material. However, some of the material may apply to a variety of different-aged populations. Later chapters will refer the reader back to previous chapters when appropriate.

ASSESSMENT

When assessing oral motor skills in infants, it is important to consider two important factors: (1) the newborn's oral anatomy is significantly different from the adult's oral anatomy and (2) young infants exhibit a number of reflexes and responses that are not typically seen in adults. These anatomical differences and reflexes impact on the child's feeding and oral motor development, which is discussed in great detail in Chapter 1.

During oral motor assessment it is important to attain a detailed case history and to use an appropriate assessment tool with individuals of all ages. A generic case history form is included in this chapter. Several assessment tools that may be used with infants will be discussed or presented. See Appendix A for a reference list of all assessment tools presented in the book.

Case History

When completing any assessment, it is important to have a thorough case history. Figure 4.1 is a general case history form that can be used for infants as well as individuals of all ages with oral motor concerns. Some clinical experience or supervision may be needed for the clinician to initially interpret the results of the case history information as many of the questions reflect developmentally appropriate skills. The clinician must make a clinical judgment about which information from the case history form reflects areas of need for the client. This is particularly important when assessing infants. Checklists such as the Developmental Pre-Feeding Checklist (Morris & Klein, 1987, pp. 69–82; Klein & Morris, 1999, pp. 480–509; Morris & Klein, 2000, Appendix B) and the Developmental Self-Feeding Checklist (Morris & Klein, 1987, p. 306) may be beneficial in assisting the clinician in making appropriate clinical judgments about the material presented in the case history.

Assessment Tools

After obtaining a thorough case history, it is important to observe the child's oral motor behaviors. This portion of the chapter describes a number of assessment tools, consisting primarily of checklists to assist the clinician during the observation of the child's feeding, eating, and drinking. As previously mentioned, the Developmental Pre-Feeding Checklist developed by Suzanne Evans Morris and Marsha Dunn Klein (Morris & Klein, 1987, pp. 69–82; Klein & Morris, 1999, pp. 480–509; Morris & Klein, 2000, Appendix B) may be used to accomplish this goal. This is an excellent checklist to use in the assessment of infant feeding. It is also a good way for the clinician to learn about normal development. Two additional checklists from the book *Pre-Feeding Skills* (Morris & Klein, 1987) may also provide important assessment information: the Developmental Self-Feeding Checklist (p. 306) and the Positioning Checklist (p. 169). In the second edition of *Pre-Feeding Skills,* Morris and Klein (2000, p. 305) developed another tool, entitled "Body Alignment for Seating and Positioning Checklist."

INTERACTIVE EXPERIENCE: NORMAL DEVELOPMENT

Observe an infant who is developing feeding skills at a normal rate. Visit the infant monthly, if possible, for the first two years of life. Complete the Developmental Pre-Feeding Checklist found in *Pre-Feeding Skills* (Morris & Klein, 1987, pp. 69–82), the *Mealtime Participation Guide* (Klein & Morris, 1999, pp. 480–509) or *Pre-Feeding Skills,* 2nd edition (Morris & Klein, 2000, Appendix B), as you make your observations. How does the infant's development compare to the behaviors noted in the checklist? What did you learn about normal development?

FIGURE 4.1 Oral Motor Case History

Client's name ______________________________

Birth date __________

Age ______________

Person completing form ______________________________

Date _________

Eating/Drinking

What are the individual's current difficulties with eating and drinking? When did the current difficulties with eating and drinking begin? Describe.

Describe the individual's appetite.

Describe a typical breakfast, lunch, and dinner for the individual.

What types of foods and liquids can the individual safely manage (e.g., regular liquid, thickened liquid, regular table food, soft table food, etc.)?

Does the individual prefer certain food or liquid tastes, textures, or temperatures? Describe.

Does the individual have difficulty with: (describe)

Voluntary opening or closing of mouth? ______________________________

Sucking? ______________________________

Biting on nipple, cup, or utensils? ______________________________

Keeping food in mouth? ______________________________

Chewing? ______________________________

Food temperatures? ______________________________

Food textures? ______________________________

Food tastes? ______________________________

Drinking from a cup or bottle? ______________________________

Eating from a spoon? ______________________________

Swallowing (e.g., food, liquid, medication, etc.)? ______________________________

Choking/Gagging? ______________________________

Reflux? ______________________________

Tooth grinding? ______________________________

FIGURE 4.1 Oral Motor Case History *(Continued)*

Does the individual self-feed or is the individual fed by someone else? If so, who feeds the individual?

What feeding/eating/drinking methods does the individual use (e.g., breast, bottle, G-tube, spoon, cup, etc.)? If the individual drinks from a cup, describe the type of cup (e.g., cutout cup, spouted cup, regular open cup, etc.).

Does the individual use any specialized equipment when eating and drinking?

Where and how is the individual positioned when eating and drinking (e.g., in a chair, in bed, in a special seat)?

How long does it take for the individual to complete an average meal?

Does the individual eat enough food and drink enough liquid in a reasonable amount of time? ______ Yes _____ No

Approximate Amount 1. liquids ______________________

2. solids ______________________

Does the individual have upper respiratory concerns (e.g., colds, food or environmental allergies, asthma, etc.)?

Is there a family history of upper respiratory concerns?

What is the individual's weight and height?

Has the individual gained or lost weight suddenly? Explain.

Does the individual have any other health concerns that impact on eating, drinking, or speaking?

Oral Motor and Dental

Has the individual had oral motor treatment (e.g., oral massage, oral brushing, oral exercises/activities, etc.)? Describe.

Does the individual chew on:

toys? _____	straws? ____	pens/pencils? ___
fingernails? ____	tongue? ____	other? ___________

(Continued)

FIGURE 4.1 Oral Motor Case History *(Continued)*

Does the individual suck his or her:

thumb? ____ fingers? ____ tongue? ____

pacifier? ____ blanket? ____ other? ______

Describe the individual's dental history/needs.

Speech, Language, and Communication

What are the individual's current difficulties with speech, language, and communication? Describe.

Has the individual received speech-language therapy in the past or does the individual currently receive speech-language therapy? Describe treatment goals.

Does the individual have a history of hearing difficulties (e.g., middle ear infections, hearing loss, etc.)? Please describe.

How does the individual currently communicate? Does the individual use gestures, sign language, or other forms of alternative/augmentative communication (e.g., picture symbols, word or alphabet board, etc.)? Describe.

Is the individual's speech intelligible to

familiar people? ______________________________

unfamiliar people? ______________________________

Does the individual appear frustrated if he/she is not understood? Please describe.

Questions and Other Information

Does the individual have other medical concerns (e.g., heart problems, diabetes, etc.)? Describe.

Do you have any other questions, or is there any other information about the individual that you feel is important to describe here?

What other services does the individual receive (e.g., occupational therapy, physical therapy, etc.)?

Sources: Developed by Diane Chapman Bahr and Rebecca Miller with ideas from case histories by J. M. Jelm, *Assessment and Treatment of Verbal Dyspraxia* (Baltimore, MD, workshop, 1995); S. E. Morris and M. D. Klein, *Pre-Feeding Skills* (Tucson, AZ: Therapy Skill Builders, 1987), pp. 105–106; R. B. Pierce, *Swallow Right: An Exercise Program to Correct Swallowing Patterns* (Tucson, AZ: Communication Skill Builders, 1993). Reprinted by permission.

Neonatal Oral-Motor Assessment Scale (Braun & Palmer, 1986)

The Neonatal Oral-Motor Assessment Scale (NOMAS) assesses oral motor function in newborn infants. Tongue and jaw function is evaluated during nutritive and nonnutritive suckling. The scale contains 42 items and each item is scored on a 4-point scale (i.e., 0 to 3). The scale can be used with infants who are at risk for feeding difficulties (e.g., infants born prematurely). "The NOMAS was found to differentiate tongue from jaw movements and oral-motor disorganization from dysfunction" (Arvedson, 1993).

Oral Motor Assessment Checklist (Bockelkamp, Ferroni, Kopcha, & Silfies, 1997)

The Oral Motor Assessment Checklist (see Figure 4.2) was developed by graduate students at Loyola College in Maryland. This general checklist can be used with children as well as adults. It is best suited for individuals 6 months of age or older. When working with infants, it is best to use developmental checklists such as the Developmental Pre-Feeding Checklist (Morris & Klein, 1987, pp. 69–82; Klein & Morris, 1999, pp. 480–509; Morris & Klein, 2000, Appendix B) and the Developmental Self-Feeding Checklist (Morris & Klein, 1987, p. 306) in addition to this checklist. Some clinical experience or supervision may be needed for the clinician to interpret the results of the Oral Motor Assessment Checklist as developmentally appropriate skills need to be taken into consideration. The speech-language pathologist will then make clinical judgments about information from the checklist for treatment.

FIGURE 4.2 Oral Motor Assessment Checklist

Name ____________________

Date ____________________

D.O.B. ____________________

Age ____________________

Sex ____________________

Location ____________________

Examiner ____________________

Body Positioning

Sitting Position

90 degree hip, knee, and ankle flexion ____
Slouching in chair ____
Leaning to one side ____ (____Right ____Left)
Reclined ____ Angle? ____ (e.g., 45 degrees)

(Continued)

FIGURE 4.2 Oral Motor Assessment Checklist *(Continued)*

Head Position

Head supported ____yes ____no
Normal alignment ____
Chin tucked ____
Hyperextended ____

Shoulder Position

Normal alignment ____
Elevated ____
Rounded ____
Symmetrical ____
Asymmetrical ____

Additional Observations

____

____

Food Consistencies Presented

Regular ____
Mechanical soft ____
Puree ____
Thin liquids ____
Thick liquids ____

Additional Observations

____

____

Oral Structure and Function

Mouth at Rest

Open ____
Closed ____
Tongue protruded ____
Drooling ____
Tremor ____
Low muscle tone ____
High muscle tone ____

Additional Observations

____

____

FIGURE 4.2 Oral Motor Assessment Checklist *(Continued)*

Lips

Symmetrical ____
Asymmetrical ____ (____Right Weak ____Left Weak)
Active use of lips ____
Ability to pucker ____
Adequate lip closure ____
Lip retraction ____

Additional Observations

____

____

Jaw

Munching pattern ____
Rotary pattern ____
Jaw retraction ____
Jaw thrust ____
Wide jaw excursions ____

Additional Observations

____

____

Tongue

Moves tongue independently of jaw ____
Tongue lateralization ____
  Which side(s)? ____Right ____Left
Fasciculations ____
Deviation ____
  Which side(s)? ____Right ____Left
Tongue thrust ____
Range of motion ____Good ____Fair ____Poor

Additional Observations

____

____

Dentition

Normal ____
Overbite ____
Underbite ____
Missing teeth ____Yes ____No

Additional Observations

____

____

Source: Denise Bockelkamp, Danielle Ferroni, Allison Kopcha, and Donna Palumbo Silfies (1997). Reprinted by permission.

Oral-Motor/Feeding Rating Scale (Jelm, 1990)

Judy Michels Jelm (1990) developed the *Oral-Motor/Feeding Rating Scale,* which can be used with individuals 12 months of age to adult. Lip/cheek, tongue, and jaw movements are evaluated in eight areas of function and are scored on a 6-point scale (i.e., 0 to 5). The areas include "breast feeding, bottle feeding, spoon feeding, cup drinking, biting (soft cookie), biting (hard cookie), chewing, and straw drinking" (Jelm, 1990). Areas such as "self-feeding, adaptive feeding equipment, diet adaptations, position, sensitivity, food retention, swallowing, and orofacial structures" (Arvedson, 1993, p. 263) are also taken into consideration.

Oral Motor Evaluation Protocol (Beckman, 1997)

Debra Beckman (1997) has also developed an assessment tool that may be used with individuals of all ages exhibiting oral motor concerns. Clinicians need to be specifically trained to administer this tool. Workshops are offered by Debra Beckman. The tool assesses concerns with specific muscle group function. It is a "hands-on" assessment tool in that the clinician is required to physically examine the muscle tone, strength, and responses of the muscle groups responsible for specific oral function.

TREATMENT

A broad range of treatment ideas may be considered when working with children in the birth to 2-year age or developmental range. For example, the inhibition and facilitation techniques used with an infant born prematurely may be considerably different from the techniques used with an infant born full term with Down syndrome. Techniques used with younger infants may be significantly different from techniques used with older infants. As previously discussed, the majority of the young child's oral motor development is completed in the first two to three years of life. Therefore, if an infant is exhibiting any deviation from typical oral motor development, then it is important to begin treatment as early as possible. This treatment can begin in the first weeks of the child's life if needed. As the speech-language pathologist develops a treatment plan for an infant or young child, these issues as well as the many sensory and motor ideas presented in Chapters 2 and 3 need to be taken into consideration.

This portion of the chapter begins with a brief discussion of the treatment of infants born prematurely. The remainder of the chapter focuses on the specifics of treatment. Treatment sources and interactive case experiences are also presented.

Treatment of Infants Born Prematurely

Infants born prematurely need to be therapeutically managed with great care. Speech-language pathologists and others working in the neonatal intensive care unit (NICU) *must be specially trained.* The speech-language pathologist in the NICU provides the following services:

- Attends rounds
- Assesses nippling readiness

- Promotes nippling readiness
- Assesses feeding
- Evaluates swallowing function
- Provides feeding intervention
- Completes developmental evaluations
- Provides and recommends developmentally appropriate care
- Provides parent education
- Completes discharge evaluations
- Refers to early intervention programs (Ziev, 1999, p. 33)

Infants born prematurely often have unstable vital signs. The clinician must work closely with other medical staff to ensure that handling techniques do not stress the fragile newborn. For the most part, gentle handling techniques are used for short periods of time. University of Miami's Tiffany Field and colleagues have completed a significant amount of research on this population (Kuhn, Schanberg, Field, Symanski, Zimmerman, Scafidi, & Roberts, 1991; Field, 1995, 1998; Scafidi, Field, & Schanberg, 1993; Wheeden, Scafidi, Field, Ironson, Valdeon, & Bandstra, 1993). Field and coresearchers discovered that infants born prematurely who received 15 minutes of carefully applied massage three times each day gained weight faster, were discharged from the hospital sooner, and demonstrated more mature motor behaviors than similar infants who did not receive the massage.

Clinicians working in neonatal intensive care units may wish to consider implementing a program similar to the one described by Field and colleagues. Massage can assist the infant in the development of body awareness and the integration of tactile and proprioceptive input. It may also support general growth and development as well as immune system function. This helps prepare the infant for interactions with people and the environment. The appropriately trained speech-language pathologist can establish an oral motor program in the NICU that combines infant massage with oral massage as well as other oral motor work. It is important to note that *clinicians working in neonatal intensive care units need specialized training to safely do this job.*

Treatment Specifics

The timing and sequence of the segments involved in the oral motor treatment session are flexible and should be modified according to the infant's needs. However, a suggested timing and sequence has been presented in this chapter to provide the speech-language pathologist who is beginning to use this approach with suggested guidelines. As the speech-language pathologist develops skill and his or her own style in this area of oral motor treatment, the timing and sequence may change.

The first two segments of an oral motor treatment session for the infant (i.e., whole-body massage/movement and oral massage/other facilitation techniques) may take 10 to 20 minutes. The timing of oral sensory exploration, feeding therapy, and sound play will vary according to the needs of the child. If feeding is the main focus of the treatment session, then each of the first three parts of the session (i.e., whole-body massage/movement, oral massage/other facilitation techniques, and oral sensory exploration) may take only about 5 minutes each. It is important to realize that although the segments of the treatment session are presented and discussed as somewhat separate entities, there are aspects of each that can be incorporated throughout the treatment session. For example, oral sensory exploration could be used extensively during feeding, eating, and drinking activities as well as during oral motor activities. Massage and movement may also need to be incorporated throughout the session to assist the child in becoming more focused and organized in movement responses.

A treatment session for the young infant could include some of each of the areas (e.g., whole-body massage and movement—10 minutes, oral massage and other facilitation techniques—5 minutes, oral sensory exploration—10 minutes, feeding therapy—10 minutes, sound play—10 minutes). The treatment session for the older infant or young toddler may include 5 minutes of whole-body massage and movement activities, 5 minutes of oral massage and other facilitation techniques, 5 to 10 minutes of oral sensory exploration and oral motor activities (these may include feeding/eating/drinking activities), 5 to 10 minutes of feeding/eating/drinking activities (if needed), and the remainder of the session on early speech production activities. Language tasks are incorporated throughout the session. Oral motor work is completed within the context of language activities. Many language concepts can be targeted throughout the treatment session. A certain portion of the session may also be reserved for work on specific language activities.

The treatment recommended in this book requires the involvement of parents and caregivers. Many of the techniques also involve "hands-on" work with the child and must be applied with the understanding and consent of the child's parent or legal guardian. A weekly 45-minute treatment session will usually provide the parent or caregiver with enough ideas and techniques to use until the next treatment session. It is important for the parent and/or care provider to attend the session with the infant and to carry out demonstrated techniques and activities at home. Techniques and activities completed one time per week will usually not provide the infant or young child in need of oral motor treatment with the intensity needed to make changes in the oral motor system. Oral motor treatment is most effective when applied on a regular basis (i.e., at least three to five times per week and daily if possible), similar to an exercise program.

Oral Motor Treatment: Young Infant*

- Whole-body massage/Movement activities
- Oral massage/Other facilitation techniques
- Oral sensory exploration
- Feeding therapy
- Sound play

Oral Motor Treatment: Older Infant/Young Toddler*

- Whole-body massage/Movement activities
- Oral massage/Other facilitation techniques
- Oral sensory exploration
- Oral motor activities
- Feeding/Eating/Drinking activities
- Early speech production activities

Whole-Body Massage and Movement Activities

It is suggested that a typical oral motor treatment session for an infant begin with massage and movement activities. These strategies are also incorporated throughout the session as needed by the child.

*Lists adapted from unpublished workshop materials developed by Diane Chapman Bahr and Libby Kumin (see Kumin & Bahr, 1997).

Infant massage can be taught to the parents or caregivers by a certified infant massage instructor. A certified infant massage instructor can be located by contacting the International Association of Infant Massage (see Appendix D). As previously mentioned, massage has been found to have many benefits for the infant. These include improved circulation, body awareness, bowel function, sleeping patterns, and general level of contentedness. Infants require touch; it is the first means of communication between the parent and the child. The book *Touching: The Human Significance of the Skin* by Ashley Montagu (1986) discusses this topic in detail. Infants who are massaged tend to be more organized in their responses to the environment, as they often demonstrate improved attention, focus, and concentration. This is true of infants with and without disabilities. The book entitled *Infant Massage: A Handbook for Loving Parents* by Vimala Schneider McClure (1989) discusses and illustrates general massage techniques for infants. Parents may wish to apply the massage just prior to the child's therapy session, using strokes that will alert or calm the infant, depending on the child's muscle tone and state of arousal. Carefully applied vigorous strokes can assist in increasing muscle tone in the body, whereas stokes applied slowly can assist in decreasing muscle tone in the body.

As the child matures, the clinician may choose to incorporate "ball massage" into the treatment session. This technique is recommended for older infants, and it may not be appropriate for individuals who remain very fragile. A small therapy ball or lightweight playground ball can be rolled over the front and back of the child's body as the child is lying on a mat or soft surface. Firm but gentle pressure is applied with the ball. Some children prefer the contact of a ball, on the body, as the tactile and proprioceptive input provided in this manner is often more consistent than the input provided by the caregiver's hands.

Neuro-developmental treatment and Feldenkrais's "Awareness through Movement" are effective treatment modalities to use with an infant. They assist the infant in developing more typical movement patterns. "Awareness through Movement" activities provide the infant with information regarding the ease and efficiency of movement. These activities were developed by Moshe Feldenkrais, who originated the functional integration system to improve the "functions of the human motor system" (Kimmey, 1985, cover). Movement done with ease and efficiency requires less effort on the behalf of the child. This can lead to greater willingness to continue the particular movement. The application of techniques from Feldenkrais's "Awareness through Movement" is generally done in a slow, gentle, consistent manner, whether the child has high muscle tone or generalized low muscle tone. Feldenkrais (1975) described his method as a way to facilitate maturation of the central nervous system using the relationship between the muscular and nervous systems. Feldenkrais practitioners teach the client how to move with ease. This is particularly important for infants exhibiting neurological concerns. The Bobaths, who developed neuro-developmental treatment (NDT), also stressed the concept of establishing ease and efficiency of movement. See Chapter 3 for more information on neuro-developmental treatment.

If the clinician is not trained in infant massage or movement techniques, he or she may begin by gently rocking the infant. This provides the infant with rhythmic vestibular stimulation that tends to be organizing and calming to many infants. However, the clinician should *consult with an occupational therapist, physical therapist, or another movement specialist* who is familiar with appropriate movement techniques to facilitate improved muscle tone and movement patterns in the infant's body.

Specific movement techniques are used to therapeutically handle infants with different types of tonal concerns (e.g., generalized low muscle tone, hypertonicity, fluctuating muscle tone, or mixed muscle tone). For the infant with hypertonicity or fluctuating muscle tone (e.g., infants with cerebral palsy), a treatment plan would often include handling techniques to facilitate ease of movement in the body. The infant with generalized low muscle tone throughout the body (e.g., infants with Down syndrome, Prader-Willi syndrome, Williams syndrome, and fetal alcohol syndrome) may respond better to more vigorous movement than the child with hypertonicity. However, it is important to apply handling techniques in a rhythmic and organized manner and not to move the infant too vigorously. Infants are fairly delicate, and movement that is too vigorous may injure the child. Some infants exhibit low muscle tone in the trunk of the body and high muscle tone or "fixing patterns" in the shoulder girdle, oral area, or extremities. Movement activities must be carefully chosen for these individuals to increase muscle tone in the trunk of the body while facilitating ease of movement in the more distal areas of the body. Consult with the infant's physical therapist and/or physician prior to initiating movement activities.

Many infants with oral motor concerns also exhibit other health issues that may affect their participation in movement activities. Some infants with tonal concerns also exhibit gastroesophageal reflux. This is often seen in infants with low muscle tone in the trunk of the body. Bouncing or rigorous movement activities may exacerbate gastroesophageal reflux. Heart or pulmonary issues may preclude certain movement activities. The clinician should ask the parents or guardians for permission to *consult with the child's doctor* regarding these concerns.

As the infant matures and becomes more mobile, the environment can be structured to facilitate the child's development of movement patterns. The child can crawl and climb on equipment set up in an obstacle course or bounce on a bouncing horse. Appropriate activities can facilitate postural stability and control needed for oral development. The movement activities must be carefully chosen to improve muscle tone and body movement. Certain activities may actually cause an increase in abnormal muscle tone and movement. For example, rigorous bouncing may elicit increased extensor tone in the child with cerebral palsy, whereas gentle, rhythmic movement may improve muscle tone.

Although it is important to use massage and movement in the treatment session, the clinician must be aware that the child may become overloaded or overwhelmed by too much of this type of stimulation. The massage and movement may also bring about memories stored within the body from previous touch-pressure or movement experiences. This may be very positive for the child *or* may result in crying. The crying may be a sign of distress or a sign of release. In the article "Crying," Schneider (1987) discusses the importance of crying as a release. She says that "often after a good cry babies are happier, their digestion improves, and they sleep more deeply" (p. 20). Schneider suggests that the baby be provided with love and support while crying as opposed to being "ignored or hushed" (p. 20). This can be done by holding, rocking, and talking to the baby.

The application of touch and movement in oral motor treatment is like a "dance" between the child and the clinician and must be carefully applied. The concept of a "dance" is used here because dancing involves the coordinated movement among partners. If one partner is out of synchrony with the other, the "dance" is not well executed. One partner may "trip" over the other partner.

This can occur figuratively in therapy if both partners do not work well together and do not establish synchronicity.

Oral Massage and Other Facilitation Techniques

As the infant or young child becomes comfortable with therapeutic handling, oral massage may be applied. This may be modified according to age, size, and level of acceptance by the child. Massage may be used to increase awareness in the child's oral structures, particularly the oral musculature. If the child demonstrates atypical oral motor patterns, such as a hyperresponsive gag reflex or tonic bite reaction, massage can be used to bring about an improved response. The oral massage can also help to improve the infant's other tactile and proprioceptive responses.

When the infant is small, the caregiver can apply the intraoral portion of the massage with a finger. If the infant's mouth is very small, the care provider may initially use "the pinky finger" to massage the inside of the child's mouth. As the infant's mouth increases in size, the caregiver will want to use the index finger to achieve greater control in the application of the massage. The Infa-Dent Finger Toothbrush has soft bristles near the tip and can be placed on the caregiver's index finger to provide increased stimulation. The Infa-Dent Finger Toothbrush can be purchased from a variety of companies that carry oral motor supplies (see product sources in Appendix D).

As the child's oral structures grow, a Nuk oral massage brush made by Gerber (see product sources in Appendix D) may become the implement of choice when applying massage techniques inside the child's mouth. This brush is available in two sizes (i.e., small and large). The small brush may be a better choice for children with small mouths and may be more readily accepted by some children than the large Nuk. However, some individuals cannot tolerate the stimulation provided by either Nuk oral massage brush. The input from these brushes can be perceived as quite intense by some individuals. There may also be other reasons not to use the Nuk oral massage brush with a particular individual (e.g., certain health and dental issues).

In addition to these considerations, the clinician should be aware that the large Nuk oral massage brush is a two-piece brush. The brush portion can become detached from the handle if the individual bites with great pressure. This is unlikely to occur with the small Nuk oral massage brush, as it is constructed differently than the large brush. However, it is recommended that the Nuk oral massage brushes be used *under supervision,* if the individual cannot use the brush safely and independently or is in danger of swallowing parts of objects. This would be true of children in the birth to 2-year age group. Also, the protrusions on either Nuk oral massage brush can become worn with use. It is important to dispose of the brush and replace it if this occurs. Despite these concerns, Nuk oral massage brushes remain good tools for oral brushing with many clients. Firm, consistent input can be provided with a Nuk oral massage brush, and the brush allows the clinician to apply massage inside the dental arch without the danger of accidentally being bitten by the client.

The *oral massage sequence* is a general massage sequence that can be used with most individuals receiving oral motor treatment. This general oral massage can help bring greater awareness to the individual's oral mechanism as well as improved responses in the oral area so that more specific oral motor techniques can be applied. Although the sequence is introduced here in the

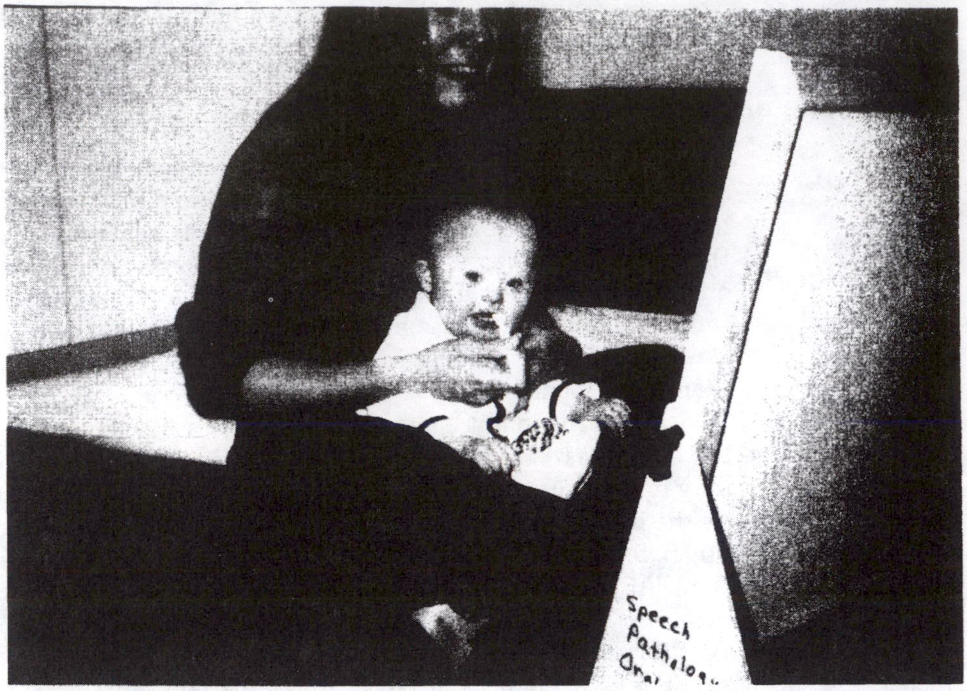

Michael, a 6-month-old child with Down syndrome, receives oral massage with the large Nuk oral massage brush. The clinician can monitor Michael's reactions to the massage by looking into the therapy mirror.

chapter on the treatment of infants and young children, it may be an integral part of oral motor treatment programs for individuals of any age.

The sequence is modified according to the age and the needs of the individual. Some older children and adults can apply this sequence themselves. However, care must be taken when assigning the application of the sequence to the client. As previously discussed, many individuals with oral motor concerns also exhibit other fine motor concerns. Therefore, these individuals may have difficulty applying the oral massage with the specificity needed to make a change in the oral motor system. Turn taking is certainly encouraged between a care provider and the client in the application of many oral motor techniques, but the client may not exhibit the strength or precision of hand movement needed to apply the techniques adequately.

When working in and around the individual's mouth, it is important for the clinician to observe universal precautions. This includes wearing gloves when working inside the individual's mouth as well as on or around the individual's lip area. It is also important to wear gloves when working on the outside of the individual's mouth if the individual drools or has any open sores or lesions. Some children respond in a negative manner to the gloves being worn by the clinician. These are often children who have been hospitalized and may associate the wearing of gloves with medical procedures. These children need to learn that gloves are not threatening and are part of oral motor assessment and treatment. This can be done through play activities and by consistent use of gloves by all individuals completing oral motor work requiring touch to the oral area. Some individuals are also sensitive to latex products. Gloves are available in materials other than latex, as well as different colors, scents, and flavors. See information on universal precautions in Chapter 3 for further information.

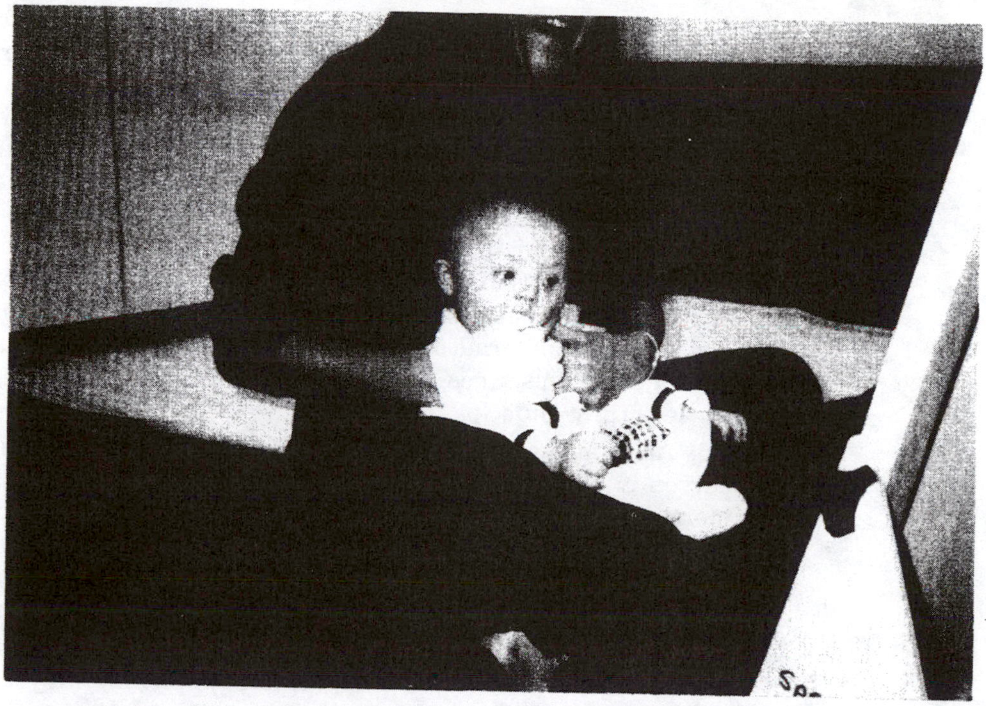

Michael, a 6-month-old child with Down syndrome, is accustomed to the clinician wearing of gloves during oral massage. He has received oral massage since he was a young infant.

Oral Massage Sequence*

1. When doing massage work with an individual, be certain to explain what you are doing and why in easy-to-understand terms. This is also important when working with patients in comas and those who seem cognitively unable to understand what you are saying.

2. Determine an area on the individual's body where touch is readily accepted. This is often the back, shoulders, or arms. Begin your massage in this area. Individuals who are very sensitive to touch may respond better to gentle but firm squeezes as opposed to long massage strokes. Apply the gentle but firm squeezes in a rhythmic manner. Music or song can be used to establish the rhythm. A rhythm of 60 to 70 beats per minute is recommended. For many individuals, the face and oral areas are very sensitive. Therefore, beginning in an area away from the face will often assist the individual in becoming accustomed to the care provider's touch prior to the application of touch to the face.

3. Work your way toward the individual's face with your massage. If the person becomes distressed or rejects your touch-pressure at any time, move back to an area where the individual previously accepted the touch-pressure and then re-approach the area where touch-pressure was rejected. If the individual rejects your touch-pressure again, move back to the area where touch-pressure was accepted previously. Re-approach an area approximately three times. If the individual continues to reject the touch-pressure, complete the massage work in an area of the body where the individual accepted the touch. Be sure to respect all communication from the individual.

*Adapted from an unpublished protocol used at Maryland School for the Blind; originally written by Suzanne Wayson, speech-language pathologist.

4. When the individual allows you to touch his or her face, begin your massage near the temporomandibular joint (TMJ) and move toward the lips. Anchor your thumbs on the person's mandible so that you have control over the movements of your index, middle, and ring fingers. These are the fingers that provide the massage. If the person is very sensitive, use gentle but firm presses. As the person becomes more accepting, add a rotary component to the massage. If the person has high muscle tone, use slow, relaxing motions. If the person has low muscle tone, your movements can be more vigorous and you may want to use tapping or vibration. It is important to massage the area of the masseter and buccinator muscles. The masseter muscles are important in the attainment of jaw stability and graded jaw movement. The buccinator muscles assist in activation of the lips. See Chapter 1 for further information regarding the importance of these muscles.

5. Apply presses with your index fingers *around* the individual's lips. If the person is very sensitive, use gentle but firm presses. As the person becomes more accepting, add a rotary component to the massage. Anchor your thumbs on the individual's mandible to give your index fingers more control during the massage. Begin applying the presses near the corners of the person's lips and move toward midline. Do this *above* the top lip and *below* the bottom lip.

6. When working directly *on* the person's lips, use your fingertips, the Nuk oral massage brush, or other appropriate implement. If you are using your fingertips, *wear gloves,* as lips and fingers frequently have small cuts through which disease can be communicated. Begin by pressing *on* the person's top lip and then the bottom lip from the corners toward the center. Add a rotary component with your fingertips as the individual can tolerate this input. If the person has low muscle tone in the lip area, tapping can be used. The individual can also be asked to participate in resistance activities (e.g., pressing the lips against your finger, a tongue blade, etc.).

7. Use a Nuk oral massage brush inside the person's mouth if possible. A finger or the Infa-Dent Finger Toothbrush may need to be used with a young infant or someone who cannot tolerate the use of the Nuk oral massage brush. Unflavored toothettes may also be used if the individual does not tolerate the intense input of the Nuk oral massage brush (Rosenfeld-Johnson, 1999a). The use of toothettes is discussed in Chapter 5. These are sponge brushes that should not be used with individuals who may bite off and swallow the sponge. Massage the insides of the person's cheeks using short back-to-front strokes beginning near the front of the individual's cheek area and moving toward the back of the cheek area. Massage the sulci and the gums. If the person has sensitivities, move carefully. Gentle but firm presses, top down/bottom up movements, or a rolling motion may be used in place of the brushing motion. It is important to massage the inside of the cheeks to bring awareness to the medial and lateral pterygoid muscles, which are important in the attainment of jaw stability and graded jaw movement. See Chapter 1 for further detail.

8. Gently but firmly press the Nuk oral massage brush or other appropriate implement on the individual's gum areas (if the individual does not have teeth) or the chewing surfaces of the individual's teeth (if the individual has teeth). Remember that the teeth and gums have sensory receptors and can be an area of extreme sensitivity.

9. Stroke the individual's entire tongue with the Nuk massage brush or other appropriate implement. This can be done using short back-to-front strokes beginning near the front of the tongue and moving toward the back of the tongue. Firm but gentle presses can also be applied if the individual does not

accept stroking. The stimulation to the individual's tongue can vary according to the tone in the muscles. If the muscle tone in the individual's tongue is low, use careful but vigorous movement. If the muscle tone is high, use slow, firm but gentle movement. Observe the movements of the individual's tongue and give extra attention to the areas of the tongue that seem most limited in movement. At this point, you can have the individual participate in resistance activities by pressing the tongue against a surface such as a tongue blade (e.g., laterally) if appropriate.

10. Gently but firmly press the Nuk oral massage brush or other appropriate implement against the outside edge of the individual's hard palate (i.e., just inside the teeth or just inside where the teeth would be). Be sure to apply this technique to the alveolar ridge and the lateral areas of the palate near the molars or near where the molars will be. It is extremely important to massage the alveolar ridge, as this is the tongue's target when producing many speech sounds and when a mature tongue resting posture is established. The lateral areas of the hard palate near the molars are also important to stimulate. In most individuals, the molars provide external stability for the tongue when producing connected speech (Boshart, 1998, 1999; Rosenfeld-Johnson, 1999a). Stimulation of the lateral hard palate in addition to the molars themselves may bring increased awareness to this area.

11. These are some basic oral massage ideas that can be modified according to the individual's needs. Oral massage is most effective when completed three times each day before an activity that requires the individual to use his or her mouth (e.g., eating, drinking, speaking, and toothbrushing). The massage routine can take as little as three to five minutes.

12. Once an oral massage routine has been established, many individuals can participate in or carry out their own routine. Caution must be taken in allowing the individual to carry out the routine independently if the individual cannot apply the techniques in the specific manner described. The protocol is simple and can be easily taught to parents, caregivers, and other professionals who work with the individual.

In conjunction with the general oral massage, *Beckman facilitation techniques* are some of the easiest techniques to use with an infant and young child. These are both easy to apply and to demonstrate. The majority of the Beckman (1997) facilitation techniques involve a particular movement of the surface tissue and underlying musculature for three repetitions. There are facilitation techniques for the facial and oral musculature. Parents and caregivers can be instructed to apply these techniques in conjunction with the oral massage protocol at least one time each day. These techniques can be used with very young infants as long as they are medically stable and have no other condition that contraindicates this type of work. The techniques are also easy to apply to older infants and toddlers, as three repetitions of a particular facilitation technique do not require the child to remain still for a long period of time. The application of the techniques can be made into a fun activity for the child where the clinician and/or the caregiver can sing a song or make funny noises to go along with the techniques.

There are approximately 25 facilitation techniques. Parents and caregivers appear to easily fit 5 or 6 of the Beckman facilitation techniques into the child's oral motor routine (at least three to five times per week, daily if possible). As previously mentioned, Debra Beckman has an assessment protocol for the clinician to determine the child's progress with the facilitation techniques. As the clinician determines that particular facilitation techniques have accomplished the goal of improved muscle function, the clinician may then teach the parents and caregivers new facilitation techniques while deleting any techniques from the routine that may no longer be as important. Both the use of the assessment and the facilitation techniques require *specific training from Debra Beckman.* Beckman offers workshops to teach her facilitation techniques at various locations each year throughout the United States. See Appendix D for website information.

Myofascial release techniques can also be a powerful tool when working with young children exhibiting oral motor concerns. In order to effectively use myofascial release in oral motor treatment, the clinician must learn about fascia. Fascia "covers the muscles, bones, nerves, organs, and vessels down to the cellular level" (Barnes, 1990, p. 3). It is the fascia that separates one muscle from another. The fascia allows the muscles to work in a dissociated manner gliding over one another and performing specific functions. When an individual does not use the musculature in a normal way, fascial restrictions can and often do occur. This restricts the dissociated movement of the musculature. Myofascial release is "a whole-body, hands-on approach for the evaluation and treatment of the human structure" (Barnes, 1990, p. 17) that uses "gentle tractioning forces" (p. 18) to release fascial restrictions. A myofascial release requires approximately 90 to 120 seconds for the release to occur. Therefore, children who are extremely movement oriented may not remain in a position long enough for the clinician to effect a fascial release. Clinicians need to be specifically trained in this form of treatment. John F. Barnes who developed a unique approach to myofascial release and Regi Boehme are two of the most prominent individuals teaching this type of treatment to clinicians. See Appendix D for how to access information on workshops provided by these two individuals.

The techniques used in *proprioceptive neuromuscular facilitation (PNF)* are attributed to the work of Herman Kabot, Maggie Knott, and Dorothy Voss (Sullivan, Markos, & Minor, 1982). Kabot, Knott, and Voss

> described functional patterns of movement that were used to improve muscle control of patients having both orthopedic and neurological problems. Many techniques were also developed by them to enhance relaxation or to increase strength by promoting irradiation from stronger to weaker muscle groups. (Sullivan, Markos, & Minor, 1982)

This manual treatment accesses the neuro-reflexive responses in the body. It is applied to the client, and the client does not need to participate in the treatment. Proprioceptive neuromuscular facilitation is used to improve postural control and movement patterns. Specific PNF techniques have been developed to address oral motor concerns that affect eating, drinking, and speech production. Karel and Berta Bobath were influenced by the work completed in this area when they developed the concepts of neuro-developmental treatment (Langley & Thomas, 1991). (See Chapter 3 for further discussion.) Proprioceptive neuromuscular facilitation is usually applied to the adult population; however some PNF techniques may be useful with infants and children exhibiting oral motor concerns.

Children are often more observant than adults around them realize. Children tend to want to do what they see others doing. Some children accept oral massage and other facilitation techniques for a period of time and then suddenly reject it. It is possible that the sensory input may have changed in some way or that the child may be perceiving the sensory input as different. It is also possible that the child has become more aware of the activities in which others typically engage. If oral massage and other facilitation techniques are not a part of this process, then the child may reject the massage. Puppets and family members have been used as role models in this situation (i.e., oral massage and other facilitation techniques have been completed on puppets and family members). This topic will receive further attention in Chapter 5.

The oral massage portion of the treatment session prepares the infant's mouth for the remainder of the therapy activities in the session and addresses some of the sensory input needs of the individual. Moore (1988) discusses the importance of working with the sensory systems in the book *Neuroanatomy Simplified.* She stresses the complexity of the sensory systems and states that in treatment, motor output is frequently stressed without adequate consideration of the complex sensory input needed for the motor output. Chapters 2 and 3 provide great detail on this topic.

After the application of oral massage and other facilitation techniques, the remainder of the treatment session can include a variety of activities focusing on motor output while continuing to attend to the individual's sensory needs for learning. These activities include oral sensory exploration, oral motor activities, feeding, eating, drinking, sound play, and early speech production. Language activities can be readily incorporated throughout the treatment session.

Oral Sensory Exploration

Infants exhibiting muscle tone and movement issues at birth often do not provide themselves with the oral experiences needed for adequate oral motor development. These infants frequently must be assisted in learning to mouth toys as well as their own hands and feet. Infants with oral motor concerns often have difficulty bringing their hands and feet to midline. Mouthing is a midline activity. When they are observed mouthing items on their own, infants with oral motor concerns frequently do not complete this exploration in an organized and thorough manner. By comparison, some infants who are typically developing have been observed via sonography to suck their thumbs while in utero. According to Boshart (1998), mouthing is greatest between 5 and 7 months of age in the child who is typically developing. Many individuals working with infants do not realize the significance of oral exploration for later development of eating, drinking, and speaking

It is extremely important for the infant to have a large variety of oral experiences. Information received by the infant via oral exploration appears to provide the infant with a great deal of information about an object. The mouth seems to act like a "third hand" in the exploration of objects. Prior to the child being mobile, this type of exploration assists the infant in learning about the environment in which he or she lives. The child also develops a variety of motor plans when mouthing objects of different shapes, sizes, and textures. Children continue to mouth toys and objects until this is no longer needed for exploration (i.e., the child has found another or more appropriate means to explore the environment) or to provide sensation to the oral mechanism. It is a concern to the clinician when a parent or caregiver reports that a child has never mouthed hands, feet, or toys. The child has then skipped a stage of development needed for later developing skills and has not benefited from the effects that mouthing can have on attention and organization. (See information in Chapter 3 on the connection between oral sensory input and attention.)

After completing oral massage and other facilitation techniques, the oral motor treatment session for an infant may include activities that involve oral sensory exploration. For young infants, the clinician may position the infant in such a way that he or she may easily bring the hands and feet toward the mouth (e.g., side lying or supine). An occupational therapist or physical therapist may assist the speech-language pathologist in this work. The clinician would want to introduce the infant to a variety of sensory experiences. Providing a variety of similar but slightly unique experiences is the key to assisting the infant in developing more sophisticated oral motor skills. Infants with oral motor concerns frequently will approach an activity in the same manner each time the activity is introduced as opposed to exploring different ways of approaching the activity. Learning is more complete when the infant discovers the variations that can take place within an activity. Therefore, when the infant explores a toy with the mouth, the care provider can assist the infant in discovering the variety of ways that the toy can be explored with the mouth. This type of exploration can also be done with foods. When the infant adjusts or changes oral exploratory patterns, the motor planning required for these activities is also adjusted or changed.

Parents, caregivers, and clinicians are often concerned about whether to use a *pacifier* with an infant with oral motor concerns. If the infant has a weak suckle-swallow pattern, then the clinician may suggest that the caregiver provide the infant with a pacifier to give the infant more practice with the pattern. This may be particularly useful with infants born prematurely. Some infants with oral motor concerns have difficulty establishing and maintaining a rhythmic suckle-swallow pattern. The clinician and care provider may assist the infant in establishing this pattern by rhythmically pressing and/or stroking the infant's tongue. Once the infant begins using the rhythmic suckle with this method, the care provider may then give the infant a pacifier for further practice.

A pacifier with a short, narrow nipple may be the most similar to the mother's nipple. This type of pacifier may help to establish a "natural" suckling pattern (Rosenfeld-Johnson, 1999a). However, other types of pacifiers (e.g., orthodontic) are available and may be appropriate for a particular child. This will require a clinical decision by the professional working with the child. Nonnutritive suckling on a pacifier will hopefully assist the infant in establishing the suckling pattern needed to express milk or formula from the breast or bottle. In addition, nonnutritive suckling on a pacifier, breast, or finger can also be calming and organizing for the infant. This is particularly important for infants with sensory concerns.

Infants who exhibit exaggerated tongue protrusion or tongue thrust patterns may also have difficulty taking a pacifier, as the pacifier will be ejected from the mouth with the tongue protrusion. This is particularly true in young infants with Down syndrome and cerebral palsy. In older infants and young children who exhibit exaggerated tongue protrusion or tongue thrust patterns, pacifier use must be carefully considered. A pacifier generally requires the infant to use the mouth in one way (i.e., the suckle pattern). The suckle-swallow pattern is a single plane, front-back tongue movement. In order for the older infant and young child to develop increasingly sophisticated oral motor skills for eating, drinking, and speaking, the tongue must learn to move in a variety of directions. Through pacifier use, exaggerated tongue protrusion or tongue thrust patterns may actually be strengthened in the older infant and young child, and the clinician and caregiver may have difficulty assisting the child in the development of other tongue movements (e.g., lateralization, elevation, and depression). Tongue lateralization is important for the development of tongue and jaw dissociation as well as the adequate management of solid food. Tongue elevation and depression are critical processes for precise speech production.

A variety of *mouth toys* are available with different surfaces, protuberances, and textures. The infant and young child can be assisted in the oral exploration of these toys. If the individual is posturally unstable, side lying, supine, and prone positions can be used during oral exploration. The clinician can place toys into the infant's hands and assist the infant in bringing the toys to his or her mouth. Changing the infant's position varies the activity. It is also important to provide the child with a variety of mouth toys so that he or she can learn to plan the movements needed to explore the different surfaces, protuberances, and textures.

As the infant matures, toys and other implements that encourage the child to "chew" can be introduced. Chewing is a good activity for developing the jaw musculature. Some toys with protuberances fit perfectly into the area of the infant's mouth that will eventually hold his or her molars. Chewing different textures provides the child with a variety of chewing experiences. Mouth toys, Chewy Tubes,® plumbing tubing, and bite blocks can be used to provide these experiences. The clinician is advised against using items to which the infant is sensitive. For example, some individuals are sensitive to latex. Therefore, nonlatex items need to be used with these individuals. It is important to provide mouth toys that are safe for oral use (Rosenfeld-Johnson, 1999a). Some toys contain materials or dyes that may not meet this criterion.

Boshart (1996) developed a booklet entitled *Mouthing Toys! An Instructional Booklet* and a set of mouth toys to accompany the booklet. Although the toys are designed for children ages 2 to 5 years, many of the ideas in the booklet are useful when working with children under the age of 2 years. Boshart suggests that mouthing sessions last for 5 to 15 minutes. The purpose of the mouth-

Carmen, a 21-month-old child with Down syndrome, seems to enjoy biting on the Massaging Action Teether while receiving massage to her arms and shoulders. The vibration from the toy seems to improve the muscle tone in Carmen's oral structures.

ing session can vary (e.g., to decrease hyperresponsivity, to increase sensory responsiveness, to improve dissociated movements of the oral structures, to grade oral movements, etc.).

Cheesecloth, which can be purchased in the cleaning section of the grocery store, can be used as a treatment tool. Cheesecloth is similar to gauze but has a slightly finer mesh. It can be used to present foods that may be unsafe for the infant or young child to eat. Dried fruit, meats, and other foods can be wrapped within the cheesecloth and presented to the child. A square of cheesecloth is cut using a single, double, or triple thickness. A triple thickness would be used if the clinician or caregiver does not want any of the food to come through the mesh. This would depend on whether the infant can manage food that may come through a single or double thickness. The food is placed in the center of the square of cheesecloth, and the remainder of the cheesecloth in gathered and twisted so that the food is held in a "sack" created by the fabric. The cheesecloth sack can then be placed on the child's gum surfaces in the area where the molars will emerge, and the child can be allowed to "chew." If the infant does not enjoy the feel of the dry cheesecloth within the mouth, the clinician or caregiver may moisten the cloth with water or another appropriate liquid. It is important that the liquid used to moisten the cloth does not conflict in any way with the food presented in the cloth. Water works well to moisten the cloth, as it does not disguise the tastes of the foods being presented. Fruit juice would generally be compatible with the taste of fruit.

Organza, which is a fabric that can be purchased in a fabric store, has been used by some clinicians to hold food for chewing (Beckman, 1997; Rosenfeld-Johnson, 1999a). This fabric can be used in a similar fashion as the cheesecloth described in the previous paragraph. It is reportedly a better tool than cheesecloth to use with individuals who tend to shred the cheesecloth with their teeth. Shredded cheesecloth may be aspirated (Rosenfeld-Johnson, 1999a).

The Baby Safe Feeder (see product sources in Appendix D) also allows the infant to experience table foods. It is comprised of a mesh bag that attaches to a handle the infant can hold. The feeder can be cleaned in the dishwasher and is advertised as appropriate for children ages 4 months to 2 years of age.

The topic of oral motor activities will be presented in Chapter 5. Some of the oral motor activities discussed in Chapter 5 will be appropriate for children in the birth to 2-year age group. However, many oral motor activities for children in this age group incorporate the use of food and liquid. This is discussed in the next section of the chapter.

Feeding/Eating/Drinking Activities

Feeding therapy is often an important portion of the oral motor treatment session for the infant. Many infants have difficulty with feeding or have gastrointestinal difficulties that affect feeding from birth. The type of feeding therapy incorporated into treatment is dependent on the maturation of the infant.

Young infants with oral motor concerns frequently have difficulty developing a *nutritive suckle* (i.e., the infant's tongue is under the nipple and moves front and back to express the liquid). As previously mentioned, stroking the infant's tongue in a rhythmic manner may assist the infant in establishing the necessary rhythm for the suckle. The strength of the suckle may also be an issue for the infant. In addition to the practice of suckling activities over time, the use of strategies, such as Beckman (1997) and other facilitation techniques, may assist in strengthening the musculature. Parents and caregivers can be taught to provide the infant with suckling practice throughout the day by providing the infant with frequent feedings for shortened periods of time. This strategy will help eliminate fatigue.

Rosenfeld-Johnson (1999a) suggests that a short, narrow nipple similar to the mother's nipple be used with most infants, including those with a weak suckle. According to Rosenfeld-Johnson (1999a), this type of nipple provides the infant with a "natural" suckling experience that can promote typical oral motor function. In addition, she suggests that a vacuum-type bottle be used. These bottles have a plastic pouch containing the formula or breast milk that can be compressed until the liquid meets the nipple. Playtex and other companies produce bottles of this type. If the infant has a weak suckle, Rosenfeld-Johnson (1999a) suggests that the feeder may assist the infant by rhythmically compressing the plastic pouch as the infant suckles. Using this type of bottle also allows the feeder to position the child in a fairly upright position so that the child's ear is above the mouth. In this position, liquid will be less likely to travel through the eustachian tubes to the middle ear spaces (Rosenfeld-Johnson, 1999a).

In addition to the method suggested by Rosenfeld-Johnson, some bottle nipples (e.g., Haberman premie nipple and Avent nipples) are easier for the infant to suckle than the standard bottle nipple. The Avent bottles also allow the child to be fed in an upright position and reportedly prevent colic secondary to the bottle design (i.e., the flow of the formula is controlled so that air is not swallowed). When the infant has developed an effectively strong suckle, nipples that require a stronger suckle are then introduced. There are a variety of Avent nipples designed for this purpose. This would also be a time when the child could move to using the method suggested by Rosenfeld-Johnson (1999a). The proper equipment and techniques can assist the infant in moving toward the development of a mature sucking pattern (i.e., the tongue moves up and down and the lips are active). The parents or caregivers may provide the infant with longer, less frequent feedings as the infant becomes more adept at bottle-feeding.

During *bottle* or *breast-feeding,* it is important for the clinician to observe whether the infant is using a wide excursion of the jaw while suckling or sucking. If the child is moving the jaw in wide excursions, then jaw support may be applied. Jaw support is given along the bony portion of the mandible. It is important for the infant's feeder to support the bony portion and not inhibit the movements of the tongue. The base of the tongue is connected to the soft tissue found posterior to the chin. Jaw support is supplied until the infant has the idea of suckling or sucking while using the jaw, tongue, and lips in a graded manner.

When working with young infants with oral motor difficulties, it is important to use a bottle with an appropriate nipple if the infant is bottle-fed. As previously mentioned, a short, narrow nipple similar to a mother's nipple may be an excellent choice (Rosenfeld-Johnson, 1999a). Enlarging the hole of a nipple is *usually not* recommended. Although this strategy may significantly increase the flow of the formula, it may also make the formula more difficult to control. The infant may then attempt to compensate for the increased flow by protruding or retracting the tongue in the mouth. Children with low muscle tone frequently protrude the tongue, whereas children with high muscle tone frequently retract the tongue to decrease formula flow (Rosenfeld-Johnson, 1999a). Tongue retraction ultimately may cause some significant difficulties with later developing eating and drinking skills, as the tongue has learned to retract to protect the airway. It is then more difficult for the tongue to learn to move in a dissociated manner (i.e., elevate, depress, and lateralize). Once the individual feels the need to protect something as life sustaining as the airway, he or she often has difficulty changing this pattern even after the danger has passed. *At times,* the hole in the nipple may be cross-cut, because cereal or other thickening agents are being mixed with the formula to increase calories, to thicken the formula so that the infant can more effectively manage the bolus, or to increase the weight of the formula to decrease reflux (Rosenfeld-Johnson, 1999a). These are valid reasons to enlarge the hole of the nipple.

As the infant matures, *spoon-feeding* is typically introduced around 4 to 6 months of age (Walter, 1994). It is important to use a spoon that is shaped similarly to the bowl formation made by the tongue when creating a bolus. It is also important to use a spoon that fits the size of the infant's mouth. A plastic coated or heavy plastic spoon (e.g., the Maroon Spoon) may feel more comfortable in the infant's mouth than a metal spoon. Some infants with oral tactile hypersensitivities may not like the feel of a metal spoon. The Maroon Spoon is available in two sizes and has a shallow bowl that approximates the natural tongue bowl shape. See Appendix D for companies that carry the Maroon Spoon. It should be noted that some infants with very small mouths might need to use a spoon that is smaller than the small Maroon Spoon.

When spoon-feeding an infant with oral motor concerns, certain concepts should be kept in mind. It is important to position the infant in the most stable position for the child. For many infants who are beginning spoon-feeding, this position is a semireclined position in an infant seat. As the infant gains postural stability, the child is moved gradually into a more upright position. When presenting the spoon to the infant, it is important to present the spoon in a level manner. This means that the spoon enters the infant's mouth from the front and not from above. The infant's head should also be level if possible. When most infants begin spoon-feeding, it is typical for them to exhibit slight extension in the head-neck area as they use the suckle-swallow pattern to manage the food from the spoon. At times, infants are extending their necks without the clinician or caregiver noticing. Individuals who have poor postural stability and difficulty developing mature oral movements during feeding may continue to exhibit extension in the head-neck area beyond the typical developmental period. These individuals often lean their heads back onto their shoulders. When the young child's head-neck area is hyperextended, the child may be at risk for aspiration. As the infant's oral and pharyngeal structures mature, there is less natural protection from aspiration (see Chapter 1).

In addition to placing the spoon in the infant's mouth in a level manner, it is recommended that the person feeding the infant apply a small amount of "weight" to the spoon while waiting for the child's lips to close around the spoon (Rosenfeld-Johnson, 1999a). This provides the infant with increased input regarding the placement of the spoon and also allows the child to process the movements needed for the lips to actively clear the spoon. When removing the spoon from the infant's mouth, the feeder should also remove the spoon in a level manner after the child's lips have closed around the spoon. *Do not tip the spoon upward* when removing it from the infant's mouth, as this does not require the child to actively use the lips to clear the spoon. One technique that is widely used while spoon-feeding individuals with oral motor concerns is the application of pressure into the body of the tongue. This technique must be used with *caution,* for the child's body must be appropriately aligned and the pressure into the tongue must be applied so that the tongue is depressed and not retracted. Applying too much pressure to the tongue often results in the tongue being pressed toward retraction, and this may actually strengthen the tongue protraction-retraction pattern.

Overland (1999) teaches a method of spoon feeding that encourages active lip movements and appropriate tongue position (i.e., inside of the mouth, waiting to form the bolus). She suggests that the child be spoon-fed using a lateral spoon position. The Maroon Spoon is a good spoon for this technique and, as previously mentioned, is available in two sizes (i.e., large and small). The spoon is presented laterally to the child's mouth so that the child's lips can actively remove the food from the edge of the spoon. The spoon handle touches the corner of the child's mouth. The spoon position is alternated so that the spoon handle alternately touches each corner of the child's mouth as the child removes the food from different sides of the spoon. The child's tongue, then, remains in the mouth, and only his or her lips are active in removing the food from the spoon (Overland, 1999). Active upper and lower lip movement during spoon-feeding is typically seen in children around 10 months of age (Morris & Klein, 1987). Suzanne Evans Morris, Sara Rosenfeld-Johnson (1999a), Lori Overland (1999), and others provide many practical techniques in their workshops.

Foods that require *chewing* are needed to stimulate the infant's chewing responses. Chewing is not generally stimulated with smooth spoon foods. The emergence of munching/chewing occurs between 5 and 7 months of age in the typical infant (Walters, 1994). As previously mentioned, the phasic bite reaction may be a precursor to the development of chewing (see Chapter 1). Therefore, it is important for the infant to have food or toys on which to chew during the period when this reaction is present (i.e., prior to 9 to 12 months). Some children with oral motor concerns experience limited opportunities to chew food during

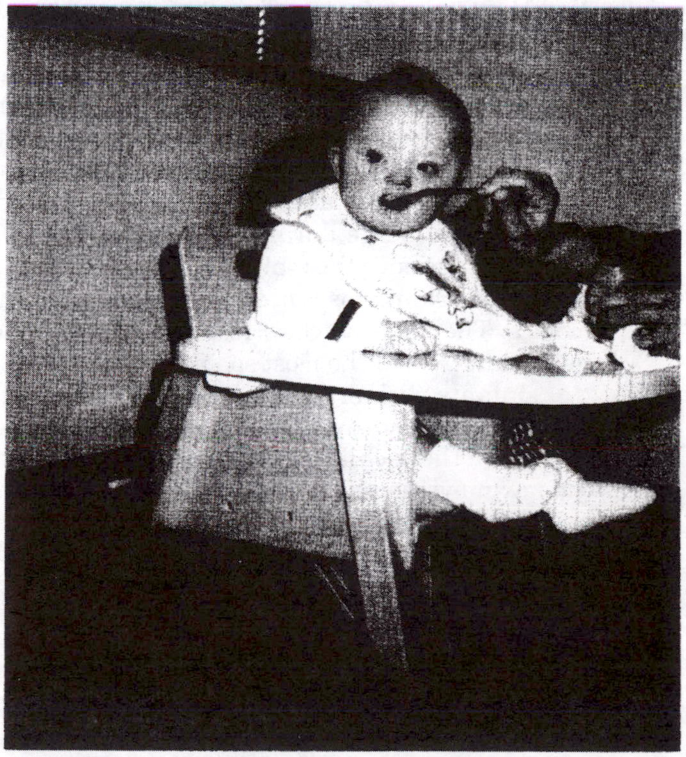

Michael, a 6-month-old child with Down syndrome, has active lip closure on the spoon, and his tongue is in an appropriate position for swallowing. He is seated in a Rifton Toddler Chair.

this critical learning period. These may be the individuals who are later reported to chew on "everything" but have not made the connection between chewing and swallowing food. Chewing also assists in the development of the musculature of the jaw. Therefore, it is important to provide the infant with safe, early chewing experiences.

As the typical infant matures, chewing movements become increasingly graded. The tongue and the jaw work together in this process. According to Alexander (1990), unsophisticated lateral tongue movements and lateral-diagonal jaw movements are seen in the 7-month-old child. The 10-month-old child can transfer food with the tongue from "side-to-center and center-to-side" and can move the jaw in "up-down, forward-backward, and circular-lateral-diagonal movements" (Alexander, 1990, p. 67). Side-to-side tongue lateralization and increased circular-diagonal jaw movements are noted in the 12- to 15-month-old child. "Well integrated rotary jaw movement with controlled grinding and shearing activity" continues to develop during the first 3 years of the child's life (Alexander, 1990, p. 67).

During chewing activities, the clinician can observe the strength of the infant's oral musculature, the infant's ability to create a bolus, and the quality of the child's chewing. The clinician can then address these concerns in treatment.

The infant's body needs to be as stable as possible during chewing activities, so the child has control over the distal movements in the mouth. For some infants and young children with oral motor concerns, chewing activities may need to begin in antigravity positions (i.e., side lying or prone). Chewing can also be facilitated with nonfood items or in supine. Supine is often not considered a good position for feeding, as the child may aspirate in this position. The child can be positioned in a semireclined position instead of supine and can be moved into a more upright position as stability develops in the body.

Foods can be placed in cheesecloth or organza as previously described to allow the infant to chew on the food without the risk of loosing control of the bolus. Certain foods, such as graham crackers and Veggie Stix (i.e., processed snack made from vegetables), have been used to provide children with early chewing experiences. These foods tend to dissolve in the mouth if they are not chewed. It is important for foods to be placed on the child's gums where the molars will emerge during chewing activities. This placement will allow the child to experience the typical location for food placement during chewing. Children with oral motor concerns frequently do not chew foods in the area of the molars. They tend to chew foods with the side teeth. The molar area plays an important part in the most sophisticated level of chewing (i.e., rotary chewing).

Infants with oral motor concerns may exhibit large, ungraded jaw movements beyond those seen in the typical developmental process. It may be helpful to provide these children with some jaw support until the child learns to grade the jaw movements during chewing. As previously mentioned, jaw stability is best provided by placing a hand along the bony portion of the mandible so that the soft tissue of the base of the tongue is not inhibited from movement. When providing jaw support, the clinician or care provider must be careful to maintain the child's head and jaw in appropriate alignment and not limit the jaw movement so much that the temporomandibular joint is adversely affected (i.e., moved out of alignment).

As the infant begins to develop chewing skills, a vertical munching pattern is usually observed. This may be related to the phasic bite reaction (see Chapter 1). Lateral, diagonal, and eventual rotary movements are seen as the child develops increasingly sophisticated chewing skills. Many children with oral motor concerns have difficulty developing rotary jaw movements for chewing. During feeding therapy, the clinician and caregiver can provide external support to stabilize the jaw as well as facilitate increasingly sophisticated movement patterns for chewing. This can provide the child with the knowledge of how the sophisticated movement may feel and can assist the child in developing the motor plan for these patterns. However, the facilitator must be *cautious* when manipulating the child's jaw, as the musculature must be physically and developmentally ready to move in lateral, diagonal, and rotary motions. The temporomandibular joint must also be properly aligned during chewing activities. This joint can be easily damaged or can become painful if not properly aligned. Children with oral motor concerns frequently do not have adequate muscle function to support the sophisticated patterns required in chewing and need to develop this prior to the active facilitation of these patterns. Many children will actively move the jaw in a graded manner once they have adequate muscle function. It is important for the clinician or caregiver to allow the child to do as much of the movement as possible without assistance, as the motor system learns best through active movement.

During chewing, the tongue moves the food toward the gums and what will eventually become the molar surfaces. The tongue also collects the food from these surfaces and creates a bolus so that the food can be safely and effectively swallowed. Tongue and jaw dissociation is seen when the infant begins to move the tongue laterally to place food on or retrieve food from the gum/molar surfaces.

Tongue lateralization is a developmental process. Refer to a resource such as *Pre-Feeding Skills* (Morris & Klein, 1987, 2000), for specific information on this process. According to Morris and Klein (1987, 2000), the child's tongue usually demonstrates an unrefined rolling motion or center-to-side movement at 7 months of age. By 24 months of age, the child typically exhibits sophisticated tongue tip lateralization to place and retrieve food.

Many young children with oral motor concerns have difficulty establishing tongue and jaw dissociation and accurate tongue movement. The child can participate in a variety of activities to improve these skills. The clinician can place food wrapped in cheesecloth or organza in a variety of locations on the child's gum surfaces to encourage the tongue to follow the placement of the food. As the child becomes more proficient in managing foods of increased texture, the clinician and the caregiver can create a game where food is placed in the child's cheek area or on the gum surfaces in a variety of locations and the child is required to retrieve the food with the tongue. Overland (1999) and Rosenfeld-Johnson (1999a) both recommend activities similar to these to encourage tongue and jaw dissociation. It is important to note whether the child is moving the jaw along with the tongue during these activities. As the child is developing tongue and jaw dissociation, the tongue and jaw may move together. As the child's oral motor skills become increasingly sophisticated, the tongue and jaw will move with greater dissociation. However, a significant amount of jaw movement may be noted in individuals who are having difficulty developing tongue and jaw dissociation. Jaw stabilization may need to be carefully provided for these individuals so that the tongue can learn to move separately from the jaw.

When the individual begins to lateralize the tongue, the jaw often starts to swing slightly to one side or the other as the individual manages food. This is the beginning of the movement pattern that will eventually develop into rotary chewing. Rotary chewing is a more sophisticated and efficient pattern than munching, as the lateral movement and grind used in this pattern can break the food down more efficiently for digestion than the vertical movement of the munching pattern. When the individual becomes efficient with chewing, he or she will typically lateralize the food to both molar surfaces while demonstrating a preference for chewing on one side.

When the individual's tongue can move independently of the jaw and lateralize food, a preferred side for food management and tongue lateralization is often noted. This is consistent with the lateral preferences occurring in motor function in other areas of the body (e.g., preference to use one hand or one foot more than the other during motor tasks). However, the side that the individual prefers for munching and chewing may or may not be the same one the individual prefers for other motor functions.

Biting also requires the individual to have graded control of the jaw. Many individuals with oral motor concerns do not take complete bites of food (i.e., biting completely through the food and not holding the food with the teeth while pulling the food away from the mouth with the hand). As the infant's teeth emerge, the clinician and caregiver can begin to encourage the child to take controlled bites of food. The central incisors typically erupt between 6 and 10 months of age (Perkins & Kent, 1986). The child will often begin by taking bites centrally. However, after the side teeth erupt, the young child may be observed to take bites using the side teeth. All of the deciduous teeth typically erupt by the time the child is 2 years of age (Perkins & Kent, 1986). Children can typically take a controlled, sustained bite from a soft cookie at 12 months of age and from a hard cookie by 21 months (Morris & Klein, 2000). If the child cannot take a sustained, controlled bite of food, graded jaw activities (e.g., chewing) and manual facilitation techniques (e.g., Beckman facilitation techniques, 1997; myofascial release, etc.) may assist the child in developing the muscle function needed for graded jaw movements. External jaw stabilization may again need to be carefully applied while the child is learning to take controlled bites. The use of external jaw stabilization has been discussed in a variety of contexts in this book. The analogy of the "dance" can again be used with the concept of jaw stabilization. The feeder must stabilize the child's jaw "just enough" to provide the child with the support and guidance needed to attain the desired movement. This is like one partner leading the other in a dance.

As the infant begins to develop jaw stability and control, the child gradually becomes ready for cup and straw *drinking.* Many parents begin providing infants with cup and straw-drinking experiences around 6 months of age. This usually begins with the parent or caregiver providing the infant with a single sip from a cup or straw held by the parent. Infants with oral motor difficulties frequently have difficulty transitioning from the bottle to the cup.

The use of a cut-out cup containing thickened liquid is often a good first step in moving the infant toward effective cup drinking. When the liquid is thickened, both the caregiver and the child have more control over the movement of the liquid. Juice may be thickened with applesauce, fruit puree, or stage 1 baby food fruit. Milk or formula may be thickened with baby rice cereal, unflavored yogurt, or smooth flavored yogurt. Liquids may also be thickened with commercially available thickeners such as Thick-It. The thickened liquid provides the child with increased sensory input. It is also easier for the child to control orally than thin liquids.

In the beginning stages of cup drinking, a small amount of liquid may be placed in the cup with a small amount of thickener. Cutout cups are available in several sizes to fit the size of the child's mouth. The cutout portion of the cup allows the clinician or caregiver to observe the flow of the liquid as it moves from

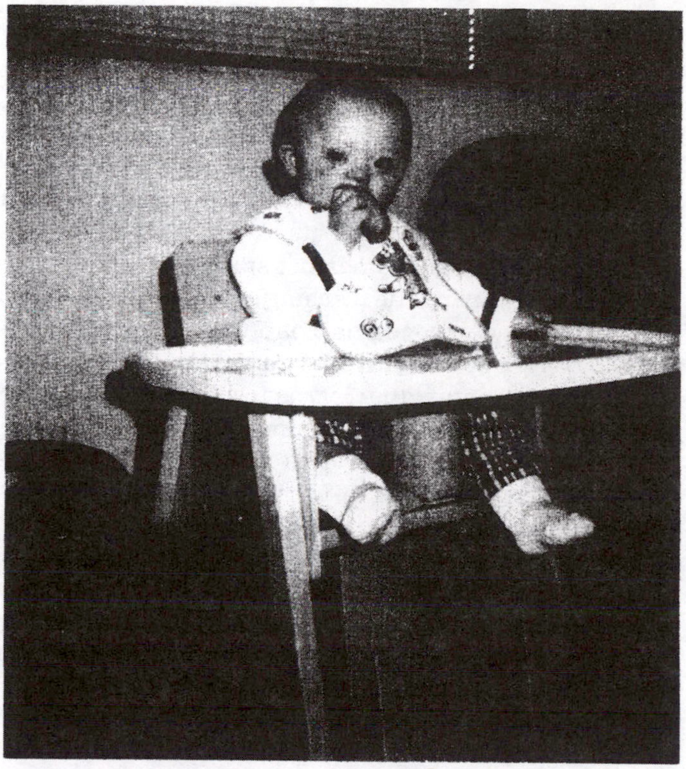

Michael, a 6-month-old child with Down syndrome, bites on a piece of Zwieback toast. Michael uses graded jaw movements to bite the large piece of toast.

the cup into the child's mouth. The cutout also allows the child to maintain appropriate head alignment during drinking (i.e., head and neck in alignment with the body or slight flexion of the head and neck; *no hyperextension* of the head or neck). Cutout cups are generally made of a strong but slightly flexible plastic so that the child may bite on the rim of the cup to initially attain jaw stability while learning to dissociate the movements of the lips and tongue from the jaw during drinking. Children may typically bite on the cup rim until 24 months of age (Morris & Klein, 1987).

The Sassy Infa-Trainer Cup is another type of cup that can be helpful in the teaching of cup drinking. This is a hard plastic, cylindrical cup with a lid. The cylinder is approximately the size of an infant's bottle. The flow of the liquid can be controlled by adjusting the positions of the lid. Slightly thickened liquid may also be placed into this cup. However, the liquid must be able to flow through the holes in the lid. The cup lid has a lip on which the infant may bite for stability. However, the lip is not flexible. The lip of the lid also provides the infant with the opportunity to use the lips to draw the liquid into the mouth. Cutout cups and the Sassy InfaTrainer Cup are available from a variety of sources. (See products list in Appendix D).

Many types of spouted cups are also available. Cups with hard spouts should be used with caution. Although they often provide a fairly easy transition from the bottle to a cup, the oral movement used by the child is usually similar to the oral movement used in drinking from a bottle. The use of the hard, spouted cup may actually strengthen the child's tendency to use a protraction-retraction pattern while drinking. However, some clinicians have found that the use of a soft, spouted cup not only assists the child in transitioning from the bottle to the cup, but can assist the child in developing the active lip movements required during cup drinking. The soft spout can be cut down as the child becomes more adept with the drinking process. This is one way to move a child toward the use of a cup with a recessed lid. Unfortunately, most cups with recessed lids have been taken off of the market. These are good cups to use when transitioning the child from the bottle to the cup, as the child can use jaw, lip, and tongue movements as though drinking from a regular cup with the cup lid providing safety against spillage.

During the teaching of cup drinking with individuals who are experiencing oral motor concerns, it is often important to provide the individual with external jaw support until the graded jaw movements for drinking begin to be learned. As the individual learns to stabilize the jaw, the jaw support may be gradually removed. Wide excursions of the jaw are frequently seen in infants who are learning to drink from a cup. The excursions decrease by about 18 months (Morris & Klein, 1987), when the child develops greater control over the musculature of the jaw, cheeks, lips, and tongue.

Straw drinking is frequently taught to the older infant. This can be done by placing a small amount of liquid in the straw (i.e., placing one end of the straw in the liquid while a finger is placed over the other end of the straw). The liquid may be thickened if needed. The child then sucks the small amount of liquid from the end of the straw while maintaining the head and neck in appropriate alignment (Morris & Klein, 1987). Liquid may also be frozen inside of a straw and the child can be taught to suck the liquid from the straw as it melts. Once the child has the idea of sucking small amounts of liquid from a straw, the child may be ready to learn to drink from a straw in the typical manner.

The clinician or caregiver may wish to create a straw from plumbing tubing that will allow the child to bite on the straw for jaw stability if needed. Plumbing tubing is available in many sizes and is safe for drinking. Other types of tubing, such as aquarium tubing, may not be safe for drinking (Beckman, 1997). Once the child learns to drink from a straw, it is important to observe the manner in which the child manages the straw. If the child's tongue is under the straw, then the clinician would want to find a way to teach him or her to use the lips more actively. When the tongue is placed under the straw, the child uses a protraction-retraction tongue pattern as opposed to the up and down tongue movement used in mature sucking. If the child has difficulty learning to place only the lips on the straw (rather than the upper lip and tongue on the straw), there are methods to teach active use of the lips for straw drinking. For example, a lip bumper can be created by placing a drilled cork (Morris & Klein, 1987) or a sponge rubber hair curler toward the end of the straw. A small amount of the straw protrudes from the cork or sponge rubber curler. The child is then required to place only the lips on the end of the straw as opposed to placing the tongue under the straw. Morris and Klein (1987, 2000) discuss the teaching of straw drinking in the book *Pre-Feeding Skills*.

Overland (1999) and Rosenfeld-Johnson (1999a) have also developed a variety of strategies for teaching appropriate straw drinking skills. Overland (1999) suggests the use of a Honey Bear container with a straw made of tubing to teach straw drinking. The Honey Bear container can be compressed so that the liquid can reach the child's mouth through the tubing during the learning process. Rosenfeld-Johnson (1999b) has developed a systematic Straw Drinking Hierarchy to assist the child in the development of graded jaw, lip, and tongue movement. Information about these techniques as well as products used with the techniques are available from Innovative Therapists International. (See product sources list in Appendix D.)

Many individuals with oral sensory and motor concerns also exhibit *constipation* and *liquid intake* issues. Liquid intake must be carefully monitored for these individuals. Children with these concerns are usually followed by the child's pediatrician and/or a pediatric gastroenterologist who may refer the child to be seen by a dietician or nutritionist. Although constipation may be exacerbated by low muscle tone in the body, inadequate liquid intake is frequently a concern for individuals with constipation. Liquid can be increased in an individual's diet using a variety of means. Pureed foods (i.e., homemade foods or baby food) often contain a significant amount of liquid. Popsicles can be made from fruit juice and/or fruit puree and may help facilitate liquid intake and acceptance of fruits. Fruit smoothies can also be served. These are cold, thick drinks made with fruit, milk/milk substitute/water, and ice. The acceptance of whole fruit is important for the individual with constipation, as the pectin under the "skin" of the fruit is said to be very helpful in alleviating the concern. As the child's oral motor skills become more sophisticated, he or she can safely learn to manage whole fruits containing the "skins." A variety of experiences with fruit tastes and textures can prepare the child for the acceptance of whole fruits when the child has developed the skill to safely manage them.

Finger feeding is introduced as soon as the infant is ready to use the hands and the mouth together to explore foods. This usually occurs at about 8 to 12 months of age (Walter, 1994). The clinician or caregiver may place the younger infant's fingers into foods and allow the child to taste the foods placed on his or her fingers. As the child matures and is able to manage foods of increasing texture, the older infant and caregiver can take turns placing pieces of food within the child's mouth. Food can be positioned on the child's lateral gum surfaces to encourage the development of tongue lateralization.

Young children appear to enjoy the act of feeding themselves. Although it is helpful for the child to learn to finger feed, it may also be important for the clinician and the caregiver to maintain the ability to feed the child. This can be established through *turn-taking* activities where the child learns that turn taking is part of the accepted routine during therapy and during meals. When children are learning to control their environment, they may initially reject the idea of taking turns. However, it is important for the clinician and caregiver to impress this idea on the child by being a good role model. This may entail allowing the child to take turns feeding the clinician, caregiver, other members of the family, and so on.

Based on their keen observational ability, children learn many skills during the first two years of life. Children tend to want to do what they see others doing. If a particular feeding strategy is being used only with the child exhibiting an oral motor concern, the child may notice this and begin to reject the strategy. This may occur after the child has been accepting the strategy for a period of time. Therefore, it may be important to *use the strategy with other members of the family* as well.

Children also respond well to the use of a *predictable routine,* where variations from the routine are introduced slowly. Feeding therapy should involve a predictable routine when possible. It is important to feed children at consistent times at home with the use of consistent oral motor techniques and strategies. The clinician can assist the parent or caregiver in establishing predictable routines for the child's mealtimes.

Another issue that often arises during feeding therapy is *food and liquid selectivity*. As previously discussed, children may not want certain foods or liquids based on taste, texture, smell, or temperature. Many individuals with oral motor concerns do not feel, taste, smell, or experience foods and/or liquids in the same way as many other people. Often, they require changes in the foods/liquids that will suit their particular sensory needs or preferences. It is important to observe factors affecting the child's acceptance or rejection of foods/liquids and make changes accordingly.

During feeding therapy, the transitions from one type of food or liquid to another can be systematically managed. Foods and/or liquids can be modified in a systematic manner to accommodate the individual's olfactory, taste, texture, and temperature preferences. The individual can move from a level of overselectivity to a more typical level of food/liquid acceptance. It is important to observe the foods and liquids accepted by the individual and move systematically toward acceptance of a more balanced diet at the individual's own pace.

The clinician can discover the types of foods and liquids preferred by the child via the case history and caregiver report. The child may prefer sweet foods, smooth foods, foods of increased taste, foods of increased texture, room-temperature food, thickened liquids, tart liquids, and so forth. Once the clinician discovers the child's preferences, a systematic plan can be made for introducing the child to varying food/liquid tastes, temperatures, textures, smells, and the like. It is important to introduce changes in foods/liquids slowly with the child who is very sensitive to small changes in the foods/liquids presented.

It is also important not to attempt to "trick" the child by placing or hiding other foods into the foods accepted by the child (e.g., meats placed in yogurt). It is crucial not to mix foods or liquids that would not normally be mixed (e.g., eggs and applesauce). The chart shown in Figure 4.3 may assist the clinician and caregiver in discovering the child's preferences and in planning a systematic approach to expanding the child's acceptance of a variety of foods/liquids.

The clinician would list the specific foods accepted or rejected (e.g., chocolate, yogurt, Welch's Grape Juice, etc.) or more general categories (e.g., cold drinks, bland foods, etc.). Factors that seem to have an impact on acceptance or rejection of the food or liquid (e.g., taste, temperature, texture, smell, etc.) can be identified by placing a check mark in the appropriate column. The clinician and care provider may then identify appropriate foods to try with the child based on this systematic analysis of the food or liquid characteristics accepted by the child. For example, if the child seems to prefer foods with intense tastes,

FIGURE 4.3 Systematic Evaluation of Foods and Liquids

FACTORS IMPACTING ACCEPTANCE/ REJECTION	TASTE	TEXTURE	TEMPERATURE	SMELL	OTHER
Foods or Liquids Accepted (list)					
Foods or Liquids Rejected (list)					
Foods or Liquids to Try (list)					

then other similar foods with intense tastes may be tried. See Chapter 2 for detailed information on each of the sensory systems.

Safe foods and liquids can be provided that will challenge the individual's sensory system and skill level. Safety must be considered first, as someone with an unrefined oral motor system may choke on foods or liquids that he or she is unable to manage. As previously discussed, foods for chewing may be initially wrapped in cheesecloth or organza. Liquids can be thickened to slow the liquid flow and increase sensory input. Textured foods that easily form into a bolus or dissolve quickly in the mouth are often considered safe first foods (e.g., some graham crackers, Lorna Doone cookies, cheese curls, and Veggie Stix). Small pieces of banana and lightly steamed fresh vegetables cut in strips may also be safe foods for some individuals. It is important that the individual's oral motor system is ready to safely manage foods and liquids prior to these being introduced.

Foods and liquids of increased texture allow the oral sensory system to know that food/liquid is present and needs to be acted upon. Individuals with oral motor concerns often exhibit difficulties with oral awareness and may respond well to textured food/liquid. At times, a care provider or clinician may be concerned that the child is not ready to manage foods of increased texture. When given the textured food, the individual may actually use more sophisticated oral motor patterns than he or she used with foods of a soft or smooth texture. Foods of increased texture can challenge the oral motor system to respond in a more sophisticated manner. However, these foods must be introduced to the child in a safe and systematic manner, so that the child is not placed at risk for choking.

Foods of mixed texture may be a significant challenge for some children with oral motor issues. The clinician should be aware that fruits and vegetables are foods of mixed texture that require the child to manage both the fiber and the juice of the food. Fruits and vegetables with skins have three textures that the individual will need to manage. For example, when eating a fruit, the child must chew the pulp and the skin while swallowing the juice that is being extracted in the chewing process. The skin will often require more chewing than the pulp. When sandwiches are presented or toppings are added to crackers, the child is required to manage mixed textures and tastes. Some children will reject foods of mixed texture or taste. These individuals frequently demonstrate sensory issues. However, other children will eat foods of mixed texture and taste as long as the foods easily form into a bolus. These individuals frequently have muscle function concerns. Many parents give their children peanut butter and jelly sandwiches or grilled cheese sandwiches without the crust. These are foods of mixed taste and texture that can form into a bolus easily. When beginning to present the older infant with foods of increased texture, it may be important to present single textures at first, progressing systematically toward foods of mixed texture.

When a child exhibits *difficulty accepting changes in texture,* it is important for the clinician to discern whether the child is having difficulty managing the texture or whether the child does not like the way the texture feels in the mouth. If the child is having difficulty managing the texture, then the skills needed to manage the food must be taught (e.g., tongue lateralization, sustained chewing, etc.). If the child does not like the feel of the food, then the food must be introduced in a systematic manner according to his or her preferences. The clinician and caregiver may begin by slowly increasing the texture of the food (e.g., thickening or adding less liquid to pureed foods, adding very small pieces of appropriate ground or crumbled food to a pureed food, etc.). As previously stated, it is important to mix only those foods that would be logically mixed. The clinician and care provider should not mix foods that they would not mix for themselves. The application of oral massage as well as providing the child with a variety of oral sensory experiences may also assist the child in accepting foods of increasing texture.

In the book *Pre-Feeding Skills* (1987, 2000), Morris and Klein discuss food transitions (i.e., moving from liquids to smooth solids, moving from smooth solids to lumpy solids, and moving from lumpy solids to chewy solids). They also discuss foods that can facilitate more normal movement and foods that can interfere with normal oral movement. These texture issues are very important to consider when working with infants and young children with oral motor concerns.

Another factor to be considered is *taste.* It is important to determine the infant's taste preferences. In the *Pre-Feeding Skills* book, Morris and Klein (1987, 2000) mention that infants seem to prefer sweet tastes. Breast milk is reportedly sweet in taste. This apparent taste preference may have something to do with the location of taste receptors on the tongue. The receptors for sweet tastes are reported to be found on the front of the tongue. This is the area of the tongue that young infants use initially in feeding. This early experience with sweet tastes may also explain why so many individuals seem to have a preference for sweet foods. Salty and sour tastes are experienced a little further back and toward the sides of the tongue. Bitter tastes are sensed toward the back of the tongue. This is the area where the child's gag response is still elicited after oral sensory experiences have apparently inhibited the response in other areas of the tongue. Poisonous items are often bitter tasting. Therefore, the ability to sense bitter tastes in the same area as the gag response may be a protective mechanism for the child.

For some children, certain food tastes may be too intense. However, many individuals prefer foods of increased taste, such as sweet or spicy foods. The individual may sense the taste of these foods more readily than bland foods. Adding appropriate spices and condiments to food may increase the individual's acceptance of a food. For example, cinnamon may be added to fruits, and spices, such as "Mrs. Dash," may be added to vegetables. Children may more readily accept fruits and vegetables if taste is increased. Appropriate sauces can also be added to foods to change taste; however, this will also change the texture of the food. Many children exhibiting exaggerated tongue protrusion or a tongue thrust pattern seem to prefer the addition of sauces to foods.

For those children who exhibit difficulty with the intensity of food tastes and seem to become overloaded by certain food tastes, the taste of the food may be gradually increased. A systematic approach would again be used in this process. The clinician and care provider would begin by adding small amounts of flavoring to the bland tasting foods that are accepted by the child. Flavoring, such as vanilla or maple flavoring, can be added, a "drop" at a time, to foods such as oatmeal. Jams and jellies can also add flavor to foods. A thin spread of jam, jelly, or cream cheese can be placed on a cracker, bagel, or piece of bread.

Food *temperature* may be another consideration when working with children with oral sensory concerns. Some individuals are not interested in foods at room temperature. Refrigerating or warming appropriate foods may stimulate an individual's interest in these foods. Fruits can be chilled, for example, or bananas can be served frozen. Supplements can be chilled or warmed according to an individual's preference. Other children prefer their foods at room temperature. These individuals may not accept foods that are warmed or chilled. The clinician and care provider will need to prepare foods for these individuals as close to room temperature as possible.

The *smell* of food is one factor that is frequently overlooked by the clinician when using food in treatment. The sense of smell and taste are interrelated. It seems to be the sense of smell that allows the individual to tell one sweet, salty, sour, or bitter taste from another. Some children with food preferences may be overwhelmed by the smell of some foods. Other children may seem to crave the smell of certain foods. Children with upper respiratory issues may not smell food as well as children who do not have these issues. The olfactory system has a powerful effect on how an individual responds to food. A human being's appetite may immediately increase when the smell of a food considered appetizing is perceived (e.g., the smell of baking bread for some individuals). On the other hand, a person may begin to feel sick if a smell is perceived as noxious (e.g., the smell of certain strong cheeses for some individuals). See Chapter 2 for greater detail regarding the responses of the various sensory systems.

New skills are learned most effectively through *variations* as opposed to doing an activity the same way each time (Morris, 1986, 1987a). This applies to feeding as well as other areas. For example, when learning to chew foods, it is important that the individual learn to chew a variety of foods that provide at least a slightly different chewing experience. Once the individual has demonstrated skill with a certain food, a caregiver can provide other foods that are similar to that food but different in some quality. Crackers, cookies, and bagels are examples of foods available in many different shapes, sizes, tastes, and textures. Fruits can also be prepared in many different ways. Small variations in the presentation of food or liquid can be used to systematically assist an individual in expanding his or her food repertoire. For example, if the child only accepts one brand of graham cracker, the care provider can buy other graham crackers that are similar to the cracker accepted by the child. When the child accepts similar graham crackers (e.g., honey graham crackers made by different manufacturers), then other types of graham crackers can be systematically introduced.

Many other eating and drinking activities can be used with the young child to facilitate improved use of the oral motor system. The book *Pre-Feeding Skills* by Morris and Klein (1987, 2000) contains many of these ideas.

Sound Play and Early Speech Production Activities

Sound play is a natural outgrowth of most oral motor work with infants and young children. As the infant becomes more aware of the oral structures through oral massage and other oral stimulation, the child is more likely to produce vocalizations. With increased oral awareness, the infant is also more likely to repeat vocalizations. The infant's vocalizations and other oral sounds (e.g., "raspberries") are encouraged whenever they occur during the treatment session. This can be done by responding to the child's sounds in the context of the conversation, imitating the child's sound and/or praising the child for making the sound. Responding to the child's sounds as if they are meaningful in the context of the conversation seems to be a very powerful reinforcer (e.g., "Oh, is that what happened? What happened next?"). The imitation of the child's sounds is also reinforcing to the child. A turn-taking routine where the infant and adult take turns producing sounds can be established using both of these strategies. This turn-taking routine is a first step in helping the child understand the turn-taking nature of conversation. Praising the child for producing sounds (e.g., "Nice talking!") seems to be a less powerful reinforcer for sound production than participation in an actual communication routine.

It is suggested that the clinician maintain an inventory of the sounds produced by the child. Initially, the infant will usually produce back vowel sounds. As the infant becomes more aware of the lips and tongue, sounds made with the lips and apex of the tongue may be heard. The sound that is perceived as a /d/ sound is initially produced by the infant using the apex or blade of the tongue as opposed to the tongue tip. During initial sound production, the infant may produce sounds with wide jaw excursions and minimal tongue and jaw dissociation. As the child matures, greater precision and dissociation is noted in his or her oral movements during sound production and early speech production.

A segment of each therapy session can easily focus on sound production. As the infant begins to produce certain sounds routinely, the clinician and caregiver can encourage the child to vary the sound. This may be a variation in intonation, length of sound production, or actual sound. If he or she is producing one particular back vowel sound, then perhaps the child can be encouraged to produce a different back vowel sound. If he or she is producing a particular lip sound, then perhaps the child can be encouraged to produce a different lip sound. This can be done using one of the cueing systems discussed here.

Hayden (Square, Goshulak, & Hayden, 1997) has developed a hierarchical system of moving the child's articulators into appropriate positions so that different speech sounds can be formed. This is called the *PROMPT system.* To effectively use the PROMPT system, the child must allow the clinician to therapeutically handle the oral mechanism and the clinician must be trained in the PROMPT approach. Major areas addressed by the PROMPT system are "postural support," "jaw-labial-lingual control," and "speech sequencing" (Square et al., 1997, p. 22).

Another approach to physically teaching sound production was described by Young and Hawk (1955) in the book entitled *Moto-Kinesthetic Speech Training.* Young and Hawk stressed the importance of considering the whole child (i.e., physically, mentally, and psychologically) in the process of moto-kinesthetic speech training. Children are placed in supine when initially receiving this type of treatment, decreasing the effect of gravity on the jaw. Auditory input is provided simultaneously with the physical manipulation of the musculature. The oral musculature is assisted in attaining a standard goal that is related to the shaping of the air current for speech sound production. When using this method, sounds are not taught in isolation but are coarticulated. This is consistent with the way speech is produced. Consonant sounds are taught by combining them with the back vowel sound "a" as in the word *cat.* This back vowel sound is one that most children can produce. With the exception of the "h" sound, the consonant sounds presented initially in the book are easy for the child to see (e.g., "wh," "f," voiceless "th," and "p"). It should be noted, however, that this sequence is not developmental in nature. Voiceless sounds appear to be taught first, vowels other than the "a" sound appear to be taught next, and voiced sounds appear to be taught last based on the sequence presented in the book. Once consonant-vowel combinations are established by the child, consonant-vowel-consonant combinations are developed. The sounds "l" and "r" are described as vowel-like in nature and are some of the last sounds to be described. The directions for establishing each sound are described in Appendix

C. Note that the sequence is different from that described earlier as voiceless and voiced cognates have been placed together. The clinician may choose to teach the voiceless and voiced cognates together or may wish to separate the teaching of these, depending on the needs and abilities of the client. Moto-kinesthetic speech training is presented in this chapter on infants, because the clinician may begin to use some of these techniques with infants and young children as they are beginning to produce and combine sounds. If this approach is used, it may be important for the speech-language pathologist to consider the developmental sequence of sound acquisition during the facilitation of speech sounds. Many resources are available on this topic (e.g., Kent, 1999).

Jelm (1995b) has developed a system of visual-tactile cues. She has developed a cue for most phonemes. In the Jelm cueing system, voiced and voiceless cognates have similar cues. For example, the /p/ and /b/ phonemes are cued by tapping the puffed cheek once lightly, as if pushing the air from the cheek. The cues are performed by the clinician or caregiver and are observed by the child. The child is also encouraged to perform the cues. The visual-tactile cues work well with older infants and young children. The cues can be easily incorporated into the child's gestural system. If the child is learning to use sign language to augment communication, visual-tactile cues can become part of his or her signal language system. The consistent use of visual-tactile cueing can significantly boost the child's speech intelligibility. This type of cueing works particularly well when motor planning concerns are present.

Encouraging the infant or young child to vocalize can be a challenge at times. If the child has only weak vocalizations or cannot sustain the vocalizations, the clinician must examine the infant's respiratory and vocal mechanisms. Some infants do not have adequate respiratory support to produce strong, sustained vocalizations. If this is the case, consult with the child's physical therapist for assistance in developing a program to improve respiration. This may involve the use of therapeutic techniques, such as myofascial release, neuro-developmental treatment, or Feldenkrais's "Awareness through Movement." Some infants require physical assistance in learning to breathe properly. If the infant's vocal mechanism is weak, stronger closure of the vocal folds may occur when the child is exerting energy (e.g., pushing up while in prone, grasping a finger or toy).

An increase in vocalization is often observed in infants and young children during movement activities. Therefore, the movement activities introduced in the beginning of the therapy session may enhance the child's ability to vocalize. The increase in vocalization during movement is believed to occur at least partially as a result of stimulation to the vestibular system. Refer to Chapter 2 for a thorough discussion of the vestibular system and its potential connections to other sensory systems.

Once the infant or young child has the ability and the idea of how to vocalize, this can be further encouraged through activities that involve vocal reverberation. The child may enjoy vocalizing into containers that echo the voice (e.g., plastic milk bottles with the tops cut off, paper towel cardboard tubes, etc.). There is an inexpensive toy that echos the child's voice and is shaped like a microphone called the Echo Mic. This can often be purchased in toy stores. Some tape recorders with microphones can also act as amplifiers. Infants and young children appear to enjoy hearing their voices amplified, and this activity can reinforce vocalization. The child and the clinician or caregiver can take turns vocalizing into the devices. The clinician and caregiver can encourage the child to extend and vary vocalizations using this technique.

Treatment Sources

For 13 years, the book *Pre-Feeding Skills* by Morris and Klein (1987) has been an excellent resource for oral motor treatment ideas when working with infants and young children. The book clearly explained the many processes involved in feeding and suggested a menu of treatment ideas for each type of difficulty encountered (e.g., jaw instability, jaw thrust, exaggerated tongue protrusion, etc.). The treatment section of the book was extremely user-friendly in that it suggested the many possible causes for the limiting oral motor patterns observed and then suggested a great number of options for working with each pattern. The treatment ideas presented in *Pre-Feeding Skills* were particularly helpful when working with children experiencing significant physical involvement. The book also had sections devoted to infants born prematurely and infants receiving feeding through a gastrostomy tube. Topics such as reflux and toothgrinding (i.e., bruxism) were discussed. This book was a highly recommended resource for clinicians working with infants and young children demonstrating oral motor concerns.

Pre-Feeding Skills: A Comprehensive Resource for Mealtime Development (Morris & Klein, 2000) is the greatly expanded and revised second edition of this outstanding resource. Morris and Klein have added many new chapters on topics such as sensory issues that affect feeding, failure to thrive, children with autism, and diagnostic testing. Most of the original chapters have been updated, expanded, and refined. The new book's focus is expanded to cover the complete mealtime experience and feeding relationship. Klein and Morris (1999) also published another book entitled *Mealtime Participation Guide.* This book contains many of the mealtime participation experiences that provided experiential learning for the clinician in the original *Pre-Feeding Skills* book.

Disorders of Feeding and Swallowing in Infants and Children: Pathophysiology, Diagnosis, and Treatment (1994), edited by Tuchman and Walter, is another excellent source of information regarding oral motor and swallowing concerns in infants and young children. This book has chapters on swallowing physiology and neurology, feeding and swallowing issues and disorders, the roles of the speech-language pathologist and occupational therapist, the management of behavioral and nutritional concerns, videofluoroscopy and other diagnostic tools, gastroesophageal reflux and pulmonary issues, as well as other topics. The many medical issues related to pediatric oral motor and swallowing concerns are explained in a clear and concise manner.

Pediatric Swallowing and Feeding: Assessment and Management (1993), edited by Arvedson and Brodsky, is an extremely useful resource for the clinician. This book covers the assessment and treatment of children with oral motor and swallowing concerns. Both medical and therapeutic management is discussed. Specific chapters are presented on the management of swallowing difficulties, nutrition, drooling, and craniofacial disorders. The book contains many charts and photographs to illustrate the information presented as well as a user-friendly oral-motor and feeding evaluation form in a checklist format.

INTERACTIVE CASE EXPERIENCES

The interactive experiences allow the reader to practice using the information from the chapter. These experiences challenge the reader to think of the possibilities for each of the cases. The answers to the questions in the interactive case experiences are for the reader to decide. Given the following information, what treatment ideas might you try with these infants?

Corey

Corey is a 3-month-old child with Down syndrome. She was born following a full-term pregnancy. Her delivery was uncomplicated, and her general health at birth was good. Corey appears to have normal hearing; she has not had any episodes of otitis media. She seems to be a very alert child who is visually attentive to her environment. Corey has moderate low muscle tone throughout her body as well as loose ligaments connecting bones in her joints. When she is lying on her back (in supine), she exhibits an extensor pattern (i.e., she extends her neck, arches her back, and extends her arms and legs). Corey exhibits an open mouth posture. She accepts touch to her cheeks and to the inside of her mouth. However, she seldom brings her hands or toys placed into her hands to her mouth. Corey continues to drink formula from a three-holed nipple, as she reportedly tires easily when drinking from the single-holed nipple. While drinking, Corey's jaw moves rhythmically but in wide excursions. She exhibits a significant amount of reflux. Corey does not yet eat solid food.

1. What positions might you try with Corey?
2. What types of movement might you use with Corey?
3. What types of oral stimulation might you provide Corey?
4. What changes might you suggest in Corey's feeding?
5. What resource(s) might you use to find more information on reflux?
6. What components would you include in an oral motor treatment session for Corey?

Jeremy

Jeremy is a 16-month-old child who was born prematurely at 30 weeks gestation and was diagnosed with cerebral palsy. He has a history of ear infections and reflux. He is being treated for both his otitis media and reflux with medication. Jeremy exhibits low muscle tone in the trunk of his body. His shoulders are often elevated, and he frequently rests his neck and head on his shoulders. He exhibits lip retraction and tongue retraction, and he has high muscle tone in his arms and legs.

Jeremy is fed primarily via a gastrostomy tube but is beginning to accept some foods and liquids by mouth. He will drink several ounces of thickened juice from a soft, spouted cup but will not accept any other liquid from the cup. When he drinks from a cup, he bites on the spout for stability. When he eats from a spoon, he moves his jaw in an ungraded manner and occasionally bites on the spoon.

Jeremy exhibits a hypersensitive gag response and does not appear to want touch on his face or in his mouth. He resists toothbrushing. Jeremy will only accept smooth foods such as some stage I baby food fruits and vanilla yogurt. He also appears to prefer that his foods be presented at room temperature. He seems to prefer food that is sweet but not too intense in taste. When presented with food containing any type of "lumps," he immediately gags.

When a small piece of graham cracker is placed in Jeremy's mouth, he does not gag. However, his tongue moves in a protraction-retraction pattern and the small piece of graham cracker is pushed out of Jeremy's mouth. He bites and chews on mouth toys. Jeremy is very responsive to praise, and he appears to be a "visual learner." He is cognitively delayed.

1. What would be some positioning considerations for Jeremy?
2. What type of movement activities would you choose for Jeremy, considering the mixed muscle tone in his body?
3. What would you do to inhibit Jeremy's hypersensitive gag response and facilitate his acceptance of touch?
4. How would you systematically expand Jeremy's repertoire of acceptable foods and liquids?
5. How would you teach Jeremy to move his tongue in a more sophisticated manner?
6. What components would you include in an oral motor treatment session for Jeremy?

5

Ages 2 to 4

A Time to Refine Oral Motor Development

This chapter will focus on appropriate oral motor tools and techniques for individuals in the 2- to 4-year age group. Many of the tools and techniques described for younger children can continue to be used. Oral motor work is a continuum of care. For some children who are developmentally functioning at the birth to 2-year level, ideas from Chapter 4 may be appropriate. It should be noted that the placement of information according to age levels in this book is meant only as a general guide. For example, the Assessment of Oral Motor Functions by Elizabeth Mackie (1996a) discussed in this chapter may be an appropriate assessment for children ages 12 months to 2 years in addition to the Developmental Pre-Feeding Checklist by Suzanne Evans Morris and Marsha Dunn Klein (1987, pp. 75–82; 2000, Appendix B; Klein & Morris, 1999, pp. 480–509) discussed in Chapter 4. Another example would involve the use of cueing strategies. Although cueing techniques are discussed in this chapter, some children are ready for the cueing of sounds as early as 8 months of age. Decisions to use specific assessment and treatment tools should be based on the needs of each individual.

ASSESSMENT

When assessing children in the 2- to 4-year age range, it is important to have the parent or caregiver provide a thorough case history. (See Chapter 4 for suggested case history form.) During the assessment process, the clinician will observe the child's body and oral structures at rest and when the child is performing oral motor tasks. It is also important to observe the child during eating and drinking activities as well as during imitative oral movement and speech production tasks. Eating and drinking activities provide important information about the function of the oral musculature. Muscle function and motor planning issues can be identified during the oral motor assessment. A few assessment tools will be discussed here. See Appendix A for a complete reference list of the assessment tools presented in the book.

The Assessment of Oral Motor Functions, found in the book *Oral Motor Activities for Young Children* by Elizabeth Mackie (1996a, pp. 9–22), is a very thorough and user-friendly assessment of the oral motor skills of young children. Oral motor function is assessed while the individual is performing a quiet activity, producing speech, performing oral motor tasks, as well as eating and drinking. The assessment is a checklist format and may also be modified for various populations and age groups.

The general assessment tool entitled Oral-Motor Assessment Checklist (Bockelkamp, Ferroni, Kopcha, & Silfies, 1997) in Chapter 4 may also be used with any variety of age groups and populations. If the clinician is in need of a short assessment format, this checklist may be the tool of choice.

Components of an Oral Motor Evaluation

The following is a comprehensive list* of components that may be part of the oral motor evaluation. The oral motor evaluation for each client is tailored for that client's needs and may or may not consist of all of the components listed. A detailed discussion of the information provided in this list will be presented in sections of the chapter following the list. The clinician may choose to develop his or her own assessment tool based on the information provided here.

Body and Mouth

- Posture and stability
- Responses to sensory input
- Respiration and phonation
- Oral and facial structures
- Oral muscle tone/jaw posture
- Lip posture and muscle tone
- Tongue position and muscle tone
- Drooling
- Tooth grinding (bruxism)
- Involuntary oral movements (e.g., fasciculations, tics, etc.)
- Overflow of movement

Eating and Drinking

- Management of foods (jaw, lip, and tongue movements)
  —Intake method (e.g., spoon, finger-feeding, fork, etc.)
  —Spoon-feeding
  —Biting
  —Chewing
  —Bolus formation
  —Swallowing
- Management of liquids (jaw, lip, and tongue movements)
  —Intake method (e.g., bottle, cutout cup, etc.)
  —Bolus formation
  —Swallowing

**Sources:* C. Boshart, *Oral-Motor Seminar: "Hard Tissue Analysis" Supplement* (Temecula, CA: Speech Dynamics, Inc. [video], 1995); J. M. Jelm, *Assessment and Treatment of Verbal Dyspraxia* (Baltimore, MD, workshop, 1995); L. Kumin, M. Goodman, and C. Councill, "Comprehensive Speech and Language Intervention for School-Aged Children with Down Syndrome," *Down Syndrome Quarterly, 1,* (1) (1996): 1–17; A. D. Long, D. C. Bahr, and L. Kumin, *The Battery for Oral-Motor Behavior in Children* (unpublished test, 1998); E. Mackie, *Oral-Motor Activities for Young Children* (E. Moline, IL: LinguiSystems, Inc., 1996).

Oral Motor Tasks

- Jaw
  —Movement (open, close)
  —Strength
  —Coordination and accuracy
- Lips/Cheeks
  —Movement (puckering, retraction)
  —Strength
  —Coordination and accuracy
- Tongue
  —Movement (protrusion, retraction, elevation, depression, lateralization)
  —Strength
  —Coordination and accuracy

Speech Production

- Jaw
  —Movement
  —Strength
  —Coordination and accuracy
- Lips/Cheeks
  —Movement
  —Strength
  —Coordination and accuracy
- Tongue
  —Movement
  —Strength
  —Coordination and accuracy

The components of an oral motor evaluation can apply to the assessment of an individual at any age. However, the evaluator needs to have a working knowledge of development, so that developmental variations can be taken into consideration. For example, "well integrated rotary jaw movement and controlled grinding and shearing activity" continues to develop during the first three years of the child's life (Alexander, 1990, p. 67). Therefore, the jaw movements of a 2-year-old child are not expected to be as sophisticated as the jaw movements of a 3-year-old child. As another example, "the presence of tongue thrust may be a normal but transient occurrence during mixed dentition" (Pierce, 1978, p. 17). Mixed dentition (i.e., when the mouth contains both deciduous teeth and permanent teeth) can occur until children are 10 to 13 years of age (Perkins & Kent, 1986). Developmental checklists as well as articles and books on development can provide the clinician with the developmental information needed to make accurate judgments during assessment. (See developmental information provided in Chapter 1.)

Assessment of the Body and Mouth

It is important to observe the individual's body at rest and while the individual is performing other motor tasks, such as speech. The individual's *posture, stability, responses to sensory input, as well as respiratory and phonatory control* can be assessed while the individual is seated and while the individual is standing or moving. The following questions are important to consider (Long, Bahr, & Kumin, 1998; Mackie, 1996a):

- Does the individual have adequate postural control?
- Are the individual's trunk, shoulders, neck, and head in appropriate alignment? If not, can a change in position assist with alignment (e.g., placing the individual in a chair where hips, knees, and ankles are at 90 degrees)?
- How does the individual respond to sensory stimulation (e.g., vestibular, tactile, proprioceptive, etc.)? Is the individual hyporesponsive or hyperresponsive? Does the individual exhibit sensory defensiveness or sensory overload? (See Chapter 2 for more detail on this topic.)
- Does the individual have adequate respiratory control for speech or sound production? If not, can a change in position or an applied technique assist with improved respiration?
- Does the individual have adequate phonatory control for speech and sound production? If not, can a change in position or an applied technique assist with improved phonation?

The individual's *oral structures* can be assessed while the individual is at rest and while performing gross and fine motor activities. Photographs may be taken to assist with this assessment and can be useful in documenting treatment progress. Structural deviations and sensory concerns can have a significant impact on the individual's adequate production of speech. These issues can also be the reason that an individual continues to demonstrate unsophisticated eating and drinking skills. The following questions may be considered during the assessment (Boshart, 1995a; Long, Bahr, & Kumin, 1998; Mackie, 1996a; Shipley & McAfee, 1992):

- Is the horizontal width of the individual's face approximately the width of the eye times five (Boshart, 1995a)? If not, a narrow face may indicate the presence of a narrow palate and a wide face may indicate the presence of a wide palate. This can affect tongue placement for adequate oral motor function.
- Are the center corners of the individual's eyes in line with the widest part of the individual's nose (Boshart, 1995a)? If not, a narrow nose may indicate difficulties with breathing through the nose. This can also affect jaw position and tongue placement for adequate oral motor function.
- If imaginary lines were drawn at the individual's hairline, base of eyebrow, base of nose, and base of chin, would the individual's face be divided into equal thirds (Boshart, 1995a)? If not, the jaw, hard palate, and tongue may be out of position for adequate oral motor function.
- If an imaginary line was drawn from the bridge of the individual's nose, to the philtrum, and then to the front of the chin while the individual is viewed from the side, would the individual's facial structures follow this line (Boshart, 1995a)? If not, does the individual's face appear convex or concave? This structural deviation can result in the jaw, hard palate, and tongue being out of the appropriate position for adequate oral motor function.
- If an imaginary line was drawn from the bottom of the individual's ear to the point of the individual's chin while the individual is viewed from the side, is the angle of the line 26 degrees (plus or minus 4 degrees) to the horizon (Boshart, 1995a)? If not, the size of the nasopharynx and oropharyn-

ynx may be reduced or expanded and may affect adequate oral motor function.

- If the individual is viewed from the side, is the angle of the nose and the philtrum 90 degrees to 100 degrees (Boshart, 1995a)? This may indicate the type of occlusion exhibited by the individual.
- What is the relationship of the mandible to the maxilla at rest? Is the mandible separated from the maxilla by more than 1 to 3 millimeters in the molar area (Boshart, 1995a)? Is the mandible protruded, retracted, or misaligned in some other fashion?
- Do the individual's lower first molars rest one-half tooth ahead of the upper first molars, and are the top front teeth resting 1 to 3 millimeters in front of the lower front teeth (Boshart, 1995a)? If not, does the individual exhibit an overbite, underbite, closed bite, or cross bite?
- Has the individual's dentition erupted normally? Use the checklist found in Table 5.1.
- Does the individual have a normal hard palate? If not, is the hard palate high, narrow, v-shaped, etc.?
- Does the individual exhibit hypernasality or hyponasality?

TABLE 5.1 Dentition Checklist

DECIDUOUS DENTITION	MANDIBULAR AGE OF ERUPTION	PRESENT/ ABSENT (+/–)	MAXILLARY AGE OF ERUPTION	PRESENT/ ABSENT (+/–)
Central incisors	5–9 months		6–10 months	
Lateral incisors	7–20 months		8–10 months	
First molars	10–12 months		14–16 months	
Cuspids	16–18 months		18–20 months	
Second molars	20–24 months		24–30 months	
PERMANENT DENTITION				
First molars	6–7 years		6–7 years	
Central incisors	6–7 years		7–8 years	
Lateral incisors	7–8 years		8–9 years	
First bicuspids	10–12 years		10–11 years	
Cuspids	9–10 years		11–13 years	
Second bicuspids	11–12 years		10–12 years	
Second molars	11–13 years		12–13 years	
Third molars	17–25 years		17–25 years	

Sources: W. H. Perkins and R. D. Kent, *Functional anatomy of speech, language, and hearing: A primer* (Boston: Allyn and Bacon, 1986), p. 131; R. B. Pierce, *Tongue thrust: A look at oral myofunctional disorders* (Lincoln, NE: Cliffs Notes, Inc., 1978), p. 31.

- Does the soft palate retract symmetrically when the individual produces the /a/ sound? Do any other structures assist with velo-pharyngeal closure?
- What type of oral/facial muscle tone does the individual exhibit (i.e., normal, flaccid, spastic, fluctuating)? Is different muscle tone observed in different groups of muscles?
- What type of muscle tone is observed in the individual's lips? Are the individual's lips together or separated at rest? If the individual's lips are separated, does the individual breathe through the mouth?
- In what position does the individual's tongue rest? Is it outside of the mouth, on the bottom lip or teeth, at the bottom of the mouth or in a typical resting position (i.e., tongue tip/apex to alveolar ridge)?
- How does the individual respond to sensory stimulation (e.g., tactile, proprioceptive, smell, taste, etc.) presented to the oral structures? Is the individual hyporesponsive or hyperresponsive? Does the individual exhibit sensory defensiveness or sensory overload? See Chapter 2 for more detail on this topic.
- Does the individual drool? If so, is the individual aware of this? Are there times or situations when drooling increases or decreases for the individual?
- Does the individual exhibit toothgrinding (i.e., bruxism)? Are there times or situations when the bruxism increases or decreases? Toothgrinding may indicate that the individual is seeking deep sensory input in the jaw.
- Does the individual exhibit any involuntary oral movements (e.g., fasciculations, tics, tremors, etc.)?
- Does the individual move the oral structures when moving other parts of the body (e.g., tongue out when using hands, clenching teeth when moving hands or other areas of the body)? This may indicate difficulty with dissociation of movement in the body.

Assessment of Eating and Drinking

The assessment of eating and drinking can provide the clinician with important information regarding the function of the oral musculature. Muscle tone and strength as well as coordination and accuracy can be assessed for the processes of eating and drinking. It is also important to assess food and liquid selectively concerns. (See Systematic Evaluation of Foods and Liquids in Chapter 4.)

Individuals in any age group may exhibit behavioral concerns related to eating and drinking. This can occur in children as well as adolescents and adults. The behavioral concerns are usually related to sensory issues that have gone unresolved. The appropriate assessment and treatment of individuals with behavioral feeding concerns can be extremely challenging for the clinician and the care provider. Chapters 2 and 3 contain information regarding evaluation and treatment of sensory concerns. On occasion, a behavioral approach is needed for a period of time in addition to a sensory approach during treatment to successfully manage behavioral concerns that affect eating and drinking. This is often needed if the individual is refusing food to the point that it becomes a health concern. There are a number of clinics and feeding programs in the United States that focus on this concern in children. These are frequently affiliated with hospitals, and many are listed on the Internet.

When assessing the individual's *eating skills,* the clinician can evaluate the individual's jaw, lip, and tongue movements during the management of different food textures. The following questions are important to consider (Jelm, 1995b; Long, Bahr, & Kumin, 1998; Mackie, 1996a):

- What intake method(s) are used by the individual (e.g., finger-feeding, spoon-feeding, other)?
- If the individual is eating from a spoon, how does the jaw move? Are jaw movements graded (i.e., jaw opens just enough for the spoon to enter the mouth)? Are jaw movements symmetrical?
- When eating from a spoon, does the individual actively use the lips to clear food from the spoon? Does the bottom lip actively form a seal on the spoon? Does the upper lip actively clear food from the spoon (i.e., the musculature of the upper lip moves downward and inward to clear the spoon)? If the individual is not actively using the lips, how is the spoon being cleared (e.g., with the teeth, with the jaw closing and the individual pulling the spoon from the mouth with the hand)?
- Does the individual loose any food from the mouth while eating from a spoon? If so, does the individual demonstrate awareness of this?
- Does the individual's manner of removing food from the spoon change dependant upon the food type or texture (e.g., pudding versus cereal with milk)?
- After the food is removed from the spoon, does the individual close the lips and manage the food or do the individual's lips remain open?
- Does the individual exhibit exaggerated tongue protrusion, a tongue thrust, or a tongue-pumping pattern when eating spoon foods?
- When taking bites of food, does the individual use graded jaw movement (i.e., jaw opens just enough to take the bite)? Are jaw movements symmetrical?
- Does the individual bite completely through food, or does the individual stabilize the food with the teeth and then pull the food away from the mouth with the hand? Does this change, depending on the texture of the food presented (e.g., "crisp" foods versus "chewy" foods)? Difficulty biting completely through foods may indicate that the individual has a jaw strength and/or stability issue.
- Does the individual take bites using the front teeth or does the individual take bites using the side teeth? Is this related to the individual's pattern of dentition? If the individual is missing teeth or has improperly aligned dentition, taking central bites may be difficult.
- Does the individual tend to place large amounts of food in the mouth? If so, the individual may have decreased oral awareness.
- How does the individual's jaw move while chewing food? Does the individual use an up and down munching pattern, components of a rotary chewing pattern, or a coordinated rotary chewing pattern?
- Does the individual seem to have a preferred side for chewing?
- While chewing does the individual close the lips and manage the food or do the individual's lips remain open?
- Does the individual loose any food from the mouth while chewing? If so, does the individual demonstrate awareness of this?
- Does the individual lateralize food to both molar surfaces using the tongue tip?
- Can the individual transfer food across midline using the tongue?
- Can the individual retrieve food from each molar surface and/or each sulci using the tongue?

- Does the individual adequately form a bolus? Is this different, depending on the food texture presented (e.g., foods that tend to form a cohesive bolus versus those that do not)?
- Does the individual exhibit a typical swallowing pattern or a tongue thrust/tongue-pumping pattern?
- Does food remain on the individual's tongue or in the individual's mouth after the swallow? This may indicate inadequate bolus formation and/or use of an atypical swallowing pattern.
- Does the individual cough at any time when managing foods? This may indicate incoordination of the swallow.
- Does the individual have a wet sounding voice after swallowing foods or liquids? This may indicate a swallowing concern.

When the individual is managing *liquids,* it is important for the clinician to evaluate jaw, lip, and tongue movements as the individual manages liquids of different texture, taste, and temperature. The following questions are important to consider (Jelm, 1995b; Long, Bahr, & Kumin, 1998; Mackie, 1996a):

- What intake method(s) are used by the individual (e.g., breast, bottle, cup, syringe, etc.)? If the individual is drinking from a cup, what type of cup is being used (e.g., regular cup, cutout cup; soft, spouted cup; hard, spouted cup; cup with recessed, slotted lid; straw cup)?
- Does the individual bite on the cup, straw, or bottle nipple to obtain jaw stability?
- Does the individual's jaw move in a graded manner during the activity of drinking?
- Does the individual have adequate lip closure on the cup, straw, or nipple?
- Where is the individual's tongue during the drinking process (e.g., inside the mouth; under the cup, straw, or nipple; etc.)?
- How does the individual move the tongue during the process of drinking (e.g., front/back, up/down, etc.)?
- Does the individual demonstrate a coordinated swallowing pattern?
- Does the individual drink with single-sip-swallows, a series of single-sip-swallows, or consecutive swallows? Consecutive swallows require sophisticated oral motor coordination and motor planning.
- Does the individual hold liquid in the mouth prior to swallowing? This may indicate incoordination of the swallow or the desire for increased oral sensory input.
- Does the individual make a "gulping" or any other sound while drinking? This may indicate incoordination of the swallow.
- Does the individual cough at any time during the drinking process? This may indicate incoordination of the swallow.
- Does the individual have a wet sounding voice after swallowing foods or liquids? This may indicate a swallowing concern.
- Does a change in liquid texture (e.g., thickening the liquid) affect the individual's ability to manage liquids?

Assessment of Oral Motor Tasks

The assessment of oral motor tasks allows the clinician to evaluate the individual's nonspeech oral movements. This can assist the clinician in further identifying muscle function concerns and motor planning concerns (i.e., often called *oral nonverbal dyspraxia*). Muscle strength as well as coordination and accuracy of movement can be assessed in the jaw, lips, cheeks, and tongue. Although the areas of neural control are probably different for nonspeech oral tasks compared to speech tasks, this part of an assessment can provide the clinician with information regarding the individual's ability to perform the oral movements in isolation related to speech production as well as eating and drinking. The following questions are important to consider (Jelm, 1995b; Long, Bahr, & Kumin, 1998; Mackie, 1996a):

- Can the individual open and close the jaw upon request or imitation? Is the movement graded?
- Does the individual's jaw appear to have normal strength during movement?
- Are jaw movements coordinated and accurate?
- Does the individual move the head or other parts of the body when moving the jaw? This may indicate difficulty with dissociation of movement in the body.
- Can the individual pucker or round the lips? Can the individual retract the lips? Can the individual compress the lips (i.e., the lips actively move together as opposed to the jaw only closing)? Can the individual alternately pucker and retract the lips (e.g., as in repeating /u-i/ several times)? Can the individual place the top teeth on the bottom lip? These lip movements are used during speech production.
- Do the individual's lips appear to have normal strength during movement?
- Are lip movements graded, coordinated, and accurate? Do lip movements improve when the individual's jaw is stabilized?
- Can the individual protract, retract, elevate (tip and body), depress (tip and body), and lateralize (tip) the tongue inside of the mouth? If not, can the individual protract, retract, elevate, depress, and lateralize the tongue tip outside of the mouth. The assessment of tongue movements inside the mouth would seem to be more functional than the assessment of tongue movements outside of the mouth, since the tongue primarily moves inside the mouth for speech production, eating, and drinking.
- Does the individual's tongue appear to have normal strength during movement?
- Are tongue movements graded, coordinated, and accurate? Do tongue movements improve when the individual's jaw is stabilized?
- Does the individual stabilize the jaw during lip or tongue movements by opening the mouth completely, biting down, or some other manner (e.g., leaning on a hand)?

Assessment of Speech Production

The assessment of speech production is an extremely important part of the oral motor evaluation. The following questions should be considered (Jelm, 1995b; Long, Bahr, & Kumin, 1998; Mackie, 1996a):

- How does the individual's jaw move during the production of syllables, words, sentences, and connected speech?
- Does the individual's jaw appear to have normal strength during speech production?
- Are the individual's jaw movements graded, coordinated, and accurate during speech production? Does the individual's jaw move in a graded manner between high, medium, and low jaw positions or does the individ-

ual tend to hold the jaw in a certain position during speech production (Rosenfeld-Johnson, 1999a)? Difficulties with graded jaw movement during speech production often indicate jaw stability and control issues.

- Does the individual move the head or other parts of the body during speech production? This may indicate difficulty with dissociation of movement in the body.
- How do the individual's lips move during the production of syllables, words, sentences, and connected speech?
- Do the individual's lips appear to have normal strength during speech production?
- Are the individual's lip movements graded, coordinated, accurate, and symmetrical during speech production?
- How does the individual's tongue move during the production of syllables, words, sentences, and connected speech?
- Does the individual's tongue appear to have normal strength during speech production?
- Are the individual's tongue movements graded, coordinated, and accurate during speech production?
- Is the individual's speech completely intelligible? If not, what percentage of the time is the individual's speech intelligible?
- Does the individual have any difficulty sequencing sounds for speech production?

Assessment of Motor Planning

Motor planning concerns are not as easily assessed as physiologic oral motor concerns. Many times, oral groping and struggle behaviors may be initially identified as a motor planning concern when the real concern is jaw instability or some other muscle-based issue. If the clinician stabilizes the individual's jaw by holding the bony portion of the jaw and the individual can then move the oral structures without the previously seen groping or struggle behaviors, then jaw instability (a muscle function concern) is likely to be present. If, however, the individual continues to exhibit groping and struggle behaviors after the jaw has been stabilized, then he or she may have a motor planning concern (Jelm, 1995b). Many children with developmental difficulties (e.g., cerebral palsy, Down syndrome) exhibit what appears to be a motor planning concern when they have not had the appropriate movement experiences to establish appropriate motor plans for speech production or other oral motor activities. It is common for individuals to exhibit a combination of muscle function and motor planning concerns. Muscle function concerns reflect a difficulty with muscle tone, strength, and coordination of movement. Motor planning concerns reflect the brain's inability to sequence the movements of the muscles appropriately for function. During oral motor assessment, the speech-language pathologist can analyze each of these areas to better determine appropriate treatment strategies.

The terms *dyspraxia* and *apraxia* have been used to describe motor planning concerns. In this book, the term *dyspraxia* will be used instead of the term *apraxia* the majority of the time, because the prefix *dys* denotes "difficulty" whereas the prefix *a* denotes "without" (Nicolosi, Harryman, & Kresheck, 1989, pp. 1, 86). Individuals with motor planning concerns usually have *difficulty* establishing or reestablishing the motor plans for speech and nonspeech tasks. They often can develop sufficient motor plans with appropriate treatment (Rosenfeld-Johnson, 1999a).

One way to assess motor planning concerns is to consider the characteristics of dyspraxia. By observing these characteristics, the clinician can often determine whether the individual exhibits or is at risk for dyspraxia. The following questions would be important to consider when determining the presence of motor planning concerns in children (Crary, 1993; Hickman, 1997; Jelm, 1995b; Kumin, 1997; Long, Bahr, & Kumin, 1998; Macaluso-Haynes, 1978):

- Did the child exhibit limited sound play as an infant?
- Does the child produce a limited number of consonant sounds accurately?
- Does the child produce "multiple speech sound errors" with "omissions (most prominent), substitutions, additions, and distortions of consonants and vowels" (Crary, 1993, p. 129)?
- Does the child produce vowel sounds more accurately than consonant sounds? Does the child have more difficulty producing diphthongs than other vowels?
- Does the child produce consistent consonant articulatory errors in spontaneous speech and inconsistent consonant articulatory errors during imitative speech production tasks?
- Are consonant clusters or complex sounds such as affricates more difficult for the child to produce than singletons?
- Does the child exhibit "difficulties with sound sequencing, including transposing sound sequences and inability to use sounds in sequences that are acceptable in isolation" (Crary, 1993, p. 129)?
- Does the child substitute voiced for unvoiced consonants?
- Does the child omit fricatives more often than nasal or stop consonants?
- Does the child omit lingual sounds more often than labial sounds?
- Does the child demonstrate irregularities in rhythm and intonation?
- Does the child have difficulty imitating speech?
- Does the child demonstrate difficulty initiating speech movements? Does the child exhibit groping, struggle, or trial and error behaviors during speech attempts or production? Does the child exhibit silent posturing during speech attempts or production?
- Does the child's speech performance improve when visual, tactile, and/or movement stimuli are provided?
- Is the child's speech telegraphic in nature? Are the child's single words more intelligible than words in conversation?
- Does the child produce words or phrases "out of the blue?" If so, does the child have difficulty repeating these (Jelm, 1995b)?
- Does the child demonstrate increased difficulty as word or utterance length increases?
- Are the child's diadochokinetic rates slower than normal?
- Has the child required a prolonged period of speech remediation?
- Are the child's receptive language skills far superior to the child's expressive language skills?
- Does the child exhibit oral nonverbal and/or limb dyspraxia?
- Does the child exhibit soft neurological signs such as difficulties with fine motor coordination during hand use, "gait, and alternate movements of the extremities" (Macaluso-Haynes, 1978, p. 245)?
- Does the child exhibit oral sensory concerns?
- Does the child exhibit eating and drinking skills that are far more sophisticated than the child's speaking abilities?
- Does the child exhibit greater intelligibility when reading aloud than when speaking spontaneously?

Additional Tools for the Assessment of Dyspraxia in Children

A few tools have been developed for the assessment of dyspraxia in children. Two of the tools are commercially available and one tool is available via workshop attendance. These are discussed here.

Jelm (1995b, pp. A-9–A-23) has developed the Assessment of Verbal Dyspraxia. This assessment contains a checklist consisting of 14 statements, which may indicate that the child is at risk for a motor planning difficulty. One characteristic of dyspraxia listed by Jelm that seems particularly predictive of motor planning concerns is "words out of the blue." Many children who exhibit limited verbal output and are eventually diagnosed with motor planning concerns are reported to say words and phrases that are completely intelligible at times. These words and phrases, however, are often heard one time and not again. If a child can produce intelligible words and phrases with near perfect speech production, then the child may be exhibiting a motor planning concern as opposed to a muscle function or physiologic issue.

The Assessment of Verbal Dyspraxia (Jelm, 1995b, pp. A-9–A-23) analyzes oral motor function as the child completes a variety of tasks. Lip, cheek, tongue, and jaw movement are assessed on the Analysis of Oral-Motor Movement Function in Feeding section of the assessment during spoon-feeding, cup drinking, biting, and chewing. Jelm rates these areas according to whether atypical oral movements are noted consistently or inconsistently as well as whether atypical oral movements prevent the individual from completing the task. Atypical oral movements indicate muscle function or physiologic concerns that affect the child's oral performance during eating and drinking tasks. These are assessed because muscle function concerns can usually be seen when the child is using the oral mechanism to eat and drink. A lack of sophistication in oral movement for eating and drinking may indicate difficulties with jaw stability; tongue and jaw dissociation; graded jaw, lip, and tongue movement; and so on.

Jelm also analyzes lip, cheek, tongue, jaw, and transitional movements as the child completes imitative oral movements (e.g., lip rounding, lip spreading, tongue elevation, etc.). She uses a rating scale for this analysis as well as the analysis of the child's imitation of consonant, vowel, and consonant-vowel combinations. The rating scale for both parts of the assessment (i.e., Analysis of Imitative Oral-Motor Movement Skills and Analysis of Imitative Verbal Skill: Level I) rates the child on one characteristic of dyspraxia, the amount of struggle or searching behaviors noted during these imitative tasks. Jelm's assessment also analyzes the child's spontaneous verbal skills in words and sentences by asking nine yes/no questions about the child's spontaneous speech production in a section entitled "Analysis of Spontaneous Verbal Skills in Words and Sentences: Level II." A positive response indicates the presence of dyspraxic characteristics. This assessment is available to individuals who take Jelm's workshop on dyspraxia.

The Preschool Profile of *The Apraxia Profile* (1997) by Hickman is comprised of an oral motor exam, a word repetition subtest, a phrase and sentence repetition subtest, a connected speech sample, and a checklist of dyspraxic characteristics. The oral motor exam consists of automatic oral movements, such as those occurring during eating and drinking activities; imitated nonspeech lip and tongue movements; as well as imitated lip and tongue movements during sound production. The oral motor exam also consists of a diadochokinetic subsection for children ages 3 to 5 years. Omissions, distortions, substitutions, and additions are noted on the word repetition subtest. The evaluator varies the rate, pitch, intonation, and volume of the items presented in the phrase and sentence repetition task as the child is asked to imitate the prosodic features of each utterance. The child's connected speech is rated for intelligibility, and mean length of utterance is calculated. Comments can also be made regarding the child's use of syntax, morphology, voice, fluency, and prosody during connected speech. The dyspraxia checklist itemizes 49 characteristics. The first 10 items on the checklist are those most characteristic of dyspraxia. Many of the other 39 characteristics are indicators of dyspraxia; however, some of these characteristics could also indicate a muscle function concern. The test information is summarized both quantitatively and descriptively.

The *Kaufman Speech Praxis Test for Children* (1995), developed by Kaufman, can be administered in 5 to 15 minutes. It was developed for children ages 2 years to 5 years, 11-months. This tool is organized in a hierarchy, beginning with simple motor speech tasks (i.e., pure vowels) and ending with complex motor speech tasks (i.e., polysyllabic combinations). It is a norm-referenced test. A standard score and a percentile ranking can be derived from each section.

Both the Assessment of Verbal Dyspraxia (Jelm, 1995b, pp. A-9–A-23) and the Preschool Profile (Hickman, 1997) assess the individual during eating and drinking as well as during various other oral motor tasks. It is important to compare the child's automatic eating and drinking skills to the child's speech production skills. If the child has limited speech production skills but fairly sophisticated oral motor skills during the processes of eating and drinking, then the child may be exhibiting developmental dyspraxia of speech. If the child exhibits unsophisticated and unrefined oral motor skills during the processes of eating and drinking, the child is probably exhibiting muscle function concerns. Some children exhibit both muscle function concerns and developmental dyspraxia of speech. This is the reason that the clinician must assess the many characteristics of dyspraxia discussed in this chapter.

TREATMENT

A treatment session for a child at the 2- to 4-year developmental level may include the following:*

- Gross motor activities/ball massage
- Oral massage/Other facilitation techniques
- Oral motor activities
- Eating and drinking activities
- Specific speech and language activities with cueing strategies

Children at the 2- to 4-year developmental level respond well to treatment that is play based and movement oriented. The session may begin with gross motor activities, but movement activities may be incorporated throughout the treatment session. The child may also need a variety of sensory activities incorporated into the session. (See Chapters 2 and 3 for specific information on this topic.)

*List adapted from unpublished workshop materials developed by Diane Chapman Bahr and Libby Kumin; see Kumin & Bahr, 1997.

Gross Motor Activities

The first part of the treatment session can focus on a variety of *gross motor activities* to assist the child in improving postural tone and stability. The gross motor portion of the treatment session may take 5 to 10 minutes at the beginning of the treatment session. The 2- to 4-year-old child is usually in a stage of development where the child seeks out and enjoys gross motor activities. There are many whole-body, gross motor activities in which the child can engage. Many of the activities suggested in this part of the chapter work particularly well with children who demonstrate at least mild low muscle tone and a variety of sensory issues in the body. Other types of movement activities and experiences would need to be used with children who exhibit hypertonicity, fluctuating muscle tone or mixed muscle tone in the body (e.g., children with cerebral palsy, children with some neurological diseases, etc.). These children tend to respond better to slow, easy movement experiences, such a gentle rocking or Feldenkrais's (1972) "Awareness through Movement" activities as opposed to vigorous gross motor activities. Neuro-developmental treatment techniques also work well with children who exhibit a variety of tonal concerns in the body. See information on Feldenkrais's "Awareness through Movement" and neuro-developmental treatment in previous chapters. If the child has a movement disorder, consult with his or her occupational and/or physical therapist regarding appropriate movement activities for the child.

In a speech clinic where gross motor activities are a part of most oral motor treatment sessions, it is suggested that a room be developed for gross motor activities. An obstacle course can be devised from mats of various sizes and shapes. A tunnel and indoor playground equipment (e.g., slides and swings) can be added to the obstacle course sequence. These movement activities are ideal to encourage some of the whole-body movement that assists the child in the development of postural tone and organization of movement in the body. Other pieces of equipment, such as a rocking or bouncing horse and a mini-trampoline with a handle, can also be placed in this room. As previously mentioned, bouncing activities can facilitate an increase in muscle tone in the body of individuals with low muscle tone but may not be activities of choice for a child with hypertonicity, certain health concerns (e.g., gastroesophageal reflux), or certain physical concerns (e.g., atlantoaxial instability). Clinicians may take turns using the gross motor treatment room with their clients.

If an occupational and physical therapist is consulting or working in the program, they can assist the speech-language clinician in developing an appropriate sensory and movement program for each child. Different types of swings and a vestibular bowl may be added to the room. As previously mentioned, appropriate vestibular activities can encourage oral output and improved visual function. These and other appropriate sensory and movement activities can assist the child in producing organized adaptive responses. Refer to information in Chapters 2 and 3 regarding this topic.

Many gross motor activities can be done with the child at this age level without the use of much equipment. Activity songs such as *Head, Shoulders, Knees, and Toes* and the *Hokey Pokey* can facilitate movement. Children with low muscle tone and sensory issues can play "jumping" games and perform simple calisthenics.

Children in the 2- to 4-year range are often very mobile. This may cause them to be more reluctant to accept the type of massage work that they received more passively as an infant. *Ball massage* is an excellent way to apply massage to the child's body. The ball massage may serve to calm the child if he or she has

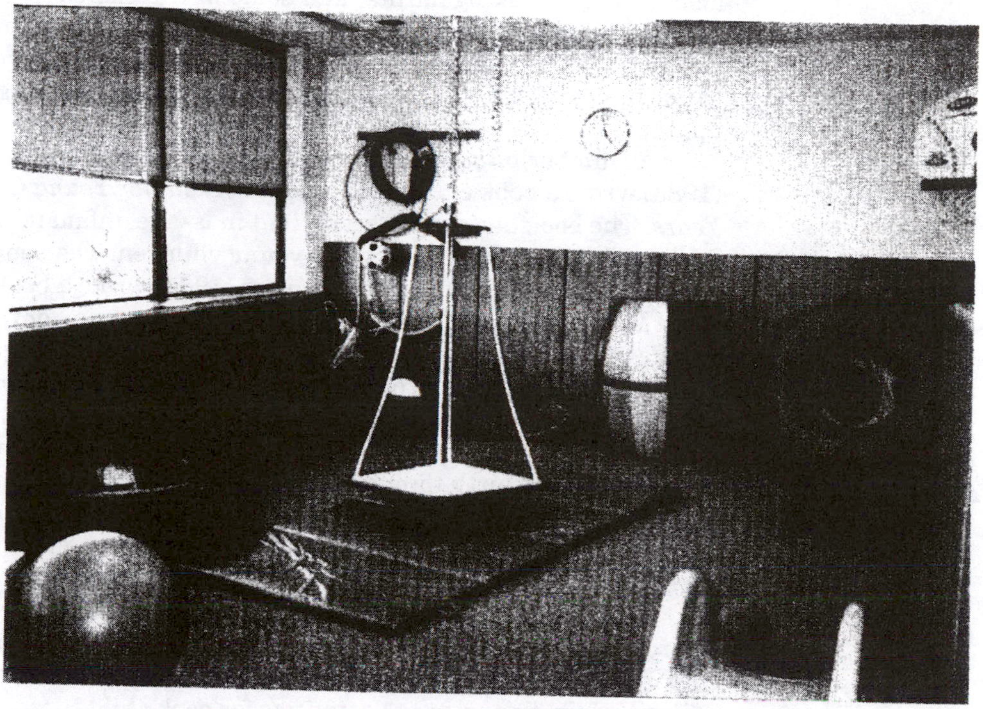

Gross motor/sensory integration room at Loyola College in Maryland.

become overstimulated during vigorous movement activities. It may also serve as a precursor to oral massage activities. This activity can be used with children exhibiting sensory concerns and tonal issues (e.g., hypertonicity, hypotonicity, etc.).

Ball massage may be completed with different ball sizes; however, it is often done with a large therapy ball. The child will lay on a mat or other soft surface, and the clinician or care provider can roll the large therapy ball over each side of the child's body. For children who appear to have difficulty with direct hands-on contact initially, this is a way to use an intermediary object to provide the deep touch pressure that the child may require.

Other ball sizes may also be used. If the ball massage is completed while the child is sitting or standing, a playground-sized ball may be used. This ball can be rolled over the child's back, arms, and legs. Some children will not initially accept direct touch to the facial area. A small ball covered with soft vinyl or cloth can be used to massage the child's face. The ball can be pressed against the child's face and mouth or rolled over the child's facial muscles and lips. This type of massage may act as a precursor to the use of other types of oral massage with the child.

When working with the young child, it is important for the clinician to carefully plan and understand the purpose of each activity. It is recommended that the clinician find information on appropriate movement activities for young children, such as a book on exercise for young children. However, it is also important to understand that the activities in these books have generally been developed for children with typical muscle tone and movement patterns. The activities may be suited for children with low muscle tone but may not be suited for children with high muscle tone. Some children with very low muscle tone also may have lax ligaments, and some of the exercises and activities recommended for children with typical muscle tone may not be appropriate for these children. When working with children with tonal concerns, *consult with the child's occupational therapist and/or physical therapist* regarding the choice of appropriate activities.

A number of *books* have been written on exercise for children. Prudden (1983) wrote a book entitled *Exercise Program for Young Children: 4 Weeks to 4 Years.* The book has chapters on infant massage, infant movement activities, as well as exercises for toddlers and young children. The benefits of each activity and exercise are also presented. Meyer (1984) wrote a book entitled *Help Your Baby Build a Healthy Body: A New Exercise Program for the First Five Formative Years,* which includes chapters on exercise and massage. Activities are suggested according to age group. Gerard's (1988) *Teaching Your Child Basic Body Confidence: The Gerard Method for Enhancing Physical Development Through Creative Play in Only Minutes a Day* also has activities presented by age group addressing ages birth through 6 years. It provides information on developmental milestones as well as activities in the areas of gross motor development, balance, strength, coordination, and fine motor development. The activities in all three books are illustrated and simply explained.

The following checklist can assist the clinician in the process of selecting appropriate sensory and movement activities. As previously mentioned, it is important to *consult with the child's occupational and/or physical therapist* to select the most appropriate activities for each child.

Movement and Sensory Activity Checklist

Activities to Increase Postural Tone (Consult with PT and OT)

- ☐ Vigorous movement
- ☐ Running
- ☐ Jumping
- ☐ Bouncing
- ☐ Climbing
- ☐ Fast dancing

Activities to Decrease Excessive Extensor Tone (Consult with PT and OT)

- ☐ Slow rocking
- ☐ Facilitation of slow, easy movement (e.g., Feldenkrais's "Awareness through Movement" activities, neuro-developmental treatment techniques)

Activities to Improve Postural Stability (Consult with PT and OT)

- ☐ Resistance activities (i.e., safe pushing or pulling activities using the arms and shoulders)
- ☐ Exercises and activities to strengthen the abdominal, chest, back, and shoulder musculature

Activities to Improve Sensory Awareness and Organization (Consult with OT)

- ☐ Songs that incorporate movement (e.g., *Head, Shoulders, Knees, and Toes*)
- ☐ Carefully selected vestibular activities
- ☐ Swinging on a swing
- ☐ Ball massage
- ☐ Swaddling (e.g., rolling the individual's body in a blanket)
- ☐ Sitting in a bean bag chair

- ☐ Sitting in a tub of balls
- ☐ Having the individual lay on a therapy ball and slowly moving the ball in a variety of directions
- ☐ Sitting on a therapy ball while performing fine motor activities

Oral Massage and Other Facilitation Techinques

Oral massage can be completed in a playful manner when working with a child in this age range. Children in the 2- to 4-year group often seem to notice that the oral massage routine is something that they alone may be doing. This may complicate treatment, as children who had previously been allowing oral massage may suddenly begin to reject this activity. Many parents and care providers may stop doing the work secondary to the child's apparent wishes.

It is often important during this period for the child to see others participating in oral massage activities; for example, a sibling may also participate in oral massage. Also, parents and care providers may begin taking turns with the child. The child can apply the oral massage to the care provider, and then the care provider may apply the oral massage techniques to the child.

When taking turns during this type of activity, the care provider must be careful to work in a sanitary manner. For example, the care provider and the child would not share an oral massage brush. The care provider would also want to be sure that both the care provider and the child wash their hands prior to touching one another's faces. If the child or care provider has any open sores on the face, then both the child and the care provider should wear gloves. Some children at this age level seem to enjoy trying on and wearing the gloves, even though the smallest gloves will not yet fit them. See information on universal precautions in Chapter 3.

Puppets with mouths, such as those designed by Patsy Fann, often become an important part of treatment with children in the 2- to 4-year age range. If a child has not been introduced to the idea of oral massage prior to this time, the child may begin this process by massaging the puppet's arms and face as well as brushing the puppet's mouth. Again, the same brush would not be used in the puppet's mouth as the clinician would use in the child's mouth if possible. At times, young children will become very enthusiastic in this process and take the brush from the puppet's mouth to the child's mouth before the clinician, parent, or care provider can assist the child in switching brushes. If this occurs, the puppet may be laundered.

Patsy Fann has created a variety of "Puppets That Swallow." These are available with many customized options for oral motor treatment. If the child enjoys a particular story, many of the puppets are designed to resemble the characters in popular children's stories and songs (e.g., *Itsy Bitsy Spider*). All of the puppets have mouths and can swallow pretend food. However, the puppets can be customized to include teeth and tongues.

These puppets have many applications in addition to assisting the child in the acceptance of the oral massage work. The puppets may help the child work through selectivity issues experienced while eating and drinking (i.e., the child can be encouraged to sample foods and liquids as the puppet pretends to sample the same foods and liquids). The puppets can also assist the clinician in demonstrating appropriate tongue placement for articulation and swallowing. The puppets can be used to stimulate language and early literacy skills. Parents often purchase these puppets for carry-over and play activities at home. Joanne Hanson (1998) has written a book about the use of the "Puppets That Swallow," entitled *Progress with Puppets: Speech and Language Activities for Young Chil-*

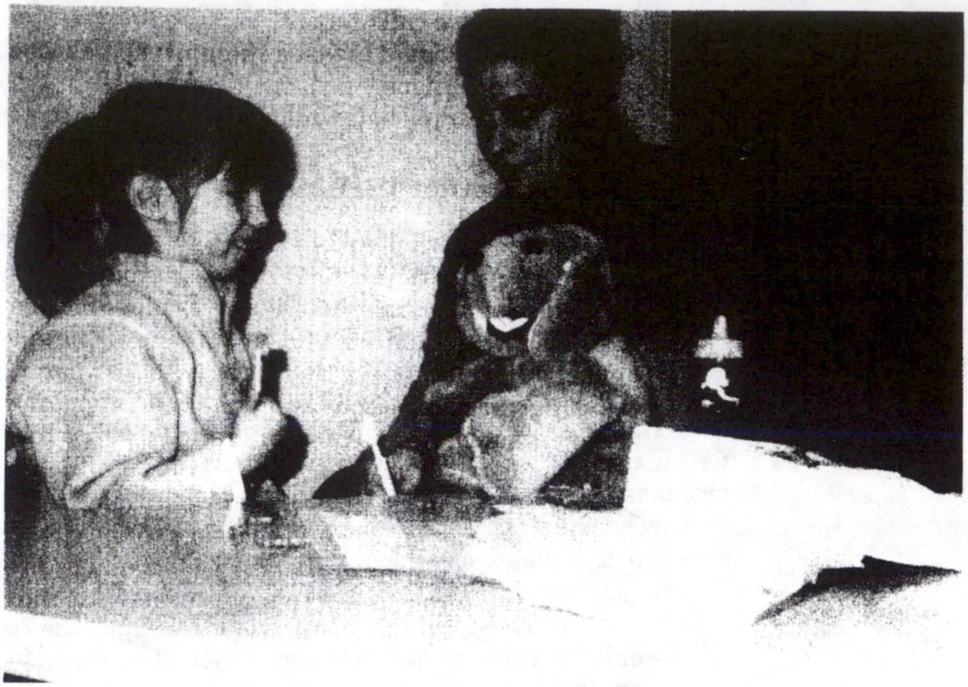

Nicole, a 5-year-old child with Pierre Robin sequence, prepares to participate in oral massage with a puppet made by Patsy Fann. This activity is facilitated by her clinician Felicia.

dren. The book covers the use of puppets in the areas of "chewing, feeding, and oral-motor therapy; language stimulation; articulation; fluency and voice training; sensory integration; as well as language arts and reading" (Hanson, 1998, Table of Contents). See product sources in Appendix D for information on where to order the puppets by Patsy Fann.

It is important for the oral massage work to continue during the 2- to 4-year period if a child continues to demonstrate oral motor concerns. This portion of the treatment session prepares the child for the oral motor activities that follow. The oral massage work can be completed in as little as 3 to 5 minutes. Refer to oral massage sequence in Chapter 4.

As discussed in Chapter 4, an oral massage brush may be an effective tool to use when massaging inside the child's mouth. Children in the 2- to 4-year age group usually have a full set of teeth and can bite the facilitator if the facilitator places gloved fingers inside the child's dental arch. As discussed in Chapter 4, Gerber produces two *oral massage brushes.* The larger brush can be used if the child *does not* have a tonic bite response or is not likely to bite off the tip of the brush. The smaller Nuk oral massage brush may be the brush of choice with children who may bite hard enough on the larger Nuk oral massage brush to break off the tip. Both Nuk oral massage brushes have pliable rubber protrusions. These may begin to show wear after many uses or if the child consistently chews on the brush. If the brush begins to look worn, it is important to dispose of the brush.

The Nuk oral massage brushes can be dipped in foods and liquids to add flavor to the oral brushing experience if the child prefers or enjoys this. This can make the brushing activity more fun and more interesting. Flavored seltzer water can add flavor as well as increase the intensity of the experience through the effervescence of the seltzer. It is also a clear liquid and usually will not stain clothing. Some children greatly enjoy the use of the seltzer water (i.e., often those who exhibit hyporesponsivity in the oral tactile system), whereas children with hypertonicity in the body may experience an increase in atypical muscle tone when the seltzer water is used. The Nuk oral massage brushes can be sanitized by washing them in the dishwasher, in hot soapy water, or in a sanitizing solution safe for items that are used in the mouth. These brushes can be purchased in bulk from the Gerber Products Company (see products list in Appendix D). The large Nuk oral massage brushes can be purchased separately, but the small Nuk oral massage brushes must be purchased as part of a set.

A soft child's toothbrush can also be used to brush the oral structures. However, the child's toothbrush does not allow the clinician or the care provider to apply the specific pressure needed when working to deeply stimulate the child's tongue muscles (e.g., when applying Beckman [1997] facilitation techniques). The soft toothbrush may also be uncomfortable for the child when the clinician or care provider stimulates the edges of the child's hard palate.

The toothette is another implement that may be used in oral motor treatment with children at this age level. The toothette is a sponge brush on a cardboard stick used to stimulate the child's lips, internal cheek areas, tongue, and hard palate. Some children prefer the feel of the unflavored toothette to the feel of the Nuk oral message brush in the mouth. The unflavored toothette can be used to stimulate the oral structures of some individuals demonstrating hyperresponsivity to sensations in the mouth. Other individuals may prefer the clinician to use a gloved finger or some other implement (e.g., a small round lollipop) if these can be used safely with the child. Flavored toothettes (e.g., mint) should be used primarily with individuals exhibiting extreme hyporesponsivity in the mouth (Rosenfeld-Johnson, 1999a). Some chldren who like intense tastes prefer the toothette with taste.

Caution must be taken when using a toothette during treatment. It is made of a sponge-type material, and an individual could bite off a portion of the brush and swallow it. Therefore, the child must have the cognitive ability to understand that the brush is not to be chewed. The toothette can provide the child with a different oral experience than a Nuk oral massage brush. An advantage of using the toothette is that it is disposable and can be discarded after a single use. However, the clinician or care provider may not be able to apply the same amount of pressure when massaging the oral structures with a toothette as can be applied when using a Nuk oral massage brush. Toothettes can be purchased through a pharmacy or medical supply company.

As previously mentioned, children at the 2- to 4-year level are frequently quite mobile. Therefore, the clinician and the care provider may need to set up a *routine* to facilitate the child's cooperation with oral massage. On a daily basis, oral massage can be done prior to a meal, prior to speech practice, or as part of a toothbrushing routine. The clinician or care provider may sit the child in a particular chair or in a lap. Children at this age level often appear to enjoy looking in a mirror as the care provider does the routine with the child. It is generally helpful to make the activity a "game." A game-like situation can be established by adding certain words (e.g., rhymes), sounds (e.g., funny noises), or music (e.g., songs) to the activity.

Music can be used to establish a rhythm for the massage. For example, the firm but gentle rotary presses recommended in the oral massage protocol can be applied to the rhythm of the music. Children's folk music is particularly good for this type of activity. Any music with a steady rhythm of approximately 60 beats per minute may be useful if it appeals to the child. Refer to information on the use of music in treatment in Chapter 3.

Other facilitation techniques can be added to this portion of the child's treatment session. The Beckman facilitation techniques (1997) may be particularly useful with children in this age range. The clinician can learn these techniques by taking a workshop from Debra Beckman (see Appendix D). The techniques can be easily added to the oral massage routine. They are also applied in a manner that many children at this stage find easy to tolerate after the routine is established. While these techniques are being described as part of a therapy session in this chapter, the techniques are demonstrated to parents and care providers for use at home one or more times each day. Approximately five Beckman facilitation techniques can be added to the oral massage activity without a significant increase in time commitment.

Other types of body work such as myofascial release and proprioceptive neuromuscular facilitation can be used with this age group. However, it is more difficult to use techniques that require the child to remain in a still position for any length of time. If a child is not very mobile, then these types of techniques are easier to apply. See information presented on myofascial release and proprioceptive neuromuscular facilitation in previous chapters.

Oral Motor Activities

Oral motor activities for the child in the 2- to 4-year age group may be developed by using a variety of resources. It is most important for the clinician to choose activities that appropriately suit the child's specific oral motor needs. These needs are determined by oral motor assessment and diagnostic treatment observations. The amount of time spent in a therapy session on oral motor activities will be determined by his or her specific needs. For example, a child with multiple misarticulations related to significant muscle function issues may need to spend 10 to 15 minutes on these types of tasks, whereas a child with a motor planning difficulty may only require 5 minutes to work on oral sequencing activities. Again, it is important that the child work on these tasks and then move on to functional speech and language activities as soon as possible.

The *Pre-Feeding Skills* book by Morris and Klein (1987, 2000) contains many ideas pertaining to children in this age group. This book has been discussed in previous chapters and is particularly useful when working with children exhibiting developmental concerns.

The book entitled *Oral Motor Activities for Young Children* by Mackie (1996a) contains the Assessment of Oral Motor Functions previously discussed in this chapter. Once this assessment is completed, Mackie provides a checklist for the clinician to systematically identify the areas of oral weakness (e.g., jaw instability, difficulties with tongue and jaw dissociation, etc.). The remainder of the book contains many creative and fun activities to address the child's identified oral motor needs. These take the form of lip and tongue activities and are associated with specific speech sounds that require the oral movement patterns being addressed in each lesson. Many of these activities involve the use of foods, and pictures are used with all of the activities to provide the child with a visual image of what each task involves.

The book entitled *Oral-Motor Exercises for Speech Clarity* (Rosenfeld-Johnson, 1999b) is an outstanding resource containing appropriate oral motor activities for persons of all ages. Rosenfeld-Johnson (1999b) developed systematic treatment protocols involving the use of horns, straws, bubbles, bite blocks, and other tools to facilitate graded respiratory control as well as graded jaw, lip, and tongue movement needed for precise speech production. The activities can be fun, and parents can easily incorporate them into the home routine. See Chapter 6 for a more detailed description of this resource.

M.O.R.E. Integrating the Mouth with Sensory and Postural Functions (1995) by Oetter, Richter, and Frick contains many activities for the 2- to 4-year-old child as well as other age groups. The authors discuss the importance of the suck/swallow/breathe synchrony. Treatment principles and activities are also discussed. An outstanding characteristic of this book is the rating scale used to rate the level of difficulty in activating or using certain mouth toys or oral exercisers. The acronym M.O.R.E. represents Motor components, Oral organization, Respiratory demand, and Eye contact/control (pp. 3–4). Each mouth toy or oral exerciser is rated according to the level of difficulty in each of these areas. The lower the score, the easier the task is considered. The higher the score, the more difficult the task is considered. The book rates many different types of oral equipment (i.e., whistles, music makers, oral exercisers, bubbles, blowers, and infant/toddler toys). It also contains a quick reference guide to the use of the oral equipment and an oral motor grocery list. The oral motor grocery list contains recommended food and nonfood items that can be useful in strengthening sucking and blowing, improving jaw control during munching and rotary chewing, and increasing arousal and alertness. When using mouth toys and oral exercisers in treatment, it is important that the items are *safe* for oral use (Rosenfeld-Johnson, 1999a). The clinician can check the package or call the manufacturer for this information.

Once the clinician has systematically identified appropriate oral motor toys and exercisers using *M.O.R.E. Integrating the Mouth with Sensory and Postural Functions* as a guide, activities using the toys and exercisers can be expanded to address a variety of treatment goals. The child can be initially taught to activate mouth toys and oral exercisers while in a stable position. Appropriately completed blowing activities (e.g., lips only on whistle) can encourage tongue retraction (Rosenfeld-Johnson, 1999a). This is very important for children exhibiting exaggerated tongue protrusion or tongue thrust. When a child can activate a mouth toy in a stable position, a group of children can form a marching band with whistles, kazoos, and music makers. The marching activity is a gross motor activity that may promote postural tone and stability in children with low muscle tone. When the child has mastered the ability to operate a mouth toy, the clinician can ask the child to imitate the clinician's performance with a matching toy (e.g., the child can imitate a specific number of "toots," duration of "toots," or sequence of "toots" on a whistle). This can encourage the child to develop good listening or auditory discrimination skills as well as improved respiratory control. By imitating sequences of activations with a mouth toy, the child will need to use controlled respiration. Controlled respiration is very important for effective speech production. It can also help the clinician introduce concepts such as "short" and "long," as related to auditory signals.

The materials discussed here respresent only a small portion of what is available for the development of oral motor activities related to the child's specific oral motor needs. Many other materials are available to address this area of treatment. Companies such as Innovative Therapists International, Speech Dynamics, Inc., and Super Duper Publications carry a variety of oral motor materials, including mouth toys and oral exercisers. LinguiSystems, Inc., also carries many manuals addressing oral motor assessment and treatment. See product sources in Appendix D for more information on these companies. Again, it is most important that the clinician systematically use these materials based on the child's established oral motor needs.

INTERACTIVE EXPERIENCE: ORAL MOTOR ACTIVITIES

Brainstorm activities that would be appropriate to address the areas of jaw strengthening, stability, and control; tongue strengthening, mobility, and control; as well as lip strengthening, mobility, and control. Some activities have been suggested in each area to assist you with this process. After thinking of the activities, identify the purposes of each activity. (See the example.) This activity is a modified version of one used by Jelm (1995b).

Example:

Activity for Jaw Strengthening, Stability, and Control

Chewing foods of increased texture using the back molars

Purposes:

- can strengthen the jaw musculature and improve jaw stability
- can be used to teach rotary and other graded jaw movements
- can increase oral awareness in a natural manner

Activity:

Activities for Jaw Strengthening, Stability, and Control

- Chew foods of increased texture using the back molars
- Open and close the jaw in a graded manner
- Open and close the jaw against carefully applied resistance
- Suck thickened liquids through a straw
- Use mouth toys and tools appropriately (Rosenfeld-Johnson, 1999b; Oetter, Richter, & Frick, 1995)
- Beckman (1997) facilitation techniques
- Others?

Activities for Tongue Strengthening, Mobility, and Control

- Elevate or lateralize tongue against carefully applied resistance
- Move tongue in a variety of directions without moving jaw
- Move tongue to accurately remove cake gel or cake decos from various locations on the lips or in the mouth
- Hold a mint Lifesaver against the alveolar ridge until it melts
- Move tongue to a variety of locations in the mouth while holding half of a stale marshmallow between the molars to stabilize the jaw
- Use mouth toys and tools appropriately (Rosenfeld-Johnson, 1999b; Oetter, Richter, & Frick, 1995)
- Beckman (1997) facilitation techniques
- Others?

Activities for Lip Strengthening, Mobility, and Control

- Actively use upper lip to clear spoon
- Press the lips outward against carefully applied resistance
- Smile
- Pucker
- Alternately smile and pucker
- Use mouth toys and tools appropriately (Rosenfeld-Johnson, 1999b; Oetter, Richter, & Frick, 1995)
- Beckman (1997) facilitation techniques
- Others?

Eating and Drinking Activities

Although eating and drinking activities may be included in the oral motor activities just discussed, some children in the 2- to 4-year age group require specific treatment in this area. Many children with oral motor concerns exhibit functional eating and drinking skills but continue to demonstrate *unsophisticated eating and drinking patterns.* The refinement of these skills may lead to more sophisticated oral motor patterns needed for speech production. For example, sucking involves tongue elevation and active lip movement, whereas the more primitive pattern of suckling involves primarily protraction and retraction of the tongue. Tongue elevation is important for the many speech sounds produced within the mouth. Tongue and jaw dissociation is needed for the lateralization of food. Although the tongue movement is different for speech (i.e., elevation versus lateralization), tongue and jaw dissociation is imperative for the development of mature sounding speech.

Some children will require specific treatment for the development of eating and drinking skills because they are having difficulty *obtaining adequate sustenance.* Many of these children have moderate to severe physical difficulties. However, some of the children may have sensory-based concerns. The *Pre-Feeding Skills* book (Morris & Klein, 1987, 2000) contains many therapeutic techniques for working with these children. Eating and drinking activities may address sensory as well as motor needs. Some children in the 2- to 4-year age range are very selective in the foods that they will accept. As discussed in Chapter 4, foods can be systematically introduced to the child to address this need. *Behavioral concerns* are frequently attached to food selectivity issues by the time children reach ages 2 to 4 years. Many of these concerns began with sensory issues and can be resolved by working with the child's sensory systems. However, children with severe behavioral feeding issues may benefit from involvement in a behavioral feeding program. There are many behavioral feeding programs throughout the United States, often affiliated with hospitals. Check the Internet for further information on these programs.

Some children in the 2- to 4-year age range have not developed adequate motor abilities for eating and drinking. Skills required for eating and drinking may be difficult or may take additional time to establish, since these children may be beyond the "critical learning period" for learning many of these skills. Although this is certainly a consideration in treatment, it is best if the clinician maintains a positive expectation for the child's development of these skills.

Some children in the 2- to 4-year age range may still be fed via *gastrostomy tubes.* The weaning of the child from the gastrostomy tube may take a little more time than expected. Some children may need to use compensatory strategies for eating and drinking while they are working on the development of sophisticated oral motor skills. For example, a child having difficulty moving the bolus from the oral cavity to the pharynx may need to clear the oral cavity by taking a drink of thickened liquid if this is a safe activity for the child. Although this may not reflect the clinician's ultimate goal for the child, it may be a necessary step in the process of teaching the child to clear the mouth. As the child develops more sophisticated oral motor skills for eating and drinking, compensatory strategies can be replaced with functional eating and drinking skills. Specific details regarding the weaning of children from a gastrostomy tube can be found in the *Pre-Feeding Skills* book (Morris & Klein, 1987, 2000).

The amount of time spent in a therapy session on eating and drinking activities will be determined by the child's specific needs. For some children, the development of eating and drinking skills will be the focus of treatment. In this case, the majority of the session may be composed of eating and drinking activities.

Specific Speech and Language Activities with Cueing Strategies

Specific speech and language activities with cueing strategies are also an important part of the oral motor therapy session for the 2- to 4-year-old child. If the clinician has targeted an increase in intelligibility or overall speech productions as a primary goal, these activities may account for much of the treatment session. Children with oral motor concerns frequently exhibit concomitant language difficulties as well. Therefore, specific speech and language activities may require 20 to 25 minutes of a 45-minute treatment session. The activities are chosen based on the specific needs of the child. Speech-language pathologists are well trained in choosing appropriate speech and language activities for each child. As previously mentioned, the books *Oral Motor Activities for Young Children* (Mackie, 1996a) and *Oral-Motor Exercises for Speech Clarity* (Rosenfeld-Johnson, 1999b) have many oral motor activities related to the specific production of speech sounds.

When working with the 2- to 4-year-old child, treatment will usually need to involve some type of *play* in order to engage the child. Children in this age range respond well to structure and routine, but they frequently do not respond as well to traditional drill and practice. Some of the same materials used with older children can be used with children in this age group (e.g., picture cards targeting specific speech sounds). However, they will be more likely to attend to activities if they are presented as a game or part of a play activity. Many children in this age group enjoy pretend play. Activities involving books can also encourage verbal output.

Cueing strategies work well with this age group when addressing speech sound production. Moto-kinesthetic cueing (Young & Hawk, 1955) involves physical movement of the child's oral structures toward the position of correct sound production. A system of tactile-kinesthetic cueing taught by Deborah Hayden is called the PROMPT system (Square, Goshulak, & Hayden, 1997). For many children, this type of hands-on prompting is of great assistance in establishing the correct placement for the production of speech sounds. See Chapter 4 for detailed information on cueing.

Visual-tactile cueing is another very effective cueing system. In this system, each speech sound is represented by a hand signal. The child observes the clinician or care provider using the cue and will often imitate the hand signal and the speech sound. Many of the cues are performed at (i.e., touching) or near the mouth and are related to some characteristic of the speech sound being cued. Visual-tactile cueing is recommended for individuals experiencing muscle function concerns and/or motor planning issues. This system works particularly well with children experiencing speech motor planning difficulties. It appears that individuals with motor planning concerns respond well to speech activities that incorporate some type of body movement as well as some type of routine. Visual-tactile cueing uses both of these strategies. Jelm (1995b) has developed a system of visual-tactile cueing in which she has devised a cue for each speech sound. The same or a similar cue is used for cognates such as /p/ and /b/ sounds in this system.

When working with a visual-tactile cueing system such as the one developed by Jelm (1995b), the clinician will often initially introduce sounds that are more easily seen by the child. The /p/, /b/, and /m/ sounds are often good sounds for the clinician to begin working on, as these are lip sounds and can be readily seen by the child. The clinician may also want to cue sounds and the cognates of sounds that the child can already produce. For example, the child may be producing the /g/ sound. The clinician may then wish to assist the child in producing the /g/ sound more consistently as well as in establishing the production of the /k/ sound. This type of visual-tactile cueing can be easily used to cue the production of the speech sounds in words. The clinician will often begin by cueing the sound in the initial position of single-syllable words. However, the cue can be used to establish the production of the targeted sound in all positions of words.

Another type of visual-tactile cueing system is the pacing system. The pacing system was originally used with adults exhibiting dyspraxia. When working with children in the 2- to 4-year age group, a pacing board can be used. The pacing board can be created by placing or drawing a series of images on a rectangular piece of tagboard. The images can be drawn shapes (e.g., circles, squares, stars, etc.), stickers, and the like. The number of images in the series depends on the child's level of speech and language output. For example, if the child is working on adding sounds to the ends of single-syllable words, a pacing board with two images (e.g., dots or circles) would be used. The clinician would point to one circle while saying the first part of the word (e.g., /kæ/), then point to the second circle while saying the final sound (e.g., /t/). The child would imitate the clinician to produce the word *cat*.

The pacing board can be used to assist the child in adding sounds or syllables to words. It can also be used to assist the child in expanding the length of utterance. The pacing board provides the child with visual, tactile, and movement cues. The clinician points to images on the pacing board as the clinician says the sounds, syllables, or words that the clinician is asking the child to imitate. The child then points to the images on the pacing board while repeating the sounds, syllables, or words. When first using the pacing board, the clinician and care provider may need to assist the child physically in the use of the board via hand-over-hand assistance. However, many children will imitate the use of the board.

A tactile pacing board can be made for individuals who are visually impaired by placing a series of glue dots on a tongue depressor or a series of tactile images on a piece of tagboard. Tactile graphics can be created on a computer with a tactile graphics program, or they can be manually placed on the board. Materials such as sponge, carpet, or sandpaper can be used to create the images on the pacing board. Children with vision may also benefit from a pacing

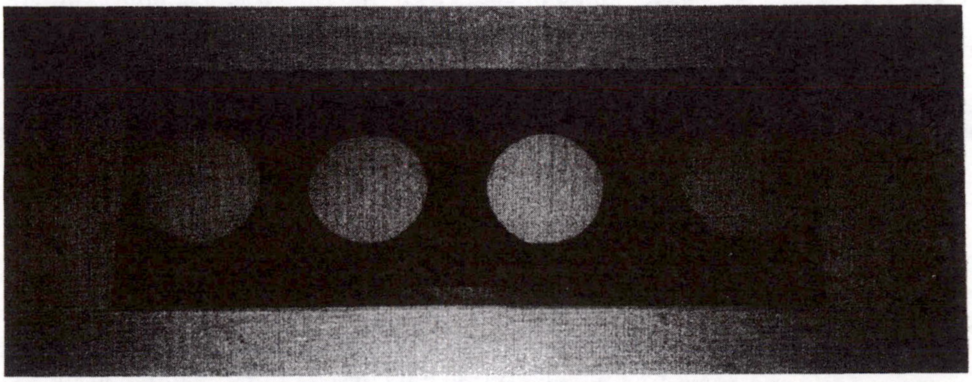

A homemade pacing board with four symbols (i.e., dots) used in the expansion of word and utterance length.

board made out of a material that they can feel. This tactile input may provide some children with information needed to process the task. In addition to its use with individuals demonstrating visual or sensory concerns, a smaller pacing board made from the tongue depressor and raised glue dots can also be used with adolescents and adults. This allows them to carry the pacing board in a pocket for use in communication exchanges outside the clinic setting. A good resource for information about the use of this implement with young children is "The Pacing Board: A Technique to Assist the Transition from Single Words to Multiword Utterances" by Kumin, Councill, and Goodman (1995).

Auditory cueing is usually used in conjunction with moto-kinesthetic, tactile-kinesthetic, and visual-tactile cueing. The sound is provided with the cue. Many children in the 2- to 4-year age group who exhibit oral motor concerns do not respond as well in treatment when the auditory cue is used alone. This may be related to the age and/or cognitive abilities of the child. Some individuals do not seem to respond well to the auditory cues presented alone. Children who have had a history of chronic middle ear concerns frequently require another type of cue in addition to the auditory cue. Children with Down syndrome frequently do not seem to respond well to information presented in a pure auditory format. These children often appear to require at least a visual cue in addition to the auditory cue, as many of them seem to be "visual learners."

Cueing works effectively with individuals exhibiting muscle function issues, and it works particularly well to facilitate motor planning. Moto-kinesthetic and tactile-kinesthetic cueing physically assist the individual in establishing the motor plan for articulatory movements. Visual-tactile cueing and pacing slow down the process of articulation as well as provide additional input. Cueing and pacing seem to assist the individual in finding the pathway to the motor plan. As previously mentioned, these methods provide additional input and may also "distract" the individual from the speaking process so that the "pressure" is removed from the communicative attempt. This allows the process to become "automatic." Individuals with motor planning issues perform poorly in demand situations and need to find a way for speech to become habitual or automatic. The *Easy Does It for Apraxia and Motor Planning-Preschool* program (1994) by Strode and Chamberlain, as well as other approaches to the treatment of developmental apraxia of speech, will be discussed in Chapter 6.

CASE EXAMPLE

In the following case example concerns are placed in parentheses and in bold. This will assist the clinician in understanding the impact of the behaviors being described.

Description

Casey is a 3-year-old child exhibiting generalized low muscle tone in her body. Her back and shoulders are rounded when she is seated on the floor. However, her posture improves when she is seated in a chair with her hips, knees, and ankles at 90 degrees. **(difficulties with postural stability and control)** Casey has an open mouth posture, and she breathes through her mouth. She has allergies and sinus concerns. She also has frequent otitis media; PE tubes were placed at 2 years of age and are still in place. Casey's tongue rests in the bottom of her mouth, and she occasionally drools. **(jaw and tongue out of position for adequate speech production and swallowing, difficulty with lip closure, possible decreased awareness)**

When eating from a spoon, Casey opens her mouth in wide excursions, and her upper lip moves weakly to clear the bowl of the spoon. **(ungraded jaw movement and weak lip movement)** She frequently has food on her face while she is eating, and she does not seem to be aware of this. **(decreased awareness)** Casey uses exaggerated tongue protrusion to swallow soft food textures. **(tongue out of position for mature swallow, unsophisticated tongue movement)** When taking a bite of food, she bites down on the food and then pulls the food away from her mouth with her hand. **(jaw instability)** She also takes bites using her side teeth and cannot take an adequate bite with her front teeth. She has an overbite. **(jaw instability and dentition concern)** When chewing food, Casey primarily uses a munching pattern. However, she also exhibits components of rotary chewing. She chews with her mouth open. **(difficulty with graded jaw movement)** Casey's tongue transfers food primarily to her right side teeth using a center to side motion. However, when chewing foods of increased texture, she transfers food to both molar surfaces using her tongue tip. **(foods of increased texture provide greater input, and Casey uses a more sophisticated pattern)** Casey drinks from a straw with consecutive swallows, but her tongue is typically under the straw, and she uses a protraction-retraction tongue movement pattern. **(poor grading of tongue, lip, and jaw movement)** She drinks with slow, consecutive swallows from an open cup and makes a "gulping" noise during swallowing. **(difficulty with swallowing coordination)**

Casey can imitate a variety of oral movements. However, wide excursions of her jaw are frequently noted. **(difficulty with graded jaw movement)** Her lip closure appears weak. **(weak lip closure)** She can move her tongue to a variety of locations in her mouth; however, her jaw moves with her tongue. **(difficulty with tongue and jaw dissociation)** Casey's speech production is imprecise. She has inadequate lip compression during the production of lip sounds. **(weak lip closure)** Her jaw moves with her tongue during the production of tongue sounds. **(difficulty with tongue and jaw dissociation)** Casey thrusts her tongue forward during the production of most sibilant sounds. **(difficulty with graded tongue movement)** She demonstrates some difficulty sequencing the sounds in words, phrases, and sentences. **(possible motor planning concerns related to generalized low muscle tone and inability to set up an appropriate motor plan)** Casey spontaneously produces two- and three-word sentences. **(possible difficulty with respiratory support for speech production)** Her intelligibility is affected by her imprecise speech production. **(muscle function and motor planning concerns)** Casey's receptive language skills are age appropriate. She does not have any health or physical issues that preclude her involvement in regular gross motor activities.

Treatment Plan

Gross Motor Activities Provide Casey with appropriate rigorous movement, such as jumping and bouncing to increase postural tone. She may also benefit from appropriate resistance activities. Gross motor activities may need to be incorporated throughout Casey's session to increase postural tone and stability as needed. Consult with her occupational and physical therapists regarding appropriate movement activities for Casey.

Oral Massage Provide Casey with oral massage and other facilitation techniques to increase oral awareness and oral muscle tone.

Oral Motor Activities Provide activities to facilitate jaw stability, graded jaw movement, appropriate jaw and tongue position, tongue and jaw dissociation, tongue elevation within the mouth, graded tongue movement, swallowing coordination, lip strength and mobility, graded lip movement, and motor planning with Casey.

Specific Speech and Language Activities Strengthen the production of Casey's speech sounds /p/, /b/, and /m/. Work toward accurate tongue placement for the sounds /t/, /d/, and /n/ with Casey. Use visual-tactile cueing to improve intelligibility and assist with motor planning. Incorporate appropriate expressive language activities throughout the treatment session.

Recommendations

1. Speak with Casey's parents regarding the management of her allergies and sinus concerns. Recommend that her parents speak with Casey's primary care physician regarding possible referral to an ENT physician or allergy specialist if this has not occurred.
2. Speak with Casey's parents regarding the management of her dental issues. Recommend a visit to a dentist if this has not occurred.
3. When Casey is working in a seated position, position her in an appropriate chair where her hips, knees, and ankles are at 90 degrees. Work with an occupational therapist to find an appropriate chair and table for Casey. Table height may need to be relatively high if she needs to stabilize her trunk and shoulder girdle by bearing weight on the table using her arms.
4. Consider presenting activities to Casey using a slant board or other vertical surface (e.g., easel) to encourage improved postural control and subsequent fine motor function.
5. Consult with Casey's occupational therapist and physical therapist regarding activities to encourage improved postural control.

INTERACTIVE CASE EXPERIENCE

The interactive case experience in this chapter will allow the reader to practice using the information from the chapter. This experience is meant to challenge the reader to think of possibilities for the case presented. The answers to the questions in the interactive case experience are for the reader to decide.

Review the case just presented. Develop activities for each part of the treatment plan. What other recommendations need to be made? What other comments or ideas do you have concerning Casey?

6

Ages 4 to 6

Working with Preschool-Aged Children

Many of the concepts discussed in this chapter are similar to those found in previous chapters. A number of the assessment and treatment tools and strategies discussed in previous chapters can be used with the preschool-aged child. However, the approach to oral motor assessment and treatment may vary from approaches discussed previously, as the 4- to 6-year-old child typically has different interests and abilities than the younger child. It is important for the clinician to be familiar with the continuum of oral motor assessment and treatment strategies to appropriately address the needs of each individual with oral motor concerns.

Many children in this age group are referred for speech therapy when it becomes apparent that speech difficulties exhibited by these individuals are not resolving on their own. The child as well as his or her peers frequently demonstrate awareness of the child's speech and language difficulties. Children with significant speech difficulties are frequently viewed as less competent or able than their peers without speech concerns. In addition to the social limitations caused by a speech difficulty itself, parents and care providers may attempt to protect these children by limiting their social contacts with other children. This could further affect the child's development of social skills.

It is important to determine whether the speech difficulty demonstrated by the child has an oral motor basis. Oral motor concerns can have a significant impact on the phonological development of the child. Most speech-language pathologists are well trained in the assessment and treatment of phonological concerns. Through careful assessment, the clinician can determine whether the speech difficulties are movement based. Some assessment tools to assist in this process are discussed here.

ASSESSMENT

The components of an oral motor assessment could be the same for any age group. These will often include the assessment of the child's body and mouth at rest and during movement activities, the child's eating and drinking patterns, the child's performance during nonspeech oral motor tasks as well as the child's speech production. A discussion of these components is found in Chapter 5.

Again, it is important for the clinician to choose an assessment tool that suits the needs of the individual client. It is also important to obtain an oral motor case history from the child's parents or care providers. See Chapter 4 for a suggested case history form.

Children in the age group of 4 to 6 years who have severe oral motor concerns may benefit from assessments discussed in earlier chapters. Checklists such as the Developmental Pre-Feeding Checklist (Morris & Klein, 2000, Appendix B; Klein & Morris, 1999, pp. 480–509; Morris & Klein, 1987, pp. 75–82), the Body Alignment for Seating and Positioning Checklist (Morris & Klein, 2000, p. 305), the Positioning Checklist (Morris & Klein, 1987, p. 169), and the Developmental Self-Feeding Checklist from *Pre-Feeding Skills* (Morris & Klein, 1987, p. 306) may be very useful. The Beckman Oral Motor Assessment Protocol assesses the oral structure and oral muscle function of the jaw, cheeks, lips, tongue, and soft palate. The use of this protocol is taught by Debra Beckman (1997) in her workshops and can be used with clients exhibiting a range of oral motor concerns. Children with severe neuromotor disorders (e.g., cerebral palsy, strokes due to sickle-cell anemia, traumatic brain injury, Batten's disease, etc.) often require team assessment involving the child, care providers, speech-language pathologist, occupational therapist, physical therapist, and others. The development of strategies for adequate nutrition and communication are often a main focus of the assessment.

A variety of assessment tools are available to evaluate individuals demonstrating mild to moderate oral motor concerns that may impact on eating and drinking as well as speech production. Some aspects of these assessment tools will also be useful during the evaluation of individuals with more severe oral motor concerns. The appropriateness of the assessment tool will be determined by the speech-language pathologist and will require the use of clinical judgment. Appendix A contains a reference list of all assessment tools presented in this book. A number of tools are described here to assist the speech-language pathologist in determining the most appropriate tool for the child.

The Assessment of Oral Motor Functions from the book *Oral-Motor Activities for Young Children* by Mackie (1996a) is one assessment tool that can be used with children in the 4- to 6-year age range. This tool is described in Chapter 5. The Verbal-Motor Production Assessment for Children (VMPAC) was developed by Hayden and Square (1999) and is available from the Psychological Corporation. This is a protocol for children ages 3 through 12 years with normative information on speech and nonspeech oral motor skills. The test assesses muscle tone; respiration; phonation; reflexes; jaw, lip, and tongue muscle function; as well as oral motor execution, integration, and sequencing. It should be noted that this tool includes the assessment of respiration and phonation in addition to other aspects of oral motor function. The evaulation of respiration, phonation, and resonation are very important in an oral motor assessment, as these processes provide the air stream, voicing, and quality of sound for speech.

The lists of assessment questions presented in Chapter 5 may also be used to assess body and mouth function, including respiration, phonation, and resonation; eating and drinking skill development; the child's ability to perform nonspeech oral motor tasks; speech production, including intelligibility; and motor planning. The clinician could use items from these lists of questions to customize an assessment tool for the particular population with which the clinician works. If the clinician needs a quick assessment of oral motor function, the Oral-Motor Assessment Checklist may be the tool of choice (see Chapter 4).

It is particularly important to determine the factors affecting the speech production of children in this age group. The clinician will need to assess whether the child is exhibiting an oral motor difficulty related to a muscle function or another physiologic concern, an oral motor difficulty related to motor planning concerns, or an oral motor difficulty related to some combination of the two issues. Refer to discussions in previous chapters regarding ways to determine physiologic concerns versus motor planning issues.

Several assessment tools have been developed for the evaulation of motor planning skills in children ages 4 to 6 years. The Assessment of Verbal Dyspraxia (Jelm, 1995b), the Apraxia Profile (Hickman, 1997), and the Kaufman Speech Praxis Test for Children (Kaufman, 1995) were discussed in Chapter 5. Another tool for the evaluation of motor planning skills is discussed here.

The Screening Test for Developmental Apraxia of Speech (Blakeley, 1980) contains eight subtests assessing the various aspects of dyspraxia found in 4- to 12-year-old children. This tool can be administered in 10 minutes, and the results are quantitative. Subtest I screens for the discrepancy between receptive language and expressive language skills in children with dyspraxia (i.e., receptive language skills are often significantly greater than expressive language abilities). The second subtest screens the child's ability to produce the full range of vowels and diphthongs within single-syllable words. The third subtest screens the child's ability to imitate nonspeech oral movements. Subtest IV screens the child's diadochokinetic skills. The child is asked to produce single sequences of three syllables over five trials and is then asked to produce triple sequences of three syllables over three trials. Subtest V is an imitative articulation task screening the child's production of consonant sounds in the initial, medial, and final positions in words. On the sixth subtest, the child is asked to imitate complex multisyllabic words over three trials. On subtest VII, the child is asked to imitate one- to three-syllable words. The words are scored for the presence of transpositions or redundancies. On subtest VIII, the child's connected speech is screened for prosodic concerns.

It is also important for the clinician to assess speech intelligibility, since intelligible speech production is the desired functional outcome of speech therapy. An intelligibility test is one way for the clinician to observe functional changes in the child's speech intelligibility over time. An intelligibility measure can reflect the changes in the child's speech production resulting from oral motor therapy.

Weiss (1982) developed the Weiss Intelligibility Test "designed to quantify intelligibility of isolated words, contextual speech, and overall intelligibility of children and adolescents" (p. 5). In part A, the client is asked to name 25 pictures of single items. In part B, the client is asked to tell the clinician about one or more pictures to obtain a 200-word speech sample. A percentage of intelligible speech production is calculated for each part of the test, and an overall percentage of intelligibility is also calculated. Wilcox and Morris (1999) developed the Children's Speech Intelligibility Measure (CSIM), a standardized measure of single-word intelligibility for children 3 years of age to 10 years, 11 months of age. It was designed for use with children who exhibit unintelligible speech. Fifty words are imitated by the child, recorded on an audiotape, and then scored by an independent evaluator.

TREATMENT

An oral motor treatment session for the 4- to 6-year-old child may consist of the following:*

- Gross motor activities/exercise program/ball massage
- Oral massage/Other facilitation techniques
- Oral motor activities/exercises
- Specific speech activities with cueing strategies
- Articulation and language therapy

During a 45-minute treatment session the timing of each portion of the session may be as follows. The gross motor/exercise portion may be completed in the first 5 minutes of the session. The oral massage/other facilitation techniques portion may be completed in another 5 minutes of the session. Oral motor activities and exercises may require 10 minutes of the session. Specific speech activities with cueing strategies may require 10 or more minutes, depending on the oral motor needs of the child. Articulation and language activities may comprise the remainder of the session and will often be combined with the specific speech activities. These are only suggested guidelines for the timing of an oral motor treatment session. The child may also need a variety of sensory and motor activities incorporated throughout the session. See Chapters 2 and 3 for specific information on these topics. Treatment should always be specifically tailored to the needs of the client.

The areas listed here may provide a basic structure for an oral motor treatment session, but each area is not meant to be exclusive of the others. Oral motor treatment is a wonderful "dance" among overlapping and integrated areas of treatment. It is also important to note that some of the programs and materials discussed in this chapter may already define activities for the different portions of the oral motor treatment session. For example, each chapter in the program *Easy Does It for Articulation: An Oral Motor Approach* by Strode and Chamberlain (1997) includes "whole body wake-ups," "body positioning and jaw stability" activities, "face wake-ups," "vocal warm-ups," "taste and food activities," as well as "direct facilitation techniques" to encourage the production of specific consonant sounds (Therapy Manual, pp. 7–8).

Special Treatment Considerations

Children in this age group often seem to be aware of activities that may differ from the norm. This can be true of children with cognitive delays as well as children exhibiting typical cognitive development. Oral motor work needs to be carried out on a routine and consistent basis. However, some of the activities (e.g., oral massage, oral exercises, etc.) may not be activities in which the child sees other people engaging on a regular basis. Therefore, it is important for the clinician to assist the care provider and the child in developing routines at home that incorporate suggested oral motor techniques. To be effective, these activities need to be completed three to five times a week and daily if possible (similar to any exercise or motor development program). Siblings and other family members have often been responsive to participation in oral motor activities in order to encourage the child to participate. Puppets can also be used to demonstrate

*List adapted from unpublished workshop materials developed by Diane Chapman Bahr and Libby Kumin; see Kumin & Bahr (1997).

and participate in oral motor tasks. (See information in Chapter 5 regarding the use of puppets in treatment.)

At times, clinicians will stop applying oral massage and other "hands-on" facilitation techniques to children in this age group. This may occur because the children are being treated in a school setting where the parents and care providers may not be attending the treatment session. However, oral massage and other facilitation techniques continue to be an important part of an oral motor treatment program. When working in a school setting, it is important for the clinician to provide the parents with information letters, opportunities to observe and discuss treatment, as well as home activities. Regular home activities are essential for the success of the program. A signed release for the child's participation in oral motor treatment is also recommended, in addition to a signed individualized education plan (IEP). The release should be approved by the school administration. It is important to educate school administrators, teachers, and other appropriate school personnel regarding the nature and importance of oral motor assessment and treatment.

Children may also be treated in a group in a school setting, and the clinician may find it difficult to apply oral motor techniques in a sanitary manner while working with more than one child. In group situations, additional staff can be used to apply the techniques (e.g., assistants, occupational therapists, volunteers, etc.). If the clinician must treat the group of children without the assistance of others, then he or she can devise activities that may provide appropriate oral stimulation for the child. For example, children can use washcloths to massage their own faces. They can massage their own mouths with the Nuk oral massage brush while the clinician quickly massages each child's mouth in a more specific manner. However, care must be taken to do this in a sanitary manner. This will involve the clinician changing gloves or using an antibacterial gel before working with another child.

Gross Motor Activities/Exercise Program/Ball Massage

Gross motor activities continue to be important if postural tone and stability concerns continue to be present. In children with disorders such as cerebral palsy and Down syndrome, these concerns are usually present. In children with mild oral motor difficulties, postural concerns may be subtle. Many of these children sit with a rounded back. They lack stability in the shoulder area and in the jaw. When seated in a chair, they will often wrap their legs around the legs of the chair for stability. Children with mild postural stability concerns may frequently move their bodies while sitting in their chairs. Some evaluators may label children with these tendencies as hyperactive when the actual reason that they are moving in the chair may be a continuous or frequent need for movement to increase muscle tone in the trunk of the body.

Appropriately chosen gross motor activities can build postural tone and stability in children with postural concerns. If the child has a neurological disorder with concomitant hypertonicity or fluctuating muscle tone, the clinician must be careful to choose gross motor activities that will improve postural tone and stability without increasing muscle tone in areas of the body where tone is already high. Slow, organized movement activities may be best for children who tend to have excessive extensor tone in the body. For children with generalized low muscle tone, the gross motor activities must be vigorous enough to increase tone in the body. The clinician should *consult with a physical and/or occupational therapist* regarding appropriate gross motor activities for children with significant postural concerns.

An exercise program may begin to be incorporated into the child's treatment and home programs. Children who exhibit postural stability and control issues will often benefit from being involved in activities that develop the upper body, particularly the shoulder girdle. Resistance and weight-bearing activities can assist with this development. Again, the activities must be carefully chosen for the child exhibiting hypertonicity in the body. Many children in the 4- to 6-year age group become involved in activities such as gymnastics and swimming. These can be particularly good activities for building muscle tone and stability in the upper body. Swimming can also be a good activity for children with high muscle tone, if the water is warm and movements are slow and organized. During the therapy session, the clinician may choose to have the child with low muscle tone participate in 5 minutes of calisthenics that include jumping jacks, wall push-ups, and so on. See the Gross Motor and Sensory Activity Checklist in Chapter 5 for further ideas. Again, it is important to consider any health or physical issues exhibited by the child prior to choosing gross motor activities.

Ball massage may be used with a child in this age group if the child becomes overstimulated by gross motor or other activities or if the child requires the overall tactile and proprioceptive input to act in a focused and organized manner. Ball massage can be relaxing for individuals exhibiting hypertonicity. Refer to information in Chapter 5 on ball massage.

Oral Massage and Other Facilitation Techniques

Oral massage and other facilitation techniques for the 4- to 6-year-old child are similar to those used with the younger child (see information presented in

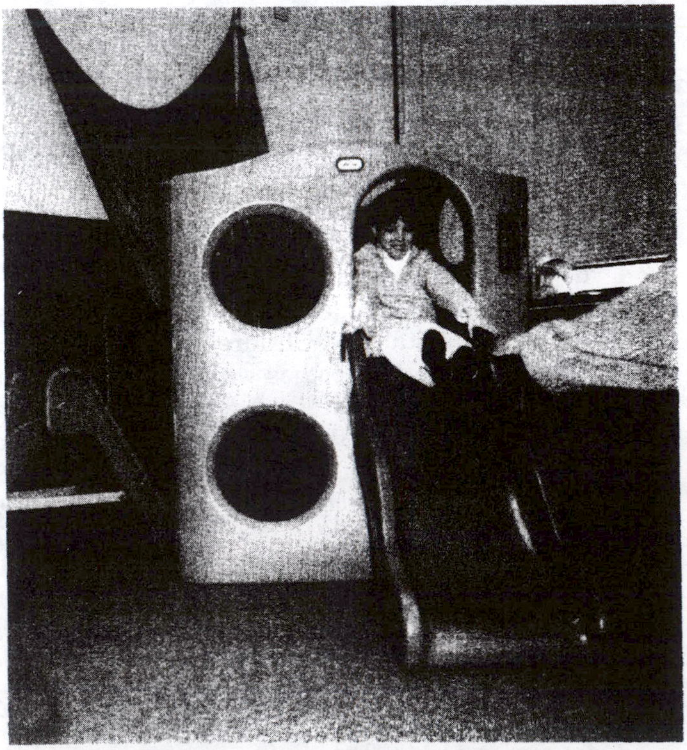

Nicole, a 5-year-old child with Pierre Robin sequence, participates in gross motor activities prior to oral motor, speech, and language treatment.

Chapters 4 and 5 on oral massage and other facilitation techniques). Massage is completed on both the external and internal oral structures. Intraoral massage continues to be an important part of the treatment process, as this can increase intraoral awareness and has the potential to improve the child's responses to sensation in the oral area. The child at this age can often be an active participant in the oral massage process, such as taking turns with the clinician or care provider in brushing the oral area. Although the child is often an active participant in this process, most children at this age do not apply the massage in a specific manner. Therefore, it is important for the clinician and care provider to continue to take part in the massage. The massage can often be accomplished in a game-like format. Some clinicians have created games where the child chooses a picture of an oral area or structure and then that area is the next area to be brushed or massaged. It should be noted that the oral massage protocol can be modified to address the individual needs of each client.

In addition to general oral massage, Beckman (1997) facilitation techniques can be used to improve oral muscle function. If a child has been receiving systematic oral motor treatment prior to reaching ages 4 to 6, then the child will often be amenable to the hands-on nature of the Beckman techniques. However, if a child is just beginning treatment at this age, then the clinician may wish to introduce these facilitation techniques as well as oral massage and brushing techniques by demonstrating them on a puppet (see Chapter 5), care provider, or sibling. As discussed previously, children are great imitators and learn their routines by observing others.

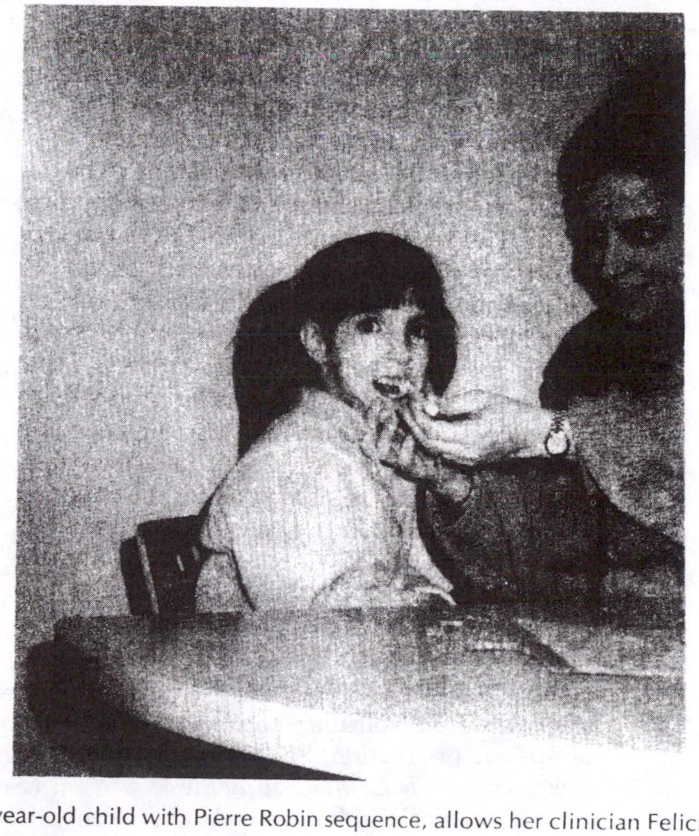

Nicole, a 5-year-old child with Pierre Robin sequence, allows her clinician Felicia to massage her oral structures.

Some preschool children will allow the clinician to apply myofascial release and proprioceptive neuromuscular facilitation techniques. This can often be accomplished by explaining the importance of the use of these techniques to the child in terms that he or she can understand. Myofascial release and proprioceptive neuromuscular facilitation require the child to remain in a position where the clinician or care provider can apply the technique. In particular, myofascial release techniques require the clinician or caregiver to apply the hold until a fascial release is attained. Each release may require as much as 90 to 120 seconds. The clinician must be specifically trained to administer either proprioceptive neuromuscular facilitation or myofascial release techniques. These techniques are described in Chapter 4.

There are also some oral motor tasks that may provide the child with stimuli similar to the oral massage work. For example, chewing very chewy foods may provide the child with some of the deep sensory input attained by the massage work. However, it should be noted that many oral motor tasks do not provide the specific input achieved in oral massage.

Oral Motor Activities/Exercises

There are many oral motor activities and exercises for children with oral motor difficulties in the 4- to 6-year age range. These are determined by careful assessment. It is important to choose the *specific oral motor activities and exercises that suit the individual child's needs* and implement them in a systematic fashion. Most exercise programs require the individual to complete a certain number of repetitions of each exercise in order to gain the desired outcome (i.e., improved muscle function and/or motor planning). Exercise programs usually require an individual to work toward 10 to 15 *controlled* repetitions of an exercise in sets of 3. A number of specific exercises make up the exercise program that is completed at least three to five times per week.

For children with significant feeding and severe oral motor concerns (e.g., children with severe neuromotor issues), the *Pre-Feeding Skills* book by Morris and Klein (1987, 2000) will continue to be a good resource for treatment ideas. Also see previous chapters for treatment ideas.

The resource entitled *M.O.R.E. Integrating the Mouth with Sensory and Postural Functions* by Oetter, Richter, and Frick (1995) contains a description of the many available oral exercisers (e.g., mouth toys, musical instruments, etc.) for children in the 4- to 6-year age group. When using mouth toys and oral exercisers in treatment, it is important that the items are *safe* for oral use (Rosenfeld-Johnson, 1999a). Children who continue to exhibit oral motor concerns in this age group may also continue to need to work toward *adequate respiration during speech production.* Activities that require the controlled use of respiration may be used to assist the child in establishing the quick inspiration and extended expiration needed during speech production. These activities may include the use of whistles, bubbles, and musical instruments. For example, when working with bubbles, the clinician may ask the child to blow the bubbles in a slow and controlled manner similar to the slow expiration needed in speech production. The child can also be taught to imitate sounds of changing rate and rhythm when activating whistles, kazoos, and musical instruments. These can approximate respiratory patterns for speech as well as other prosodic features of speech production. See Chapter 5 for a more thorough description of the resource *M.O.R.E. Integrating the Mouth with Sensory and Postural Functions.*

Systematic and controlled use of horns, straws, and bubbles can encourage graded jaw, lip, and tongue movement in addition to respiratory control. This is described by Rosenfeld-Johnson (1999b) in the book *Oral-Motor Exercises for Speech Clarity*. This book uses task analysis to approach oral motor treatment and includes controlled and systematic oral motor activities to assist the client in developing the motor control needed to produce each consonant and vowel sound. Exercises for respiration, phonation, resonation, and articulation are described in great detail, with the number of repetitions for each exercise noted. The book was developed for clients of all ages and ability levels. Innovative Therapists International is a company that carries a variety of oral motor products developed by Rosenfeld-Johnson, Overland, and their colleagues. Oral motor books, videos, and treatment tools are available through this company. Appendix D contains information on products and resources listed in this and other chapters.

Marshalla (1992) recorded a two-day workshop for clinicians on video discussing oral motor treatment concepts. The workshop is entitled *Oral-Motor Techniques in Articulation Therapy.* Marshalla specifically addresses tactile issues, facilitation techniques for jaw stability, as well as specific techniques for improving oral motor function of the lips and tongue. She discusses the use of these techniques relative to the production of speech sounds such as /l/, /k/, /g/, and /r/. The video series has sections specifically dedicated to the correction of lisps (i.e., frontal and lateral), drooling, and dyspraxia. Marshalla also addresses speech development on the videotapes. In addition to the videos discussed here, Marshalla has developed a variety of oral motor treatment materials. These are available from Speech Dynamics, Inc. This company also carries products developed by Charlotte Boshart, whose materials are discussed in the next chapter.

Easy Does It for Articulation: An Oral-Motor Approach by Strode and Chamberlain (1997) is another resource designed for children ages 4 to 12 years. It is comprised of a Therapy Manual and a Materials Book. The Therapy Manual includes explanations of each component of the program as well as

> program guidelines and suggestions, illustrated techniques for body positioning and oral-motor facilitation, suggestions for creating an oral-motor materials box, a classroom program with sample lesson plans, a tracking sheet for oral-motor stimulation . . . , a tracking sheet for speech practice . . . , answers to common questions, sound group chapters organized by articulator placement . . . , and a reference list. (p. 6)

The Materials Book includes "worksheets for practice of consonant phonemes in isolation; syllables; initial, final, and medial positions in words; multisyllabic words; and phrases and sentences" (p. 6). It also includes stimulus pictures representing target consonant phonemes "in initial, medial, and final positions of words and multisyllabic words" (p. 6). Hand signal pictures and descriptions for visual cueing are included in the Materials Book. Each chapter includes "whole body wake-ups," information on "body positioning and jaw stability," "face wake-ups," "vocal warm-ups," "taste and food activities," as well as "direct facilitation techniques." The chapters address specific consonant sounds according to place of production (i.e., bilabial, labiodental, lingua-alveolar, velar, lingua-alveolar strident, palatal, lingua-alveolar glide, palatal glide, and linguadental sounds). The chapters appear to be arranged generally according to developmental sequence and according to the sound placements that are most easily seen. For example, the first chapter addresses the lip sounds /p/, /b/, /m/, and /w/, whereas the /r/ and "er" sounds are addressed in Chapter 8.

The Complete Oral-Motor Program for Articulation (1996) by Pehde, Geller, and Lechner was developed for children ages 3 to 12. This program can be purchased as a complete kit, containing the manual, picture cards, and a variety of oral motor supplies. The manual can also be purchased separately. Section 1 of the manual addresses early developing sounds (i.e., /p/, /b/, /m/, /w/, /k/, /g/, /t/, /d/, and /l/) and contains activities for the development of jaw stability as well as preschool awareness activities. Section 2 provides specific remediation techniques for the later developing sounds /s/, /z/, "sh," "ch," "j," and /r/. Home activities are included in each section of the program. The program also includes some tools for clinicians, such as a "materials list," "guidelines for classroom lessons," a "parent letter," parent questionnaires, a "sound character and initial sound cards list," and an "oral motor checklist" (p. 3).

Many oral motor materials and supplies are available from Super Duper Publications. These include games, activity books, kits, videotapes, audiotapes, CDs, puppets, and other supplies needed to complete oral motor treatment. Some of the materials include *"Can Do" Oral-Motor Fun and Games* (1997), *"Can Do" Oral-Motor Game Boards* (1998), and the *"Can-Do" Oral-Motor Fun Deck* (1997). The "Can Do" products by DeNinno and Gill focus on activities to increase tongue sensation, strength, and movement as well as activities to increase lip strength and movement. *The Mighty Mouth Game* (1998) by Robbins and Jackson is available from Super Duper Publications. It encourages children to perform 17 pictured oral motor exercises while moving pawns around a game board. The company also carries materials by Marshalla, Boshart, and Morris.

The planning guide shown in Figure 6.1 can be used with individuals of all ages and can assist the speech-language pathologist in systematically planning and tracking treatment activities. Child-specific concerns are listed in the first

FIGURE 6.1 Treatment Plan

Client's name:

Date:

Clinician's name:

CONCERN	ACTIVITY OR EXERCISE	NUMBER OF TARGET REPETITIONS	RESOURCE	DATA COLLECTION

column (e.g., respiratory control, jaw instability, tongue and jaw dissociation, graded jaw/lip/tongue movement, etc.). Activities or exercises are selected to address each specific concern listed. If appropriate, the target number of repetitions for each activity or exercise is listed. Resources for activities and exercises, including specific page numbers, can be listed in the next column. Data can then be collected. See Chapter 9 for related information on goal writing and treatment notes.

INTERACTIVE EXPERIENCE: ORAL MOTOR ACTIVITIES AND EXERCISES

Brainstorm and list appropriate oral motor activities and exercises for children ages 4 to 6 years in the following areas (this activity is a modified version of one used by Jelm [1995b]):

- Activities/exercises for jaw strengthening, stability, and control
- Activities/exercises for tongue strengthening, mobility, and control
- Activities/exercises for lip strengthening, mobility, and control

Specific Speech Activities with Cueing Strategies

Many traditional articulation and phonological activities are appropriate for this portion of treatment. Specific speech activities with cueing strategies are useful with children in this age group who demonstrate muscle function and/or motor planning issues. Moto-kinesthetic, tactile-kinesthetic, and visual-tactile cueing are effective tools, as well. (Refer to information on cueing in the previous chapters.) The characteristics of motor planning concerns often become more apparent as a child develops speech. (See information in Chapter 5 on developmental dyspraxia of speech.)

The *Easy Does It for Apraxia—Preschool* program by Strode and Chamberlain (1994) uses a traditional, bottom-up approach to the treatment of developmental dyspraxia of speech. This program consists of a Therapy Manual and a Materials Book. The goals of the program as described in the Therapy Manual are to "establish interactive, turn taking, and imitative behaviors"; "produce vowel sounds and sequences" as well as "isolated consonants"; "combine consonants and vowels to form syllables"; "produce one-syllable CVC words"; "produce multisyllabic words"; and "produce consonant blends in words" (p. 8). This program includes visual cues called hand signals, which are described as well as pictured. The program was developed for the 2- to 6-year-old client and uses a VAKT (i.e., visual, auditory, kinesthetic, tactile) approach.

Easy Does It for Apraxia and Motor Planning is another program by Strode and Chamberlain (1993). This program, developed for children ages 4 to 12, uses a traditional, bottom-up approach to the treatment of developmental dyspraxia of speech. The goals for the child as described in the Therapy Manual include producing "vowel sequences and isolated consonants," combining "consonants and vowels to form syllables," producing "one-syllable words using consonant-vowel-consonant (CVC) combinations," producing "multisyllabic words," producing "phrases and sentences," and producing "consonant blends in words" (pp. 4–5). The program consists of a Therapy Manual and a Materials Book and uses a VAKT (i.e., visual, auditory, kinesthetic, tactile) approach.

Jelm (1995b) developed a system of treatment for children that is somewhat different from the approach used by Strode and Chamberlain. She calls her approach "a hierarchical model of treatment" (p. T-8). This model has five levels. Level I is comprised of spontaneous movement at the automatic level. Level II provides the child with experience and awareness activities. Level III involves imitation and repetition activities while the child is in a stable position. Level IV involves imitation and repetition activities as the child is involved in movement. Level V consists of functional activities. This approach considers the ideas that individuals with dyspraxia generally have developed some automatic spontaneous speech but require awareness activities as well as consistent practice to add items to their speech repertoire. Jelm developed a system of visual-tactile cues (discussed previously) that are easily learned. She has also created a guide to explain verbal dyspraxia to parents. This guide, entitled *A Parent Guide to Verbal Dyspraxia* (Jelm, 1995a), is very useful in explaining a motor planning concern versus a muscle function concern to parents.

Articulation and Language Therapy

The traditional forms of articulation and language therapy may be used in conjunction with the preceding approaches and activities. In addition to the specific sounds in error, it is important to consider the phonological processes involved. Oral motor treatment may assist the child in resolving phonological issues, such as fronting, backing, cluster reduction, final consonant deletion, and so on. Many excellent resources are available on the treatment of phonological process concerns, but it is beyond the scope of this book to discuss these.

Language treatment can certainly be incorporated throughout the treatment session with a segment of the session focused specifically on this area as needed by the child. The child's language development is extremely important to facilitate and monitor. Children with oral motor concerns frequently demonstrate receptive and expressive language concerns. If the child is not developing expressive language in a typical manner, then the child may not be receiving appropriate feedback to refine receptive language concepts. For example, a child who thinks all furry, four-legged animals are dogs may not be able to express this concept intelligibly. The child, therefore, cannot receive the feedback from others regarding the refinement of this and other concepts. This difficulty may affect the development of the child's reasoning abilities. Pragmatic concerns are also frequently noted in individuals with oral motor issues. As previously mentioned, children with articulation concerns may have less opportunities to develop social communication skills and/or may be treated differently (e.g., as less capable) by others who interact with them.

CASE EXAMPLE

Description

Johnny is a 5-year-old child exhibiting the characteristics of developmental dyspraxia of speech. He has normal hearing and his receptive language skills are age appropriate, but his expressive language skills are significantly below age level. Johnny's gross and fine motor skills appear to be age appropriate. However, he exhibits some sensory integrative concerns (e.g., apparent hypersensitivity to oral and other tactile input, as well as apparent desire for deep proprioceptive input).

As an infant, Johnny reportedly demonstrated limited sound play. He was described as a very quiet baby. Johnny was said to be a "late talker." He did not say his first word consistently until 18 months of age, and he did not put words together until 3 years of age. However, Johnny reportedly produced clear words and phrases on occasion that were not heard again until he was much older.

Currently, Johnny's speech contains many articulation and phonological errors. He omits many sounds, particularly those at the ends of words. He consistently substitutes error sounds for the correct sounds when he is speaking in a spontaneous manner. However, when asked to imitate words and phrases, he produces inconsistent sound substitutions. Johnny has great difficulty producing words containing consonant clusters. He frequently reduces the clusters to single consonant sounds. Johnny transposes consonant sounds in words. However, his production of vowel sounds is generally accurate. He often voices unvoiced consonant sounds. He exhibits a very fast speaking rate, and he demonstrates irregular speech rhythm and intonation. Johnny does not exhibit any groping or struggle behaviors during speech production. However, he demonstrates groping and struggle behaviors when attempting to imitate nonspeech motor acts (e.g., imitative lip and tongue movements). As Johnny's length of utterance increases, his speech becomes increasingly less intelligible. When asked to imitate diadochokinetic activities, his production is slow and irregular. However, when provided with visual and tactile cueing, Johnny's speech production improves significantly.

Treatment Plan

Gross Motor Activities Provide Johnny with gross motor activities that are accompanied by sound and speech production. The *Easy Does It for Apraxia—Preschool* program suggests movements to accompany sound production. Activities that incorporate body movements with the words of a song (e.g., *Head, Shoulders, Knees, and Toes, Hokey Pokey,* etc.) may assist Johnny in developing a more organized motor plan. Body movement can facilitate sound and speech production.

Oral Massage Provide Johnny with oral massage to improve responses to oral sensation and increase oral awareness.

Oral Motor Activities and Exercises Provide activities to facilitate motor planning with Johnny. Ask him to participate in oral motor activities that are rhythmic and organizing (e.g., lip and tongue movements synchronized to the rhythm of music or a drum beat). Have Johnny practice lip and tongue movements that are similar to the movements used in the production of the speech sounds he is learning to motor plan.

Specific Speech Activities with Cueing Strategies Use a traditional or hierarchical approach to treatment. Provide Johnny with a large amount of speech practice so that he has the opportunity to establish and routinize motor plans for speech. Be sure that Johnny has regular home practice activities. Use visual-tactile cueing and the pacing board to facilitate speech production in all appropriate settings.

Recommendations

1. Suggest that Johnny be screened by an occupational therapist trained in sensory integrative treatment regarding apparent tactile and proprioceptive needs.
2. Educate Johnny's parents, teachers, and others, regarding the nature of developmental dyspraxia of speech.
3. Provide consistent home practice activities for Johnny. Provide carry-over activities for the classroom.

INTERACTIVE CASE EXPERIENCE

The interactive case experience will allow the reader to practice using the information from the chapter. This experience is meant to challenge the reader to think of possibilities for the case presented. The answers to the questions in the interactive case experience are for the reader to decide.

Review Johnny's case. Using the treatment-planning guide presented in this chapter (Figure 6.1), identify Johnny's concerns that need to be addressed. What resources, materials, or tools might you use as part of treatment? If available, review these resources and materials. Develop activities or exercises for each part of the treatment plan. Include the number of target repetitions for each activity or exercise if appropriate. What other recommendations need to be made? What other comments or ideas do you have concerning Johnny?

7

Ages 6 to 12

Working with School-Aged Children

School-aged children with oral motor concerns frequently receive speech-language assessment and treatment through services provided in the school setting. Providing effective oral motor assessment and treatment can present a particular challenge to the clinician in the schools. Caseloads in the school setting are often large, and children receiving oral motor treatment often require at least some individual treatment. However, the clinician can creatively incorporate many oral motor activities into group treatment. A number of treatment materials have been developed with this idea. Group treatment was briefly discussed in Chapter 6 and will be further discussed in this chapter.

Children with severe oral motor difficulties that affect eating and drinking as well as sound production may attend schools with staff specifically trained in oral motor assessment and treatment. However, many children with severe difficulties are included in school settings where the staff may not be specifically trained. It is often a challenge for the clinician in the school to handle the very specific oral motor needs of these children. This chapter will provide information on assessment and treatment techniques as well as materials and resources to assist clinicians working with the school-aged population.

ASSESSMENT

It is important for the clinician working with school-aged children to attain an oral motor case history from the child's parents or guardians. This may require some extra effort from the clinician, as parents and guardians are not often as available to the school clinician as they are during the infant, toddler, and preschool years. The gathering of case history information can be used as part of the initial educational process for parents and guardians, for it is important to educate parents and guardians about oral motor assessment and treatment. Chapter 4 contains a suggested case history form. After gathering case history information, the clinician can choose an appropriate oral motor assessment tool for the individual child.

The components of the oral motor assessment may include some or all of those discussed in Chapter 5. Posture, positioning, and whole-body movement patterns continue to be important to take into account with this age group. The child's oral structures at rest as well as his or her oral motor function while performing a variety of oral motor tasks (e.g., eating, drinking, nonspeech tasks, speech tasks) need to be evaluated. Some clinicians may choose to skip the assessment of the child's eating and drinking skills secondary to time constraints or some other reason. However, the child's eating and drinking skills may provide some significant diagnostic information about muscle function versus motor planning concerns. Refer to discussions on motor planning in previous chapters. Also, children with muscle function concerns may continue to demonstrate unsophisticated oral motor patterns while eating and drinking. This may have an impact on their social interactions during mealtimes as well as their ability to manage food and liquid. A small snack as part of the assessment process can provide the clinician with important information about the child's oral movement patterns. A variety of assessment tools are discussed in this chapter. The clinician will need to choose appropriate tools based on the client's individual needs. See Appendix A for a complete reference list of the assessment tools presented in the book.

For children in this age group with severe oral motor concerns, the assessments discussed in earlier chapters may be most useful. Checklists such as the Developmental Pre-Feeding Checklist (Morris & Klein, 2000, Appendix B; Klein & Morris, 1999, pp. 480–509; Morris & Klein, 1987, pp. 75–82), the Body Alignment for Seating and Positioning Checklist (Morris & Klein, 2000, p. 305), the Positioning Checklist (Morris & Klein, 1987, p. 169), and the Self-Feeding Checklist from *Pre-Feeding Skills* (Morris & Klein, 1987, p. 306) may continue to be very useful with children demonstrating severe oral motor concerns that affect eating and drinking.

The Oral Motor Assessment Checklist in Chapter 4 of this book may be a useful tool for the clinician working with school-aged children. This checklist can be used with individuals exhibiting a variety of severity levels. It is also quick and easy to administer. Time is often a factor for the very busy clinician.

The assessment questions presented in Chapter 5 may also be used by the clinician to evaluate school-aged children. The clinician may decide to use these questions as a guide in developing an assessment tool specific to the population of children being served. The Verbal-Motor Production Assessment for Children (VMPAC) by Hayden and Square (1999) as well as the Beckman Oral Motor Assessment Protocol (Beckman, 1997) would both be appropriate oral motor assessments for children in this age group. See Chapters 4 and 6 for a description of these assessment tools.

The Assessment of Oral-Motor Functions from the book *Oral-Motor Activities for Young Children* (Mackie, 1996a) is another assessment tool that can continue to be used with children in the 6- to 12-year range (see Chapter 5). Mackie (1996b) also developed two other assessments that can be found in the book entitled *Oral-Motor Activities for School-Aged Children:* the Assessment of Oral-Motor Functions during Non-Speech Tasks and the Assessment of Oral-Motor Functions during Speech Tasks. Eating and drinking skills are not evaluated on these two assessments. On the Assessment of Oral-Motor Functions during Non-Speech Tasks the following are assessed: the body and mouth at rest; the strength and stability of the jaw, lips, and tongue; and the mobility and differentiation of the jaw, cheeks, lips, and tongue. On the Assessment of Oral-Motor Functions during Speech Tasks, the child's oral motor function is assessed during the production of conversational speech as well as during other speech production tasks. This assessment is meant to be used in conjunction with an articulation test. Both assessments (i.e., Assessment of Oral-Motor Functions during Non-Speech Tasks and Assessment of Oral-Motor Functions during Speech Tasks) use a checklist format for recording observations. The possible indications of each observation are also listed in each assessment for the clinician (e.g., a "straight and erect" body and trunk position may indicate "good trunk support for speech production" [p. 9]). A Student Profile Sheet (p. 22) is used to summarize the results of both assessment tools.

Boshart (1998) developed a simple one-page assessment entitled Oral Sensory—Motor Analysis to observe "tactile sensitivity" and "oral-motor differentiation" (p. 28). The client's neck, face, and oral structures are evaluated for normal responsivity, hyperresponsivity, or hyporesponsivity. Dissociated movements of the lips and tongue are assessed by asking the client to complete a variety of oral movements. These movements are rated on a scale of 1 to 5, with 1 representing independent movement of the articulator being assessed.

It is often during the school years that clinicians assess children for myofunctional (i.e., tongue thrust) concerns affecting dental and speech development. The acquisition of a mature swallowing pattern by the child is a developmental process. Graber (1976, as cited by Pierce, 1978, p. 16) states that the infantile swallowing pattern "remains dominant until five or six months of age and starts to change only with the eruption of the lower incisor teeth." According to Pierce (1978), the primary tongue thrust stage extends from "infancy until the beginning of mixed dentition (the period when both 'baby teeth' and permanent teeth are present)" (p. 16). A study by Hanson and Cohen (1973) revealed that 57.9 percent of children age 4 years, 9 months exhibited a tongue thrust swallowing pattern. The transitional tongue thrust stage seems to occur in children between the ages of 6 and 10 years. This is a time when children have mixed dentition, the mandible and maxilla may be growing at uneven rates, the extrinsic tongue muscles change orientation, and the intrinsic tongue muscles develop finer coordination and control (Pierce, 1978).

Pierce (1978) suggests that the sequence in which the teeth erupt is more important than the age at which the teeth erupt. (See Dentition Checklist in Chapter 5 for information regarding the typical age and sequence of tooth eruption.) "The presence of tongue thrust may be a normal but transient occurrence during mixed dentition" (p. 17). Fletcher (1974, as cited by Pierce, 1978, p. 17) states that children should exhibit "a mature swallowing pattern" by 10 to 12 years of age. According to Pierce, "the research seems to indicate that if the child has not developed a normal swallowing pattern by age 10, he is not likely to self-correct" (p. 13). Approximately 30 percent of the general population maintain a tongue thrust swallowing pattern at age 18 without intervention (Fletcher, Casteel, & Bradley, 1961).

Pierce (1993) developed the Checklist for Tongue Thrust Evaluation and the Tongue Thrust Evaluation. These can be found in the book entitled *Swallow Right: An Exercise Program to Correct Swallowing Patterns.* The Checklist for Tongue Thrust Evaluation assesses the swallowing of liquids, solids, and saliva; eating and drinking patterns and concerns; dentition and dental alignment; structure and movement of the lips, tongue, hard palate, and soft palate; speech production; breathing patterns; feeding and family dental history; as well as other oral behaviors. The Tongue Thrust Evaluation reflects the results of the Checklist for Tongue Thrust Evaluation and can be sent to a referring dentist or orthodontist.

A variety of tools to assess motor planning concerns in children were discussed in Chapters 5 and 6. The Assessment of Verbal Dyspraxia (Jelm, 1995b) and the Screening Test for Developmental Apraxia of Speech (Blakeley, 1980) are both appropriate assessment tools for school-aged children. Hickman developed a School-Age Profile as part of *The Apraxia Profile* (1997). The School-Age Profile is comprised of an oral motor exam, a word repetition subtest, a phrase and sentence repetition subtest, a connected speech sample, and a checklist of dyspraxic characteristics. The oral motor exam consists of automatic oral movements, such as those occurring during eating and drinking activities; imitated nonspeech lip and tongue movements; sequences of imitated nonspeech lip, tongue, and jaw movements; imitated lip and tongue movements during sound production; as well as imitated sound sequences. Omissions, distortions, substitutions, and additions are noted on section A of the word repetition subtest. On section B of the word repetition subtest, the child is asked to repeat challenging multisyllabic words over three trials. On the phrase and sentence repetition subtest, the child is required to repeat phrases and sentences as well as count from 1 to 10. Some of these imitated utterances are evaluated for omissions, distortions, substitutions, and additions; others are assessed for appropriate prosody. The child's connected speech sample is rated for intelligibility, and mean length of utterance is calculated. Comments can also be made regarding the child's syntax, morphology, voice, fluency, and prosody during connected speech. The dyspraxia checklist itemizes 50 characteristics; the first 10 items on the checklist are most characteristic of dyspraxia. Many of the other 40 characteristics are indicators of dyspraxia; however, some of these characteristics could also indicate a muscle function concern. The test is summarized both quantitatively and descriptively.

Tests of intelligibility assist the clinician in tracking the child's progress in oral motor treatment. Speech intelligibility is the desired functional outcome of an oral motor treatment program addressing improved speech production. The Weiss Intelligibility Test (Weiss, 1982) and the Children's Speech Intelligibility Measure (CSIM) (Wilcox & Morris, 1999) are both appropriate tools for children in this age group. Both tools were described in Chapter 6.

School-aged children may exhibit overt oral motor concerns, such as postural instability, jaw instability, low oral muscle tone, difficulty with tongue and jaw dissociation, sensation issues, myofunctional issues, motor planning concerns, and so on. However, a number of school-aged children will exhibit subtle muscle function or motor planning concerns that may be difficult to assess. Some children have developed compensatory strategies (e.g., maintaining the jaw in a high position while speaking) that may not initially be apparent to the clinician. The clinician will learn to discern the subtle characteristics demonstrated by these children with increased experience in assessment and treatment of individuals with oral motor concerns.

TREATMENT

Children with severe oral motor concerns may continue to require treatment techniques similar to those used with a younger child. Again, the *Pre-Feeding Skills* book by Morris and Klein (1987, 2000) is a good resource for assessment and treatment ideas for individuals with severe oral motor concerns that affect feeding. Neuro-developmental treatment, Feldenkrais's "Awareness through Movement," myofascial release, and proprioceptive neuromuscular facilitation may be useful when working with children who exhibit severe oral motor concerns in the 6- to 12-year age group. These techniques were discussed in previous chapters.

When providing oral motor treatment to school-aged children, the clinician must make a special effort to educate parents, caregivers, and school personnel. Permission forms for oral motor assessment and treatment should specify the hands-on nature of the process, so that parents and care providers have a clear understanding that some of the techniques require the clinician to touch the child. Education of parents, care providers, and school personnel regarding the reasons for using these techniques is important. It is often easy for parents, care providers, and school personnel to understand that oral motor treatment is similar to the work done in physical therapy and occupational therapy to address sensory and motor concerns in other areas of the body. The techniques (e.g., massage, awareness activities, exercises and activities for improved muscle tone and precision of movement, etc.) are often used in physical and occupational therapy programs. Rationales for the use of techniques discussed in this chapter were provided in Chapters 1 through 3.

It is recommended that the school clinician provide information sessions for school personnel, parents, and guardians. Letters to parents and care providers can be sent to explain treatment techniques as well as to reinforce information provided in information sessions. Individual conferences with parents, care providers, and school personnel can assist the clinician in establishing an effective oral motor program for the child. As previously mentioned, it is also recommended that the clinician obtain a signed consent from the child's parent or guardian to perform oral motor treatment techniques that may require hands-on work.

Education of others involved with the child can assist the clinician in attaining the carry-over of oral motor activities at home and in school. Oral motor treatment is most successful if someone in the child's environment is applying the techniques used in treatment on a regular basis (i.e., at least three to five times per week, and daily if possible). This is similar to most exercise or physical activity programs. In order to change muscle function and/or improve motor planning, it is important to establish a regular oral motor treatment routine for the child.

The speech-language clinician may also wish to involve other school personnel as well as parents and other volunteers in the oral motor treatment program. This may be particularly important if the clinician provides the treatment in a group session. Occupational therapists and physical therapists may want to cotreat with the speech-language pathologist. Classroom assistants or teachers may be called on if a number of students in a class require this type of treatment. Treatment can occur within the classroom setting if the majority of the students in a small class require oral motor treatment. In some settings, oral massage is provided prior meals or oral language time in the classroom. In other settings, where only a few children in a class require the oral motor treatment, a speech pathology assistant, parents, or other volunteers may assist the speech-language pathologist during group treatment outside of the classroom. If the speech-language pathologist is providing individual oral motor treatment in a school setting, the clinician may consider providing the treatment in an area where others (e.g., parents, guardians, school personnel, and others as appropriate) can observe. This assists with the education of others regarding the techniques used and protects the clinician from concerns others may have regarding the hands-on work involved in oral motor treatment.

Oral motor treatment for the school-aged child may consist of the following components:*

- Gross motor activities/exercise program/ball massage

*List adapted from unpublished workshop materials developed by Diane Chapman Bahr and Libby Kumin; see Kumin & Bahr (1997).

- Oral massage/Other facilitation techniques
- Oral motor activities/exercises
- Specific speech activities with cueing strategies
- Articulation and language therapy

An oral motor treatment session for a child in this age group may involve 5 minutes of gross motor/exercise activities to improve postural tone and stability, 5 minutes of oral massage/other facilitation techniques to increase oral awareness and oral muscle function, and 10 minutes of oral motor activities and exercises to improve specific oral movements or functions. The remainder of the session would involve specific speech activities as well as language tasks. As previously discussed, the timing and sequence of the segments involved in the session should be modified according to the needs of the clients. However, the suggested timing and sequence has been provided for the speech-language pathologist who is beginning to use this approach to oral motor treatment. As the speech-language pathologist develops skill and his or her own style in this area of treatment, the timing and sequence may change. A 45-minute treatment session is recommended.

Gross Motor Activities/Exercise Program/Ball Massage

As previously mentioned, the gross motor/exercise portion of the session may require the first 5 minutes of the session. This may include vigorous aerobic activities or calisthenics for children with generalized low muscle tone. Children with high muscle tone, fluctuating muscle tone, or mixed muscle tone may require a more careful selection of movement activities. The physical and/or occupational therapist can assist the speech-language pathologist in the process of choosing appropriate gross motor activities or exercises for each child. Children in this age group often respond well to activities on video. For example, a children's aerobic exercise tape could be used with children demonstrating generalized low muscle tone. A T'ai Chi video may provide appropriate movements for individuals with a variety of tonal as well as movement coordination concerns. The Gross Motor and Sensory Activity Checklist in Chapter 5 contains many activities that would continue to be appropriate for the school-aged child. Children in this age group are also frequently involved in organized sport and exercise programs. As mentioned in Chapter 6, swimming, gymnastics, and other activities that develop the trunk and shoulder girdle could assist in the child's development of postural stability and control as well as motor organization. Some children may participate in an appropriately supervised lightweight training program to accomplish this goal. It continues to be important to consider any health or physical limitations that may preclude certain forms of physical activity for the child.

The ball massage may continue to be appropriate for children who require calming after gross motor or other activities or for those who do not have a good sense of body awareness. The ball massage may also be modified. Instead of using a large therapy ball, a smaller ball may be used for this activity. The smaller ball can be rolled along the surfaces of the child's arms and back. The child can also roll the ball over his or her own body surfaces.

Oral Massage and Other Facilitation Techniques

The oral massage can be administered as previously described (see protocol/sequence in Chapter 4). Many school-aged children will be interested in massaging and brushing their own mouths. It is important to empower children by allowing them to be partners in treatment. However, the clinician may not wish to fully relinquish the application of these activities, as the child may not apply the techniques as specifically or deeply as needed to achieve increased awareness. Beckman (1997) facilitation techniques can continue to be used with the school-aged child. A game may need to be devised for younger children in this age group to participate in the oral massage and other facilitation techniques. Some children in this age group may allow the clinician to apply techniques such as myofascial release and proprioceptive neuromuscular facilitation with an explanation that the child can understand. Chapter 4 describes these techniques.

Oral Motor Activities/Exercises

Oral motor activities/exercises *must be carefully selected* for the school-aged child. This involves careful assessment of the child's oral motor concerns and task analysis of his or her goals. The exercises and activities must directly relate to the child's goals. For example, if the child needs to improve tongue and jaw dissociation for precise speech production, then activities should address jaw and tongue movements that are used in speech production. The Treatment Plan in Chapter 6 (Figure 6.1) can be used to plan appropriate oral motor activities

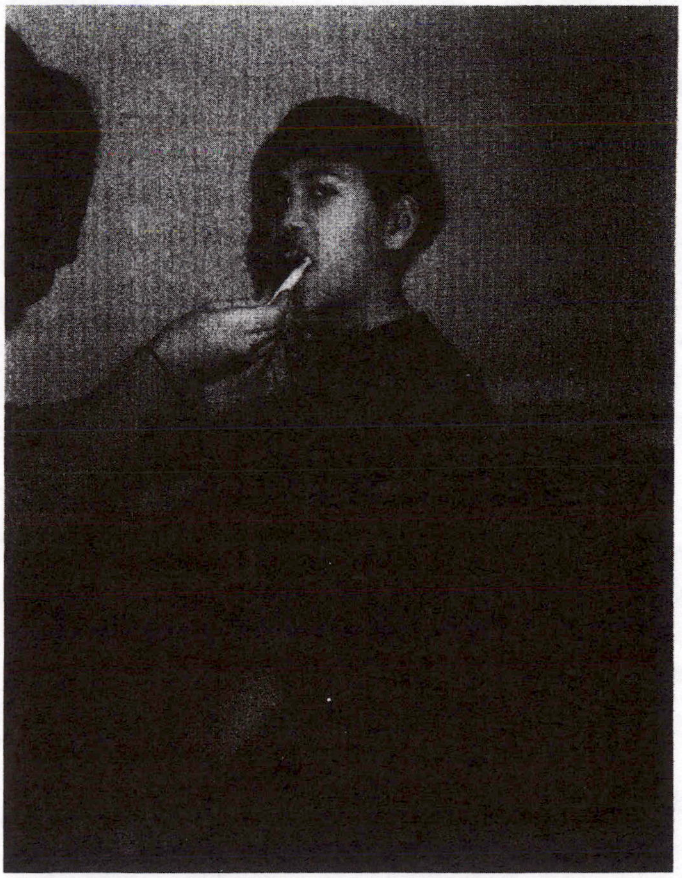

Daniel, a 10-year-old child with imprecise speech and a reverse swallowing pattern, allows his clinician Amy to complete the oral massage.

based on the client's identified oral motor needs. Figure 7.1 can be used in addition to the Treatment Plan to analyze the steps needed to accomplish an oral motor goal.

Children who continue to exhibit oral motor concerns in the school-aged population may also continue to need to work toward adequate *respiration* during speech production. Activities that require the controlled use of respiration may be used to assist the child in establishing quick inspiration and extended expiration during speech production. These activities may include the use of whistles, bubbles, and musical instruments, as suggested in the book *M.O.R.E.: Integrating the Mouth with Sensory and Postural Functions* by Oetter, Richter, and Frick (1995). Discussion of this resource can be found in Chapters 5 and 6. Rosenfeld-Johnson (1999a, 1999b) has also developed a number of techniques and materials addressing the graded abdominal control needed for speech respiration. She analyzed each step of the process and has the clients complete activities involving bubbles and horns in a systematic, hierarchical manner. These techniques are described in the book *Oral-Motor Activities for Speech Clarity* (1999b).

There are many programs and materials containing oral motor activities/exercises for the school-aged population. *M.O.R.E.: Integrating the Mouth with Sensory and Postural Functions* by Oetter, Richter, and Frick (1995), *Easy Does It for Articulation: An Oral-Motor Approach* by Strode and Chamberlain (1997), *The Complete Oral-Motor Program for Articulation* by Pehde, Geller, and Lech-

FIGURE 7.1 Task Analysis

Client's Name:

Clinician's Name:

Date:

Goal:

STEPS TO ATTAIN GOAL	ACTIVITIES/ EXERCISES	NUMBER OF TARGET REPETITIONS (IF APPROPRIATE)	RESOURCES/ MATERIALS/ TOOLS	DATE ACHIEVED
1.				
2.				
3.				
4.				
5.				
6.				
7.				
8.				
9.				
10.				

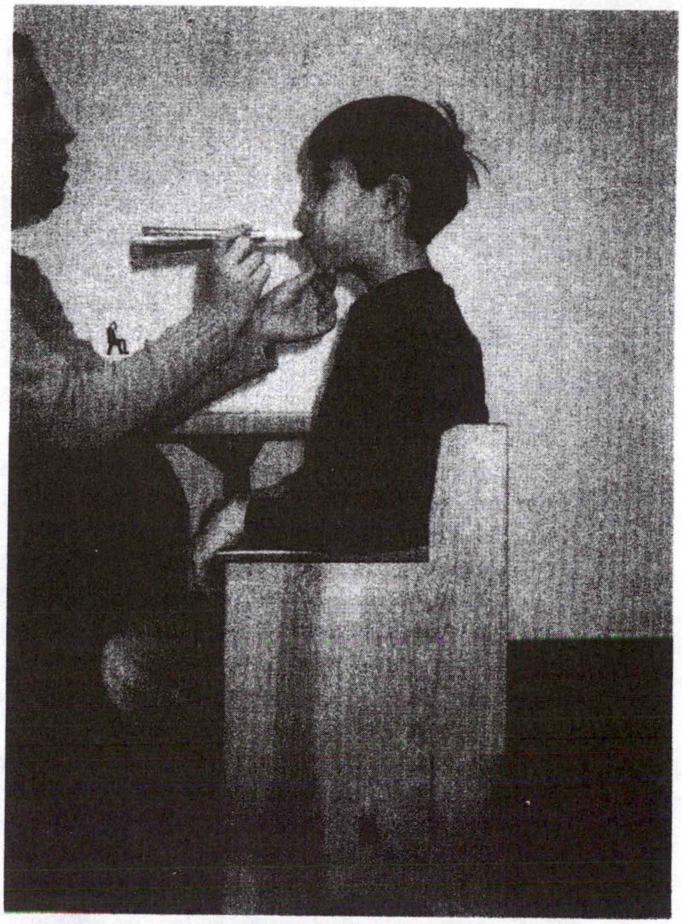

Daniel, a 10-year-old child with imprecise speech and a reverse swallowing pattern, works on a horn-blowing activity (Rosenfeld-Johnson, 1999b) with his clinician Amy. He is seated in a chair that was specifically designed to promote appropriate posture in someone Daniel's size.

ner (1996), and *Oral-Motor Exercises for Speech Clarity* by Rosenfeld-Johnson (1999b) were discussed in Chapters 5 and 6. The straw and horn programs developed by Rosenfeld-Johnson (1999b) can be particularly effective with this age group. Their systematic nature and the amount of home practice suggested in the programs can significantly reduce overall therapy time for the child. Many oral motor materials and supplies for the school-aged child are available from Innovative Therapists International, Speech Dynamics, Inc., Super Duper Publications, and others (see product sources in Appendix D). Puppets (see Chapter 5) can continue to be used in treatment to demonstrate oral motor activities and exercises as well as the placement of the articulators for the production of specific speech sounds.

In addition to these activities and materials, a number of other individuals have developed oral motor materials and tools for the school-aged child. The book *Oral-Motor Activities for School-Aged Children* by Mackie (1996b) contains an oral motor program of 20 mandatory lessons. Specific areas of oral motor need are targeted in these activities. These include "enhancing proprioceptive and kinesthetic awareness," "improving oral sensory awareness," differentiating tongue movement from jaw movement, "improving jaw control and stability," "improving tongue control and mobility," "improving tongue control for elevation," "improving lateral tongue stability and mobility," and other important oral motor skills needed for effective speech production. The program also includes specific oral motor activities that address the oral movements needed for the production of the /r/, /s/, /l/, "sh," "ch," and "j" sounds.

The book *MA CAT: Motor Activities for Children in Articulation Therapy* by Kuratomi (1997) contains oral motor activities for the body, neck, head, face, jaw, mentalis muscle, lips, tongue, gums, palate, and cheeks. This manual was developed to accompany systems to facilitate the production of specific speech sounds by Boshart and Jutila. The systems will be discussed at a later point in this chapter. Each activity in the *MA CAT* contains the activity code number (corresponding with an activity in the Boshart and Jutila systems), the skill developed by the activity, pictured tools needed for the activity, and pictured steps to complete the activity. The activity pages can be sent with the child for home practice. Activities are chosen from this resource based on the child's performance on Boshart's (1998) Oral Sensory—Motor Analysis. *MA CAT* activities address the improvement of sensation, "proprioception, muscle tone, lip closure, resting posture, relaxation, differentiation, stabilization, and flexibility."

Myofunctional therapy can often be completed with children in this age group who exhibit a tongue thrust (also called a *reverse swallow*) pattern when swallowing. This type of treatment is frequently used with adolescents as well as adults. The tongue thrust pattern may affect the individual's production of certain speech sounds (e.g., sibilant sounds are often fronted) and the development of the individual's dentition. Charles Straub, an orthodontist, was the "first professional to create and publish a tongue thrust therapy program" (Boshart, 1995b). The American Speech-Language-Hearing Association developed two documents entitled *The Role of the Speech-Language Pathologist in Assessment and Management of Oral Myofunctional Disorders* (1991) and *Oral Myofunctional Disorders: Knowledge and Skills* (1993). These documents clarify the clinician's role and define necessary skills needed by the clinician who works with individuals exhibiting myofunctional concerns.

Garliner (1974) authored a text entitled *Myofunctional Therapy in Dental Practice: Abnormal Swallowing Habits: Diagnosis—Treatment.* The book was written for dental practitioners and speech pathologists and provides a thorough discussion of myofunctional assessment and treatment. Garliner states the following goals for myofunctional therapy:

1. The primary goal for Myofunctional therapy before dental intervention is to establish a more normal orofacial muscle balance to aid in the eventual growth and development of the dental form.
2. The primary goal for Myofunctional therapy during dental intervention is to adapt the orofacial muscles to the changing dental form and thus aid in the eventual establishment of a more normal occlusal relationship.
3. The primary goal for Myofunctional therapy after dental intervention is to adapt the orofacial muscles to the changed dental form. (p. 271)

In addition to a complete description of treatment techniques, Garliner also provides the clinician with the answers to many important questions about myofunctional therapy (e.g., At what age should myofunctional treatment begin?).

Swallow Right: An Exercise Program to Correct Swallowing Patterns by Pierce (1993) provides a description of the etiology, anatomy, diagnosis, and treatment of myofunctional disorders. The program can be used with children, adolescents, and adults exhibiting myofunctional concerns and can be applied using individual or small group instruction. It is comprised of 12 lessons divided into three stages of treatment. Lessons 1–5 comprise the first stage of muscle training, lessons 6 and 7 are focused on training the swallow, and lessons 8–12 are devoted to habituation of the new oral motor and swallowing patterns for the client. The program also includes an evaluation for tongue thrust, methods for charting progress at home and in the clinic, guidelines for parents, and information on the elimination of fingernail biting and thumb or finger sucking. A recommended therapy schedule (i.e., the time recommended for each aspect of the program) is also provided.

Swalloworks, developed by Boshart (1995b), is a program for the remediation of myofunctional concerns in children, adolescents, and adults. The program is comprised of 10 lessons and a final meal exam. Each lesson emphasizes appropriate oral resting position, muscle training activities, as well as functional swallowing activities (e.g., saliva swallowing, swallowing from a cup, swallowing during meals, etc.). The program stresses the importance of daily practice. Boshart also provides the clinician with background information on oral motor function and development, comparison of the deviant and normal swallow, tongue resting position, and respiration. The importance of stability for mobility; dissociation of movement among the different oral structures; "tongue strength, tone and endurance"; (p. 2) as well as "tactile sensitivity and proprioception" (p. 3) are discussed.

Taming the Tongue Thrust, developed by Barnes (1994), is another program for addressing myofunctional concerns in children, adolescents, and adults. The goals of the program are as follows: "Develop correct posture and

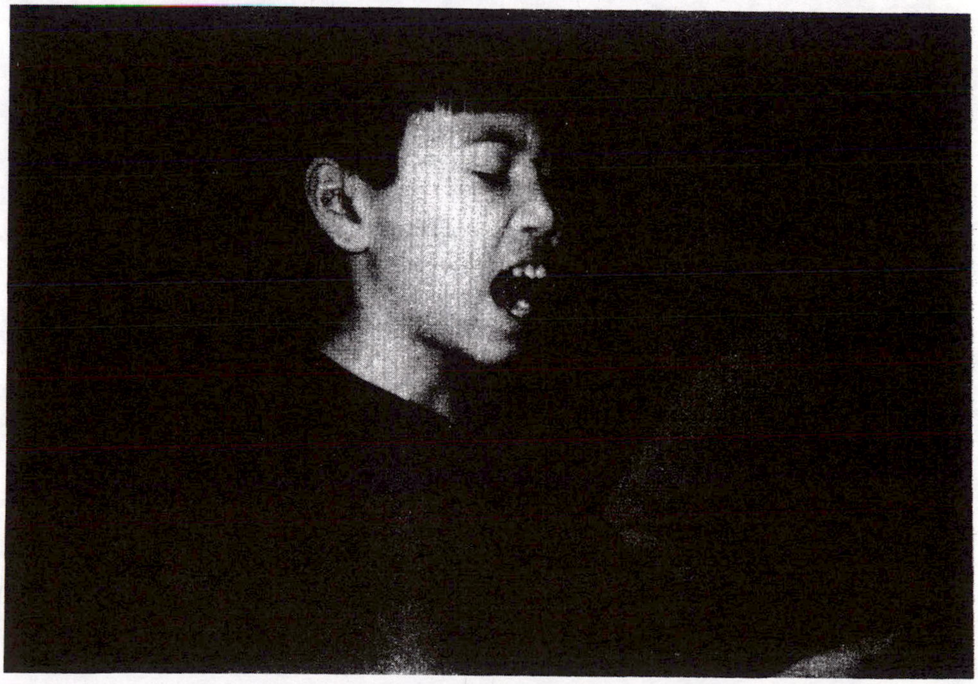

Daniel, a 10-year-old child with imprecise speech and a reverse swallowing pattern, works on placing his tongue on the alveolar ridge. He is just beginning myofunctional therapy.

improve muscle tone of tongue, lips, and facial muscles; synchronize the muscles and steps associated with the correct swallow; eliminate detrimental oral habits"; and "create normal function for resting, chewing, swallowing, and speaking" (p. 6). The program is comprised of a treatment manual and a video, in which the exercises in the program are demonstrated. The manual provides information on causes, concerns, and effects of tongue thrust (pp. 1–4) as well as specifics about how to implement the program. A time table for the training, stabilization, and habituation of the "normal" swallow is recommended. The importance of charting progress and home practice is stressed.

INTERACTIVE EXPERIENCE: THE COMPLEX NATURE OF ORAL MOTOR TASKS

This interactive experience is designed to assist the clinician in developing awareness of the complex nature of most oral motor tasks. Appropriate oral motor treatment requires the clinician to choose appropriate tasks to address the specific needs of the client. Tasks such as those listed in this experience may or may not be appropriate for a particular client. When choosing appropriate oral motor tasks for a client, the clinician can analyze a task in this manner to see if the activity matches the client's needs. Answer the following questions as you complete the activities:

1. What structure(s) are you facilitating? (e.g., jaw, lips, tongue, etc.)
2. What process(es) are you facilitating? (e.g., breath control, voicing, articulation, eating, drinking, etc.)
3. Are you working on improving awareness, muscle tone, strength, stability, mobility, control, or something else?

Use a cocktail straw to blow a cotton ball across a table surface in a smooth, controlled fashion.

Hold a button attached to a string with your lips *(not your teeth)* while another person pulls on the string.

Bite down on one-half of a large, stale marshmallow with your molars and move your tongue to specified locations in your mouth.

Hold a mint Lifesaver between your tongue tip and your alveolar ridge as long as you can.

INTERACTIVE EXPERIENCE: ORAL MOTOR ACTIVITIES AND EXERCISES

Brainstorm and list appropriate oral motor activities and exercises for school-aged children in the following areas (this activity is a modified version of one used by Jelm [1995b]):

- Activities/exercises for jaw strengthening, stability, and control
- Activities/exercises for tongue strengthening, mobility, and control
- Activities/exercises for lip strengthening, mobility, and control

Specific Speech Activities with Cueing Strategies

Although specific speech activities with cueing strategies can be used with school-aged children exhibiting muscle function concerns, these are particularly important for use with children who exhibit *motor planning concerns.* It is important to remember that many children demonstrate both muscle function and motor planning concerns.

Moto-kinesthetic, tactile-kinesthetic, and visual-tactile cueing were discussed in previous chapters. These cueing systems can be applied to the specific speech activities completed with school-aged children. If the child has difficulty establishing the sound in isolation, moto-kinesthetic or tactile-kinesthetic cueing may be needed. If the child can produce the sound, visual-tactile cueing can assist the child in producing the sound in a variety of contexts.

Several programs have been developed to address the needs of children who exhibit motor planning concerns. The *Easy Does It for Apraxia—Preschool* (1994) and the *Easy Does It for Apraxia and Motor Planning* (1993) programs by Strode and Chamberlain both contain cueing systems. Although the *Easy Does It for Apraxia—Preschool* program was developed for children ages 2 to 6 years, it can be very useful in the treatment of school-aged children who are developmentally delayed. Jelm's (1995b) "hierarchical model of treatment" (p. T-8) also uses a simple visual-tactile cueing system that can be easily learned by children and parents. All three of these programs were discussed in Chapter 6.

The remediation of factors affecting *intelligibility* is important to address with school-aged children. These include rate, rhythm, stress, and intonation.

Rate is often a factor that significantly affects the child's intelligibility of speech. In *A Voice Assessment Protocol for Children and Adults,* Pindzola (1987) uses the rate of 140 to 160 words per minute as the standard to which she compares the individual's conversational rate. Speaking rate seems to increase with age during childhood (i.e., the 3-year-old child speaks more slowly than the 6-year-old child, who speaks more slowly than the 12-year-old child). Slowing the child's speaking rate can frequently assist children with muscle function as well as motor planning issues in improving intelligibility. The pacing board or a pacing system is a visual-tactile cueing strategy that can help the child slow the rate of speech. This strategy may also assist the child in developing the motor plan for the production of words, phrases, and sentences. A portable pacing board may be developed for a child in this age group. For example, a small pacing board can be made by placing glue dots on a tongue depressor or popsicle stick. The use of the pacing strategy was discussed in Chapter 5.

Children in this age group may be initially assisted in developing other prosodic features (e.g., rhythm, stress, intonation) through the use of a pacing system. However, auditory and visual feedback can be used to help the child in establishing a more natural speaking style. This type of feedback would include the use of audiotaping and videotaping. As previously mentioned in Chapters 5 and 6, children can also practice imitating rhythm, stress, and intonation while using sound producing instruments such as a kazoo or a whistle. Play acting is another good way to work on the development of rhythm, stress, and intonation.

Articulation and Language Therapy

Articulation and language therapy is incorporated into the oral motor treatment session for children in the 6- to 12-year age group as appropriate. The clinician can address specific error sounds by teaching articulatory placement. These sounds can be practiced in isolation, syllables, words, phrases, sentences, and conversation. Concerns with phonological processes can be addressed as well. The language needs of the child can be addressed specifically in this portion of the session and throughout the session as appropriate.

Boshart and Jutila have developed systems for working with specific speech sounds. These are *The "K" and "G" Systems* (1996), *The "L" System* (1995), *The "Sh" and "Ch" Systems* (1995), *The "S" System* (1995), *The "R" System* (1995), and *The "Th" System* (1996). The systems are systematic articulation practice programs on cassette tape and can be used with preschool and school-aged children. Each system contains 10 practice cassette tapes of five to seven minutes in length. The tapes can be used in therapy and in the classroom as well as in home practice. Record-keeping forms are provided for clients and clinicians. The cassettes contain "an auditory stimulus model for the client to imitate," "practical stimulus words, phrases, and sentences" (e.g., linguistically simple phrases and sentences used in everyday communication), stimulus words used in "a variety of linguistic categories" and "a variety of phonetic contexts," word shapes that progress from the "least motorically demanding" to the "most motorically demanding," "stimulus words without conflicting speech sounds," as well as sentences that are "linguistically and phonetically" complex (*The "SH" and "CH" Systems,* p. 2). The *MA CAT: Motor Activities for Children in Articulation Therapy* by Kuratomi (1997) was developed to accompany these systems.

CASE EXAMPLE

Description

Jill is a 10-year-old child exhibiting characteristics of a myofunctional disorder. Her hearing and cognitive skills are within normal limits. She has mild to low muscle tone in the trunk of her body and in her oral structures. Jill sits in a chair with her hips extended, and she sits on the floor using a "w" sitting pattern. When swallowing, she tenses the orbicularis oris and has poor movement of the masseter muscles. Jill has an overbite and spaces between her top front teeth. Her tongue rests in the bottom of her mouth, and her tongue and mandible move as a unit. She has difficulty elevating the back of her tongue. Jill had her tonsils and adenoids removed at age 7. Her palatal vault is high and narrow, and she has a diminished gag response. Jill's upper lip is relatively inactive, and she has an open mouth posture. She has a history of sinus concerns, but these have been resolved. She can currently breathe through her nose. She has no health or physical concerns that would preclude regular exercise. Jill drinks liquids to clear food from her mouth, and she prefers to eat foods with some type of sauce. She also swallows some food whole. Jill bites her fingernails. She drank from a bottle until 3 years of age and sucked her thumb until 5 years of age. Jill has a history of articulation difficulties. She currently continues to front the production of /s/ and /z/ sounds.

Treatment Plan

Gross Motor Activities/Exercise Program Provide Jill with appropriate gross motor activities that will promote improved muscle tone in the trunk of her body (e.g., wall push-ups, jumping jacks, running in place, etc.). She might become involved in an exercise program outside of therapy (e.g., swimming, gymnastics, or a light-weight program) focusing on the development of the musculature on the front and back of the body as well as in the area of the shoulder girdle.

Oral Massage Provide Jill with oral massage and other facilitation techniques to increase oral awareness and muscle function.

Oral Motor Activities/Exercises Implement a myofunctional treatment program with additional oral motor activities to address specific oral motor concerns such as Jill's poor movement of the masseter muscles, poor tongue and jaw dissociation, difficulty elevating the back of the tongue, and upper lip inactivity.

Specific Speech Activities Treat the fronted production of the /s/ and /z/ phonemes via traditional articulation therapy.

Recommendations

1. Suggest to Jill's parents that she be seen by an orthodontist for evaluation of her occlusion. Coordinate treatment with the orthodontist's plan.
2. Educate Jill's parents, teachers, and others regarding the nature of a myofunctional disorder.
3. Provide consistent home practice activities for Jill. *Consistent* home practice is essential for the remediation of a myofunctional concern.

INTERACTIVE CASE EXPERIENCE

The interactive case experience will allow the reader to practice using the information from the chapter. This experience is meant to challenge the reader to think of possibilities for the case presented. The answers to the questions in the interactive case experience are for the reader to decide.

Review Jill's case. What resources, materials, or tools might you use as part of treatment? If available, review these resources and materials. Develop activities for each part of the treatment plan. What other recommendations need to be made? What other comments or ideas do you have concerning Jill?

8

Age 13 and Beyond

Working with Adolescents and Adults

Oral motor assessment and treatment is a continuum that spans the age groups from birth to advanced age. This final chapter on assessment and treatment will discuss the use of the approach described throughout the book as it applies to adolescents and adults. The area of motor speech disorders in adults has been covered extensively in a great number of texts. Many of the techniques discussed for use with the pediatric population have originated in work completed with the adult population. An example of this is the use of the pacing board in treatment to assist with motor planning and speaking rate reduction.

The approach to working with adolescents and adults can be similar to the approach used with children. Many of the sensory and motor needs or concerns may be similar. However, assessment and treatment techniques are modified to address the specific needs of adolescents and adults. This is particularly important, because adolescents and adults have different learning styles than children. Technique modification must be done in such a way that the individual understands the rationale for completing the activity and the activity does not seem child-like. This should be considered when developing activities for adolescents and adults who are developmentally disabled or who have acquired disabilities.

The chapter contains a discussion of oral motor assessment and treatment tools for adolescents and adults. In the assessment portion of the chapter, a listing of questions regarding the characteristics of dyspraxia and the different types of dysarthria is presented. This has been included to assist clinicians in making an accurate differential diagnosis. The treatment of adolescents is discussed separately from the treatment of adults in the chapter, as the clinician will work with adolescents in a somewhat different manner than with adults. The chapter contains a section on the treatment of adults who are dependent on others for care. These individuals often require some special considerations during the oral motor treatment process.

ASSESSMENT

It is important for the clinician working with adolescents and adults to attain an oral motor case history. Some of the history may be obtained from the client, but the clinician may need to contact the client's family members for this information. The gathering of case history information can become part of the initial educational process for the client and appropriate family members regarding oral motor assessment and treatment. See Chapter 4 for a suggested case history form. After gathering case history information, the clinician can choose an appropriate oral motor assessment tool for the individual. Appendix A contains a complete reference list of the assessment tools presented in the book.

The choice of an appropriate assessment tool should be based on the needs of the client. Clients with developmental disabilities in this age group may have completely different assessment needs than clients with acquired disabilities in terms of the tool chosen. However, many of the evaluation components discussed in Chapter 5 would be applicable to most populations.

It is important to assess the individual's posture and oral structures at rest and during movement. The assessment of the individual's eating and drinking skills can provide the clinician with important information about muscle function. In addition, adolescents are often particularly self-conscious about any differences they may have from the typical adolescent population. Differences in eating and drinking abilities may prove to be embarrassing for them. Adolescents and adults with acquired disabilities (e.g., stroke, traumatic brain injury, etc.) may need assessment and treatment of their eating and drinking skills for nutrition purposes. As part of the assessment process, it continues to be important to assess nonspeech oral movements in both adolescents and adults to observe difficulties with movements in isolation that may impact on the individual's eating, drinking, or speaking abilities. Speech production is another vital area to address during the assessment of adolescents and adults. Throughout the assessment and treatment process, the individual's sensory as well as motor difficulties need to be considered. See Chapters 2 and 3 for further detail on sensory motor function.

Some of the assessment tools discussed in previous chapters may be used with adolescents and adults. For example, the clinician may choose to develop an assessment tool from the assessment questions presented in Chapter 5. This tool could be custom-designed for the particular population being served. The Oral Motor Assessment Checklist discussed in Chapter 4 was developed for use with individuals of all ages. This checklist is particularly useful when assessing adolescents and adults, as it is quick, easy to administer, and covers essential areas impacting on oral motor function. The assessments by Mackie found in the book entitled *Oral-Motor Activities for School-Aged Children* (1996b) may be used as written or may be modified to assess adolescents and adults. The Checklist for Tongue Thrust Evaluation and the Tongue Thrust Evaluation by Pierce (1993) may be used with both adults and adolescents. These assessments were discussed in Chapter 7. In addition to these instruments, a number of instruments have been developed for adults specifically but may be used with adolescents as well.

The Orofacial-Swallowing Evaluation and Rating Scale from *The Source for Oral-Facial Exercises* by Gangale (1993) is particularly useful in evaluating individuals with concomitant medical concerns. It contains areas for gathering information about the client's medical history, medications, nutritional status, dietary concerns, respiratory status, general physical condition, gross and fine motor skills, and other assessment results. Swallowing and oral motor function can be evaluated using this instrument. A rating scale of 1 to 7 is used to evaluate lip, tongue, jaw, and neck movements. The gag reflex as well as the client's ability to chew, cough, and clear the throat are assessed. This tool also evaluates factors that affect intelligibility such as phonation, vocal quality, loudness, pitch, rate, intonation, and resonance.

The *Dworkin-Culatta Oral Mechanism Examination* (Dworkin & Culatta, 1996) is a very thorough assessment of the oral mechanism. This tool can be used with children as well as adults and adolescents. It is comprised of a screening test to evaluate "facial status, lip functioning, jaw functioning, hard palate status, tongue functioning, velopharyngeal functioning, status of dentition, and motor programming abilities" (Screening Test Checklist Form). If a concern is noted in any area of the screening test, a deep test can be performed. The deep tests evaluate the appearance of the structures, the movements of the structures, the muscle tone and strength in the structures, sensation, and speech abilities.

The *Assessment of Intelligibility of Dysarthric Speech* by Yorkston and Beukelman (1984) is an objective way to measure the intelligibility concerns of individuals with muscle function and physiologic concerns. Both single-word and sentence intelligibility are assessed. The single-word intelligibility segment of the test requires the individual to read or repeat 50 words. An independent evaluator (i.e., a clinician who did not administer the test) transcribes the utterances or identifies words from a multiple-choice format. The percentage of intelligible words produced by the client is then calculated. On the sentence intelligibility portion of this test, the client reads or repeats sentences of increasing length (i.e., 5 to 15 words). The percentage of intelligible speech is determined from the transcription completed by an independent evaluator. "Speaking rate" and "rate of intelligible speech" (i.e., number of "intelligible words per minute") are assessed (p. 11). A "communication efficiency ratio" is established by comparing the "rate of intelligible speech produced" by the client to a typical speaking rate (p. 12). This instrument is easy to administer and useful in tracking a client's progress over time.

The *Frenchay Dysarthria Assessment* (Enderby, 1983) can be used with clients ages 12 years to adult. It is a standardized instrument and provides differential diagnosis of dysarthria. The test assesses reflexes, sensation, and respiration. The function of the structures involved in speech are separately addressed (i.e., jaw, lips, tongue, palate, and larynx). Speaking rate and intelligibility are evaluated.

Many books and articles have been written about the assessment and treatment of dysarthria. The clinician can use the results of the Dworkin-Culatta Oral Mechanism Examination (Dworkin & Culatta, 1996), the Orofacial-Swallowing Evaluation and Rating Scale from *The Source for Oral-Facial Exercises* (Gangale, 1993), the *Assessment of Intelligibility of Dysarthric Speech* (Yorkston & Beukelman, 1984) and/or the *Frenchay Dysarthria Assessment* (Enderby, 1983) to determine the characteristics of dysarthria exhibited by the client. This will enable the clinician to provide more effective treatment.

Darley, Aronson, and Brown (1975, p. 246) define *dysarthria* as "a collective group of speech disorders resulting from disturbances in muscular control over the speech mechanism due to damage of the central or peripheral nervous system." It affects the speech processes of respiration, phonation, resonation, and articulation and results from difficulties with sensation, paresis, paralysis, and coordination in the muscles used for speech production. According to Brookshire (1997, p. 417) "Assessment of dysarthria is as much a search for interactions among processes underlying speech [i.e., respiration, phonation, resonation, and articulation] as it is a diagnosis of abnormalities within speech itself." There are several types of dysarthria that are differentially diagnosed by the characteristics demonstrated in the processes of respiration, phonation, resonation, and articulation. This differential diagnosis is often applied to adults with acquired or degenerative disabilities. However, Crary (1993) as well as

Caruso and Strand (1999) have used the term *developmental dysarthria* in the discussion of children with these characteristics. Therefore, the lists of questions in the next section of this chapter may have some application to pediatrics as well as adults.

The clinician can determine the *type of dysarthria* exhibited by the client by asking pertinent questions related to each type. The types of dysarthria each have specific characteristics. Many of these characteristics were defined by research completed at the Mayo clinic by Darley, Aronson, and Brown (Rosenbek & LaPointe, 1978; Wertz, 1978). The questions listed in the sections that follow can assist the clinician in determining the type of dysarthria exhibited by the client (Duffy, 1995; Murdoch, Thompson, & Theodoros, 1997; Rosenbek & LaPointe, 1978; Wertz, 1978; Yorkston, Beukelman, & Bell, 1988).

Flaccid Dysarthria

According to Duffy (1995), "Flaccid dysarthria is . . . produced by injury or malfunction of one or more of the cranial or spinal nerves. It reflects problems in the nuclei, axons, or neuromuscular junctions that make up the motor units of the final common pathway" (p. 99). It can affect the individual's respiration, phonation, resonation, and/or articulation. Hypotonia and muscle weakness are two predominant characteristics of flaccid dysarthria. These can result in decreased speed, range, and precision of oral movement required for accurate speech production as well as adequate eating and drinking skills. Therefore, individuals with flaccid dysarthria may also require assessment of eating and drinking abilities. As previously discussed throughout the book, the assessment of eating and drinking skills can provide important information about muscle function. The following questions can assist the clinician in identifying flaccid dysarthria in clients (Duffy, 1995; Rosenbek & LaPointe, 1978; Wertz, 1978; Yorkston, Beukelman, & Bell, 1988):

- Does the individual exhibit flaccid paralysis, hypotonia, muscle weakness, muscle atrophy, and/or fasciculations?
- Does the individual exhibit audible inspiration?
- Does the individual exhibit reduced respiratory support for speech production?
- Does the individual exhibit abnormal respiratory movements?
- Does the individual demonstrate difficulties with glottal closure (e.g., breathy voice quality, frequently continuous; harsh voice quality; monopitch; hoarseness; diplophonia; aphonia)?
- Does the individual exhibit monoloudness?
- Does the individual exhibit inadequate velo-pharyngeal closure (e.g., hypernasality, frequently with nasal emission)?
- Does the individual exhibit flaccid paralysis, hypotonia, muscle weakness, muscle atrophy, decreased sensation, and/or fasciculations in the tongue or other oral musculature resulting in imprecise production of speech sounds?
- Does the individual speak in short phrases and/or at a slow rate?
- Does the individual have neuropathology of lower motor neurons (i.e., cranial nerves, particularly the Vth, VIIth, Xth, and XIIth, and/or spinal nerves serving the speech musculature)?
- Does the individual have or has the individual had poliomyelitis, a tumor or surgery that has affected the function of lower motor neurons, a stroke (e.g., brain stem stroke), a congenital neuromuscular disorder (e.g., mus-

cular dystrophy), myasthenia gravis, a demyelinating disease (e.g., Guillain-Barre), bulbar palsy, facial palsy, or a traumatic brain injury?

Spastic Dysarthria

"Spastic dysarthria is . . . produced by damage to the direct and indirect activation pathways of the central nervous system, bilaterally" (Duffy, 1995, p. 128). It usually affects more than one aspect of speech production (i.e., respiration, phonation, resonation, and articulation). Hypertonicity and muscle weakness are two predominant characteristics of spastic dysarthria. These can result in decreased speed, range, force, and precision of movement required for accurate speech production as well as adequate eating and drinking skills. Therefore, individuals with spastic dysarthria may also require assessment of eating and drinking abilities. The following questions can assist the clinician in identifying spastic dysarthria in clients (Duffy, 1995; Murdoch, Thompson, & Theodoros, 1997; Rosenbek & LaPointe, 1978; Wertz, 1978; Yorkston, Beukelman, & Bell, 1988):

- Does the individual exhibit spastic paralysis; hypertonia; muscle weakness; "little or no muscle atrophy" (Murdoch et al., 1997); pathological reflexes (e.g., suck, snout); hyperactive reflexes (e.g., gag, jaw-jerk); and/or limited range, force, or speed of movement?
- Does the individual have flattened nasolabial folds?
- Does the individual exhibit shallow breathing?
- Is the individual's voice strained, strangled, harsh, or breathy (continuous) sounding?
- Does the individual speak with monopitch, a low pitch, or pitch breaks?
- Does the individual exhibit monoloudness?
- Does the individual produce voicing on voiceless stop phonemes?
- Does the individual exhibit slow and/or insufficient velopharyngeal closure resulting in hypernasality?
- Does the individual have dysphagia and/or drooling?
- Does the individual have spastic paralysis, hypertonia, and/or muscle weakness in the oral musculature?
- Does the individual exhibit limited or reduced range, force, or speed of movement in the musculature of the articulators?
- Does the individual produce imprecise consonant and/or distorted vowel sounds resulting from incomplete articulatory contacts?
- Does the individual prolong speech sounds, syllables, and/or words?
- Does the individual feel fatigued when speaking, and does the individual's speech deteriorate with fatigue?
- Does the individual exhibit difficulty with control of emotional expression?
- Does the individual speak in short phrases and/or at a slow rate?
- Does the individual produce slow and regular alternating motion rates (AMRs, e.g., /pʌ pʌ pʌ/)?
- Does the individual use excessive or equal stress when speaking?
- Does the individual have bilateral neuropathology of the upper motor neurons (i.e., pyramidal and/or extrapyramidal tracts)?
- Does the individual have or has the individual had a stroke, a brain tumor, encephalitis, a traumatic brain injury, spastic cerebral palsy, pseudobulbar palsy, a degenerative disease (e.g., amyotrophic lateral sclerosis, progressive supranuclear palsy), or a demyelinating disease (e.g., multiple sclerosis)?

Ataxic Dysarthria

"Ataxic dysarthria . . . is a disorder of sensorimotor control for speech production that results from damage to the cerebellum or to its input and output pathways" (Cannito & Marquardt, 1997, p. 217). It may affect the individual's respiration, phonation, resonation, and/or articulation. However, the individual's articulation and prosody seem most affected (Duffy, 1995). Hypotonia and coordination concerns are two predominant characteristics of ataxic dysarthria. These can result in decreased speed, force, range, timing, and overall precision of movement required for accurate speech production as well as adequate eating and drinking skills. Therefore, individuals with ataxic dysarthria may also require the assessment of their eating and drinking abilities. The following questions can assist the clinician in identifying ataxic dysarthria in clients (Cannito & Marquardt, 1997; Duffy, 1995; Rosenbek & LaPointe, 1978; Wertz, 1978; Yorkston, Beukelman, & Bell, 1988):

- Does the individual exhibit hypotonia; slow, awkward movement (i.e., dysmetria); inaccurate range, timing, and direction of movement; hyporeflexia; muscle fatigue; "disordered stance or gait" (Duffy, 1995, p. 147); rhythmic rocking of the trunk or head (titubation); "rotated or tilted head postures; ocular motor abnormalities" (Duffy, 1995, p. 147), dysdiadochokinesis; or tremor (Cannito & Marquardt, 1997; Duffy, 1995; Rosenbek & LaPointe, 1978)?
- Does the individual reportedly bite his or her tongue and/or cheek when speaking or eating (Duffy, 1995)?
- Does the individual sound as though he or she has had too much alcohol to drink when the individual has not had any alcohol?
- Does the individual's speech production reportedly deteriorate when drinking alcohol?
- Does the individual exhibit reduced respiratory support for speech production?
- Does the individual exhibit abnormal respiratory movements?
- Does the individual have difficulty coordinating respiration with speech production?
- Does the individual's voice sound harsh, monopitch, and/or tremorous?
- Does the individual have difficulty controling the loudness of speech, or does the individual exhibit monoloudness?
- Does the individual have difficulty initiating speech?
- Does the individual exhibit hypotonia; reduced speed of movement; and/or inaccurate range, timing, and direction of movement in the speech musculature?
- Does the individual produce imprecise consonant and/or distorted vowel sounds?
- Does the individual prolong speech sounds/syllables or intervals between speech production?
- Does the individual repeat syllables when speaking?
- Is the individual's speech production dysrhymic, and does the individual have irregular articulatory breakdowns?
- Does the individual produce slow and irregular alternating motion rates (AMRs, e.g., /pʌ pʌ pʌ/)?
- Does the individual speak at a slow rate?
- Does the individual use excessive or equal stress when speaking?
- Does the individual "stumble over words" (Duffy, 1995, p. 157)?

- Does the individual have neuropathology of the cerebellum or its input/output pathways?
- Does the individual have or has the individual had a stroke, brain tumor (e.g., brain stem, cerebellopontine angle), traumatic brain injury, ataxic cerebral palsy, Friedreich's ataxia, alcohol or drug toxicity, infection (e.g., menigitis, encephalitis), or a demyelinating disease (e.g., multiple sclerosis).

Hypokinetic Dysarthria

Hypokinetic dysarthria is associated with pathology of the "basal ganglia control circuit" (Duffy, 1995, p. 166). Although symptoms may be seen in the individual's respiration, phonation, resonation, and/or articulation, the "characteristics are most evident in [the individual's] voice, articulation, and prosody" (Duffy, 1995, p. 166). Rigidity is the predominant characteristic of hypokinetic dysarthria. This can result in reduced speed, force, range, and precision of oral movements needed for accurate speech production and adequate eating and drinking skills. Therefore, individuals with hypokinetic dysarthria may also require assessment of their eating and drinking abilities. The following questions can assist the clinician in identifying hypokinetic dysarthria in clients (Adams, 1997; Duffy, 1995; Rosenbek & LaPointe, 1978; Wertz, 1978; Yorkston, Beukelman, & Bell, 1988):

- Does the individual exhibit rigidity; "slow initiation and speed of movements" (Duffy, 1995, p. 167); "markedly reduced range [of motion]; variable speed of repetitive movements; movement arrest" (Rosenbek & LaPointe, 1978, p. 256); "loss of automatic aspects of movement" (Wertz, 1978, p. 82); resting tremor of the head, limbs, fingers, jaw, lips, and/or tongue; masked facial features; reduced gesturing during speech production; reduced eye movements; reduced swallowing frequency; and/or flexed posture?
- Does the individual exhibit decreased respiratory capacity, "increased respiratory rate," "irregular breathing patterns," "paradoxic rib cage and abdominal movements," and/or "difficulty altering automatic breathing patterns for speech" (Duffy, 1995, p. 182)?
- Does the individual produce decreased vowel durations and/or decreased syllables per breath?
- Does the individual produce short rushes of speech and/or inappropriate silences?
- Does the individual speak in short phrases?
- Does the individual exhibit monoloudness or reduced loudness?
- Does the individual exhibit monopitch and/or a low pitch?
- Does the individual exhibit a harsh or a continuous breathy voice quality?
- Does the individual exhibit "continuous voicing in segments with voiceless consonants" (Duffy, 1995, p. 182)?
- Is the individual hypernasal, or does the individual nasalize sounds across syllables (Adams, 1997; Duffy, 1995)?
- Does the individual exhibit decreased jaw stability; decreased range, speed, and duration of lip movements secondary to lip rigidity; and/or decreased tongue strength and endurance (Duffy, 1995)?
- Does the individual produce imprecise consonant sounds?

- Does the individual produce stop and affricate sounds as fricative sounds (i.e., spirantization)?
- Does the individual nonvolitionally repeat phonemes or what he or she previously said (i.e., palilalia)?
- Does the individual produce "rapid or blurred" (Duffy, 1995, p. 176) alternating motion rates (AMRs, e.g., /pʌ pʌ pʌ/)?
- Does the individual have "indistinct boundaries between syllables" (Duffy, 1995, p. 183)?
- Does the individual exhibit a variable speaking rate, increased overall speaking rate, and/or reduced stress?
- Does the individual have neuropathology of the basal ganglia and their connections (Duffy, 1995)?
- Does the individual have or has the individual had Parkinson's disease, Parkinsonism, progressive supranuclear palsy, degenerative neurological disease (e.g., Alzheimer's), drug induced symptoms (e.g., reserpine and phenothiazine), Shy-Drager syndrome, or a stroke?

Hyperkinetic Dysarthria

"Hyperkinetic dysarthria . . . is most often associated with diseases of the basal ganglia control circuit" (Duffy, 1995, p. 189). The individual's respiration, phonation, resonation, and articulation may be affected by hyperkinetic dysarthria. However, it most often affects the individual's prosody and can impact on just one aspect of speech production with the involvement of only a few muscles (Duffy, 1995). Hyperkinetic dysarthria is characterized by "abnormal, rhythmic or irregular and unpredictable, rapid or slow *involuntary* movements" (Duffy, 1995, p. 189). Although these characteristics most often affect speech production, they may also affect the individual's eating and drinking abilities. Therefore, eating and drinking skills may need to be assessed in some individuals with hyperkinetic dysarthria. The following questions can assist the clinician in identifying hyperkinetic dysarthria in clients (Brookshire, 1997; Duffy, 1995; Nicolosi, Harryman, & Kresheck, 1989; Rosenbek & LaPointe, 1978; Wertz, 1978; Yorkston, Beukelman, & Bell, 1988; Zraick & LaPointe, 1997):

Predominantly Quick

- Does the individual exhibit variable muscle tone and/or quick, random, involuntary movements?
- Does the individual exhibit "quick, unpatterned involuntary head/neck, jaw, face, tongue, palate, pharyngeal, laryngeal, thoracic-abdominal movements at rest, during sustained postures and [during] movement" (Duffy, 1995, p. 202) characteristic of chorea?
- Does the individual exhibit "sudden, forced inspiration or expiration," "voice stoppages," and/or "transient breathiness" (Duffy, 1995, p. 201)?
- Does the individual exhibit sudden or excess variations in loudness?
- Does the individual exhibit monoloudness?
- Does the individual have a harsh, strained-strangled, and/or monopitch voice quality?
- Does the individual exhibit "rhythmic phonatory interruption" (Rosenbek & LaPointe, 1978, p. 256)?
- Does the individual exhibit sudden and/or excessive grunting, throat clearing, screaming, or moaning; unprovoked obscene language (i.e.,

coprolalia); echolalia; or palilalia characteristic of Gilles de la Tourette syndrome?

- Does the individual exhibit episodic or "rhythmic hypernasality" (Rosenbek & LaPointe, 1978, p. 256)?
- Does the individual exhibit highly variable imprecise articulation?
- Does the individual produce imprecise consonant sounds and/or distorted vowel sounds?
- Does the individual produce "slow and irregular" (Duffy, 1995, p. 202) alternating motion rates (AMRs, e.g., /pʌ pʌ pʌ/)?
- Does the individual produce prolonged intervals and/or inappropriate silences during speech production?
- Does the individual prolong phonemes?
- Does the individual exhibit a variable speaking rate?
- Does the individual speak in short phrases?
- Does the individual exhibit excessive, inefficient, and/or variable stress patterns on syllables and words?
- Does the individual have dysphagia?
- Does the individual have neuropathology of the basal ganglia control circuit (Duffy, 1995)?
- Does the individual have myoclonus (i.e., involuntary single or irregular, repetitive brief jerks of a body part), tics (i.e., rapid, irregular, patterned movements partially under volitional control as seen in Gilles de la Tourette syndrome), chorea (i.e., rapid, irregular, "involuntary, random, purposeless movements of a body part" [Duffy, 1995, p. 192] as seen in Huntington's chorea or Sydenham's chorea), or ballism (i.e., appearance of extreme form of chorea)?

Predominantly Slow

- Does the individual exhibit variable hypertonia; sustained, "distorted movements and postures" (Rosenbek & LaPointe, 1978, p. 256); "twisting and writhing movements," "slow movements," and/or "involuntary movements" (Wertz, 1978, p. 82)?
- Does the individual exhibit "audible inspiration" (Duffy, 1995, p. 204)?
- Does the individual speak with variable loudness, or is the individual monoloud?
- Does the individual exhibit phonatory stenosis (Rosenbek & LaPointe, 1978, p. 256) or voice stoppages?
- Does the individual have a monopitch, harsh, and/or strained-strangled voice quality?
- Does the individual exhibit a vocal tremor?
- Does the individual exhibit hypernasality?
- Does the individual produce imprecise consonants and/or distorted vowels with irregular articulatory breakdowns?
- Does the individual produce "slow and irregular" (Duffy, 1995, p. 207) alternating motion rates (AMRs, e.g., /pʌ pʌ pʌ/)?
- Does the individual prolong phonemes or intervals?
- Does the individual exhibit inappropriate silences?
- Does the individual exhibit a slow and/or variable speaking rate?
- Does the individual use excessive, inefficient, and/or variable stress patterns when speaking?

- Does the individual speak in short phrases?
- Does the individual have neuropathology of the basal ganglia control circuit (Duffy, 1995)?
- Does the individual have dysphagia?
- Does the individual have or has the individual had athetosis (congenital or acquired), dystonia (e.g., facial dystonia and Meige's syndrome), dyskinesia (i.e., irregular, involuntary movements as seen in orofacial/face/neck/axial dyskinesia, drug induced dyskinesia, tardive dyskinesia, or spasmodic torticollis), a stroke, or a brain tumor?

Unilateral Upper Motor Neuron Dysarthria

Unilateral upper motor neuron dysarthria "is associated with damage to the upper motor neurons (UMNs) that carry impulses to the cranial and spinal nerves that supply the speech muscles" (Duffy, 1995, p. 222). It primarily affects the individual's articulatory production and results from muscle weakness and possible motor incoordination (Duffy, 1995). However, it may also affect the individual's eating and drinking abilities. Therefore, some individuals with unilateral upper motor neuron dysarthria may require an assessment of eating and drinking skills in addition to the assessment of speech production. The following questions can assist the clinician in identifying unilateral upper motor neuron dysarthria in clients (adapted from Duffy, 1995):

- Does the individual exhibit the following signs of damage to the pyramidal system on the side of the body opposite the damage: hemiplegia, hemiparesis, impaired fine motor skills, absence of abdominal reflex, Babinski sign, hyporeflexia, central facial weakness at rest or during volitional movements, and/or tongue weakness?
- Does the individual exhibit the following signs of damage to the extrapyramidal system on the side of the body opposite the damage: hypertonicity, spasticity, clonus, hyperreflexive stretch responses, decerebrate posturing, or central facial weakness during acts of facial expression?
- Does the individual have a soft or quiet voice (occasional finding)?
- Does the individual have a harsh and/or strained voice quality?
- Does the individual exhibit difficulties with sensation (e.g., tactile, proprioceptive, taste, etc.)?
- Does the individual exhibit unilateral facial (lower), tongue, and/or palatal weakness?
- Does the individual drool and/or have a mild swallowing concern?
- Does the individual exhibit hypernasality (occasional finding)?
- Does the individual produce "imprecise consonants" and/or have "irregular articulatory breakdowns" (Duffy, 1995, p. 228)?
- Does the individual produce slow, imprecise, and/or irregular alternating motion rates (AMRs, e.g., /pʌ pʌ pʌ/)?
- Does the individual have a slow speaking rate?
- Does the individual use "excess and equal stress" (Duffy, 1995, p. 228)?
- Does the individual have neuropathology of the "upper motor neurons (UMNs) that carry impulses to the cranial and spinal nerves that supply the speech muscles" (Duffy, 1995, p. 222)?
- Does the individual have or has the individual had a stroke, traumatic brain injury, or brain tumor?

Mixed Dysarthria

Mixed dysarthrias occur more commonly in clinical practice than any single type of dysarthria. These may result from multiple neurological insults (e.g., multiple strokes), multiple neurological diseases, or degenerative neurological illnesses that affect more than one area of the central nervous system (Duffy, 1995). Individuals with mixed dysarthrias may exhibit eating and drinking concerns in addition to the speech difficulties that characterize the dysarthrias. Therefore, it may be important to assess the individual's oral motor function during eating and drinking as well as during speech production. The following questions can assist the clinician in identifying mixed dysarthrias in clients (Duffy, 1995; Wertz, 1978; Yorkston, Beukelman, & Bell, 1988). However, the clinician will want to refer to the questions regarding the individual types of dysarthria presented previously in this chapter to discern the characteristics related to each aspect of the mixed dysarthria. For example, the individual exhibiting mixed flaccid-spastic dysarthria will have characteristics of flaccid dysarthria as well as characteristics of spastic dysarthria.

- Does the individual exhibit characteristics of flaccid-spastic dysarthria (can be seen in clients having amyotrophic lateral sclerosis, strokes, traumatic brain injury, or brain tumors)?
- Does the individual exhibit characteristics of ataxic-spastic dysarthria (can be seen in clients having strokes, a demyelinating illness, a neurological degenerative disease, brain inflammation, a brain tumor, a closed head injury, cerebellar degeneration, or spinocerebellar degeneration)?
- Does the individual exhibit characteristics of hypokinetic-spastic dysarthria (can be seen in clients having a neurological degenerative disease, progressive supranuclear palsy, strokes, or multiple disorders)?
- Does the individual exhibit the characteristics of spastic-ataxic-hypokinetic dysarthria (can be seen in clients with Wilson's disease)?
- Does the individual exhibit the characteristics of ataxic-flaccid-spastic dysarthria (can be seen in clients having amyotrophic lateral sclerosis, multiple sclerosis, or strokes)?
- Does the individual exhibit the characteristics of hyperkinetic-hypokinetic dysarthria (can be seen in clients having Parkinson's disease)?
- Does the individual have or has the individual had amyotrophic lateral sclerosis, multiple sclerosis, Friedrich's ataxia, progressive supranuclear palsy, Shy-Drager syndrome, olivopontocerebellar atrophy, striatonigral degeneration, corticobasal degeneration, Wilson's disease, hepatocerebral degeneration, hypoxic encephalopathy, central pontine myelinolysis, multiple strokes, a brain stem stroke, closed head injury, brain tumor, meningitis, encephalitis, or acquired immunodeficiency syndrome?

Dyspraxia of Speech

Dyspraxia is a term that has been used to describe motor planning concerns. The term has been used in the majority of this book instead of the term *apraxia,* because the prefix *dys* denotes "difficulty," whereas the prefix *a* denotes "without" (Nicolosi, Harryman, & Kresheck, 1989, pp. 1, 86). Individuals with motor planning concerns usually have *difficulty* establishing and reestablishing the motor plans for speech and nonspeech tasks. They often can develop sufficient motor plans with appropriate treatment (Rosenfeld-Johnson, 1999a). It is important to note that the term *apraxia* has been used to label motor planning concerns in much of the adult literature.

The *Apraxia Battery for Adults (ABA)* was developed by Dabul (1979). This tool contains six subtests that assess "diadochokinetic rate," single-word repetition with words of increasing length, "limb and oral apraxia," "latency and utterance time" during multisyllabic word production, repeated word production, and the articulatory "characteristics of apraxia." Diadochokinetic rate is evaluated by asking the client to produce one-, two-, and three-syllable sequences during designated timed trials. Words of increasing length are scored on a scale of 0 to 2. Limb and oral movements are scored on a scale of 0 to 5 for precision. A picture-naming task is used to assess latency and utterance time measured in seconds as the client produces multisyllabic words. On the Repeated Trials Test, stimulus words are repeated three times by the client and evaluated for substitutions, distortions, additions, and omissions. The Inventory of Articulation Characteristics of Apraxia is completed based on picture description, reading, and automatic speech (i.e., counting to 30). Fifteen characteristics of dyspraxia are assessed. A severity rating of "mild to moderate" or "severe to profound" is obtained for each subtest (test form). This instrument is easy to administer and useful in tracking a client's progress over time.

Another way to assess motor planning concerns is to consider the characteristics of dyspraxia. Darley, Aronson, and Brown (1975) described dyspraxia of speech in adults as "a disorder of motor speech programming manifested primarily by errors in articulation and secondarily by compensatory alterations of prosody" (p. 267). The questions listed next would be important to consider when determining the presence of motor planning concerns in adults with some type of neurological insult or disease (Brookshire, 1997; Chapey, 1986; Duffy, 1995; McNeil, Robin, & Schmidt, 1997; Wertz, LaPointe, & Rosenbek, 1991; Wertz, LaPointe, & Rosenbek, 1984). The questions listed in Chapter 5 may be used when assessing motor planning concerns in adolescents, as these difficulties are often related to the development of speech in childhood. However, the following list may be used if the adolescent has had a stroke, traumatic brain injury, or another neurological disorder with the onset after the individual's development of speech:

- Does the individual exhibit an increase in articulation errors as the movements required for sound production become more complex?
- Are the individual's articulatory errors similar to the target sound?
- When producing sounds in isolation and in connected speech, does the individual produce fewer vowel production errors than consonant production errors?
- Does the individual have greater difficulty saying sounds produced posteriorly in the mouth than sounds produced anteriorly in the mouth? Does the individual produce fewer errors on bilabial and lingua-alveolar consonants than other consonant sounds?
- Does the individual have difficulty producing affricate and fricative phonemes?
- Does the individual have difficulty producing consonant clusters?
- Can the individual repeat a single consonant sequence (e.g., /pʌ pʌ pʌ/ with greater ease than a multiconsonant sequence (e.g., /pʌ tʌ kʌ/)?
- Does the individual have more difficulty producing consonants in the beginning of words than at the end of words?

- Does the individual have more difficulty producing phonemes that occur with a low frequency within the language than phonemes that occur with a high frequency within the language?
- Does the individual produce frequent sound substitutions, additions, repetitions, or prolongations?
- Does the individual produce occasional sound distortions or omissions?
- Does the individual produce more sound substitutions than any other type of error?
- Does the individual produce more errors of placement than manner, voice, or resonance (place>manner>voice>resonance; Duffy, 1995; Wertz et al., 1991)?
- Does the individual substitute voiceless consonants for voiced consonants?
- Are the individual's misarticulations variable or inconsistent?
- Does the individual exhibit groping or struggle behaviors during speech production?
- Does the individual exhibit slow and inaccurate articulatory movements?
- Does the individual frequently produce anticipatory errors (i.e., placing the articulators in a position for a sound prior to the production of the sound)?
- Does the individual occasionally repeat sounds in words or transpose sounds in words?
- Does the individual produce fluent speech at times?
- Is the individual's use of syntactic, semantic, and morphological structures generally intact?
- Is the individual's automatic speech production significantly better than the individual's novel speech production?
- Is the individual's speech production better in natural (i.e., everyday) situations than in contrived (e.g., therapy) situations?
- Does the individual have greater difficulty on speech imitative tasks than when speaking spontaneously?
- Does the individual have greater difficulty producing nonsense syllables than meaningful words?
- Does the individual produce more articulation errors in multisyllabic words than in shorter words?
- Does the individual's intelligibility decrease as the length of utterance increases?
- Does the individual exhibit greater difficulty producing words that carry a large linguistic or psychologic weight in a sentence?
- Is the individual's speech production more consistent during oral reading than during conversation?
- Does the individual's speech production improve when visual stimuli (e.g., printed word, picture, visual cueing, etc.) are added to auditory cues?
- Does the individual's speech production improve with practice (i.e., the individual repeats a word many times until it becomes routine)?
- Does the individual exhibit difficulties with the prosodic features of language?
- Does the individual speak with a slow rate?
- Does the individual's speech improve with speaking rate reduction?
- Does the individual's speech intelligibility decrease with increased speaking rate?
- Does the individual have difficulty speaking at an increased rate upon request?
- Does the individual pause before speaking or between syllables or words?

- Does the individual exhibit "false starts" with the onset of speech production?
- Does the individual place equal stress on stressed and unstressed syllables and words in phrases and sentences?
- Does the individual demonstrate difficulties with pitch, duration, and/or loudness?
- Is the individual aware of articulatory errors? Can the individual anticipate when these will occur and attempt to correct the errors?
- Does the individual exhibit "essentially normal resonance, respiration, and phonation" (Wertz et al., 1984, cited as source in McNeil et al., 1997, p. 314)?
- Does the individual exhibit oral dyspraxia as well as dyspraxia of speech?
- Is the individual generally free of muscle weakness, paralysis, fluctuations in muscle tone, involuntary movements, and movement incoordination (McNeil et al., 1997)?
- Does the individual exhibit impaired oral sensation and/or perception?
- Does the individual have aphasia (e.g., Broca's aphasia) as well as dyspraxia?
- Is the individual's auditory comprehension of language generally intact?

TREATMENT OF ADOLESCENTS

Adolescents who require oral motor treatment are frequently those individuals continuing to exhibit postural control and stability concerns, oral sensory issues, muscle function issues, as well as motor planning difficulties. Many of these individuals have been in treatment since they were young children. Some of them may have been dismissed from treatment for a period of time and may be reentering treatment. Many of these individuals have oral motor issues that have not been resolved. Some may exhibit persistent articulatory concerns (e.g., /r/ distortion); others may exhibit myofunctional issues (i.e., tongue thrust pattern with or without concomitant speech difficulties). Individuals with myofunctional concerns may be referred to the speech-language pathologist by the dentist or orthodontist.

Individuals in this age group who are developmentally delayed may also be receiving long term oral motor treatment. The *Pre-Feeding Skills* book by Morris and Klein (1987, 2000) may continue to be the best resource for the treatment of individuals who are severely involved. Individuals who are mild to moderately developmentally delayed may be treated by determining their specific needs along the continuum discussed throughout the chapters in this book. The book *Oral-Motor Exercises for Speech Clarity* by Rosenfeld-Johnson (1999b) has many appropriate oral motor exercises and techniques for individuals who are mild to moderately developmentally delayed.

Adolescents with acquired disabilities may also require oral motor treatment. This would include individuals who have or have had traumatic brain injury, a stroke, or another neurological disorder or disease. Treatment for these individuals would be determined by the severity of the disorder and the needs of the individual client.

Oral motor treatment for the adolescent may consist of the following components:*

*List adapted from unpublished workshop materials developed by Diane Chapman Bahr and Libby Kumin; see Kumin & Bahr (1997).

- Gross motor activities/exercise program/physical therapy
- Oral massage/Other facilitation techniques
- Oral motor exercises/activities
- Remediation of factors affecting intelligibility
- Articulation and language therapy

A typical treatment session for an adolescent with oral motor concerns may include 5 minutes of gross motor activity or exercise, 5 to 7 minutes of oral massage, and 5 to 10 minutes of oral motor exercises or activities. The remainder of the session can then emphasize the remediation of factors affecting intelligibility, articulation practice, and language therapy as needed. A typical therapy session may be 45 to 60 minutes in length. The timing and sequence of the segments in the session are flexible and should be modified according to the client's needs. However, the timing and sequence has been provided for the speech-language pathologist who is beginning to use this approach to oral motor treatment. As the speech-language pathologist develops skill and his or her own style in this area of treatment, the timing and sequence may change.

Gross Motor Activities/Exercise Program/Physical Therapy

The gross motor activities/exercise program for individuals in this age group may consist of vigorous whole-body movements—such as dance, calisthenics, or other aerobic types of activity—if the individual has low muscle tone in the body. Many adolescents are interested in sports and physical fitness. However, individuals with oral motor concerns may not have had the success in physical fitness activities that individuals without oral motor concerns have had. This may be secondary to the tendency of individuals with oral motor difficulties to exhibit postural concerns as well as coordination and motor planning issues.

Dance activities, such as line dancing, can provide the individual with full-body movement as well as practice in motor planning whole-body movement. Calisthenics can be used at the beginning of the treatment session and assigned as part of a daily exercise program. Jumping jacks, wall push-ups, and so on may assist the individual in developing increased muscle tone in the body as well as postural and shoulder stability. Aerobic dance activities can develop postural tone as well as postural stability.

Continue to *consult with the individual's physical therapist, occupational therapist, and/or physician* to determine appropriate activities for individuals with physical involvement. If the individual exhibits excessive extensor tone in the body, slow controlled movement activities would usually be more appropriate than rigorous movement activities. Feldenkrais's "Awareness through Movement" activities, neuro-developmental treatment techniques, and similar activities may be more appropriate for these individuals than rigorous activities that tend to increase muscle tone in the body. Information on Feldenkrais's "Awareness through Movement" and neuro-developmental treatment can be found in previous chapters.

Oral motor treatment can be coordinated with other therapies. If the individual is receiving physical therapy, the oral motor treatment session may be scheduled after the physical therapy session. It would be important for the speech-language pathologist to collaborate with the physical therapist if this arrangement is made. The physical therapist could provide the client with appropriate movement activities to encourage improved postural control and not fatigue the client. If the client is receiving occupational therapy, it is also important to collaborate with the occupational therapist and coordinate treatment. Cotreatment with the physical and/or occupational therapist can also be a very effective approach to oral motor treatment. When the therapists work together with the client, treatment is often better coordinated and organized.

Oral Massage and Other Facilitation Techniques

The use of oral massage would continue to be important with the adolescent population to bring increased awareness and blood supply to the oral area as well as to address muscle function concerns (see oral massage sequence in Chapter 4). The individual in this age group can often take some responsibility for the massage program at home and in treatment. However, it has frequently been noted that some clients may not massage or brush the oral structures in the specific manner that the clinician or parent may massage or brush the structures. This difficulty may be secondary to issues with postural stability and control as well as resulting difficulties with fine motor function (i.e., the individual does not have the fine motor control to adequately apply oral massage). Therefore, the clinician and the parent may need to assist the client with the oral massage process. This process must be handled with care, because clients in this age group are often self-conscious. It is best to explain to the client the importance of the massage process and set up a routine where the client and clinician take turns massaging the client's face and mouth as needed to provide the required stimulation.

With appropriate explanation, the clinician may also apply techniques such as the Beckman facilitation (1997), myofascial release, and proprioceptive neuromuscular facilitation techniques. These techniques can assist with improved physiologic function (see Chapter 4 for discussion of these techniques). Individuals in this age group can usually understand the reason that a

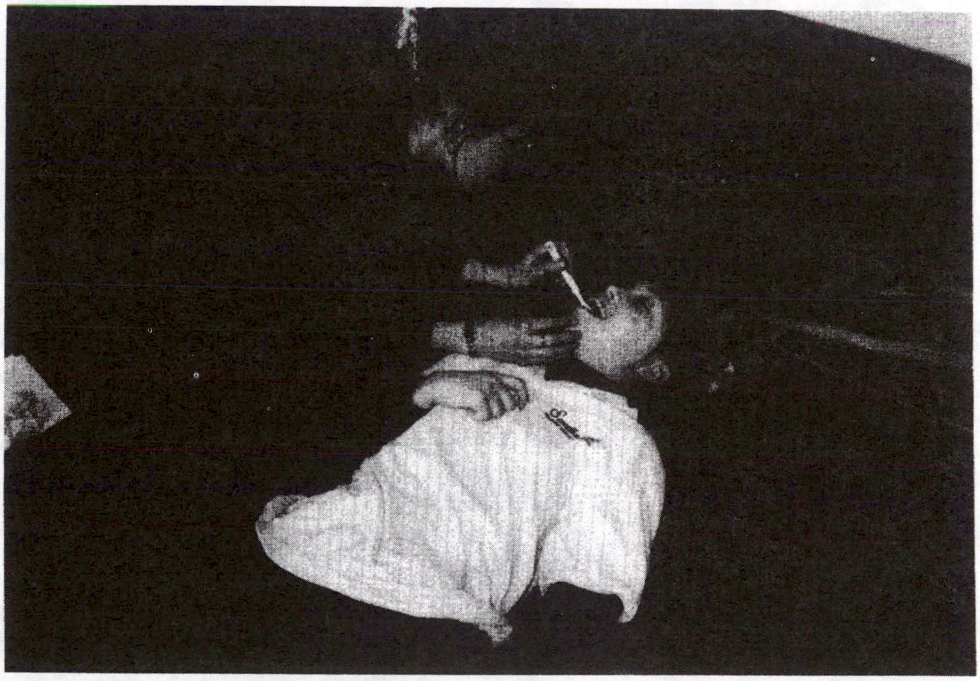

Beth, a middle school student who has had two cerebral hemorrhages, receives oral massage from her clinician Kim after completing Feldenkrais's "Awareness through Movement" and respiration activities. Specific oral facilitation techniques and oral exercise will follow.

particular technique is being applied when an explanation is offered. Again, it is important to consider any self-consciousness that may become apparent in the adolescent. The client may better understand the need for the oral brushing and the oral massage work when the similarities in this type of treatment to physical therapy or physical exercise programs are highlighted. For example, oral massage can be described as analogous to the massage an athlete may receive before running a race. If the individual is cognitively impaired and cannot understand this type of explanation, then an explanation for oral massage work needs to be provided that the individual can understand.

Oral Motor Exercises/Activities

Oral motor activities/exercises *must be carefully selected* for the adolescent. This involves careful assessment of the individual's oral motor concerns and task analysis of the individual's goals. The exercises and activities must relate directly to the individual's oral motor needs. See Treatment Plan in Chapter 6 and Task Analysis form in Chapter 7 to assist with this process.

Few oral motor treatment tools have been specifically developed for adolescents. However, the treatment tools and materials discussed in Chapter 7 and previous chapters may continue to be appropriate for many individuals in this age group. It is important to note that some of these materials may need to be modified for the age and maturity level of the individual. Materials such as

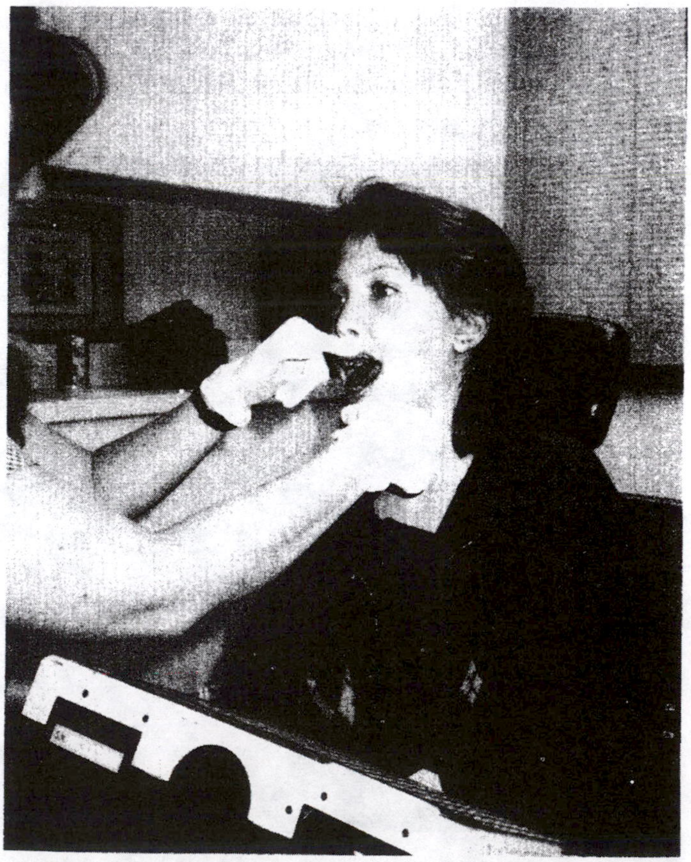

Beth receives specific oral facilitation techniques from her clinician Carla prior to completing oral exercises. Beth is appropriately positioned in her adapted wheelchair.

Easy Does It for Articulation: An Oral Motor Approach by Strode and Chamberlain (1997), *The Complete Oral-Motor Program for Articulation* by Pehde, Geller, and Lechner (1996), *Oral-Motor Activities for School-Aged Children* by Mackie (1996b), and *Oral-Motor Exercises for Speech Clarity* by Rosenfeld-Johnson (1999b) could be used with the adolescent population.

Clients with myofunctional concerns are often referred by dentists and orthodontists. Programs such as *Taming the Tongue Thrust* by Barnes (1994), *Swallow Right* by Pierce (1993), and *Swalloworks* by Boshart (1995b) would be appropriate materials to use with these individuals. Extensive information on myofunctional treatment can also be found in the book *Myofunctional Therapy in Dental Practice: Abnormal Swallowing Habits: Diagnosis—Treatment* by Garliner (1974). See Chapter 7 for further detail on myofunctional therapy.

Many appropriate oral motor exercises can also be found in materials and resources developed for the adult population. These would include *The Source for Oral-Facial Exercises* by Gangale (1993) and the Dworkin-Culatta Treatment System by Dworkin and Culatta (1996). These materials will be discussed later in this chapter.

Other appropriate oral motor activities may be found in materials discussed in previous chapters; however, these may need to be modified so that they are age appropriate. The speech-language pathologist will use clinical judgment in choosing appropriate materials and activities for the adolescent. The treatment populations in this age group may significantly differ from one another. Some clients may have persistent articulation and myofunctional concerns, others may have developmental disabilities, and still others may have acquired disabilities or neurological disease.

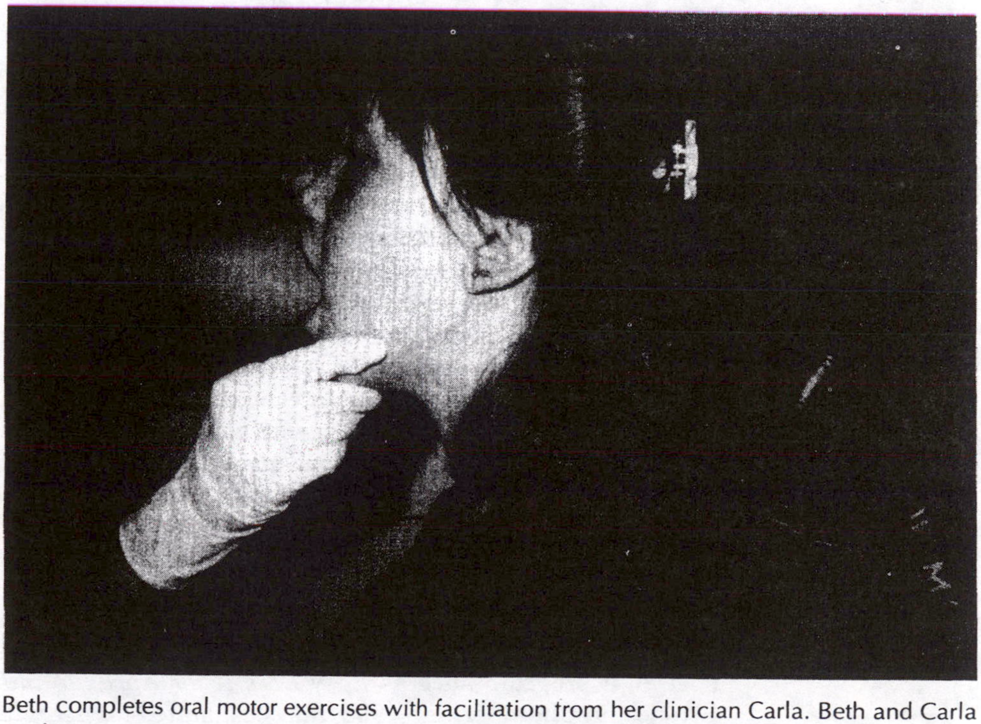

Beth completes oral motor exercises with facilitation from her clinician Carla. Beth and Carla work as a team to establish graded jaw movement while Beth maintains her body in a stable, relaxed position.

INTERACTIVE EXPERIENCE: ORAL MOTOR EXERCISES AND ACTIVITIES

Brainstorm and list appropriate oral motor exercises and activities for adolescents in the following areas (this activity is a modified version of one used by Jelm [1995b]):

- Exercises/activities for jaw strengthening, stability, and control
- Exercises/activities for tongue strengthening, mobility, and control
- Exercises/activities for lip strengthening, mobility, and control

Remediation of Factors Affecting Intelligibility

The remediation of factors affecting intelligibility would be particularly important for adolescents with oral motor concerns. A communication disorder can significantly affect the self-image of individuals who are already experiencing many physical and social changes in this stage of life. The adolescent's ability to communicate can impact on school performance as well as social interactions with peers and family. Some individuals in this age group have received many years of speech therapy and may be frustrated by lack of success. Other individuals in this age group have become accustomed to their own form of speech production and may not see a need for a change. However, this may still affect their social interactions and school performance. In addition to articulatory production, many other factors may affect intelligibility. These include speaking rate and rhythm, use of intonation and stress, vocal quality and loudness, fluency, as well as the use of appropriate pragmatic skills.

When working on speaking rate and rhythm, the clinician can use a pacing system with the client to slow the individual's speaking rate and practice appropriate rhythm. The pacing board could be constructed by placing a series of glue dots on a tongue depressor. The individual would touch each glue dot while practicing target words, phrases, or sentences. A pocket-sized pacing board is also available from Pro-Ed (see product sources in Appendix D). The use of the pacing board is discussed in Chapter 5 as well as in other chapters.

Audiotaping is also very useful in providing feedback to the client regarding rate, rhythm, and other aspects of speech production affecting intelligibility. Role-playing and drama activities are useful for improving intonation and stress, vocal quality and loudness, as well as fluency. These activities can be videotaped and reviewed. The Visi-Pitch from Kay Elemetrics Corporation can be used to help remediate vocal quality and loudness concerns. Fluency can be affected by both speech production and motor planning concerns. Techniques and materials addressing fluency concerns are widely available. Many materials are also available for working with adolescents exhibiting pragmatic issues.

Dysarthria and/or dyspraxia may be experienced by adolescents with motor speech disorders. If the individual exhibits dysarthria, materials such as the *Dysarthria Rehabilitation Program* (Tonkovich, Latham, & Rambow, 1986) and *The Source for Dysarthria* (Swigert, 1997) may be used. The *Dysarthria Rehabilitation Program* was developed for both adolescents and adults; *The Source for Dysarthria* was developed for adults. These materials will be discussed in the section on adult treatment. If the individual exhibits dyspraxia of speech, a program such as *Easy Does It for Apraxia and Motor Planning* by Strode and Chamberlain (1993) may be adapted for use with the adolescent (see Chapter 6). *The Source for Apraxia Therapy* by Tomlin (1994), and the *Workbook for the Verbally Apraxic Adult* by Richards and Fallon (1987) may also be adapted for use with adolescents. These will be discussed in the adult treatment portion of this chapter.

The use of cueing strategies can be helpful when working with adolescents exhibiting dyspraxia of speech or imprecise articulation. The use of cueing has been discussed in many chapters in this book. Moto-kinesthetic cueing (Young & Hawk, 1955) and visual-tactile cueing (Jelm, 1995b) are both methods that can be used when working with adolescents. These cueing systems were discussed in Chapter 4 and in other chapters; a listing of the moto-kinesthetic cues can be found in Appendix C. It is important for the clinician to explain the reason for using cues to the client. Moto-kinesthetic cueing requires the clinician to physically manipulate the oral structures; visual-tactile cueing does not. The type of cueing used may be determined by the comfort level of the clinician and the client.

Articulation and Language Therapy

Articulation and language therapy would be completed with adolescents as appropriate. If individuals continue to demonstrate articulatory concerns, then traditional articulation practice may serve the individual as part of a complete oral motor treatment program. Programs such as *Easy Does It for Articulation: An Oral Motor Approach* by Strode and Chamberlain, *The Complete Oral-Motor Program for Articulation* by Pehde, Geller, and Lechner, *Oral-Motor Activities for School-Aged Children* by Mackie, and *Oral-Motor Exercises for Speech Clarity* by Rosenfeld-Johnson (1999b) contain specific oral motor exercises and activities to facilitate the correct production of specific speech sounds. In persons who exhibit specific language concerns, the carry-over of speech sounds can be monitored and practiced as work is completed in areas of language need.

TREATMENT OF ADULTS

Oral motor treatment can be beneficial for adults with developmental disabilities as well as adults with acquired disabilities and neurological diseases. The speech-language pathologist will use clinical expertise and judgment to determine appropriate treatment for individuals with different types of disabilities. For example, some individuals with developmental disabilities may exhibit generalized low muscle tone and related movement patterns that impact on eating, drinking, and speech production (e.g., individuals with Down syndrome). The treatment of these individuals would be significantly different from the treatment of other individuals with developmental disabilities who exhibit hypertonicity, fluctuating muscle tone, mixed muscle tone, athetosis, ataxia, or other movement disorders (e.g., individuals with cerebral palsy). The treatment of individuals with acquired disorders (e.g., traumatic brain injury or stroke) would be based on the tonal and movement concerns demonstrated by these individuals, which can vary according to the area(s) of insult. Neurological diseases can be progressive (e.g., amyotrophic lateral sclerosis and progressive supranuclear palsy) or can take some other course (e.g., multiple sclerosis). Therefore, the approach to treatment will need to be modified based on the course of the disease.

Most individuals with dysarthria can benefit from oral motor treatment; however, there may be some exceptions. For example, many individuals with flaccid dysarthria require oral motor treatment, but someone with myasthenia gravis may not benefit from this approach secondary to the nature of the disorder (i.e., precise speech production usually returns with rest but deteriorates as the person continues to speak). An augmentative form of communication may be a better approach than oral motor treatment for someone with myasthenia gravis. Many individuals with spastic dysarthria can also benefit from oral motor treatment. However, the approach taken with progressive diseases such as amyotrophic lateral sclerosis may be different from the approach taken with a demyelinating disease such as multiple sclerosis.

When an individual has a progressive disease, the focus of oral motor treatment would be to maintain the individual's function as long as possible. Oral massage and oral exercises/activities may improve sensation and may assist the individual in maintaining oral motor function. However, when an individual has a degenerative disease and the loss of speech is inevitable, an augmentative/alternative communication system needs to be simultaneously established while oral motor treatment continues. The approach to oral motor treatment would be different for an individual with a disorder such as multiple sclerosis or Bell's palsy, where the individual is likely to recover at least some oral motor function. The focus of oral motor treatment would then be to assist the individual in regaining as much oral motor function as possible.

Ataxic dysarthria is another motor speech disorder that may not be as responsive to oral motor treatment as the other forms of dysarthria. The damage to the cerebellum or the pathways to and from the cerebellum may preclude the affects of oral motor treatment. However, these individuals also frequently exhibit hypotonia which may be responsive to oral motor treatment. The clinician may wish to provide the client with a trial period of oral motor treatment if there is a question about the efficacy of oral motor treatment with a client exhibiting a particular disorder. The decision to continue oral motor treatment can then be based on results.

Working with adults in the area of oral motor treatment can be similar to working with individuals in other age groups. Many materials are available to assist the clinician and family in the treatment of the adult with oral motor issues. Oral motor treatment for the adult may consist of the following components:

- Gross motor activities/exercise program/physical therapy
- Oral massage/Other facilitation techniques
- Swallowing therapy
- Oral motor exercises/activities
- Remediation of factors affecting intelligibility
- Language therapy

The typical oral motor treatment session for an adult may include 5 minutes of a gross motor activity if this has not been addressed in a physical or occupational therapy session prior to oral motor treatment. The oral massage and other facilitation techniques may take 5 to 10 minutes, depending on the type and extent of work completed. Swallowing therapy may be incorporated into the massage and the oral motor exercise portion of treatment. The client may work on oral motor exercises or activities for another 5 to 10 minutes, depending on the client's needs. The remainder of the session could be devoted to remediation of factors affecting intelligibility and language therapy. The timing and sequence of the segments of the oral motor treatment session should be modified according to the client's needs. However, a suggested timing and sequence has been provided for the speech-language pathologist who is beginning to use this approach to oral motor treatment. As the speech-language pathologist develops skill and his or her own style in this area of treatment, the timing and sequence may change.

Gross Motor Activities/Exercise Program/Physical Therapy

Adults who have strokes, traumatic brain injury, or a variety of neurological disorders frequently exhibit issues with sensation and postural control that may affect oral motor function. Some disorders with possible concomitant oral motor concerns include amyetrophic lateral sclerosis, Parkinson's disease, multiple sclerosis, progressive supranuclear palsy, brain stem stroke, left cerebrovascular accident, traumatic brain injury, and others. Individuals with these disorders will frequently receive physical therapy and/or occupational therapy in addition to speech therapy. Therefore, the speech-language pathologist may wish to co-treat or coordinate therapies with the occupational therapist and/or the physical therapist.

If the speech-language pathologist is *co-treating with a physical therapist,* the gross motor portion of treatment can be facilitated by the physical therapist. Techniques from Feldenkrais's "Awareness through Movement" and neurodevelopmental treatment can be incorporated into a cotreatment session (see information presented in previous chapters). If cotreatment is not occurring, then perhaps a physical therapy session can be scheduled prior to the speech and language therapy session so that the physical therapist can work with the client on postural control and stability. The speech-language pathologist can also ask the physical therapist to develop a movement or exercise program for the client to address postural and movement issues that may affect the individual's ability to complete oral motor tasks related to eating, drinking, or speaking.

If *co-treatment is scheduled with the client's occupational therapist,* improved postural control and responses to sensory input can be facilitated by the occupational therapist. Particular emphasis may be placed on the facilitation of shoulder stability for the purpose of establishing more refined fine motor control in the distal areas of the body (e.g., mouth and hands). Patients with disorders such as traumatic brain injury, progressive neurological disease, and right hemisphere syndrome may exhibit a variety of sensory integrative concerns that can be addressed by the occupational therapist. If cotreatment is not done, then perhaps an occupational therapy session can be scheduled prior to the speech and language therapy session where the occupational therapist works with the client on postural control and sensory integration.

If the client is not receiving occupational therapy or physical therapy or if the therapy schedule cannot be coordinated, then the speech-language pathologist may need to include appropriate gross motor activities into the beginning of the therapy session. This should be done with care if the client has a medical condition that may preclude certain types of activity (e.g., heart and pulmonary concerns). The speech-language pathologist should speak with the client's physician prior to beginning any type of physical exercise with the client.

Gross motor activities for *adults with generalized low muscle tone* and postural concerns can be completed while standing or while seated in a wheelchair. There are wheelchair aerobics on videotape that the client can perform. Some of the same activities described for adolescents with generalized low muscle tone can be used if the client is physically well enough to perform these. These activities could include wall push-ups, calisthenics, dance, and other activities involving resistance work for the shoulder girdle or vigorous movement of the entire body. If able, adults could begin activities outside of treatment, such as swimming, water aerobics, and weight training under supervision of the physician, physical therapist, occupational therapist, or an exercise physiologist. Properly supervised weight training can assist clients in building upper body strength, stability, and control.

Adults with hypertonicity, fluctuating muscle tone, or mixed muscle tone usually require a different approach to movement activities than adults exhibiting generalized low muscle tone. Slow, controlled movement activities are often used to facilitate more typical muscle tone and movement. As previously mentioned, techniques such as Feldenkrais's "Awareness through Movement" and neuro-developmental treatment can be used. The clinician must be specially trained in the use of these techniques or work with other professionals who are trained in the use of these techniques. Massage can also be used to decrease hypertonicity. When an individual exhibits mixed muscle tone (i.e., hypertonicity in some muscle groups and hypotonicity in others) or fluctuating muscle tone, the clinician must carefully balance movement and massage activities so that improved muscle tone and movement are facilitated throughout the body.

Oral Massage and Other Facilitation Techniques

Sensory input is often overlooked in many treatment approaches. According to Nelson and de Benebib (1991), sensory messages are used to obtain sensory changes essential in the organization of motor output and "more sensory fibers are present in the mouth than in any other part of the human body" (Nelson & de Benebib, 1991, p. 131).

> The various parts of the mouth need to relate to one another at a sensory level to coordinate their function, so the clinical objective becomes one of introducing more normal movement sensations and establishing the orientation of each segment of the whole to encourage more normal function. (Nelson & de Benebib, 1991, p. 137)

Normal function of the oral mechanism for eating, drinking, and speaking is the ultimate goal of oral motor treatment.

Oral massage is one way to increase sensation in the oral structures and continues to be very useful when working with adults. Many adults exhibit decreased sensory awareness, muscle function concerns, as well as motor planning issues. Adults who have some type of medical condition are frequently receptive to hands-on types of treatments, as many of them have experienced this type of treatment in occupational therapy and physical therapy. Many adults can learn to apply the oral massage techniques to themselves. It is important to discuss the rationale for using a particular treatment with adult clients.

The speech-language clinician will need to consult with the client's physical and occupational therapists to establish the best positioning for oral massage. Supine or side lying would be appropriate positions for clients treated in bed. If the client is lying supine in a hospital bed, the head of the bed can often be raised. Oral massage work can be applied as appropriate with the client at bedside. If the client can sit in a chair or wheelchair, it is important to work with a physical therapist and/or an occupational therapist to position the client for optimal support and stability prior to oral motor treatment.

Clients who have experienced stroke, traumatic brain injury, or neurological disease frequently exhibit oral hyperresponsivity and/or hyporesponsivity. An oral massage program can assist in improving the client's responses to sensation in the tactile and proprioceptive systems. This can be used to inhibit a hypersensitive gag response or tonic bite reflex. For example, a client's *hypersensitive gag response* can be inhibited by progressively applying the oral massage sequence in a slow, rhythmic, and systematic manner (refer to oral massage sequence in Chapter 4). The clinician can apply massage to the client's cheeks, lips, and tongue, noting where the gag response is elicited. Often, the response is elicited when stimulation is applied to the client's tongue. When completing massage work inside the client's dental arch, an implement other than the clinician's gloved finger should probably be used (e.g., Nuk oral massage brush, toothette, etc.) unless the client is biting on a bite block. The clinician applies the stimulation up to the point where the gag response is about to be elicited. This can be observed by watching the client's facial expression. The client's facial expression will begin to change as the stimulation approaches the activation of the gag response. The client's eyes may also begin to "water." When this occurs, the clinician will move the stimulation back to an area of the client's tongue or mouth where stimulation was easily tolerated. The clinician will then reapproach the area of mouth where the gag response was about to be triggered. The area in which the gag response is triggered is reapproached systematically over time in treatment. With slow, rhythmic, and systematic stimulation, the clinician can assist the client in moving the gag response further back on the tongue.

The *tonic bite reaction* may also be systematically inhibited over time by using a similar approach. Note the location where the tonic bite reaction is elicited in the client. This is usually when stimulation is applied to the client's gums or teeth. Systematically apply oral massage to the individual's oral structures using the small Nuk oral massage brush if possible. The large Nuk oral massage brush is a two-piece brush, and the tip may break off if the person bites down on it. Working through the oral massage sequence as written in Chapter 4 may reduce the individual's tonic bite reaction over time. It is extremely important that the clinician refrain from placing fingers near the individual's gums or teeth, as the pressure of the tonic bite reaction can be harmful. The clinician may wish to use a bite block when working with an individual with a tonic bite reaction. Bite blocks can be made by stacking tongue depressors and wrapping these with a tape that is safe to be placed into the mouth. Bite blocks are also commercially available from Innovative Therapist International (see product sources in Appendix D).

There are several methods for encouraging the client to release a tonic bite response. When the person is biting down, it is important for the clinician to wait until the client releases the bite if possible. Pulling on the massage brush or a bite block may cause the individual to bite harder. The clinician can encourage the client to release the bite by relaxing the oral musculature through deep, slow massage. Changes can also be made in the environment to assist the client with relaxation and release of the bite. For example, soft music can be played or the overhead lights can be lowered. When working with an individual with a tonic bite response, it is important to treat the individual in an environment that is soothing. Chapters 2 and 3 discuss the sensory systems and the sensory environment. If the client is biting on a surface that will be harmful to the client or the clinician, some clinicians have found that firm, consistent pressure applied at the temporomandibular joints will release the bite. *However, this can be painful or potentially harmful to the client and should be used only in case of an emergency.* Blowing air or sprinkling water on the client's face or plugging the client's nose may also cause the client to release the bite in an emergency situation (Morris & Klein, 1987).

Techniques such as myofascial release, Beckman's facilitation, and proprioceptive neuromuscular facilitation can be incorporated as appropriate. Speech-language pathologists will need to obtain specific training in these techniques. It is recommended that clinicians working in the area of oral motor assessment and treatment obtain training in treatment approaches such as sensory integration, neuro-developmental treatment, Feldenkrais's "Awareness through Movement," myofascial release, massage, proprioceptive neuromuscular facilitation, and so on, to use as part of oral motor treatment (see discussion of techniques in previous chapters). These approaches are particularly helpful, since oral motor treatment involves work with the entire body.

Swallowing Therapy

Swallowing therapy can be readily incorporated into an oral motor treatment program for adults. After initial oral massage work is completed, techniques such as thermal gustatory stimulation and thermal tactile stimulation can be applied. Maneuvers such as the effortful swallow, supraglottic swallow, super-supraglottic swallow, and the Mendelsohn maneuver (Logemann, 1992) can be taught during the exercise portion of the session. The assessment and treatment of swallowing disorders receive a thorough discussion in texts by Logemann (1997), Groher (1997), and others who have written on this topic. Refer to these books for detailed information on swallowing disorders.

Oral Motor Exercises/Activities

Adults exhibit many of the same types of oral motor issues as previously discussed in this book. Concerns with sensation; postural control; jaw stability; lip mobility; tongue and jaw dissociation; graded jaw, lip, and tongue movement; and motor planning are prevalent in adults with oral motor difficulties and affect the individual's ability to eat, drink, and speak. These issues have been thoroughly discussed in previous chapters. Oral motor exercises/activities to address these issues have traditionally been an important part of adult treatment. Specific oral motor activities/exercises *must be carefully selected* for the adult. This involves careful assessment of the individual's oral motor concerns and task analysis of the individual's goals. The exercises and activities must relate directly to the individual's oral motor needs. See Treatment Plan in Chapter 6 and the Task Analysis form in Chapter 7 to assist with this process. Some materials that may assist the clinician in planning appropriate oral motor activities and exercises are discussed next.

The Source for Oral-Facial Exercises by Gangale (1993) addresses both the oral motor and the swallowing needs of the adult. The book contains treatment sections on swallowing, nutrition, drooling, postural control, respiration, voice, intelligibility, communication, and "oral motor head-neck-facial exercises" in addition to the assessment protocol discussed previously in this chapter. Reference charts assist the clinician in choosing appropriate oral motor exercises and tracking client progress. The book also contains information on goal development, resources, associations, videotapes, and other instructional materials.

The Dworkin-Culatta Treatment System by Dworkin and Culatta (1996) contains exercises and activities to address each subsystem assessed in the Dworkin-Culatta Oral Mechanism Examination. The subsystems include the areas of respiration, resonation, phonation, articulation, and prosody. The activities and exercises in the book *Oral-Motor Exercises for Speech Clarity* (Rosenfeld-Johnson, 1999b) were developed for individuals of all ages. If the clinician or the client feel that some of the exercises in this book are not age appropriate based on the tools that are used, the exercises can be adpated. However, Rosenfeld-Johnson (1999a) reports that adults will readily participate in the activities as written in the book when the rationale for each activity is explained. See Chapter 6 for a description of this reference.

Adult clients with myofunctional concerns are often referred by dentists and orthodontists. Programs such as *Taming the Tongue Thrust* by Barnes (1994), *Swallow Right* by Pierce (1993), and *Swalloworks* by Boshart (1995b) would be appropriate materials to use with these individuals. Extensive information on myofunctional treatment can also be found in the book *Myofunctional Therapy in Dental Practice: Abnormal Swallowing Habits: Diagnosis—Treatment* by Garliner (1974). This topic was discussed in Chapter 7.

INTERACTIVE EXPERIENCE: ORAL MOTOR EXERCISES AND ACTIVITIES

Brainstorm and list appropriate oral motor exercises and activities for adults in the following areas (this activity is a modified version of one used by Jelm [1995b]):

- Exercises/activities for jaw strengthening, stability, and control
- Exercises/activities for tongue strengthening, mobility, and control
- Exercises/activities for lip strengthening, mobility, and control

Remediation of Factors Affecting Intelligibility

Both *The Source for Oral-Facial Exercises* (Gangale, 1993) and the Dworkin-Culatta Treatment System (Dworkin & Culatta, 1996) contain activities that address postural control as well as the remediation of factors affecting intelligibility. *The Source for Oral-Facial Exercises* contains sections on voice, intelligibility, and communication. The Dworkin-Culatta Treatment System addresses the subsystems of respiration, resonation, phonation, articulation, and prosody. Each subsystem could have an impact on intelligibility.

Some materials have been specifically developed to address *dysarthria.* The *Dysarthria Rehabilitation Program,* developed by Tonkovich, Latham, and Rambow (1986), can be used with both adolescents and adults. This program consists of sections on "exaggerating articulatory movements," "reduced speech rate via vowel prolongation," and "improving speech prosody." Each section begins with simple exercises, with the exercises becoming more complex as the client progresses through each section. The program contains forms for data collection and tracking progress. Another resource for working with adult clients exhibiting dysarthria is *The Source for Dysarthria* by Swigert (1997). It contains both assessment and treatment information regarding the areas of respiration, phonation, resonation, and articulation. Information is provided about neurology and the different types of dysarthria. Suggested goals and treatment objectives, treatment techniques, and patient handouts are provided for each area of treatment. Sample documentation and reports are included in this resource.

The adult's intelligibility may also be affected by *motor planning issues.* The *Workbook for the Verbally Apraxic Adult* by Richards and Fallon (1987) uses a traditional treatment approach beginning with simple sound combinations and progressing to the conversational level. The client initially works on producing consonant-vowel combinations and progresses to the production of conversation containing target words. This resource addresses the articulation of consonants and vowels as separate issues. One section of the book focuses on the production of consonants in consonant-vowel combinations, vowel-consonant combinations, consonant-vowel-consonant combinations, two-syllable words, multisyllable words, minimally paired words, and so on. A separate section focuses on vowels in these same contexts. A section is included in the book on prosody and addresses the use of stress and inflection in speech.

The Source for Apraxia Therapy by Tomlin (1994) provides the clinician with therapeutic suggestions for the individual with severe dyspraxia as well as the individual with mild to moderate dyspraxia. Tomlin addresses motor planning issues through the practice of speech sounds by phonemic group (e.g., bilabials, labio-dentals, etc.). She uses a functional approach to the treatment of dyspraxia by having the client work on articulation, fluency, and phrasing in rhyming words, conversational sentences and paragraphs, words and sentences of increasing length, and other types of word forms typically problematic for the adult with dyspraxia of speech. *The Source for Apraxia Therapy* also contains paralinguistic drill work on vocal pitch, word emphasis/stress, and emotional expression.

Rosenbek and associates (1973, as described in Brookshire, 1997) recommend a process for establishing or accessing the speech motor plan for the individual with dyspraxia. This process assists the individual in systematically moving from a maximally cued level to an automatic level of speech. The motor plan or speech routine is established by the individual as cueing levels are decreased.

Cues from Rosenbek and Associates

Directions for *person assisting* client (adapted from list in Brookshire, 1997, p. 281):

1. Say the word, phrase, or sentence in unison with the client.
2. Model the word, phrase, or sentence for the client. Silently mouth the word, phrase, or sentence while the client says it.
3. Say the word, phrase, or sentence. Have the client repeat it.
4. Say the word, phrase, or sentence. Have the client repeat it several times in succession.
5. Give the client the word, phrase, or sentence written on a card. Have the client read the card aloud.
6. Have the client silently read the word, phrase, or sentence. Remove the card. Have the client say the word, phrase, or sentence.
7. Ask a question for which the answer is the target word, phrase, or sentence. Have the client answer the question.
8. Role-play a situation in which the target word, phrase, or sentence would be used. Have the client use the target word, phrase, or sentence at appropriate times.

The use of *manual cueing strategies* can be helpful when working with adults exhibiting dyspraxia of speech or imprecise articulation. The use of cueing has been discussed in many chapters in this book. Moto-kinesthetic cueing (Young & Hawk, 1955) and visual-tactile cueing (Jelm, 1995b) are both methods that can be used when working with adults. Moto-kinesthetic cueing requires the clinician to physically manipulate the oral structures; visual-tactile cueing does not. These cueing systems were discussed in Chapters 4 and 5. A list of moto-kinesthetic cues can be found in Appendix C. Amer-Ind (Skelly, 1979) signal language is another type of cueing that has been widely used with adults demonstrating dyspraxia. The use of Amer-Ind or sign language can facilitate motor planning. For individuals with limited hand use, Amer-Ind signals are often easier to produce than signs found in the different forms of sign language. Either the client or the clinician can produce the cues to facilitate the client's speech production. It is important for the clinician to explain the reason for using cues to the client. The type of cueing used may be determined by the comfort level of the clinician and the client in the use of a particular type of cueing.

Whether the adult's oral motor disorder is related to dysarthria and/or dyspraxia, working with the individual on *speaking rate and rhythm* can have a tremendous impact on improving the individual's intelligibility. The typical conversational speaking rate in adults can vary from 150 to 250 words per minute (Goldman-Eisler, 1968, as cited in Yorkston, Beukelman, & Bell, 1988). Oral paragraph reading rates can range from 160 to 170 words per minute (Fairbanks, 1960, as cited in Yorkston, Beukelman, & Bell, 1988), and sentence reading rates are usually around 190 words per minute (Yorkston & Beukelman, 1984, as cited in Yorkston, Beukelman, & Bell, 1988). The clinician can use a pacing system with the client to slow the individual's speaking rate and practice appropriate rhythm. The pacing board could be constructed by placing a series of glue dots on a tongue depressor. The individual would touch each glue dot while practicing target words, phrases, or sentences. A pocket-sized pacing board is also available from Pro-Ed (see product sources in Appendix D). The use of the pacing board is discussed in Chapter 5 as well as in other chapters.

Audiotaping is very useful in providing feedback to the client regarding rate, rhythm, and other aspects of speech production affecting intelligibility. Role-playing and drama activities can also be used to improve intonation and stress, vocal quality and loudness, as well as fluency. These activities can be videotaped and reviewed. The Visi-Pitch from Kay Elemetrics Corporation is useful in the remediation of vocal quality and loudness concerns. Fluency can be affected by both speech production and motor planning concerns. Techniques and materials addressing fluency concerns are widely available.

It is particularly important to address intelligibility when working with adults. The adult's level of intelligibility can dramatically affect his or her ability to function in everyday life with family, friends, and coworkers. This may impact on the person's relationships and livelihood. The individual's intelligibility can affect self-confidence and his or her ability to acquire new employment or return to previous employment.

Language Therapy

Language therapy is an important aspect of treatment for the adult with language needs. This would be incorporated as appropriate throughout the session. Many resources are available for the clinician working with adults with language concerns.

TREATMENT OF ADULTS DEPENDENT ON OTHERS FOR CARE

The treatment of adults with oral motor concerns who are dependent on others for care may be similar to the treatment discussed in Chapter 4. However, these individuals are not infants and must be treated as adults. When speaking to adults who are dependent on others for care, it is important to interact with them in a manner consistent with other adult interactions. For example, speak to the adult as an adult. Provide simple explanations about the treatment, even if the individual does not seem to comprehend what is being said. Many of these individuals are living at home or in nursing facilities and require a significant amount of care from family members, nurses, therapists, and others. The speech-language pathologist can assist care providers in the establishment of an appropriate oral motor and communication program for the individual.

The treatment session would be structured to support the individual's quality of life. An oral motor treatment session for an adult dependent on others for care may include some or all of the following components:

- Movement and positioning
- Oral massage/Other facilitation techniques
- Swallowing therapy (as appropriate)
- Oral motor exercises/activities
- Remediation of factors affecting intelligibility (as appropriate)
- Language therapy (as appropriate)
- Use of communication devices

The clinician can consult with the client's physical and occupational therapists regarding *appropriate movement and positioning* for the individual. The clinician may be working with the individual at bedside or while the person is seated in a chair or wheelchair. While working at *bedside,* it is important to position the individual appropriately. The clinician may work with the individual in supine, semireclined (i.e., head of the bed raised), or side-lying positions. Side-lying or semireclined positions may be appropriate positions for feeding the client. Although other oral motor activities may be completed when the client is positioned in supine, feeding is generally *not* recommended in this position. If the individual is *seated in a chair or wheelchair,* it would be important for the individual to have adequate support. See information on positioning in Chapter 3 and the relationship between stability and mobility in Chapter 2. The clinician can work with the physical and/or occupational therapist to obtain appropriate seating for the individual. *Movement* can be incorporated into the treatment session to facilitate postural control and mobility. Feldenkrais's "Awareness through Movement" and neuro-developmental treatment are two approaches that can be considered. These approaches were specifically discussed in Chapters 3 and 4.

Oral massage and other facilitation techniques can be used to address oral sensory and motor concerns. These include difficulties with responses to sensory input, muscle weakness, as well as mobility and coordination issues. The oral massage protocol in Chapter 4, Beckman (1997) facilitation techniques, myofascial release, proprioceptive neuromuscular facilitation, as well as other specific techniques can also be used with this population. The application of oral massage as well as other appropriate oral stimulation can help the individual maintain a level of adequate sensation in the oral structures. This would be particularly important if the individual is being tube fed. If the oral area is not stimulated, the area may become hyperresponsive. This may affect the individual's acceptance of tooth brushing and oral care.

Swallowing therapy as appropriate can easily be incorporated into the oral motor treatment session. Many adults who are dependent on others for care require swallowing therapy (briefly discussed in an earlier section in this chapter). A number of resources are available on the assessment and treatment of swallowing.

Appropriate oral motor exercises and activities can be completed with the client. These would focus on the functional outcomes of eating, drinking, and

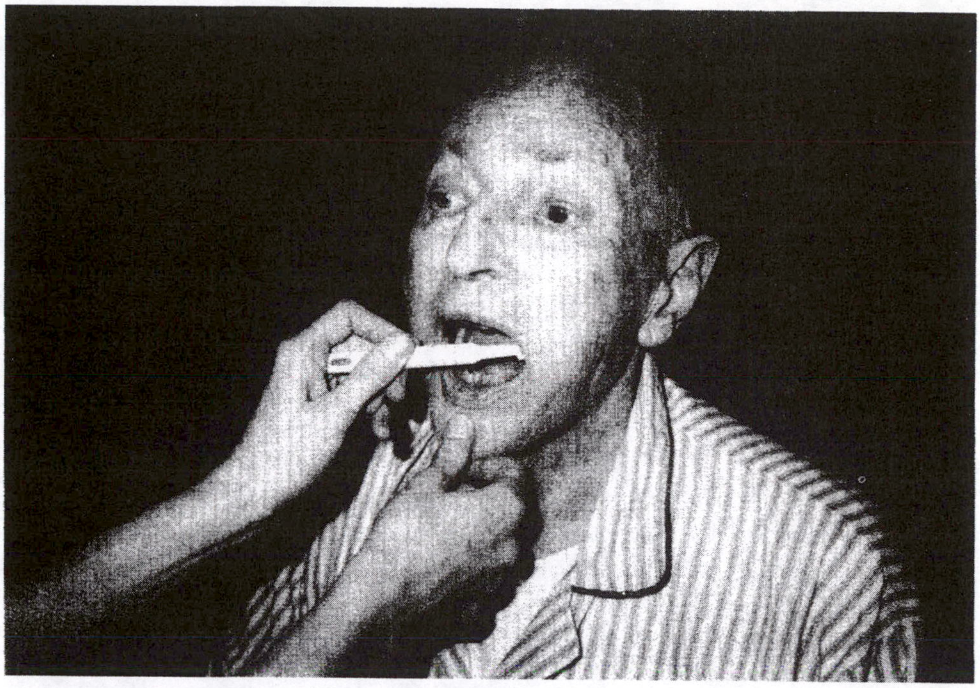

Charlie, a 90-year-old gentleman with a history of transient ischemic attacks, receives oral massage from his granddaughter Kim prior to a meal. Charlie has decreased oral sensation, which seems related to his diminished desire to eat and drink.

communication. Chapters 4 and 5 contain a great amount of information on activities to facilitate eating and drinking. Adults who are dependent on others for care may be anywhere on the continuum of oral motor treatment needs. They may therefore benefit from oral motor exercises and activities discussed in Chapters 6 through 8.

Individuals who are tube fed may also benefit from oral motor activities and exercises to help maintain the integrity of the oral mechanism. There are many exercises and activities that do not involve the use of food or liquid. However, the clinician may wish to consider providing the individual with certain food or fluid tastes *if this is approved by the individual's physician.* Tastes can be provided by dipping the Nuk oral massage brush in flavored substances (e.g., flavored Seltzer water, jelly, etc.). The individual may also enjoy chewing on foods such as dried fruits safely wrapped in cheesecloth or organza. Again, this would need to be *approved by the individual's physician,* as the use of foods and tastes for oral stimulation can increase saliva production and possibly the risk for aspiration. An individual *might* tolerate a certain amount of his or her own aspirated saliva; however, aspirated saliva mixed with anything else (e.g., molecules from food responsible for taste) may cause *aspiration pneumonia.*

When *feeding* individuals who are dependent on others for care, it is important that they be properly positioned and that the feeder is properly positioned. The individual's head should be well aligned with the body, and the individual's neck should *not* be hyperextended. Some individuals with postural control issues will raise the shoulders, extend the neck, and rest the head on the shoulders. If the individual extends the neck while eating, drinking, and swallowing, he or she might be at increased risk for aspiration. Neck extension generally opens the individual's airway. Caregivers may not have the knowledge or understanding of the importance of feeding individuals with proper head and neck alignment. Some care providers may stand rather than sit during feeding. This places the care provider in a position slightly above the individual being fed and may result in "bird feeding" (i.e., where the person being fed is extending the neck and looking up at the person doing the feeding). The client may then be placed at risk for aspiration. Individuals who are elderly and/or medically fragile may develop aspiration pneumonia if aspiration occurs.

The clinician would address *intelligibility and language* concerns as appropriate with individuals who are dependent on others for care. Augmentative and alternative means of communication may be important to explore with these individuals. See information in Chapter 3 on the use of augmentative and alternative communication.

INTERACTIVE CASE EXPERIENCES

The interactive case experiences allow the reader to practice using the information from the chapter. These experiences challenge the reader to think of the possibilities for each case. The answers to the questions in the interactive case experiences are for the reader to decide.

Review the case examples on Eddie and Drew in Chapter 1. What resources, materials, or tools might you use as part of treatment? If available, review these resources and materials. Develop activities/exercises for each part of the treatment plan. What other recommendations need to be made? What other comments or ideas do you have concerning Eddie or Drew?

9

Report Writing

Report writing in the area of oral motor assessment and treatment can be a challenging task. This chapter will provide the clinician with guidelines and sample report formats that can be used with clients of all ages receiving oral motor assessment and treatment. The first section presents some common challenges encountered by professionals in report writing. This is followed by sample report formats. It should be noted that these are only *suggested* formats; they may be particularly helpful to the new clinician and can be adapted by the experienced clinician to fit his or her own report writing style.

When writing reports, the clinician must keep several critical issues in mind. Reports need to justify the service being recommended or provided. For children in the school system, information needs to be provided about how treatment will affect or has affected the child's educational process. For adults treated in rehabilitation or other medical settings, health insurance companies want information regarding what impact the treatment will have or has had on the adult's ability to function in daily life. This information may also be required for children receiving benefits from health insurers.

COMMON CHALLENGES ENCOUNTERED IN REPORT WRITING

Following are lists of guidelines for report writing that were developed based on common practices and errors found in professional reports.

Writing Style/Preferred Practices

- *Use clear, concise language. "Short words and short sentences are easier to comprehend than long ones." (Publication Manual of the American Psychological Association,* 1994, pp. 26–27).
  Preferred: Assessment of Mr. S.'s oral structures was significantly limited secondary to the angle at which he was videotaped. Therefore, a clear view of his oral musculature was not obtained.
  Not Preferred: Assessment of Mr. S.'s oral structures was significantly limited secondary to the angle at which he was videotaped, which did not lead to a clear view of his oral musculature.
- *Use client/patient names or a pronoun reference to the client/patient in sentences discussing the client/patient.*

Preferred: Assessment of Mr. S.'s oral structures was significantly limited.
Not Preferred: Assessment of the oral structures was significantly limited.

- *Place clauses containing "due to" or "secondary to" in the second half of the sentence.*
  Preferred: Assessment of Mr. S.'s oral structures was significantly limited due to the angle at which he was videotaped.
  Not Preferred: Due to the angle at which he was videotaped, assessment of Mr. S.'s oral structures was significantly limited.
- *Use the preposition "toward" instead of "towards."*
  Preferred: Mr. S. opened his mouth as the clinician brought the spoon toward his lips.
  Not Preferred: Mr. S. opened his mouth as the clinician brought the spoon towards his lips.
- *Avoid colloquial expressions or language.*
  Preferred: Mr. S. seemed to enjoy the folk music used in treatment as he tapped his foot to the rhythm.
  Not Preferred: Mr. S. thought the music was groovy.
- *Avoid ending sentences with prepositions.*
  Preferred: Assessment of Mr. S.'s oral structures was significantly limited due to the angle at which he was videotaped.
  Not Preferred: Assessment of Mr. S.'s oral structures was significantly limited due to the angle he was videotaped at.

Grammar

- *Use active voice when possible.*
  Preferred: Mr. S. maintained lip closure around the straw while drinking several consecutive swallows.
  Not Preferred: Mr. S. was able to maintain lip closure around the straw while drinking several consecutive swallows.
- *Use idiomatic prepositions instead of unidiomatic prepositions.*
  Correct: Mr. S. appeared to lose control of the bolus.
  Incorrect: Mr. S. appeared to lose control with the bolus.

Punctuation

- *Place punctuation marks inside quotation marks.*
  Correct: Mr. S. produced the word approximations for "more," "yes," and "no."
  Incorrect: Mr. S. produced the word approximations for "more", "yes", and "no".
- *"Use a comma between elements (including before 'and' and 'or') in a series of three or more items"* (*Publication Manual of the American Psychological Association,* 1994, p. 62).
  Correct: Mr. S. safely managed oatmeal, scrambled eggs, toast, and coffee for breakfast.
  Incorrect: Mr. S. safely managed oatmeal, scrambled eggs, toast and coffee for breakfast.
- *"Use a comma to separate two independent clauses joined by a conjunction"* (*Publication Manual of the American Psychological Association,* 1994, p. 62).
  Correct: Mr. S. was well positioned in his chair, and he maintained adequate head alignment.

Incorrect: Mr. S. was well positioned in his chair and he maintained adequate head alignment.

- *"Use a semicolon to separate two independent clauses that are not joined by a conjunction"* (*Publication Manual of the American Psychological Association,* 1994, p. 63).
  Correct: Mr. S. was poorly positioned in his chair; however, he maintained adequate head alignment.
  Incorrect: Mr. S. was poorly positioned in his chair, however, he maintained adequate head alignment.

Abbreviations

- *Use "e.g.," to represent "for example."*
  Correct: Mr. S. produced a variety of single words (e.g., *hi, bye, yes, no,* etc.).
  Incorrect: Mr. S. produced a variety of single words (i.e., *hi, bye, yes, no,* etc.).
- *Use "i.e.," to represent "that is" when providing a specific idea related to the topic under discussion.*
  Correct: Mr. S. produced an approximation for the word *bye* (i.e., /bʌ/).
  Incorrect: Mr. S. produced an approximation for the word *bye* (e.g., /bʌ/).

FULL DIAGNOSTIC REPORT FORMAT

The following format may be used for a full diagnostic report. Diane Chapman Bahr, Rebecca Miller, and Karen Keilholtz developed this format for use with the pediatric population.* However, it could be modified for the adult population if appropriate. The recommendations listed in the report format represent *some* of the recommendations that can be made as a result of the oral motor assessment. The goals listed in the report are a sampling of possible goals. The report format could potentially be stored on a computer and used as a template from which individualized reports could be generated.

NAME OF DEPARTMENT/ORGANIZATION/SCHOOL/ETC.

Diagnostic Report

Name:	Date of Evaluation:
Address:	Date of Birth:
	Age:
Phone:	Gender:
Parents:	Diagnostic Code(s):
Referral Source:	Diagnosis:
Reports Sent to:	

Reason for Referral and Services Received

__________ is the _____ year, _____ month old son/daughter of __________ and __________. He/She has a diagnosis of _______________. __________ was referred for this evaluation by __________ because/to determine ____________________. __________ was accompanied to the evaluation by his/her mother/father/other. __________ currently attends __________ school/preschool/etc. __________ receives speech-language pathology/occupational therapy/physical therapy/other services _____ hours/times per week.

*Reprinted by permission of Diane Chapman Bahr, Rebecca Miller, and Karen Keilholtz.

History

Medical History

According to the case history completed by _________, _________ was born following a full term/_____ week pregnancy. His/Her general health at birth was described as _________. _________ has a/no history of ear/upper respiratory infections. *(Elaborate on these and other medical concerns.)*

Developmental History

_____________ reported that _________'s developmental patterns were _________. His/Her first tooth appeared at _____ months. He/She began sitting at _____ months of age and crawling at _____ months of age. _________ reportedly took his/her first steps at _____ months.

Oral Motor History

Report pertinent information from oral motor case history (see oral motor case history in Chapter 4).

Speech-Language History

_________ reported that _________ said his/her first words at _____ months of age. He/She reportedly produces word approximations for the words "______________." _________ is said to use signs for the words "______________." He/She began producing two word/sign combinations at the age of ______________ according to report. Currently _________ produces *(number)* word/sign combinations spontaneously/with facilitation.

Clinical Observations

_________ presented as a _________ child who ___________________. *(Describe child's sensory responses, interactions with parents, interactions with evaluator, level of attention, level of play, pragmatic skills, etc.)* Some of _________'s favorite activities during the evaluation appeared to be ___________________.

Results

Oral Motor Skills

The *(assessment name)* by *(author of assessment tool)* was used to evaluate _________'s oral motor function during a quiet activity, while eating/drinking, while performing oral movements, and during speech production.

(A table or chart with test results may be placed here.)

Strengths (list under appropriate area)
Body and mouth at rest and during eating/drinking/nonspeech tasks/speech production (these areas may be divided into separate sections)

- Sensory awareness and responsiveness
- Postural tone, stability, and control
- Head, neck, and shoulder stability as a base of support for oral motor function
- Dissociation of head-neck movement from body movement
- Presence/absence of drooling or tooth grinding
- Respiration, phonation, and resonation
- Coordination of respiration and swallowing during eating and drinking

Jaw at rest and during eating/drinking/nonspeech tasks/speech production (these areas may be divided into separate sections)

- Muscle tone
- Sensory awareness and responsiveness
- Jaw position at rest
- Jaw position(s) during swallowing and speech production
- Stability and mobility
- Grading of movement
- Dissociation of jaw movement from head-neck movement

Lips at rest and during eating/drinking/nonspeech tasks/speech production *(these areas may be divided into separate sections)*

- Muscle tone
- Sensory awareness and responsiveness
- Lip position at rest
- Lip position during swallowing and speech production
- Mobility and grading of movement
- Dissociation of lip movement from jaw movement

Tongue at rest and during eating/drinking/nonspeech tasks/speech production (these areas may be divided into separate sections)

- Muscle tone
- Sensory awareness and responsiveness
- Tongue position at rest
- Tongue position during swallowing and speech production
- Stability and mobility
- Grading of movement
- Dissociation of tongue movement from jaw movement

Motor planning during nonspeech tasks/speech production (these areas may be divided into separate sections)

(See motor planning characteristics in Chapter 5.)

Speech Intelligibility
(Use test results or speech sample.)

<u>Concerns</u>
(List under appropriate areas. See above.)
(Place language test results here.)

Language Skills
(Place language results in this section.)

Summary of Findings

__________ is the _____ year _____ month old son/daughter of __________ and __________. __________'s parents are concerned about ____________________. Based on the results of this evaluation, __________ has a diagnosis of ____________________. Test results, parental report, and clinical observation revealed ____________________. *(Note level of oral motor dysfunction/speech-language disorder, i.e., mild, moderate, severe.)* __________ requires treatment in the areas of oral motor/receptive language/expressive language skill development. This is evidenced by ______________________________. These concerns may impact upon __________'s educational process by ________________. __________'s prognosis for improvement is excellent with therapeutic intervention and current level of parental support.

Recommendations

(Consider listing recommendations according to priority in the report if possible.)

It is recommended that __________ (continue to) receive oral motor as well as speech-language therapy *(as appropriate)* for the remediation of mild/moderate/severe oral motor/speech-language delays/difficulties secondary to ______________. Therapy should focus on the following recommendations:

1. Consult with __________'s physical and/or occupational therapist regarding appropriate positioning and movement activities to facilitate postural stability/development/control so that __________ can readily participate in oral motor activities to support the processes of eating, drinking, and/or speech production.
2. Consult with __________ 's occupational therapist regarding apparent sensory integration concerns and fine motor issues. Cotreatment between the occupational therapist and the speech-language pathologist is often a very effective therapy model. Additional information on sensory integration can be found in the book *Sensory Integration and the Child* by Ayres (1979) and in the book *The Out-of-Sync Child: Recognizing and Coping with Sensory Integration Dysfunction* by Kranowitz (1998).
3. Explore the use of music and other environmental modifications to create an appropriate learning environment for __________. This may assist __________ in increasing his/her attending skills. For example, music can be played as a "background" during treatment or other instructional times to help __________ attend to tasks. Refer to the chapter entitled Facilitation of Learning by Morris (1991).
4. Use oral massage/oral facilitation techniques with __________ on a daily basis to increase oral awareness, improve responses to oral sensation, and increase oral motor skills. Provide massage and oral facilitation techniques as described and demonstrated during the visit three times per day before you require __________ to use his/her mouth in some manner (e.g., eating, speech activities, tooth brushing, etc.). This type of treatment has been successful in improving responses to sensation in the oral area as well as increasing awareness for the development of sophisticated oral motor patterns for eating, drinking, and speech production. It can require as little as 5 minutes prior to a meal, snack, tooth brushing, or speech activity. See Oral Massage Sequence and infomation on other facilitation techniques (Chapters 4–8).

   Other specific oral motor treatment ideas can be found in__________ __________________________ *(title of resource)* by ____________*(author)*. Refer to treatment ideas/activities/exercises on pages __________________. These address the areas of jaw stability/mobility/control, lip mobility/control, tongue stability/mobility/control, etc. *(List areas of need for the client.)*
5. Since __________ is currently using a pacifier, encourage __________ to use a pacifier with a short, narrow nipple. The short, narrow nipple will encourage __________ to actively use his/her lips when sucking. Long, wide nipples may promote the prolonged use of a suckle-swallow or tongue thrust pattern in __________ (Rosenfeld-Johnson, 1999a).

   Wean __________ from the pacifier as appropriate. The pacifier often promotes the use of atypical oral motor patterns. Oral massage/facilitation exploration should help satisfy __________'s need for oral stimulation.
6. Use a "heavy" plastic or plastic coated spoon with __________. The small/large maroon spoon may be a viable option. Children with oral sensitivities tend to accept these spoons more readily as they do not conduct cold as easily and often have a more acceptable feel in the mouth than metal spoons. They can also protect the child's teeth from damage if the child tends to bite on the spoon.

When presenting a spoon to __________, apply a small amount of weight with the spoon to provide __________ with the sensory input needed to encourage appropriate tongue movement and upper lip closure (Rosenfeld-Johnson, 1999a).

Present the spoon laterally to __________ to encourage active lip movement and control. Touch the corner of __________'s mouth with the spoon handle to increase sensory input. Alternate the sides of the spoon presented to __________'s lips (Overland, 1999).

__________ seems to want to feed him/herself. Give him/her his/her own spoon to explore and take turns with spoon-feeding if __________ will accept this.

7. Provide __________ with safe foods of increased texture to avoid choking episodes and facilitate his/her use of sophisticated oral patterns (e.g., tongue tip lateralization, rotary chewing, etc.). These foods may include Veggie Stix, cheese curls, butter cookies, Lorna Doone cookies, and/or graham crackers and may be introduced at the beginning of mealtime to increase awareness and promote mature eating patterns.

   If __________ cannot safely manage certain foods, these foods may be placed in a sack made from organza or a double or triple thickness of cheesecloth. This will allow __________ to experience the taste and texture of new foods without the risk of choking. The cloth may be moistened with water if __________ does not seem to like the feel of dry cloth.

   Provide __________ with foods of increased texture that __________ is capable of managing at the beginning of the meal to increase oral awareness and encourage the use of sophisticated eating patterns (e.g., tongue tip lateralization, rotary chewing, etc.).

8. Address __________'s food selectivity issues by introducing foods that represent variations of the foods that __________ will accept. For example, crackers and bagels are often foods accepted by children. These are available in many shapes, sizes, tastes, and textures. Seasoning can also be added to most foods if __________ enjoys foods of increased taste. Use appropriate seasonings for foods such as cinnamon on fruits and "Mrs. Dash" on vegetables.

9. Wean __________ from the use of the spouted cup. Spouted cups tend to promote the use of a tongue thrust pattern. Use a cup with a slotted lid or a cutout cup to promote active use of __________'s lips during drinking.

10. Thicken __________'s liquids when teaching him/her to drink from a cup. This will give __________ greater control over the flow of the liquid as the liquid moves toward and into the mouth. Thickened liquids also provide more sensory input for __________. Juice can be thickened with applesauce, and milk can be thickened with a smooth, flavored or unflavored yogurt. Several thickening agents are commercially available through a pharmacy.

    Thicken __________'s liquids to provide __________ with increased sensory input and to allow __________ greater control during swallowing. This may decrease __________'s tendency to "gulp" liquids.

11. It may be beneficial to consult with a pediatric gastroenterologist regarding __________'s difficulty with reflux. Discuss this with __________'s pediatrician. Refer to the *Pre-Feeding Skills* book by Morris and Klein (1987, 2000) for information on this topic.

12. It may be beneficial to consult with a pediatric developmental nutrition professional regarding __________'s constipation concerns. Discuss this with __________'s pediatrician. Refer to the *Pre-Feeding Skills* book by Morris and Klein (1987, 2000) for information on this topic.

13. Develop an oral motor planning program for _________ to address his/her apparent dyspraxia. Consider the use of materials from the program(s) _________________________ by ________________.
14. Investigate the use of moto-kinesthetic/tactile-kinesthetic cueing to assist _________ in improving the precision of his/her speech.
15. Investigate use of visual and tactile cueing to assist _________ in improving the precision of his/her speech.
16. Investigate the use of a pacing board with _________. This device can facilitate an increased length of expressive output. Begin with a board that can be used with two and three sound/syllable/word utterances. Model each utterance for _________ according to guidelines in "The Pacing Board: A Technique to Assist the Transition from Single Word to Multi-word Utterances" by Libby Kumin, Cheryl Councill, and Mina Goodman (1995).
17. Develop a myofunctional treatment program for _________ to remediate his/her tongue thrust pattern. Consider the use of materials from the program(s) _________________________ by ________________.
18. Use complete and grammatically correct sentences with appropriate intonation and prosody when speaking to _________. Children learn new language by hearing the complete form of the language. Use simplified language only when _________ requires this for learning new information instructionally.
19. Continue to pair simple functional signs with oral expression. Signs have been found to facilitate oral output as well as clarify what the person is trying to express.

    Explore the use of a name sign for _________. A name sign can assist _________ in the use of his/her name and aid in his/her ability to communicate about himself/herself.
20. Investigate the use of a picture and/or symbolic communication system to provide choices for _________. Photographs of actual toys, foods, etc., and/or picture symbol systems can also be used to facilitate speech production.
21. Capitalize on _________'s apparent strength in using imitation for learning. _________ demonstrated the ability to readily imitate new signs and make choices using picture communication after demonstration.
22. Investigate the use of computer assisted instruction with _________, since he/she reportedly enjoys interacting with computers. Many software programs can be accessed through alternative devices such as single switches, the Touch Window, and the IntelliKeys if needed. These alternative devices are available from a variety of companies. Contact the local assistive technology center for further information. Alliance for Technology Access Resource Centers are located in many states if the local or state education agency does not provide this service. Call the Foundation for Technology Access for further information on the center located in your state (1-415-455-4575).
23. Consider maintaining part-time inclusion along with individual treatment (i.e., occupational therapy, physical therapy, and speech/language therapy) as it seems that _________ can benefit from the more individualized and specialized instruction provided in individual treatment while inclusion provides him/her with interactive role models.
24. Provide Mr. and Mrs. _________ with information concerning oral motor, speech, and language development as well as home activities to promote generalization of skills learned during therapy.

    Provide _________'s care providers, teachers, etc. with information concerning oral motor, speech and language development as well as activities to promote generalization of skills learned during therapy.

Suggested Therapy Goals

(See information on goal writing in another section of this chapter.)

It has been a pleasure to work with __________ and his/her family, care providers, teachers, therapists, etc. Please call ______________ if you have any comments, questions, or ideas regarding the information presented in this report.

____

Speech-Language Pathologist
License Number:

SOAP NOTE FORMAT

The SOAP note format can be used for diagnostic as well as progress report writing. Diagnostic reports and progress reports are completed according to the guidelines used in a specific clinical setting. Each letter in the word *SOAP* represents a particular type of information discussed in the report.

Subjective information is reported next to the letter *S* in *SOAP* note format. This is an area where observations of the client's attention, behavior, apparent mood, level of cooperation, and so on can be reported. *Objective* information can be reported next to the letter *O*. This would include test results, data taken on client goals, and the like. Brief *assessment* statements are written next to the letter *A*. These statements summarize the client's diagnostic results or progress. The letter *P* in *SOAP* represents the client's *plan* of treatment. Recommendations and future goals may be written in this area.

The following case example was written from the sample protocol presented in the manual for the *Apraxia Battery for Adults (ABA)* by Dabul (1979). Please see the manual to review the actual protocol. Some of the sentences in the report are long sentences, because they list behaviors noted in a particular area.

Case Example: Mr. J.

DEPARTMENT OF SPEECH-LANGUAGE PATHOLOGY

Diagnostic Report

Name: Mr. J.
D.O.B: 00/00/00
Social Security Number: 123-45-6789
Address: 16 S. Street
City, State 12345
Phone: 123-456-7890
Diagnosis: Dyspraxia of speech
Diagnostic Code: (dependent on system used)
Date: 00/00/00

Reason for Referral: Mr. J. is 75 years old and is 4 months post L CVA (left cerebrovascular accident). CT (Computerized tomography) revealed ischemic brain damage in Broca's area of the brain. Mr. J. was referred for this evaluation by Dr. W. to assess Mr. J's speech production and to make recommendations regarding treatment.

S: Mr. J. was cooperative during the assessment process. His attention to tasks, language comprehension, and hearing seemed to be WNL (within normal limits). However, Mr. J. reported that he had been feeling "depressed" during the last two weeks.

O: The Apraxia Battery for Adults (ABA) was used to assess Mr. J.'s speech production. Mr. J. demonstrated characteristics of dyspraxia on all six subtests. During three, five-second trials on Subtest I, Mr. J. did not accurately produce the sequence /pʌ tʌ kʌ/. When asked to imitate 10 single-syllable words on Subtest II, Mr. J. correctly produced 7 words, had articulatory errors on 2 words, and was unable to say 1 word. When asked to imitate 10, two-syllable words on Subtest II, Mr. J. accurately produced 4 words, demonstrated visible and audible searching as well as misarticulations on 5 words, and could not produce 1 word. When asked to imitate 10, three-syllable words on Subtest II, Mr. J. accurately produced 1 word, demonstrated visible and audible searching as well as misarticulations on 4 words, and could not produce 5 words. When asked to demonstrate 10 gestures (e.g., "Make a fist") on Subtest III, Mr. J. accurately demonstrated 4 gestures, self-corrected 1 gesture, performed 2 gestures in an imprecise manner, performed 1 gesture correctly after demonstration, performed 1 gesture in an imprecise manner after demonstration, and could not perform 1 gesture. He demonstrated searching behavior while performing 3 gestures. When asked to perform 10 oral movements (e.g., "Stick out your tongue") on Subtest III, Mr. J. accurately performed 1 oral movement, performed 3 oral movements in an imprecise manner, performed 2 oral movements accurately after demonstration, performed 2 oral movements imprecisely after demonstration, and was unable to perform 2 oral movements. Mr. J. demonstrated searching behavior during 2 oral movements. When presented with pictures of 10 common objects representing multisyllabic words on Subtest IV, Mr. J. demonstrated a latency time between zero and 10 seconds with a total latency time of 27 seconds. On the same task, Mr. J. demonstrated an utterance time between zero and 9 seconds with a total utterance time of 35 seconds. When asked to repeat the 10 multisyllabic words over three consecutive trials on Subtest V, Mr. J. demonstrated no change in the number of errors on 3 of the words, an increase in the number of errors on 2 of the words, and a decrease in the number of errors on 5 of the words from trial one to trial three. On this task, Mr. J.'s total amount of change was +3. On Subtest VI, Mr. J. demonstrated 10 out of 15 articulatory characteristics of dyspraxia. He exhibited anticipatory, transposition, and voicing errors. He also demonstrated visible/audible searching, off-target attempts at words, inconsistent articulatory errors, an increase in errors with an increase in word length, a decrease in errors in automatic speech, abnormal prosodic features, and an obvious receptive-expressive language gap.

A: On the ABA, Mr. J. demonstrated severe to profound dyspraxia when producing the sequence /pʌ tʌ kʌ/ and when performing oral movements. However, the majority of his skills were within the mild to moderate range. He exhibited mild to moderate dyspraxia when repeating words that varied in length and when performing gestures. Difficulties with latency and utterance time as well as total change in performance when repeating multisyllabic words over three trials also placed Mr. J. in the mild to moderate range. Mr. J. demonstrated searching behaviors on several tasks, and he exhibited 10 out of 15 articulatory characteristics of dyspraxia.

P: It is recommended that Mr. J. receive one hour of oral motor treatment each week with follow-up activities to be completed at home on a daily basis. Important considerations for treatment follow:

1. Consider the use of oral massage with Mr. J. to increase awareness of the oral area for the purpose of improving speech production. This may provide Mr. J. with the "intrasystemic reorganization" (Brookshire, 1997, p. 283) that he needs to more effectively plan articulatory movements. It should be noted that Mr. J. does not have an apparent sensory loss. Oral massage can increase awareness in individuals with typical sensation levels. Refer to Oral Massage Sequence (Chapter 4).

2. Consider the use of materials that specifically address dyspraxia of speech with Mr. J. These would include *The Source for Apraxia Therapy* by Tomlin (1994) and the *Workbook for the Verbally Apraxic Adult* by Richards and Fallon (1987). Refer to the *O* and *A* sections of this report for specific areas that need to be addressed with Mr. J.
3. Consider the use of cues from Rosenbek and associates (Brookshire, 1997) with Mr. J. (Chapter 8). This cueing process systematically assists the client in reestablishing the motor plan for speech and can be used with the materials listed in recommendation number 2.
4. Consider the use of a visual-tactile cueing system with Mr. J. such as the one developed by Jelm (1995b). Visual-tactile cueing can assist the client in reestablishing the motor plan for speech. This can be particularly useful when the client is having difficulty producing specific speech sounds in the context of words.
5. Consider the use of a pacing system with Mr. J. to slow his speech production and to provide another form of visual and tactile cueing for Mr. J. A small pacing board can be made by placing glue dots on a tongue depressor.
6. It is suggested that Mr. J. discuss his feelings of depression with his physician.

It has been a pleasure to work with Mr. J. Please call with questions or comments regarding this report.

____

Speech-Language Pathologist
Phone Number

GOAL WRITING

Some suggested therapy goals are listed here in a *menu* format. The goals may be appropriate for either the adult or pediatric population. The wording of a goal for each client would be chosen according to individual client or patient needs. It is recommended that the goals be client or patient oriented (i.e., include the person's name in the goals), that the client or patient be the "actor" in the goal, that goals be measurable, and that goals be sequenced according to the therapy sequence if possible. It should be noted that these goals are not all-inclusive and may not suit all treatment settings. See the section titled Treatment Notes for an example of how to use the goal menu.

Goal Menu

Suggested Attending Goal

The client will attend to specified therapy tasks for _____ seconds/minutes while classical /folk/Metamusic music is played as a background.

Suggested Gross Motor/Movement Goal

The client will participate in appropriate gross motor/movement activities/exercises for a five-minute period at the beginning of each therapy session to improve postural tone/stability/control needed for improved feeding/eating/drinking/speech production (consult with the client's physician, physical therapist, occupational therapist, and others as needed).

Suggested Oral Massage Goal

The client will participate in oral massage/oral facilitation techniques for a _____ minute period to improve responses to oral sensation, increase oral awareness, and/or facilitate oral motor skills for the purpose of:

- Increasing the acceptance of food and/or liquid textures/tastes/temperatures
- Improving the precision of oral movements for feeding/eating/drinking/speech production.

Suggested Oral Motor Activity/Exercise Goal

The client will accurately complete 10 to 15 repetitions of oral motor tasks/exercises to improve stability, mobility, strength, graded movement, coordination, and/or motor planning in the jaw, lips/cheeks, and/or tongue for the purpose of improving the quality of oral movements during eating/drinking/speech production.

Suggested Motor Planning Goals

The client will:

- Motor plan the sequence of sounds in syllables, words (single syllable/bisyllable/multisyllable), phrases, sentences, reading, conversation, etc., with _____ percent accuracy with cueing/without cueing.
- Accurately complete the eight-step cueing process from Rosenbek and Associates (Brookshire, 1997, p. 281) on _____ out of _____ words, phrases, or sentences (see Chapter 8).

Suggested Articulation Goal

The client will produce the _____ phoneme(s) in _________ *(specify isolation, syllables, words, phrases, sentences, etc.)* with ___ percent accuracy/on ____ out of ____ trials/____ times within a therapy session *(specify context such as "upon imitation, while reading, in conversation," etc.)*.

Suggested Intelligibility Goals

The client will:

- Improve intelligibility from a level of _____ percent to a level of _____ percent in words/phrases/sentences/reading/conversation *(specify level of cueing or prompting used)*.
- Will speak at a rate of ___ words per minute to increase intelligibility.

Suggested Communication Goals

The client will:

- Accurately communicate his/her wants, needs, and desires ____ times per session via word approximations, gestures, signs/signals, picture communication, use of augmentative devices, etc. *(specify)*.

- appropriately comment/request ____ times per session via word approximations, gestures, signs/signals, picture communication, use of augmentative devices, etc. *(specify).*
- Appropriately initiate/maintain/terminate communication _____ times per session via word approximations, gestures, signs/signals, picture communication, use of augmentative devices, etc. *(specify).*

Suggested Carry-Over Goal

The client will accurately complete _____ *(number)* of carry-over activities at home, in the classroom, in the workplace, etc., each week. The speech-language pathologist will provide appropriate training and education for family members, care providers, teachers, employers, etc. (as appropriate) so that carry-over activities can be successfully completed.

TREATMENT NOTES

Treatment notes for the client with oral motor concerns will be specific to the setting in which the client is treated. It is suggested that daily treatment notes be maintained and that they reflect the progress that the client made in treatment that day. It is particularly helpful when the client's progress on short-term goals is reflected. The client's goals can be written at the top of the treatment record. A goal reference number can then be used as progress is reported.

Case Example: Mr. S.

Name: Mr. S.
DOB: 00/00/00
Social Security Number: 987-65-4321
Address: 16 S. Street
City, State 12345
Phone: 123-456-7890
Diagnosis: Dysarthria
Diagnostic Code: (dependent on system used)
Short-Term Goals:

1. Mr. S. will participate in gross motor exercises recommended by his physical therapist for five minutes at the beginning of each therapy session to improve postural tone, stability, and control needed for improved speech production.
2. Mr. S. will participate in oral massage/oral facilitation techniques for five to ten minutes to increase oral awareness and muscle function for the purpose of improving the precision of oral movements for speech production.
3. Mr. S. will accurately complete 10 repetitions of specified oral exercises to improve jaw stability, lip mobility, as well as tongue and jaw dissociation for the purpose of improving the quality of oral movements for speech production.
4. Mr. S. will speak at a rate of 75 words per minute to increase intelligibility of speech.
5. Mr. S. will improve speech intelligibility from a level of 75 percent to a level of 90 percent in single words with visual-tactile cueing.
6. Mr. S. will accurately communicate his wants, needs, and desires 20 to 25 times per session by using a combination of gesture, speech, and written communication.

7. Mr. S. will accurately complete two carry-over activities five to seven days per week at home and in the workplace. With Mr. S.'s permission, the speech-language pathologist will provide appropriate training and education for family members as well as Mr. S's employer and coworkers so that carry-over activities can be successfully completed.

DATE	TREATMENT CODE	COMMENTS
00/00/00	00000	Mr. S. participated in all treatment activities. **1.** 6 minutes (vigorous calisthenics); **2.** 10 minutes (oral massage, myofascial release); **3.** 8/10 (jaw stability), 9/10 (lip mobility), 7/10 (tongue and jaw dissociation); **4.** 95 w.p.m.; **5.** 85 percent intelligibility; **6.** 10 times (speech only), 5 times (speech and gesture), 5 times (written), **7.** 1 activity (oral massage) successfully completed 5 days/week. **DCB**

Appendix A
Assessment Tool Reference List

before* age 2

Tool	Age Range	Posture/ Positioning	Oral Sensation/ Structure	Feeding/ Eating/ Drinking	Nonspeech Oral Movements	Respiration	Phonation	Resonation	Speech Production	Motor Planning	Intelligibility
Feeding Tools											
The Neonatal Oral-Motor Assessment Scale (Braun & Palmer, 1986)	Newborn			+							
Developmental Pre-Feeding Checklist (Morris & Klein, 2000, Appendix B; 1987, pp. 75–82)	Birth to 24 months+	+	+	+		+					
Body Alignment for Seating and Positioning Checklist (Morris & Klein, 2000, p. 305)	Most ages	+									
Positioning Checklist (Morris & Klein, 1987, p. 169)	Most ages	+									
Developmental Self-Feeding Checklist (Morris & Klein, 1987, p. 306)	2 to 36 months			+							
Oral-Motor and Feeding Evaluation (Arvedson, 1993, pp. 283–291)	Infant	+	+	+			+				

Oral-Motor/ Feeding Rating Scale (Jelm, 1990)	1 year to adult	+	+	+							
General Tools											
Oral Motor Assessment Checklist (Bockelkamp, Ferroni, Kopcha, & Silfies, 1997)	Most ages	+	+	+							
Oral Motor Evaluation Protocol (Beckman, 1997)	Most ages		+								
Oral Sensory-Motor Analysis (Boshart, 1998)	3 years to adult		+		+				+	+	
Assessment of Oral Motor Functions (Mackie, 1996a, pp. 9-22)	Young Child	+	+	+	+				+		
Verbal Motor Production Assessment for Children (Hayden & Square, 1999)	3 to 12 years		+		+	+	+		+	+	
Assessment of Oral-Motor Functions During Non-Speech Tasks (Mackie, 1996b, pp. 9–18)	School-aged child	+	+		+						

Tool	Age Range	Posture/ Positioning	Oral Sensation/ Structure	Feeding/ Eating/ Drinking	Nonspeech Oral Movements	Respiration	Phonation	Resonation	Speech Production	Motor Planning	Intelligibility
Assessment of Oral-Motor Functions During Speech Tasks (Mackie, 1996b, pp. 19–21)	School-aged child								+		
Orofacial-Swallowing Evaluation and Rating Scale (Gangale, 1993, pp. 120–127)	Adult	+	+	+	+	+	+	+	+		
Dworkin-Culatta Oral Mechanism Examination (Dworkin & Culatta, 1996)	Child, Adolescent, Adult		+		+			+	+	+	
Dyspraxia Tools											
Assessment of Verbal Dyspraxia (Jelm, 1995b, pp. A-9–A-23)	Child		+	+	+				+	+	+
The Apraxia Profile (Hickman, 1997)	Preschool Profile and School-Age Profile		+	+	+		+		+	+	+
Kaufman Speech Praxis Test for Children (Kaufman, 1995)	2 years to 5 years, 11 months								+	+	

Screening Test for Developmental Apraxia of Speech (Blakeley, 1980)	4 to 12 years				+				+	+	
Apraxia Battery for Adults (Dabul, 1979)	Adult				+				+	+	
Intelligibility Tools											
Children's Speech Intelligibility Measure (Wilcox & Morris, 1999)	3 years to 10 years, 11 months								+		+
Weiss Intelligibility Test (Weiss, 1982)	Child and Adolescent								+		+
Assessment of Intelligibility of Dysarthric Speech (Yorkston & Beukelman, 1984)	Adolescent and Adult								+		+
Frenchay Dysarthria Assessment (Enderby, 1983)	12 years to adult		+			+			+		+
Myofunctional Tool											
Checklist for Tongue Thrust Evaluation and Tongue Thrust Evaluation (Pierce, 1993, pp. 129–131)	Child, Adolescent, Adult		+	+		+			+		

Appendix B
If in Doubt— Do Not Massage

Cautions/Contraindications	Comments
1. Bone and joint problems:	
a. Osteoporosis	a. Caution with amount of pressure, especially compression and moving client's limbs. Avoid fracture.
b. Contractures	b. Do not force movement of any body part that is contracted.
c. Inflamed tissues and joints (e.g., acute phase arthritis, bursitis)	c. Massage adjacent areas. Use Therapeutic Touch/Healing Touch. Avoid actively inflamed tissues anywhere.
d. Acute injury-breaks, strains, sprains	d. May massage adjacent areas.
2. Skin conditions (e.g., burns, rashes, open wounds, abrasions, skin infections) (Ex. boils, eczema, acne, athletes foot)	May massage adjacent area or opposite limb; never directly on area affected. Over affected areas may use Therapeutic Touch, Healing Touch.
3. General infections: Fevers, mono, TB, contagious illnesses	Already have heavily taxed immune system—do not want to tax it more with effects of massage. Options: holding, stroking, chakra, or other energy work. Goal: support the immune system.
4. Circulatory problems:	Massage adjacent areas and/or opposite limb. May use Therapeutic Touch/Healing Touch, *very* light stroking.
a. Varicosities	a. Avoid more damage to already weakened vein walls and valves.
b. Phlebitis, thrombophlebitis	b. Never massage area with "itis" inflammation. "Thrombo" means clot—danger of dislodging clot and it settling in other organs—lungs, Ht, brain, causing stroke, heart attack, lung clot.

Cautions/Contraindications	Comments
c. Edema	c. With edema, excess fluid in the interstitial tissues, there is danger of damaging the cells/ tissues. You may not affect muscles because of the amount of fluid "between" the skin and muscles.
d. Raynauds disease	d. Person experiences pain in toes and fingers when cold, due to diminished blood flow as a result of spasms of the arteries from sympathetic nervous system overactivity. Hold the digits between your hands. Do not rub. Rubbing will not cause blood flow because the problem originates at the level of the nervous system.
5. Certain diseases:	
a. AIDS and Cancer	a. Already have comprised and heavily taxed immune system.
b. Diabetes	b. Issue relates to metabolism of insulin plus complications of circulatory and neuropathy problems.
c. Kaposis sarcoma	c. No direct pressure; involves blood vessel walls. Avoid abdomen massage—could have lesion in visceral vessels.
6. a. Heart attack/stroke	Consult with physician first. a. Concerns; clots, anticoagulant therapy.
b. Severe respiratory problems	b. Respiratory: massage increases circulation and removes waste. May tax respiratory function.
7. Medications:	Concerns:
a. Long-term steroid therapy	*Steroids:* increase bone porosity, fracture potential.
b. Anticoagulant therapy	*A/C:* bruising, embolus creation.
c. Chemotherapy	*Chemotherapy:* taxed immune system, toxicity.
8. Drugs or alcohol toxicity	Tissue wastes/boundary issues.
9. Psychosis, dissociative disorders	Boundaries aren't clear, well distinguished. Could produce more confusion.
10. a. Legs and abdomen in pregnant women	a. Circulatory changes in legs. Abdomen: danger of injuring fetus, starting contractions.
b. First trimester of pregnancy	b. Possible spontaneous abortion.
c. I.U.D.s	c. Possible dislodging.

Appendix C
Moto-Kinesthetic Cueing

By Edna Hill Young (Excerpted and Adapted)

Consonants

"ha" as in hat

- Move lower jaw downward with thumb and index finger, ready for emission of air for "h." Immediately place other hand below diaphragm, and press gently but firmly inward and upward to move air outward.
- Move the jaw upward. Thumb and index finger of one hand stabilize upper jaw. Thumb and index finger on lower jaw, press inward, following curve of lower jaw, tending to bring tongue behind lower incisors for "a" as in *hat.* (Refer to positioning for "a" as in *hat.*)

"wha" as in whack *(sound is not used in all areas of the United States)*

- Thumb and index finger of each hand are placed above and below lip corners on upper jaw and lower jaw.
- Move lips toward midline, leaving an opening. Immediately place one hand below diaphragm, and press gently but firmly inward and upward to move air outward.
- Reverse the direction of the thumbs and index fingers placed on the upper and lower jaws to form the short "a" sound as in *hat.*

"wa" as in wag

- Thumb and index finger of each hand are placed above and below the lips.
- Move lips toward center, leaving an opening as for "oo" in *food*.
- As soon as the sound is heard, lower the jaw and reverse movement of the digits on the upper jaw to produce the vowel sound.

"fa" as in fat

- Using thumb and index finger, move lower lip upward and fit lower lip to curved edge of upper incisors.
- Without lifting fingers, the lip and jaw are brought downward into the vowel position.

Excerpted and adapted from E. H. Young and S. S. Hawk, *Moto-Kinesthetic Speech Training* (Stanford, CA: Stanford University Press, 1955). Reprinted by permission.

"va" as in vat

- Position mouth in same manner as for "fa" in *fat,* but bring lower lip into firmer contact with edges of upper teeth.

"tha" as in thank

- Curve index finger over lower part of upper lip, close to edge of upper incisors and press. Tongue tends to reach forward to line of pressure.
- If needed, use a tongue depressor and place tongue against edge of upper teeth.
- As soon as air begins to move between tongue and upper incisors, bring jaw downward into vowel position using thumb and index finger of other hand.

"tha" as in that

- Stimulate tongue to contact edge of upper incisors, similar to technique used to produce "tha" in *thank.* If needed, press tongue depressor on edges of upper teeth where contact with the tongue is made.
- Once tongue is in position, hold tongue more firmly against upper teeth than for the voiceless "tha."
- As soon as air begins to move between tongue and upper incisors, bring jaw downward into vowel position using thumb and index finger of other hand.

"pa" as in pat

- Using thumb and index finger, bring lower lip upward to press against upper lip. Immediately, move lower lip downward allowing emission of air. If the sound is not produced, press diaphragm in a quick, gentle movement just as jaw is lowered for the vowel sound.
- Move jaw into vowel position.

"ba" as in bat

- Place thumb and index finger of each hand above and below upper and lower lips.
- Firmly bring lips together with equal force.
- Separate lips immediately, and move jaw into vowel position.

"ta" as in tap

- Begin with mouth slightly open.
- Using a tongue depressor inserted under tongue, move tongue up quickly toward alveolar ridge.
- Release tongue quickly by lowering tongue depressor.
- Once tongue movement is established, sound may be stimulated by placing index finger at midpoint on upper jaw and bringing finger downward quickly.
- Using thumb and index finger of other hand, move lower jaw immediately downward into vowel position.

"da" as in dad

- Begin with tongue in contact with alveolar ridge. This may be assisted by the use of a tongue depressor. The "d" sound is made while the tongue is in firm contact with the alveolar ridge.
- Once tongue movement is established, sound may be stimulated by firmly pressing index finger at midpoint on upper jaw.

- Move lips slightly toward the corners using thumb and index finger of each hand.
- Move lower jaw immediately downward into vowel position.

"ka" as in cat

- Place thumb and index finger on either side of throat at base of tongue. Press gently but firmly into tongue and release. (If needed, provide downward pressure on tongue tip with a tongue depressor while simultaneously pushing tongue backward and upward until it contacts the soft palate.)
- Move jaw into vowel position.

"ga" as in gap

- Place thumb and index finger on either side of throat at base of tongue. Press gently but firmly into tongue. Do not stimulate downward movement of tongue, as for "ka" in *cat*.
- Move jaw immediately into vowel position as soon as "g" sound is heard.

"sa" as in sat

- Press toward lip corners with thumb and index finger on upper jaw.
- As soon as air emerges between incisors, move lower jaw downward into vowel position using thumb and index finger of other hand.

"za" as in zap

- Use the same stimulation as for "sa" in *sat,* but press more firmly with thumb and index finger.
- As soon as air emerges between incisors, move lower jaw downward into vowel position using thumb and index finger of other hand.

"sha" as in shall

- Move lips and surrounding tissue forward and toward center using thumb and index finger of one hand on upper jaw and thumb and index finger of other hand on lower jaw. Place pressure on upper jaw as movements are made.
- As soon as sound is heard, move lower lip and jaw downward into vowel position.

"zh" as in beige

- Follow the same procedure as for "sh," but press more firmly.
- This sound does not generally occur at the beginning of English words. Therefore, it may be practiced in nonsense words or may only be stimulated when appropriate.

"cha" as in chat

- Move mouth in same outward position as for "sha." Pressure on upper jaw is firmer than for "sha" to encourage tongue tip-alveolar ridge placement.
- Pressure on upper jaw is removed. Lower hand moves jaw and lip downward into vowel position.

"j" as in jack

- Move mouth in a similar manner as for "cha" in *chat.*

"m" as in map

- Place thumb and index finger below lower lip and equidistant from midline.
- Move the lower jaw upward until the lower lip contacts the upper lip.
- Place the index finger of the other hand firmly on central area of nose (where the nasal bone meets the lateral nasal cartilage).
- As soon as "m" sound is heard, lower jaw into vowel position.

"n" as in nat

- Using thumb and index finger lower jaw and spread lip slightly.
- Place index finger of other hand firmly on central area of nose (where nasal bone meets lateral nasal cartilage).
- If needed, a tongue depressor can be inserted to assist tongue tip in contacting alveolar ridge.
- As soon as "n" sound is heard, lower jaw into vowel position.

"ng" as in hang

- Lower jaw.
- Press gently into base of tongue with thumb and index finger (same as for "k" and "g").
- Simultaneously press on central area of nose (where nasal bone meets lateral nasal cartilage) using index finger of other hand.
- If needed, press on front of tongue with a tongue depressor and then move tongue gently back and up. Hold this while pressing on central portion of nose.
- This sound does not usually occur at the beginning of English words and must be practiced with the vowel preceding it.

"l" as in lag

- With thumb and index finger placed on lower jaw, move jaw downward a small amount and spread lower lip slightly.
- The open space seen between the incisors is a little larger than for "e" in *eat.*
- Apply firm pressure with thumb and index finger of other hand on upper jaw 3/4 of an inch to 1 inch apart equidistant from midline to encourage tongue to move forward, broaden, and fit curve of dental ridge.
- As soon as vowel-like "l" is heard, move lower jaw downward into vowel position.

"r" as in rap

- Using thumb and index finger, move jaw downward slightly from a closed position.
- With thumb and index finger of each hand placed on upper and lower jaw, spread the lips and maintain this position.
- If needed, insert a tongue depressor under tongue and tip front of tongue slightly backward.
- As soon as vowel-like "r" is heard, move lower jaw downward into vowel position.

"y" as in yap

- Move lips and jaw into position for "e" in *eat.*
- Maintain pressure on upper jaw with thumb and index finger.
- Using thumb and index finger of other hand, lower jaw into vowel position.

Front Vowels

"e" as in eat

- With thumb and index finger of each hand placed on upper and lower jaw, move lower jaw toward upper jaw, leaving a small space between incisors.
- Using thumb and index finger of each hand placed on upper and lower jaw, spread the lips.

"i" as in hit

- Using thumb and index finger, lower jaw slightly from position for "e."
- Place thumb and index finger of other hand on upper jaw and slightly spread the lip.
- Using a tongue depressor or finger, apply pressure at midline below lower lip to encourage the tongue to depress.

"e" as in egg

- Using thumb and index finger, lower jaw slightly more than for "i" in *hit.*
- Using thumb and index finger on upper jaw, slightly spread the lip.
- Apply pressure with index finger at midline below lower lip to encourage the tongue to depress.

"a" as in at

- Lower jaw slightly more than for "e" in *egg.*
- Stabilize upper jaw using thumb and index finger from one hand.
- Place thumb and index finger of other hand at equal distances from midline below lower lip. Separate fingers, pressing against jaw and moving outward from midline in an upward curve to encourage the tongue to move downward and broaden.

Central Vowel

"u" as in up

- Using thumb and index finger, lower the jaw a little more than for "a" in *at.*
- Provide auditory input (e.g., "a book," "a girl," etc.).

Back Vowels

"o" as in top

- Place thumb and index finger halfway between the midline and the lip corners below the lower lip.
- Using thumb and index finger of lower hand, press and move jaw downward slightly lower than for "u" in *up.* Press at the two points of finger contact on lower jaw to cue tongue to move back in mouth.
- Using thumb and index finger of other hand, move the upper lip outward slightly.

"a" as in all

- Using thumb and index finger, lower jaw a little less than for "o" in *top.*
- Using hand in contact with lower jaw, press lip slightly toward midline. Then bring lip and surrounding tissue forward.
- Place thumb and index finger of other hand lightly on surface of throat in a location similar to that used for the production of the "k" sound. Draw thumb and index finger forward, lightly slanting downward while moving forward to encourage enlargement of the oropharyngeal cavity.

"a" as in arm

- Move jaw slightly lower than for "a" in *at*.
- Using thumb and index finger of each hand placed on upper and lower jaw, draw lips back from midline against jaws revealing incisors.

"oo" as in foot

- Place thumb and index finger of each hand on upper and lower jaw toward the corners of the lips.
- Simultaneously bring lips toward midline and forward into protrusion.
- Press with fingers of lower hand to shape lower lip. No pressure is needed on upper lip.

"oo" as in food

- Place thumb and index finger of each hand on upper and lower jaw. Move lips toward center, leaving less lip opening than for "oo" as in *foot*.

Diphthongs

"a" as in ate

- Place thumb and index finger on lower jaw approximately halfway between midline and mouth corners. Press against lower jaw and guide jaw downward (not as low as for "a" in *at*).
- Move lower jaw upward to the position for "i" in *it*.
- Move thumb and index finger of each hand on upper and lower jaw slightly toward lip corners to assist in the production of the second sound of diphthong.

"o" as in oat

- Lower jaw with thumb and index finger (not as low as for "o" in *not*).
- Using thumb and index finger of hand on lower jaw, press toward midline to round lips as jaw is simultaneously raised.
- Use thumb and index finger of hand on upper jaw to also round the lips as lower jaw begins to ascend.
- Move lips into position for the "oo" sound in *foot*.

"u" as in use

- Shape mouth as for "e" in *eat*.
- Pressing firmly, move thumb and index finger on upper jaw toward center until the "oo" in *food* is heard.

"ou" as in out

- With thumb and index finger, move lower jaw downward into position for "a" in *arm*.
- Using thumb and index finger of each hand, move tissue above and below lips outward.
- Move tissue above and below lips toward midline until position for the sound "oo" in *foot* is produced.

"oi" as in oil

- Position mouth for "a" in *all*.
- As soon as the sound "a" in *all* is made, use thumb and index finger of each hand placed on upper and lower jaw to move lips away from midline into position for "i" in *it*.

Appendix D
Resources

A variety of product sources, associations, organizations, continuing education opportunities, websites, and listservs related to oral motor assessment and treatment are listed here. Many more can be found by searching the Internet.

Product Sources

AliMed Therapy Division
(Source for oral motor supplies and materials)
297 High Street
Dedham, MA 02026
800-225-2610
FAX 800-437-2966
www.alimed.com
e-mail: info@alimed.com

Gerber Products Company
(Source for Nuk oral massage brushes)
PO Box 120
Reedsburg, WI 53959-0120
608-524-4343

Great Ideas for Teaching!
(Source for oral motor supplies and materials)
PO Box 444
Wrightsville Beach, NC 28480-0444
800-839-8339
FAX 800-839-8498

Innovative Therapists International
(Source for oral motor supplies and materials, particularly those by Sara Rosenfeld-Johnson and Lori Overland)
3434 E. Kleindale Road, Suite F
Tucson, AZ 85716
888-529-2879
FAX 520-795-8559
www.oromotorsp.com

Interactive Therapeutics, Inc.
(Source for oral motor materials)
PO Box 1805
Stow, OH 44224-0805
800-253-5111
FAX 330-923-3030
www.interactivetherapy.com
e-mail: info@interactivetherapy.com

Kay Elemetrics Corporation
(Source for Visi-Pitch and other equipment)
2 Bridgewater Lane
Lincoln Park, NJ 07035-1488
973-628-6200
FAX 973-628-6363
www.kayelemetrics.com
e-mail: sales@kayelemetrics.com

LinguiSystems, Inc.
(Source for a variety of oral motor materials)
3100 4th Avenue
East Moline, IL 61244-9700
800-776-4332
FAX 800-577-4555
www.linguisystems.com
e-mail: www.linguisys@aol.com

Mealtimes: A Resource for Oral-Motor, Feeding, and Mealtime Programs
(Source for music tapes, videotapes, books, feeding equipment, and oral motor treatment tools)

New Visions
1124 Roberts Mountain Road
Faber, VA 22938
800-606-3665
FAX 804-361-1807
www.new-vis.com
e-mail: carmie@new-vis.com

Music in the Classroom
(Source for 60-beats-per-minute music)
PO Box 4100
Santa Cruz, CA 95063
800-772-7701
FAX 831-476-6104
www.garylamb.com
e-mail: webmaster@musicintheclassroom.com

North Coast Medical
(Source for oral motor supplies and materials)
18305 Sutter Boulevard
Morgan Hill, CA 95037
800-821-9319
FAX 877-213-9300
www.ncmedical.com

One Step Ahead
(Source for Baby Safe Feeder and other items for infants and young children)
PO Box 517
Lake Bluff, IL 60044
800-274-8440
FAX 847-615-7236
www.onestepahead.com
e-mail: osacatalog@aol.com

PDP Products
(Source for oral motor and sensory motor supplies and materials)
14398 North 59th Street
Oak Park Heights, MN 55082
651-439-8865
FAX 651-439-0421
www.pdppro.com

Playful Puppets, Inc.
(Source for Puppets That Swallow)
9002 Stoneleigh Court
Fairfax, VA 22031-3217
703-280-5070
FAX 703-280-0918
www.playfulpuppets.com
e-mail: fann@tidalwave.net

Pro-Ed: An International Publisher
(Source for tests and materials related to dysarthria and dyspraxia)
8700 Shoal Creek Boulevard
Austin, TX 78757
800-897-3202
FAX 800-397-7633
www.proedinc.com

Rifton Equipment
(Source for seating and other positioning equipment)
PO Box 901, Route 213
Rifton, NY 12471-0901
800-777-4244
FAX 800-336-5948

Sammons Preston: An Ability One Company
(Source for feeding equipment)
PO Box 5071
Bolingbrook, IL 60440
800-323-5547
FAX 800-547-4333

Southpaw Enterprises, Inc.
(Source for sensory and motor equipment, supplies, and materials)
PO Box 1047
Dayton, OH 45401-1047
800-228-1698
FAX 937-252-8502
www.southpawenterprises.com

Speech Dynamics, Inc.
(Source for oral motor supplies and materials, particularly those by Charlotte Boshart and Pamela Marshalla)
41715 Enterprise Circle, N., #107
Temecula, CA 92590
800-337-9049
FAX 909-695-4903
www.speechdynamics.com
e-mail: speech@iinet.com

Super Duper Publications
(Source for oral motor supplies and materials)
Dept. ASHA 99
PO Box 24997
Greenville, SC 29616-2497
800-227-8737
FAX 800-978-7379
www.superduperinc.com
e-mail: custserv@superduperinc.com

Therapro
(Source for oral motor and sensory motor supplies and materials)
225 Arlington Street
Framingham, MA 01702-8723
800-257-5376
FAX 888-860-6254

The Psychological Corporation/Communication Skill Builders
(Source for oral motor supplies and materials)
Order Service Center
PO Box 839954
San Antonio, TX 78283-3954
800-211-8378
FAX 800-232-1223
www.hbtpc.com

ZIMCO Products & Myofunctional Supplies
(Source for oral motor and swallowing equipment and materials)
2315 187th Avenue, NE
Redmond, WA 98052-6011
425-746-6929
FAX 425-746-2040

Associations and Organizations

Feldenkrais Guild® of North America
(Source for information on Feldenkrais, Awareness through Movement®)
3611 S. W. Hood Avenue, Suite 100
Portland, OR 97201
800-775-2118
FAX 503-221-6616
www.feldenkrais.com

International Association of Infant Massage, Inc.
U.S. Chapter
(Source of information on infant massage and location of certified infant massage instructors)
1891 Goodyear Avenue, Suite 622
Ventura, CA 93003
805-644-8524
FAX 805-644-7699
www.iaim-us.com
e-mail: iaim4us@aol.com

Neuro-Developmental Treatment Association (NDTA)
(Source of information on neuro-developmental treatment)
1550 S. Coast Highway
Suite 201
Laguna Beach, CA 92651
www.ndta.org
e-mail: ndta@alderdrozinc.com

Sensory Integration International
(Source of information on sensory integration therapy)
1602 Cabrillo Avenue
Torrance, CA 90501
310-320-9986
FAX 310-320-9934

Continuing Education

Beckman & Associates
(Workshops with Debra Beckman, SLP on her oral motor assessment and facilitation techniques)
1210 Ridge Road
Longwood, FL 32750
407-332-7409
FAX 407-332-1214
www.beckmanoralmotor.com

Boehme Workshops
(Workshops with Regi Boehme, OT, and associates on NDT and myofascial release)
8642 N. 66th Street
Milwaukee, WI 53223
888-463-4668
FAX: 414-355-6837
www.boehmeworkshops.com

Care Resources, Inc.
(Workshops with Diane Chapman Bahr, SLP on oral motor assessment and treatment; Jeannetta Burpee, OT on sensory integration therapy; and others)
1026 Cromwell Bridge Road
Baltimore, MD 21286
888-613-2275
FAX 410-583-9670

Continuing Education Resource, Inc.
(Workshops and materials by Judy Michels Jelm on oral motor assessment and treatment, specifically in the area of dyspraxia)
PO Box 1010
St. Charles, IL 60174
630-717-1710
FAX: 630-357-0298
e-mail: continuingedresource@earthlink.net

Innovative Therapists International
(Workshops with Sara Rosenfeld-Johnson, SLP; Lori Overland, SLP; and others on oral motor assessment and treatment—see information under product sources)

Institute for Effective Communication Skills
(Workshops for parents and professionals by Libby Kumin, SLP, and colleagues on assessment and treatment of children with Down syndrome)
PO Box 6395
Columbia, MD 21045-6395
410-995-0722
FAX: 410-997-8735

MFR Seminars
(Myofascial release seminars with John F. Barnes, PT, and associates)
222 West Lancaster Avenue
Paoli, PA 19301
1-800-FASCIAL
FAX: 610-644-1662
Website: vll.com/mfr/

New Visions
(Workshops with Suzanne Evans Morris, SLP on oral motor assessment and treatment—see information under "Mealtimes" in product sources)

PROMPT Institute, Inc.
(Workshops with Deborah Hayden and associates on the PROMPT technique)
63 Pan de Vida
Santa Fe, NM 87505
505-466-7710
FAX 505-466-7714
www.promptinstitute.com
e-mail: promptinst@aol.com

Speech Dynamics, Inc.
(Workshops with Char Boshart and associates on oral motor assessment and treatment—see information under product sources)

Winders, Inc.
(Workshops with Patricia C. Winders, PT, author of *Gross Motor Skills in Children with Down Syndrome—A Guide for Parents and Professionals*)
PO Box 433
North East, MD 21901-0433
410-398-2680 (voice and FAX)
e-mail: wind3829@dpnet.net

Other Websites

Apraxia-Kids Home Page: www.avenza.com/~apraxia/index.html

Developmental Verbal Apraxia: www.cs.amherst..edu/~djv/DVD.html

Cleft Lip/Palate: www.cleft.org and www.widesmiles.org

Disability Resources Monthly (DRM) Guide to Disability Resources: www.disabilityresources.org

Oral Motor Information: www.oral-motor.com

Oral Motor Resources for Children with Down Syndrome: www.altonweb.com/cs/downsyndrome/oralreso.html

The Preemie Channel: www.flash.net/~cyberkid/preemiechannel/index.html

Comeunity (resources regarding infants born prematurely): www.comeunity.com/premature/preemiepgs.html

Three Dimensional Tongue Surface during Articulation: http://soml.ab.umd.edu/~mstone/lab.html

Velo-Cardio-Facial Syndrome: www.crosslink.net/~marchett/vcfs/vcfs

Listservs

Apraxia Kids Listserv: www.jump.net/~gmikel/apraxia/aksubscribe.html

CBR-L on majordomo@po.cwru.edu (craniofacial biology research list)

CLEFT-TALK on listproc@mother.com (for parents)

DOWNS-RESEARCH on mailbase@mailbase.ac.uk (Down syndrome)

NEUROMUS on listserv@sjuvm.stjohns.edu (neuromuscular research and information)

References

Aarons, L., & Goldenberg, L. (1964). Galvanic stimulation of the vestibular system and perception of the vertical. *Perceptual and Motor Skills, 19,* 59–66.

Adams, S. G. (1997). Hypokinetic dysarthria in Parkinson's disease. In M. R. McNeil (Ed.), *Clinical management of sensorimotor speech disorders* (pp. 261–285). New York: Thieme Medical Publishers.

Alexander, M. P. (1997). Aphasia: clinical and anatomical aspects. In T. E. Feinberg & M. Farah (Eds.), *Behavioral neurology and neuropsychology* (pp. 133–150). New York: McGraw-Hill.

Alexander, R. (1987). Oral-motor treatment for infants and young children with cerebral palsy. *Seminars in Speech and Language, 8* (1), 87–100.

Alexander, R. (1990). Oral-motor and respiratory-phonatory assessment. In E. D. Gibbs & D. M. Teti (Eds.), *Interdisciplinary assessment of Infants: A guide for early intervention professionals* (pp. 63–74). Baltimore: Paul H. Brookes.

American Psychological Association. (1994). *Publication manual of the American Psychological Association* (4th ed.). Washington, DC: American Psychological Association.

American Speech-Language-Hearing Association. (1991). The role of the speech-language pathologist in management of oral myofunctional disorders. *Asha, 33* (Suppl. 5), 7.

American Speech-Language-Hearing Association. (1993). Orofacial myofunctional disorders: Knowledge and skills. *Asha, 35* (Suppl. 10), 21–23.

American Speech-Language-Hearing Association, Task Force on Central Auditory Processing Consensus Development. (1996). Central auditory processing: Current status of research and implications for clinical practice. *American Journal of Audiology, 5,* 41–52.

Arvedson, J. (1993). Oral-motor and feeding assessment. In J. C. Arvedson & L. Brodsky (Eds.), *Pediatric swallowing and feeding: Assessment and management* (pp. 249–291). San Diego: Singular Publishing Group.

Arvedson, J. C., & Brodsky, L. (Eds.). (1993). *Pediatric swallowing and feeding: Assessment and management.* San Diego: Singular Publishing Group.

Ayres, A. J. (1972a). Improving academic scores through sensory integration. *Journal of Learning Disabilities, 5,* 336–343.

Ayres, A. J. (1972b). *Sensory integration and learning disorders.* Los Angeles: Western Psychological Services.

Ayres, A. J. (1976). *The effect of sensory integrative therapy on learning disabled children: The final report of a research project.* Los Angeles: University of Southern California.

Ayres, A. J. (1978). Learning disabilities and the vestibular system. *Journal of Learning Disabilities, 11,* 18–29.

Ayres, A. J. (1979). *Sensory integration and the child.* Los Angeles: Western Psychological Services.

Barnes, J. F. (1990). *Myofascial release: A comprehensive evaluatory and treatment approach.* Paoli, PA: John F. Barnes, PT and Rehabilitation Services.

Barnes, S. M. (1994). *Taming the tongue thrust.* Arcadia, CA: Suzanne M. Barnes.

Bartlett, D. (1997). Primitive reflexes and early motor development. *Journal of Development and Behavioral Pediatrics, 18,* 143–150.

Beckman, D. (1997). *Oral motor assessment and intervention.* Longwood, FL: Debra Beckman. (workshop)

Beidler, L. M., & Smallman, R. L. (1965). Renewal of cells within taste buds. *Journal of Cellular Biology, 27* (2), 263–272.

Beukelman, D. R., & Mirenda, P. (1992). *Augmentative and alternative communication: Management of severe communication disorders in children and adults.* Baltimore: Paul H. Brookes.

Binder, J. R., & Rao, S. M. (1994). Human brain mapping with functional magnetic imaging. In A. Kertesz (Ed.), *Localization and neuroimaging in neuropsychology* (pp. 185–212). San Diego: Academic Press.

Blakeley, R. W. (1980). *Screening test for developmental apraxia of speech.* Tigard, OR: C. C. Publications.

Bly, L. (1983). *The components of normal movement during the first year of life and abnormal motor development.* Chicago: Neuro-Developmental Treatment Association.

Bobath, B. (1970). *Adult hemiplegia: Evaluation and treatment.* London, England: William Heinemann Medical Books.

Bobath, B. (1971). Motor development, it's effect on general development, and application to the treatment of cerebral palsy. *Physiotherapy, 57* (11), 526–532.

Bobath, K. (1971). The normal postural reflex mechanism and its deviation in children with cerebral palsy. *Physiotherapy, 57* (11), 515–525.

Bockelkamp, D., Ferroni, D., Kopcha, A., & Silfies, D. P. (1997). *Oral motor assessment checklist.* Baltimore: Loyola College in Maryland. (class project)

Boehme, R. (1990a). *The hypotonic child: Treatment for postural control, endurance, strength, and sensory organization.* Tucson, AZ: Therapy Skill Builders.

Boehme, R. (1990b). Integration of neuro-developmental treatment and myofascial release in adult orthopedics. In J. F. Barnes (Ed.), *Myofascial release: The search for excellence: A comprehensive evaluatory and treatment approach* (pp. 209–217). Paoli, PA: John F. Barnes.

Boshart, C. A. (1995a). *Oral-motor seminar: "Hard tissue analysis" supplement.* Temecula, CA: Speech Dynamics. (video)

Boshart, C. A. (1995b). *Swalloworks.* Temecula, CA: Speech Dynamics.

Boshart, C. A. (1996). *Mouthing toys! An instructional booklet.* Temecula, CA: Speech Dynamics.

Boshart, C. A. (1998). *Essential oral-motor techniques: A one-day seminar.* Temecula, CA: Speech Dynamics. (workshop)

Boshart, C. A. (1999). *Treatise on the tongue: Analysis and treatment of tongue abnormalities.* Temecula, CA: Speech Dynamics.

Boshart, C. A., & Jutila, M. L. (1995). *The "l" system; The "sh" and "ch" systems; The "s" system;* and *The "r" system.* Temecula, CA: Speech Dynamics.

Boshart, C. A., & Jutila, M. L. (1996). *The "k" and "g" systems* and *The "th" system.* Temecula, CA: Speech Dynamics.

de Boysson-Bardies, B., & Vihman, M. M. (1991). Adaptation to language: Evidence from babbling and first words in four languages. *Language, 67,* 297–319.

Braun, M. A., & Palmer, M. M. (1986). A pilot study of oral-motor dysfunction in "at-risk" infants. *Physical & Occupational Therapy in Pediatrics, 5* (4), 13–25.

Brooks, V. B. (1986). *The neural basis of motor control.* New York: Oxford University Press.

Brookshire, R. H. (1997). *An introduction to neurogenic communication disorders* (5th ed.). Saint Louis: Mosby Year Book.

Brown, J. R., Darley, F. L., & Aronson, A. E. (1970). Ataxic dysarthria. *International Journal of Neurology, 7,* 302–318.

Burkhart, L. J. (1993). *Total augmentative communication in the early childhood classroom.* Eldersburg, MD: Linda J. Burkhart.

Burpee, J. D. (1999). *Sensory integration, applied behavior analysis, and floor time.* Baltimore: Care Resources, Inc. (workshop)

Cacace, A. T., & McFarland, D. J. (1998). Central auditory processing disorder in school-aged children: A critical review. *Journal of Speech, Language, and Hearing Research, 41,* 355–373.

Cannito, M. P., & Marquardt, T. P. (1997). Ataxic dysarthria. In M. R. McNeil (Ed.), *Clinical management of sensorimotor speech disorders* (pp. 217–247). New York: Thieme Medical Publishers.

Carneol, S. O., Marks, S. M., & Weik, L. (1999). The speech-language pathologist: Key role in the diagnosis of Velocardiofacial syndrome. *American Journal of Speech-Language Pathology, 8,* 23–32.

Caruso, A. J., & Strand, E. A. (1999). Motor speech disorders in children: Definitions, background, and a theoretical framework. In A. J. Caruso & E. A. Strand (Eds.), *Clinical management of motor speech disorders in children* (pp. 1–27). New York: Thieme Medical Publishers.

Chapey, R. (1986). *Language intervention strategies in adult aphasia* (2nd ed.). Baltimore: Williams and Wilkins.

Chertkow, H., & Bub, D. (1994). Functional activation and cognition: The O-15 PET subtraction method. In A. Kertesz (Ed.), *Localization and neuroimaging in neuropsychology* (pp. 152–184). San Diego: Academic Press.

Chumpelik (Hayden), D. (1984). The PROMPT system of therapy. In D. Aram (Ed.), *Seminars in Speech and Language, 5,* 139–156.

Crary, M. A. (1993). *Developmental motor speech disorders.* San Diego: Singular Publishing Group.

Czesak-Duffy, B. A. (1993). *Triathlon articulation training: Tongue, body, brain exercises for improved pronounciation.* Kearney, NJ: Creative Communication Concepts.

Dabul, B. (1979). *Apraxia battery for adults.* Tigard, OR: C. C. Publications.

Darley, F., Aronson, A. E., & Brown, J. R. (1975). *Motor speech disorders.* Philadelphia: W. B. Sauders.

DeMyer, W. E. (1994). *Technique of the neurologic examination: A programmed text* (4th ed.). New York: McGraw-Hill, Health Professions Division.

DeNinno, J., & Gill, K. (1997). *"Can do" oral-motor fun deck.* Greenville, SC: Super Duper Publications.

Densem, J. F., Nuthall, G. A., Bushnell, J., & Horn, J. (1989). Effectiveness of a sensory integrative therapy program for children with perceptual-motor deficits. *Journal of Learning Disabilities, 22,* 221–229.

Duffy, J. R. (1995). *Motor speech disorders: Substrates, differential diagnosis, and management.* St. Louis: Mosby Year Book.

Dworkin, J. P., & Culatta, R. A. (1996). *The Dworkin-Culatta oral mechanism examination and treatment system.* Nicholasville, KY: Edgewood Press.

Enderby, P. M. (1983). *Frenchay dysarthria assessment.* Austin, TX: Pro-Ed.

Fairbanks, G. (1960). *Voice and articulation drillbook* (2nd ed.). New York: Harper & Brothers.

Feldenkrais, M. (1972). *Awareness through movement: Health exercise for personal growth.* New York: Harper & Row.

Feldenkrais, M. (1975). Awareness through movement. *The 1975 annual handbook for group facilitators.* San Francisco: University Associates Publishers.

Feldenkrais, M. (1985). *The potent self: A guide to spontaneity.* San Francisco: Harper & Row.

Field, T. (1990). Alleviating stress in newborn infants in the intensive care unit. *Clinics in Perinatology, 17* (1), 1–9.

Field, T. (1995). Massage therapy for infants and children. *Journal of Developmental Behavioral Pediatrics, 16* (2), 105–111.

Field, T. (1998). Massage therapy effects. *American Psychology, 53* (12), 1270–1281.

Fisher, A. G. (1991). Vestibular-proprioceptive processing and bilateral integration and sequencing deficits. In A. G. Fisher, E. A. Murray, & A. C. Bundy (Eds.), *Sensory integration: Theory and practice* (pp. 71–107). Philadelphia: F. A. Davis.

Fisher, A. G., & Murray, E. A. (1991). Introduction to sensory integration theory. In A. G. Fisher, E. A. Murray, & A. C. Bundy (Eds.), *Sensory integration: Theory and practice* (pp. 1–26). Philadelphia: F. A. Davis.

Fisher, A. G., Murray, E. A., & Bundy, A. C. (Eds.). (1991). *Sensory integration: Theory and practice.* Philadelphia: F. A. Davis.

Fletcher, S., Casteel, R., & Bradley, D. (1961). Tongue thrust swallow, speech articulation, and age. *Journal of Speech and Hearing Disorders, 26,* 219–225.

Fletcher, S. (1974). *Tongue thrust in swallowing and speaking.* Austin, TX: Learning Concepts.

Gangale, D. C. (1993). *The source for oral-facial exercises.* East Moline, IL: LinguaSystems.

Garliner, D. (1974). *Myofunctional therapy in dental practice: Abnormal swallowing habits: Diagnosis—Treatment* (3rd ed.). Coral Gables, FL: Institute for Myofunctional Therapy.

Gerard, P. C. (1988). *Teaching your child basic body confidence: The Gerard method for enhancing physical development through creative play in only minutes a day.* Boston: Houghton Mifflin.

Geschwind, N. (1965). Disconnexion syndromes in animals and man. *Brain, 88,* 237–294, 585–644.

Gill, K., & DeNinno, J. (1997). *"Can do" oral motor fun and games.* Greenville, SC: Super Duper Publications.

Gill, K., & DeNinno, J. (1998). *"Can do" oral motor game boards.* Greenville, SC: Super Duper Publications.

Glennen, S. L., & DeCoste, D. C. (1997). *Handbook of augmentative and alternative communication.* San Diego: Singular Publishing Group.

Goldman-Eisler, F. (1968). *Psycholinguistics: Experiments in spontaneous speech.* New York: Academic Press.

Graber, T. (1976). For want of T-L-C. *International Journal of Oral Myology, 2,* 7–12.

Green, J. R., Moore, C. A., Ruark, J. L., Rodda, P. R., Morvee, W. T., & VanWitzenburg, M. J. (1997). Development of chewing in children from 12 to 48 months: Longitudinal study of EMG patterns. *Journal of Neurophysiology, 77,* 2704–2716.

Greenspan, S. I. (1995). *The challenging child: Understanding, raising, and enjoying the five "difficult" types of children.* Reading, MA: Addison-Wesley.

Greenspan, S. I. (1997). *The growth of the mind and the endangered origins of intelligence.* Reading, MA: Addison-Wesley.

Greenspan, S. I., & Wieder, S. (1998). *The child with special needs: Encouraging intellectual and emotional growth.* Reading, MA: Perseus Books.

Groher, M. E. (Ed.). (1997). *Dysphagia: Diagnosis and management* (3rd ed.). Boston: Butterworth-Heinemann Medical.

Hanson, J. (1998). *Progress with puppets: Speech and language activities for young children (A guide for using the playful puppets).* Fairfax, VA: Playful Puppets.

Hanson, M., & Cohen, M. (1973). Effects of form and function on swallowing and the developing dentition. *American Journal of Orthodontics, 64,* 63–82.

Hari, M., & Akos, K. (1988). *Conductive education.* New York: Routledge.

Hayden, D. A., & Square, P. A. (1999). *Verbal motor production assessment for children.* San Antonio, TX: Psychological Corporation.

Hebb, D. O. (1949). *Organization of behavior.* New York: John Wiley & Sons.

Hickman, L. A. (1997). *The apraxia profile.* San Antonio, TX: Communication Skill Builders.

Howard, D., Patterson, K., Wise, R., Brown, W. D., Friston, K., Weiller, C., & Frackowiak, R. (1992). The cortical localization of the lexicons. *Brain, 115,* 1769–1782.

Illingworth, R. S., & Lister, J. (1964). The critical or sensitive period, with special reference to certain feeding problems in infants and children. *The Journal of Pediatrics, 65* (6), 839–848.

Jelm, J. M. (1990). *Oral-motor/feeding rating scale.* Tucson, AZ: Therapy Skill Builders.

Jelm, J. M. (1995a). *A parent guide to verbal dyspraxia.* St. Charles, IL: Continuing Education Resource.

Jelm, J. M. (1995b). *Assessment & treatment of verbal dyspraxia.* St. Charles, IL: Continuing Education Resource. (workshop)

Johnson, J. M., Baumgart, D., Helmstetter, E., & Curry, C. A. (1996). *Augmenting basic communication in natural contexts.* Baltimore: Paul H. Brookes.

Kabat, H., & Knott, M. (1948). Principles of neuromuscular re-education. *Physical Therapy Review, 28,* 107–110.

Kapit, W., & Elson, L. M. (1977). *The anatomy coloring book.* New York: Harper Collins College Publishers.

Kapit, W., & Elson, L. M. (1993). *The anatomy coloring book* (2nd ed.). New York: Harper Collins College Publishers.

Kaufman, N. R. (1995). *The Kaufman speech praxis test for children.* Detroit, MI: Wayne State University Press.

Kent, R. D. (1999). Motor control: Neurophysiology and functional development. In A. J. Caruso & E. A. Strand (Eds.), *Clinical management of motor speech disorders in children* (pp. 29–71). New York: Thieme Medical Publishers.

Kent, R. D., Netsell, R., Osberger, M. J., & Hustedde, C. G. (1987). Phonetic development in twins who differ in auditory function. *Journal of Speech and Hearing Disorders, 52,* 64–75.

Kimmey, M. (Ed.). (1985). *The potent self: A guide to spontaneity.* San Francisco: Harper & Row.

King, T. W. (1999). *Assistive technology: Essential human factors.* Boston: Allyn and Bacon.

Klein, M. D., & Morris, S. E. (1999). *Mealtime participation guide.* San Antonio, TX: Therapy Skill Builders.

Knott, M., & Voss, D. E. (1956). *Proprioceptive neuromuscular facilitation: Patterns and techniques.* New York: Harper & Row.

Koomar, J. A., & Bundy, A. C. (1991). The art and science of creating direct intervention from theory. In A. G. Fisher, E. A. Murray, & A. C. Bundy (Eds.), *Sensory integration: Theory and practice* (pp. 251–314). Philadelphia: F. A. Davis.

Kranowitz, C. S. (1998). *The out-of-sync child: Recognizing and coping with sensory integration dysfunction.* New York: Berkley Publishing Group.

Kuhn, C. M., Schanberg, S. M., Field, T., Symanski, R., Zimmerman, E., Scafidi, F., & Roberts, J. (1991). Tactile-kinesthetic stimulation effects on sympathetic and adrenocortical function in preterm infants. *Journal of Pediatrics, 119* (3), 434–440.

Kumin, L. (1997). *Oral motor assessment and treatment in infants, children, and adolescents with Down syndrome.* Columbia, MD. (workshop)

Kumin, L., & Bahr, D. C. (1997). *Oral motor skills: Assessment and intervention for infants, toddlers, children, and adolescents with Down syndrome.* Baltimore: Loyola College. (workshop)

Kumin, L., & Bahr, D. C. (1999). Patterns of feeding, eating, and drinking in young children with Down syndrome with oral motor concerns. *Down Syndrome Quarterly, 4* (2), 1–8.

Kumin, L., Councill, C., & Goodman, M. (1995). The pacing board: A technique to assist the transition from single words to multiword utterances. *Infant-Toddler Intervention, 5,* 293–303.

Kumin, L., Goodman, M., & Councill, C. (1996). Comprehensive speech and language intervention for school-aged children with Down syndrome. *Down Syndrome Quarterly, 1* (1), 1–17.

Kuratomi, C. (1997). *MA CAT: Motor activities for children in articulation therapy.* Temecula, CA: Speech Dynamics.

Langley, M. B., & Thomas, C. (1991). Introduction to the neurodevelopmental approach. In M. B. Langley & L. J. Lombardino (Eds.), *Neurodevelopmental strategies for managing communication disorders in children with severe motor dysfunction* (pp. 1–28). Austin, TX: Pro-Ed.

Lloyd, L. L., Fuller, D. R., & Arvidson, H. H. (1997). *Augmentative and alternative communication: A handbook of principles and practices.* Boston: Allyn and Bacon.

Logemann, J. A. (1992). *Diagnostic related swallowing disorders and their management (Course II).* Detroit, MI: Northern Speech Services. (workshop)

Logemann, J. A. (1997). *Evaluation and treatment of swallowing disorders* (2nd ed.). Austin, TX: Pro-Ed.

Long, A. D., Bahr, D. C., & Kumin, L. (1998). *The battery for oral-motor behavior in children.* Baltimore: Loyola College in Maryland. (unpublished test)

Love, R. J., Hagerman, E. L., & Tiami, E. G. (1980). Speech performance, dysphagia and oral reflexes in cerebral palsy. *Journal of Speech and Hearing Disorders, 45,* 59–75.

Love, R. J., & Webb, W. G. (1996). *Neurology for the speech-language pathologist* (3rd ed.). Boston: Butterworth-Heinemann.

Macaluso-Haynes, S. (1978). Developmental apraxia of speech: Symptoms and treatment. In D. F. Johns (Ed.), *Clinical management of neurogenic communication disorders* (pp. 243–250). Boston: Little, Brown.

Mackie, E. (1996a). *Oral-motor activities for young children.* East Moline, IL: LinguiSystems.

Mackie, E. (1996b). *Oral-motor activities for school-aged children.* East Moline, IL: LinguiSystems.

Marshalla, P. (1992). *Oral-motor techniques in articulation therapy.* Seattle: Innovative Concepts. (video)

Matthews, P. B. C. (1988). Proprioceptors and their contribution to somatosensory mapping: Complex messages require complex processing. *Canadian Journal of Physiology and Pharmacology, 66,* 430–438.

McClure, V. S. (1989). *Infant massage: A handbook for loving parents* (rev. ed.). New York: Bantam Books.

McNeil, M. R., Robin, D. A., & Schmidt, R. A. (1997). Apraxia of speech: Definition, differentiation, and treatment. In M. R. McNeil (Ed.), *Clinical management of sensorimotor speech disorders* (pp. 311–344). New York: Thieme Medical Publishers.

Melzack, R., Konrad, K. W., & Dubrovsky, B. (1969). Prolonged changes in central nervous system activity produced by somatic and reticular stimulation. *Experimental Neurology, 25,* 416–428.

Meyer, T. (1984). *Help your baby build a healthy body: A new exercise and massage program for the first five formative years.* New York: Crown Publishers.

Miller, J. F., & Leddy, M. (1998). Down syndrome, the impact of speech production on language development. In R. Paul (Ed.), *Exploring the speech-language connection* (pp. 163–177). Baltimore: Paul H. Brookes.

Mohr, J. D. (1990). Management of the trunk in adult hemiplegia: The Bobath concept. *Topics in Neurology: Lesson 1,* 1–11.

Montagu, A. (1986). *Touching: The human significance of the skin* (3rd ed.). New York: Harper & Row.

Moore, C. A., & Ruark, J. L. (1996). Does speech emerge from earlier appearing oral motor behaviors? *Journal of Speech and Hearing Research, 39,* 1034–1047.

Moore, C. A., Smith, A., & Ringel, R. L. (1988). Task-specific organization of activity in human jaw muscles. *Journal of Speech and Hearing Research, 31,* 670–680.

Moore, J. C. (1988). *Neuroanatomy simplified: Some basic concepts for understanding rehabilitation techniques.* Cuernavaca, Mor., Mexico: Centro de Aprendizaje de Cuernavaca, A. C.

Moore, J. C. (1999). In J. D. Burpee (Presenter), *Sensory integration, applied behavior analysis, and floor time.* Baltimore: Care Resources, Inc. (workshop)

Morris, S. E. (1982). *The normal acquisition of oral feeding skills: Implications for assessment and treatment.* Santa Barbara, CA: Therapeutic Media.

Morris, S. E. (1985). Developmental implications for the management of feeding problems in neurologically impaired infants. *Seminars in Speech and Language, 6* (4), 293–315.

Morris, S. E. (1986). *The normal acquisition of oral feeding skills: Implications for assessment and treatment.* Faber, VA: New Visions. (workshop)

Morris, S. E. (1987a). *Focus on problem solving in feeding.* Faber, VA: New Visions. (workshop)

Morris, S. E. (1987b). Therapy for the child with cerebral palsy: Interacting frameworks. *Seminars in Speech and Language, 8* (1), 71–86.

Morris, S. E. (2000). Opening the door with metamusic. *New visions learning.* Faber, VA: New Visions Website. <www.new-vis.com>

Morris, S. E. (1991). Facilitation of learning. In M. B. Langley & L. J. Lombardino (Eds.), *Neurodevelopmental strategies for managing communication disorders in children with severe motor dysfunction* (pp. 251–296). Austin, TX: Pro-Ed.

Morris, S. E., & Klein, M. D. (1987). *Pre-feeding skills: A comprehensive resource for feeding development.* Tucson, AZ: Therapy Skill Builders.

Morris, S. E., & Klein, M. D. (2000). *Pre-feeding skills: A comprehensive resource for mealtime development* (2nd ed.). San Antonio, TX: Therapy Skill Builders.

Muir, N. Y., Allard, G. B., & Greenburg, C. (1999). Oral language development in a child with Floating-Harbor syndrome. *Language, Speech, and Hearing Services in Schools, 30,* 207–211.

Murdoch, B. E., Thompson, E. C., & Theodoros, D. G. (1997). Spastic dysarthria. In M. R. McNeil (Ed.), *Clinical management of sensorimotor speech disorders* (pp. 287–310). New York: Thieme Medical Publishers.

Nelson, C. A., & de Benabib, R. M. (1991). Sensory preparation of the oral-motor area. In M. B. Langley & L. J. Lombardino (Eds.), *Neurodevelopmental strategies for managing communication disorders in children with severe motor dysfunction* (pp. 131–158). Austin, TX: Pro-Ed.

Nelson, C. A., Meek, M. M., & Moore, J. C. (1994). *Head-neck treatment issues as a base for oral-motor function.* Albuquerque, NM: Clinician's View.

Nicolosi, L., Harryman, E., & Kresheck, J. (1989). *Terminology of communication disorders: Speech-language-hearing* (3rd ed.). Baltimore: Williams & Wilkins.

Oetter, P., Richter, E. W., & Frick, S. M. (1995). *M.O.R.E.: Integrating the mouth with sensory and postural functions* (2nd ed.). Hugo, MN: PDP Press.

Oller, D. K., & Eilers, R. E. (1988). The role of audition in infant babbling. *Child Development, 59,* 441–446.

Ong, D., & Stone, M. (1998). Three-dimensional vocal tract shapes in /r/ and /l/: A study of MRI, ultrasound, electropalatography, and acoustics. *Phonoscope, 1,* 1–13.

Overland, L. (1999). *Feeding therapy: A hands-on experience.* Tucson, AZ: Innovative Therapists International. (workshop)

Palmer, J. M. (1993). *Anatomy for speech and hearing* (4th ed.). Baltimore: Williams & Wilkins.

Pehde, H., Geller, A., & Lechner, B. (1996). *The complete oral-motor program for articulation.* East Moline, IL: LinguiSystems.

Perkins, W. H., & Kent, R. D. (1986). *Functional anatomy of speech, language, and hearing: A primer.* Boston: Allyn and Bacon.

Peterson, S. E., Fox, P. T., Posner, M. I., Mintun, M., & Raichle, M. E. (1988). Positron emission tomography studies of the cortical anatomy of single word processing. *Nature, 331,* 585–589.

Pierce, R. B. (1978). *Tongue thrust: A look at oral myofunctional disorders.* Lincoln, NE: Cliffs Notes.

Pierce, R. B. (1993). *Swallow right: An exercise program to correct swallowing patterns.* Tucson, AZ: Communication Skill Builders.

Pindzola, R. H. (1987). *A voice assessment protocol for children and adults.* Tulsa, OK: Modern Education Corporation.

Prudden, S. (1983). *Exercise program for young children: 4 weeks to 4 years.* New York: Workman Publishing.

Redstone, F. (1991). Respiratory components of communication. In M. B. Langley & L. J. Lombardino (Eds.), *Neurodevelopmental strategies for managing communication disorders in children with severe motor dysfunction* (pp. 29–48). Austin, TX: Pro-Ed.

Richards, K. B., & Fallon, M. O. (1987). *Workbook for the verbally apraxic adult: Reproducibles for therapy and home practice.* Tucson, AZ: Communication Skill Builders.

Ringel, R. L., & Ewanowski, S. J. (1965). Oral perception. I. Two-point discrimination. *Journal of Speech and Hearing Research, 8* (4), 389–398.

Ringel, R. L., & Fletcher, H. M. (1967). Oral perception. III. Texture discrimination. *Journal of Speech and Hearing Research, 10* (3), 642–649.

Robbins, A., & Jackson, S. (1998). *The mighty mouth game.* Greenville, SC: Super Duper Publications.

Rood, M. S. (1954). Neurophysiological reactions as a basis for physical therapy. *Physical Therapy Review, 34,* 444–449.

Rosenbek, J. C., & Associates. (1973). A treatment for apraxia of speech in adults. *Journal of Speech and Hearing Disorders, 38,* 462–472.

Rosenbek, J. C., & LaPointe, L. L. (1978). The dysarthrias: Description, diagnosis, and treatment. In D. F. Johns (Ed.), *Clinical management of neurogenic communicative disorders* (pp. 251–310). Boston: Little, Brown.

Rosenfeld-Johnson, S. (1999a). *A three-part treatment plan for oral-motor therapy.* Baltimore: Innovative Therapists International. (workshop)

Rosenfeld-Johnson, S. (1999b). *Oral-motor exercises for speech clarity.* Tucson, AZ: Innovative Therapists International.

Royeen, C. B., & Lane, S. J. (1991). Tactile processing and sensory defensiveness. In A. G. Fisher, E. A. Murray, & A. C. Bundy (Eds.), *Sensory integration: Theory and practice* (pp. 108–133). Philadelphia: F. A. Davis.

Ruark, J. L., & Moore, C. A. (1997). Coordination of lip muscle activity by 2-year-old children during speech and nonspeech tasks. *Journal of Speech, Language, and Hearing Research, 40,* 1373–1385.

Rvachew, S., Slawinski, E. G., Williams, M., & Green, C. L. (1996). Formant frequencies of vowels produced by infants with and without early otitis media. *Canadian Acoustics / Acoustique Canadienne, 24,* 19–28.

Samuels, M., & Samuels, N. (1991). *The well baby book: A comprehensive manual of baby care, from conception to age four.* New York: Summit Books.

Scafidi, F. A., Field, T., & Schanberg, S. M. (1993). Factors that predict which preterm infants benefit most from massage therapy. *Journal of Developmental Behavioral Pediatrics, 14* (3), 176–180.

Scherzer, A., & Tscharnuter, I. (1982). *Early diagnosis and therapy in cerebral palsy.* New York: Marcel Dekker.

Schmidt, R. A. (1988). *Motor control and learning: A behavioral emphasis* (2nd ed.). Champaign, IL: Human Kinetics.

Schneider, V. (1987). Crying. *Mothering* (Spring), 19–23.

Seigert, N. B. (1997). *The source for dysarthria.* East Moline, IL: LinguiSystems.

Sensory Integration International. (1991). *A parent's guide to understanding sensory integration.* Torrance, CA: Sensory Integration International.

Sherrington, C. S. (1913). Reflex inhibition as a factor in the co-ordination of movements and postures. *Quarterly Journal of Experimental Physiology, 6,* 251.

Shipley, K. G., & McAfee, J. G. (1992). *Assessment in speech-language pathology: A resource manual.* San Diego: Singular Publishing Group.

Sieg, K. W., & Adams, S. P. (1985). *Illustrated essentials of musculoskeletal anatomy.* Gainesville, FL: Megabooks.

Skelly, M. (1979). *Amer-Ind general code based on universal American Indian hand talk.* New York: Elsevier Science Publishing.

Smith, A., Weber, C. M., Newton, J., & Denny, M. (1991). Developmental and age-related changes in reflexes of the human jaw-closing system. *Electroencephalography and Clinical Neurophysiology, 81,* 118–128.

Square, P. A., Goshulak, D. M., & Hayden, D. A. (1997). *PROMPT assessment and treatment: Clinical, theoretical, and research perspectives.* Boston: ASHA Convention. (workshop)

Square-Storer, P., & Hayden (Chumpelik), D. (1989). PROMPT treatment. In P. A. Square-Storer (Ed.), *Acquired apraxia of speech in aphasic adults* (pp. 190–219). London: Lawrence Erlbaum.

Stilwell, J. M., Crowe, T. K., & McCallum, L. W. (1978). Postrotary nystagmus duration as a function of communication disorders. *American Journal of Occupational Therapy, 32,* 222–228.

Stone, M., & Lundberg, A. (1998). Three-dimensional tongue surface shapes of English consonants and vowels. In M. P. Cannito, K. M. Yorkston, & D. R. Beukelman (Eds.), *Neuromotor speech disorders: Nature, assessment, and management* (pp. 3–25). Baltimore: Paul H. Brookes.

Stray-Gundersen, K. (Ed.). (1995). *Babies with Down syndrome: A new parents' guide* (2nd ed.). Bethesda, MD: Woodbine House.

Strode, R., & Chamberlain, C. (1993). *Easy does it for apraxia and motor planning.* East Moline, IL: LinguiSystems.

Strode, R., & Chamberlain, C. (1994). *Easy does it for apraxia—Preschool.* East Moline, IL: LinguiSystems.

Strode, R., & Chamberlain, C. (1997). *Easy does it for articulation: An oral motor approach.* East Moline, IL: LinguiSystems.

Sullivan, P. E., Markos, P. D., & Minor, M. D. (1982). *An integrated approach to therapeutic exercise: Theory and clinical application.* Reston, VA: Reston Publishing.

Tomlin, K. J. (1994). *The source for apraxia therapy.* East Moline, IL: LinguiSystems.

Tonkovich, J. D., Latham, T. J., & Rambow, M. W. (1986). *Dysarthria rehabilitation program.* Austin, TX: Pro-Ed.

Trott, M. C., Laurel, M. K., & Windeck, S. L. (1993). *SenseAbilities: Understanding sensory integration.* Tucson, AZ: Therapy Skill Builders.

Tuchman, D. N., & Walter, R. S. (Eds.). (1994). *Disorders of feeding and swallowing in infants and children: Pathophysiology, diagnosis, and treatment.* San Diego: Singular Publishing Group.

Walter, R. S. (1994). Issues surrounding the development of feeding and swallowing. In D. N. Tuchman & R. S. Walter (Eds.), *Disorders of feeding and swallowing in infants and children: Pathophysiology, diagnosis, and treatment* (pp. 27–35). San Diego: Singular Publishing Group.

Weiss, C. E. (1982). *Weiss intelligibility test.* Tigard, OR: C. C. Publications.

Weisz, S. (1938). Studies in equilibrium reactions. *Journal of Nervous and Mental Disease, 88,* 150–162.

Wertz, R. T. (1978). Neuropathologies of speech and language: An introduction to patient management. In D. F. Johns (Ed.), *Clinical management of neurogenic communicative disorders* (pp. 1–101). Boston: Little, Brown.

Wertz, R. T., LaPointe, L. L., & Rosenbek, J. C. (1991). *Apraxia of speech in adults: The disorder and its management.* San Diego: Singular Publishing Group.

Wertz, R. T., LaPointe, L. L., & Rosenbek, J. C. (1984). *Apraxia of speech in adults: The disorder and its management.* Orlando, FL: Grune and Stratton.

Wheeden, A., Scafidi, F. A., Field, T., Ironson, G., Valdeon, C., & Bandstra, E. (1993). Massage effects on cocaine-exposed preterm neonates. *Journal of Developmental Behavioral Pediatrics, 14* (5), 318–322.

Wheeler, L., Burke, C. J., & Reitan, R. M. (1963). An application of discriminant functions to the problem of predicting brain damage using behavioral variables. *Perceptual and Motor Skills, 16,* 417–440.

White, B. L. (1985). *The first three years of life* (rev. ed.). New York: Prentice-Hall.

Wilbarger, P., & Wilbarger, J. L. (1991). *Sensory defensiveness in children aged 2–12: An intervention guide for parents and other caregivers.* Santa Barbara, CA: Avanti Educational Programs.

Wilcox, K., & Morris, S. (1999). *Children's speech intelligibility measure.* San Antonio, TX: Psychological Corporation.

Winders, P. C. (1997). *Topics in Down syndrome: Gross motor skills in children with Down syndrome: A guide for parents and professionals.* Bethesda, MD: Woodbine House.

Yarrom, R., Sagher, U., Havivi, Y., Peled, I. J., & Wexler, M. R. (1986). Myofibers in tongues of Down syndrome. *Journal of Neurological Science, 73,* 279–287.

Yorkston, K. M., & Beukelman, D. R. (1984). *Assessment of intelligibility of dysarthric speech.* Austin, TX: Pro-Ed.

Yorkston, K. M., Beukelman, D. R., & Bell, K. R. (1988). *Clinical management of dysarthric speakers.* Austin, TX: Pro-Ed.

Young, E. H., & Hawk, S. S. (1955). *Moto-kinesthetic speech training.* Stanford, CA: Stanford University Press.

Zemlin, W. R. (1968). *Speech and hearing science: Anatomy and physiology.* Englewood Cliffs, NJ: Prentice-Hall.

Zemlin, W. R. (1998). *Speech and hearing science: Anatomy and physiology* (4th ed.). Boston: Allyn and Bacon.

Ziev, M. S. R. (1999). Earliest intervention: Speech-language pathology services in the neonatal intensive care unit. *ASHA,* pp. 32–36.

Zraick, R. I., & LaPointe, L. L. (1997). Hyperkinetic dysarthria. In M. R. McNeil (Ed.), *Clinical management of sensorimotor speech disorders* (pp. 249–260). New York: Thieme Medical Publishers.

Index